Learning Power Query
In Power BI Desktop Made Easy

By Indera E. Murphy

Tolana Publishing

Learning Power Query In Power BI Desktop Made Easy

Tolana Publishing
PO Box 719
Teaneck, NJ 07666 USA

Find us online at www.tolanapublishing.com
Inquiries may be sent to the publisher: tolanapub@yahoo.com

ISBN-13: 978-1-935208-43-3
ISBN-10: 1-935208-43-8

Library of Congress Control Number: 2019901230

Printed and bound in the United States Of America

v1.0

About The Power BI Tools Series

Learning Power Query In Power BI Desktop Made Easy, is part of a series of computer software books that cover a variety of Power BI tools. This book has been designed to be used as a self-paced learning tool, in a classroom setting or in an online class. All of the books contain an abundance of step-by-step instructions and screen shots to help reduce the "stress" often associated with learning new software. Some of the titles from all of the series are shown below.

ISBN: 978-1-935208-37-2

ISBN: 978-1-935208-39-6

ISBN: 978-1-935208-18-1

ISBN: 978-1-935208-34-1

ISBN: 978-1-935208-42-6

ISBN: 978-1-935208-40-2

ISBN: 978-1-935208-36-5

ISBN: 978-1-935208-35-8

ISBN: 978-1-935208-19-8

ISBN: 978-1-935208-38-9

ISBN: 978-1-935208-11-2

ISBN: 978-1-935208-26-6

Visit us online at www.tolanapublishing.com for more titles and information

Why A Book On Power Query In Power BI Desktop?

I felt that readers, especially people new to learning Power Query in Power BI Desktop, would prefer to have more assistance in learning how to import and transform data. I do not feel that flipping between web sites is the most ideal way to initially learn how to transform data.

In general, there are very few books that provide hands-on exercises for learning software or a programming language. I know that many books claim to have "step-by-step instructions". If you have tried to follow books that make this claim and you got lost or could not complete a task as instructed, it may not have been your fault. When I decided to write computer books, I vowed to really have step-by-step instructions that actually included every step. This includes steps like which file to open, which menu option to select and more. In my opinion, it is this level of detail that makes a computer book easy to follow. I hope that you feel the same way.

Over the years, I have come to realize that many people only use a small percent of the features that software or a programming language has to offer. One of my goals in all of the books that I write, is to point out as many features as possible. My theory is that if more people knew about more than 10% of the features that are available, at the very least, they would try a few of them.

About The Author

Dr. Indera E. Murphy is an author, educator and IT professional that has over 25 years of experience in the Information Technology field and has written over 50 books. She has held a variety of positions including technical writer, programmer, consultant, web designer, course developer and project leader. Indera has designed and developed software applications and web sites, as well as, manage technology driven projects in several industries. In addition to being an Executive Director and consultant, as an online adjunct professor, she has taught courses in a variety of areas including project management, technical writing, information processing, Access, HTML, Windows, Excel, Dreamweaver and critical thinking.

Thank you for purchasing this book!

CONTENTS

GETTING STARTED WITH POWER QUERY IN POWER BI DESKTOP

After reading this chapter and completing the exercises you will:

- ☑ Know what Power Query can be used for
- ☑ Understand the difference between the 32 and 64-bit versions of Power BI Desktop
- ☑ Have downloaded the practice files used in this book
- ☑ Understand terms related to Power BI Desktop
- ☑ Have learned about the Options dialog box, which is used to customize Power BI Desktop

CHAPTER 1

Welcome To Power BI Desktop!

Microsoft initially created a set of tools for Excel. This toolset includes Power Pivot, Power Query, Power View and Power Map. Power BI Desktop has the functionality of all of these Excel tools, in one interface. If you have used any of these tools for Excel, Power BI Desktop will be familiar. Power BI Desktop is a free, stand alone software package, which means that you do not have to have Excel to use it.

Power BI Desktop has functionality that Excel does not have, including, creating multi dimensional reports, table support for more than one million rows of data, using data from more than one data source in the same report file and the ability to automate the process of cleaning the data. Additionally, Excel features like slicers and conditional formatting are also available in Power BI Desktop.

While Business Intelligence enterprise solutions have their place, it is easy for them to become outdated quickly because business needs change, and much of this ad-hoc analysis is currently being created in Excel, using static data. To aid in the various types of analysis that needs to be performed, Power BI Desktop was created. This software allows more people in a company to perform Business Intelligence analysis tasks. Microsoft is raising the Business Intelligence bar with its Power BI Desktop and Power BI software. These tools can be used as part of the decision making process.

While "Desktop" is in the name of the software, the reports that are created can be viewed on smart phones, iOS and Android tablets and in Windows. Power BI Desktop can also connect to a vast and growing set of data sources, including popular cloud services like Google Analytics™.

The primary goal of this book is to teach you how to use Power Query to complete a variety of data cleansing tasks. This book is written from the prospective that you have not used Power Query before and that your main objective is learning how to clean and transform data, opposed to learning the intricacies of Power BI Desktop. This book does not cover other features in Power BI Desktop, unless they are specific to what is needed to complete the exercises in this book.

A hands-on approach is usually the best way to learn most things in life. This book is a visual guide that has over 490 illustrations that practically eliminates the guess work. I don't know about you, but it can be frustrating when you need to emulate something that you have "read" is possible, for a software package to do, and you try it on your own and it doesn't work! It is at that very moment that you realize how helpful it would be to have step-by-step instructions.

The good thing is that you have taken a great first step towards learning Power Query, by purchasing this book. Now, all you have to do, is use this book to learn how to overcome the hurdles. From time to time, I will point out functionality that may not work as expected. When I do this, I am not complaining, merely pointing out things that I think you should be aware of.

It is my sincere hope that whatever your current skill level is with Power Query, that you will learn more about features that you may already be familiar with as you go through this book, and that you learn about features that you did not know existed. Having said that, this book is written for the beginner that has not used Power Query before. I also hope that you find that this book gets you up to speed quickly, as time is money!

Learning new tips and shortcuts will let you work faster and smarter. The more you know about Power Query, the easier your day to day data transformation experiences will be.

I am sure that you looked at a few other books on Power Query for Power BI Desktop. You may have gotten the feeling that there was more "reading" about such and such topic, opposed to "these are the steps to do such and such topic". People usually learn more by doing, especially in the beginning, then just reading about the topics.

Like all of the computer books that I write, this one is also for people that want to learn a new software tool or programming language, that has step by step instructions that can be followed, and then take the knowledge and apply it to the tasks that you need to complete on your own.

Sit back and lets get started!

How This Book Is Organized

The order that the topics are covered in this book, is not an accident on my part. They are in the order that I think makes the most sense, from a data flow perspective to learn them in, whether or not you have a need to use all of the Power Query features.

To get the most out of this book, it is not advised that you skip around. The first reason is because some of the files used in later chapters are created in earlier exercises. Working through the exercises in the order that they are presented, provides a better understanding of the concepts, because you can see first hand what Power Query is capable of.

The other reason skipping around in the book is not a good idea is that a topic or option may have been covered in more detail earlier in the book. If you decide to skip around and cannot complete an exercise because there is something that you do not understand, you will have to go back and find the section that covers the topic that you have a question about. Below is an overview of what is covered in each chapter.

Chapter 1, Getting Started With Power Query In Power BI Desktop, covers information about the software, installing the software and relevant terminology. This chapter also covers options that can be set in Power BI Desktop.

Chapter 2, Loading Data Into The Data Model, covers the data source options, the options in the External section on the Home tab and importing data.

Chapter 3, Using The Data And Relationships Views, covers the options on the Data view and the Modeling tab. Relationships and the data model, including their importance in Power Query are also covered.

Chapter 4, Getting Started With The Query Editor, provides an overview of the options in the Query Editor.

Chapter 5, Creating Filters, Custom Columns And Formulas, covers using the Query Editor to create formulas to add data to a query, creating filters for different data types. Creating custom calculations is also covered.

Chapter 6, Use The Options On The Transform Tab To Transform Data, picks up where Chapter 4 left off. This chapter covers the options on the Transform tab. The options on the View tab are also covered.

Chapter 7, Use The Options On The Add Column Tab To Transform Data, covered the options on the Add Column tab, which provides another perspective on transforming data.

Chapter 8, Using The Query Editor To Mashup Data, covers the merge, append, grouping and summarize options. These options combine data and create totals.

Chapter 9, Advanced Importing And Creating Parameters, covers more ways to import and append data. Creating parameters to use with queries and drop-down lists in Power Query is also covered.

Chapter 10, Using The Pivot And Unpivot Transformations, covers using the pivot and unpivot transformation options. These options are used to reshape the data.

Chapter 11, Problem Solving, introduces ways to resolve some of the problems that you may encounter.

Objectives

The overall objective of this book is to enhance your knowledge of Power Query. This book provides the skills required to load, transform and filter data. While the process may be considered technical or "geeky", I explain the terms and concepts in a manner that is hopefully easy to understand. After completing the exercises in this book, you will be able to perform the following tasks and more:

- ☑ Learn how to discover data needed for analysis and reports
- ☑ Load data from a variety of sources into the data model
- ☑ Use the Query Editor to transform data
- ☑ Pivot and Unpivot data
- ☑ Create formulas to transform data
- ☑ Merge and append data

Conventions Used In This Book

I designed the following conventions to make it easier for you to follow the instructions in this book.

☑ The `Courier font` is used to indicate what you should type.

☑ **Right-click** means to press the right mouse button once, which will open a shortcut menu.

☑ Click **OK** means to click the OK button on the dialog box.

☑ Press **Enter** means to press the Enter key on your keyboard.

☑ **SMALL CAPS** are used to indicate an option to click on or to bring something to your attention.

☑ [Text in brackets] references a section, table or figure, that has more information about the topic being discussed. If the reference is in a different chapter, the chapter number is included, like this: [See Chapter 2, Update Options]

☑ Some toolbars or ribbons have a lot of options. When displayed, it can be hard to see each option on the toolbar or ribbon. When that is the case, I split the toolbar into two figures, so that it is easier to see all of the options.

☑ This icon indicates a shortcut or another way to complete the task that is being discussed. It can also indicate a tip or additional information about the topic that is being discussed.

☑ This icon indicates a warning, like a feature that has been removed or information that you need to be aware of. This icon can also represent what I call a quirk, meaning a feature that did not work as I expected it to.

☑ This icon indicates that some of the screen shot (figure) has been removed because it does not provide any value.

☑ When you see the phrase "**YOU SHOULD HAVE THE OPTIONS SHOWN IN FIGURE X-X**", or something similar in the exercises, check to make sure that your screen does look like the figure. If it does, continue with the next set of instructions. If your screen does not look like the figure, redo the steps that you just completed so that your screen does match the figure. Not doing so, may cause problems when trying to complete exercises later in the book.

☑ Some of the dialog boxes have OK and Cancel buttons. Viewing these buttons on all of the figures adds no value, so for the most part, they are not shown.

☑ The section heading **EXERCISE X.Y:** (where X equals the chapter number and Y equals the exercise number) represents exercises that have step-by-step instructions that you should complete. You will also see other sections that have step-by-step instructions that are not an exercise. They are not meant to be completed as you go through the book. They are for future reference, which is indicated.

☑ **HOME TAB ⇒ GET DATA BUTTON ⇒ EXCEL**, means to click on the **HOME** tab in Power BI Desktop, then click the Get Data button, then select the Excel option, as shown in Figure 1-1.

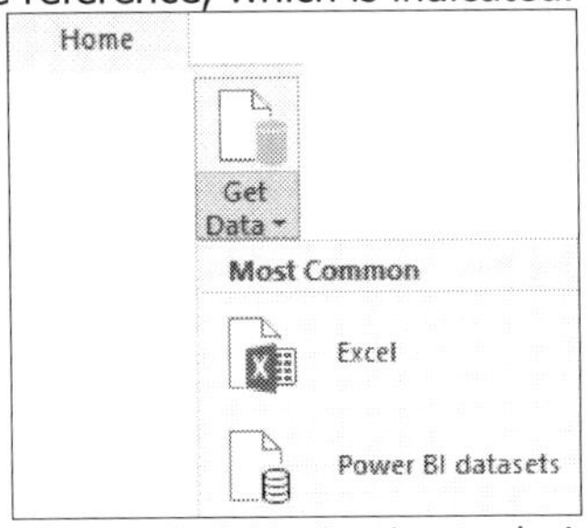

Figure 1-1 Navigation technique

☑ "E2.4 File Name" is the file naming convention for the exercise files that you will create. E2.4 stands for Chapter 2, Exercise 4. You may consider some of the file names long. I did this on purpose, so that it will be easier to know what topic the file covers. If you do not want to type the entire file name, type E2.4, as the file name. This will still let you find the correct files when needed later in the book.

Assumptions

Yes, I know one should never assume anything, but the following assumptions have been made. It is assumed that . . .

☑ You know that this book is written from the perspective that you have little to no experience with Power BI Desktop or Power Query.

☑ You know that the operating system used to write this book is Windows 8.1. If you are using a different version of Windows, some of the screen shots may have a slightly different look.

☑ When you see <smile>, you know that signifies my attempt of adding humor to the learning process.

☑ You know to click OK or the appropriate button to close a dialog box and know to save the changes (to the file) before going to the next section or exercise. Instructions like these are omitted, as much as possible.

- ☑ You know that the files created in Power BI Desktop are known as "report files". They are also called "files".
- ☑ You know that when I use the words "field" and "column", that they are one in the same. These words are interchangeable because the data is in a field in the database that you import data from and then it's called a column in Power Query.
- ☑ You know that I used the words "query" and "table" interchangeably, as they both refer to the data.
- ☑ You know that the end of each chapter in this book has a summary section. In addition to providing a recap of the topics covered, some chapter summaries contain new information, like explaining another way to accomplish a task that was already covered. I did this to not interrupt the flow of the chapter.
- ☑ You know that the links (to other web sites) in this book worked when the book went to print and that I have no control over when or if the web site owners change or remove web pages.
- ☑ You know the difference between the **SAVE** option (saves the file with the same file name) and the **SAVE AS** option (saves the file with a different file name or with the same file name in a different folder). Power BI Desktop has buttons for both of these options on the File tab. [See Figure 1-9]. The Save As button can be added to the **QUICK ACCESS TOOLBAR**, as illustrated in Figure 1-2.
  Many exercises instruct you to save an existing file with a new file name. This is when you would use the Save As button. If you want to use the Save As button, but it is not currently displayed on your Quick Access Toolbar, you will learn how to add it in this chapter.

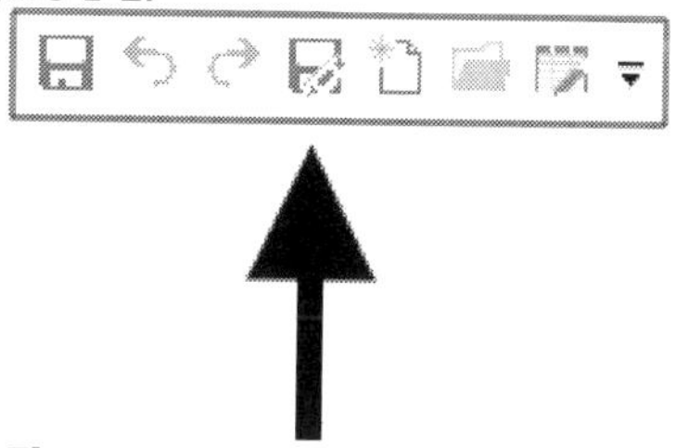

Figure 1-2 Save As button illustrated

What Is Power Query?

Power Query is a component of Power BI Desktop that is used to connect to a variety of external and local data sources and transform data. [See Chapter 2, Figures 2-2 and 2-3] This ETL (Extract, Transform and Load) tool was first introduced in Excel, as an add-in and continues to be updated on a regular basis. Power Query is not exclusive to Power BI Desktop and Excel. It has also been incorporated into Microsoft SQL Server Data Tools (SSDT) for Analysis Services (Tabular 1400 models and higher) and Common Data Services (CDS) For Apps.

Power Query uses the Power Query Editor (the interface of Power Query) to let you transform, filter and prepare the data for analysis. If you have spent hours and hours, creating formulas, then using the Fill option to add the formula to several other rows in the column or copying and pasting data in a workbook, then having to repeat the process when new rows are added to a spreadsheet, you will enjoy using the Query Editor because you complete these tasks once, and when new rows are added, these tasks (called transformations in the Query Editor) are automatically applied to the new rows, without any intervention on your part.

Depending on how you look at it, the primary purpose of Power Query is to reduce the amount of time it takes to transform data. Even though Power BI Desktop supports **R** and **PYTHON SCRIPTS** to import and clean data, these programming tools are not required to transform most data.

While Power Query can remind you of creating a macro in Excel, it is much easier to use. There are no stop and start recording buttons. Each task (transformation) that you set up is recorded, behind the scenes, using the M language and saved as a step.

Another way to think of the Query Editor is that it is the front end interface for the M language. This means that there are a lot of transformations available to you, that do not require you to know or learn anything about the M language, or that it is even running in the background, behind the Query Editors interface. Coming from a programming background, I think that this is very cool, because you do not have to think about what is going on behind the interface.

Each table of data that you import will have its own set of transformations. The formula bar or Advanced Editor is used to customize transformation formulas, if needed. Chapter 2, Figure 2-32, shows a basic change to a formula. The change was that I added which pages would be imported from the PDF file. The data and transformations are stored in a query and are accessed in the Query Editor.

Power Query Components

As you will see, Power Query has two main components, as explained below.

① The **GET DATA BUTTON OPTIONS**, are the connectors that are used to select the data source that has the data that you want to import. Once imported, the data will be cleaned as needed, so that it can be used to create reports. Connectors are revised and updated on a regular basis. Connecting to a data source is a requirement. Without data, all of the components in Power BI Desktop are useless. Using the Get Data options is covered in detail in Chapter 2.

② The **POWER QUERY EDITOR** is displayed after you connect to and either select to load or edit the table(s) of data (on the Navigator dialog box) that you selected. This is the tool in Power BI Desktop that is used to transform the data. As you will learn in Chapter 4, the Query Editor has several sections, as listed below.

- ☑ **RIBBONS** (or toolbars, if you prefer) have all of the transformation options.
- ☑ **QUERIES PANEL** displays a list of queries and parameters in the file.
- ☑ **FORMULA BAR** is used to create, edit and view the M formulas that are created.
- ☑ **DATA WINDOW** is used to view the data in a query.
- ☑ **QUERY SETTINGS PANEL** contains the name of the query (which by default, this is the name of the table that was imported) and a list of the transformation (steps) for the query. Each transformation creates a step.

Who Will Benefit From Using Power Query?

There are several categories of people that can benefit from using Power Query, as explained below.

DATA ANALYSTS While people that fall into this category may not have this job title, they will use Power Query to import the data that is needed to create data models, transform data, use DAX and/or M, as needed to create formulas, create reports and dashboards, either for their own use or for other people to use.

END USERS often benefit from the work of Data Analysts. They tend not to create the queries, reports or dashboards that they use in their decision making process. At most, some end users will create reports, but not import or create data models. People that often fall into this category are managers and executives in the company.

DEVELOPERS create Enterprise BI solutions. People in this category are usually in the IT department. They understand concepts like data warehouses, big data and cubes. People in this category know how to design and create the infrastructure needed to support and maintain the BI initiatives. They can also create any new data models or databases that may be needed. Job titles that are in the category are Programmer and Data Architect.

What Can Power BI Desktop Do?

As stated earlier, Power BI Desktop has the Excel Power tools combined in one interface. The goal of this section is to explain Power BI Desktop functionality and which component is used to complete the task. Keep in mind that Power Query is just one component in Power BI Desktop. You can use this section as a pseudo project plan for each visualization that you need to create.

Step 1: Get The Data

Each visualization needs data. In this step you need to find (often referred to as discovering the data) and connect to the data. If you know that the data is clean and in the right layout, you may be able to skip parts of step 3 below.

Step 2: Load The Data Into The Data Model

Ultimately, the data must be loaded into the data model, so that it can be used to create DAX formulas and create reports. As you will see, during the connection process, you have the options to immediately load the data into the data model or select the Edit option. Both options display the data in the Query Editor.

Step 3: Transform The Data

The goal of this step is to get the data ready for the creation of the visualization. This step mainly uses Power Query. The data may or may not be clean by the time you get to this step. You have the option of transforming the data before and after the data is loaded into the data model. Calculations that are needed for the visualization (charts or maps for example) are created in this step.

Step 4: Create The Reports Or Dashboards

Power BI Desktop offers a wide variety of visualization options that can be used to create and enhance a report, including charts, maps, filters and slicers. There are also custom visualizations that you can use. This step uses the Report view.

Step 5: Share The Data

Depending on the environment, this step may or may not be needed. This step is used to upload or publish data models and reports that you create in Power BI Desktop to your Power BI web site or publish them to Power BI from Power BI Desktop. When published to Power BI (in the cloud) or to a server, other people can use the reports. In Power BI Desktop, this functionality is known as **PUBLISHING DATA**. Reports created in Power BI Desktop can be used on a tablet that has Windows 8.1 or higher, if the Power BI App for Windows is installed.

> **What Is The Difference Between The 32 And 64-Bit Versions Of Power BI Desktop?**
> ① If you know that you will be working with large data sets (millions of records in a table), you should consider installing the 64-bit version of Power BI Desktop.
> ② The 32 and 64-bit versions can be installed on a computer that has a 64-bit processor.

Exercise 1.1: Download And Install Power BI Desktop

If you have not already installed Power BI Desktop, follow the steps in this exercise.

> **Minimum Prerequisites To Install The Software**
> To install Power BI Desktop, your computer needs to have the following installed: Internet Explorer 10 or higher, Windows 7 or higher or Windows Server 2008 R2 or higher.

Download The Software

> If you have Microsoft Office installed, you should install the same version (32 or 64-bit) of Power BI Desktop, especially if you will be importing Excel files or Access databases, because both of these file types use the Access database engine. The Access database engine bit version has to be the same of the Power BI Desktop bit version. If they are not the same, you will get the error discussed in the warning below.

> **Importing Data From An Access Database Or Excel File**
> Truth be told, it can be tricky trying to import data from an Access database or Excel file into a data model. In Power BI Desktop, this issue arises when you have the 64-bit version of Power BI Desktop installed and the version of Microsoft Office that you have installed is not the same platform. By that I mean if both are not 64-bit. The most popular error is "The provider 'Microsoft.ACE.OLEDB.12.0' is not registered".
>
> As far as I can figure out, this happens most often when the 32-bit version of Office is installed. If you get this error, there are a few software installation options that you can select from, to try and remedy the compatibility problem. The option that you select depends on which version of Office (32 or 64-bit), you have installed.
>
> If you have the 32-bit version of Office installed, you need to install the 64-bit version of the data providers, if you want to use the 64-bit version of Power BI Desktop. Each provider has a version of the Access database engine. You can download the provider from the Microsoft Access Database Engine 2010 Redistributable web page. This page has a 32 and 64-bit versions of the providers.
> https://www.microsoft.com/en-us/download/details.aspx?id=13255
>
> If you run into this issue and have the 32-bit version of Office installed, it is easier to install the 32-bit version of Power BI Desktop, then it is to install the 64-bit version of the data providers, but this is just my two cents. <smile>

1. Go to https://powerbi.microsoft.com/en-us/downloads/ (Select the Advanced download options link) or https://www.microsoft.com/en-us/download/details.aspx?id=45331 Both links have the 32 and 64-bit versions, as shown below in Figure 1-3.

2. Click the **DOWNLOAD** button ⇒

   Check one of the options shown in Figure 1-3.

   The first file shown in the figure is the 32-bit version ⇒ Click Next.

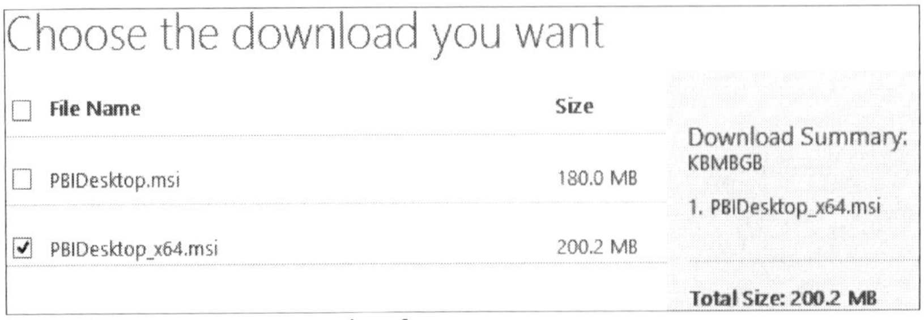

Figure 1-3 File options to select from

3. On the Opening dialog box, click the Save File button and save the file to your hard drive. The most convenient location to save the file to is the desktop <no pun intended>, so that it is easy to find when you install the software. Once the installation is complete, you can move the file to another location or delete it.

Install The Software

1. Double-click on the file that you downloaded to install the software. Follow the instructions. If you check the **LAUNCH MICROSOFT POWER BI DESKTOP OPTION** on the last screen of the installation dialog box, the software will automatically open, when the installation is completed.

2. When the installation is complete, double-click on the yellow Power BI Desktop icon. You should see the workspace shown in Figure 1-4. The options are explained below the figure.

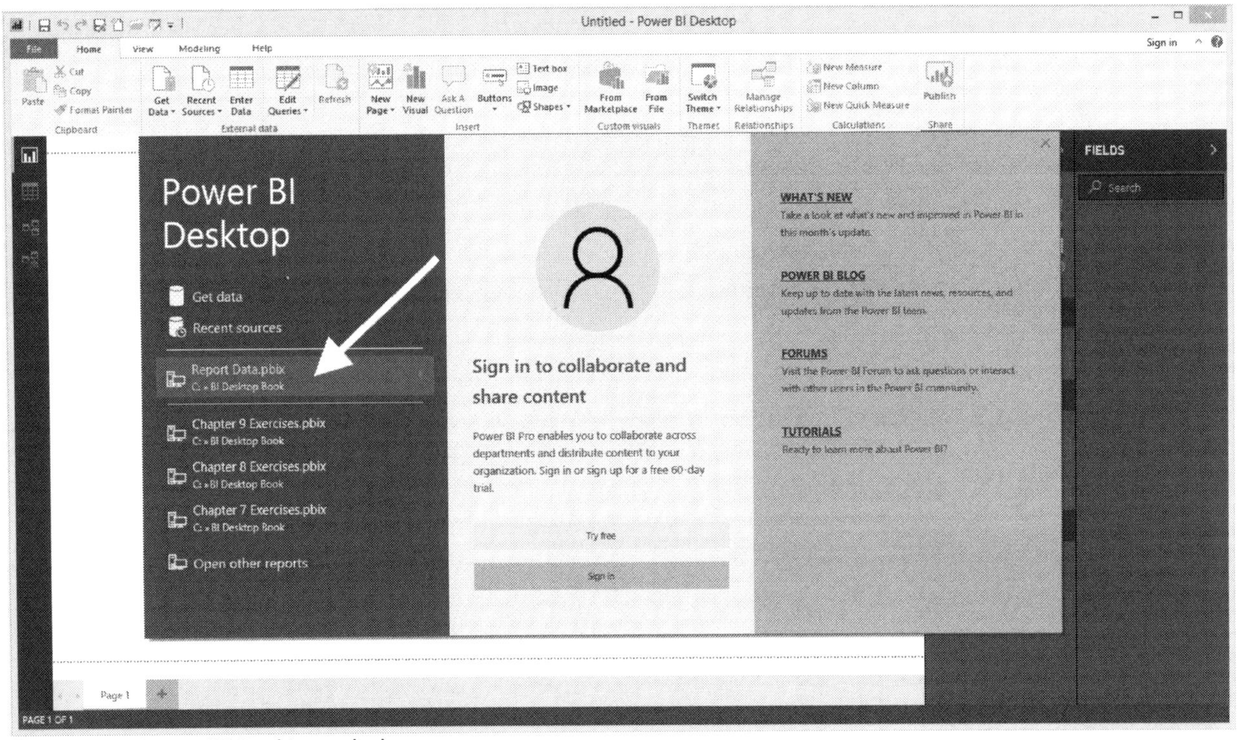

Figure 1-4 Power BI Desktop splash screen

Unlike most splash screens, this one lets you get to work right away. The **GET DATA OPTION**, opens a new file and displays the Get Data dialog box. [See Chapter 2, Figure 2-3]

The **RECENT SOURCES LINK** displays a list of data sources that you have already connected to, as shown in Figure 1-5. You can select from this list to import data.

The first section below the Recent Sources link, contains files that you have pinned to the list. Figure 1-4 illustrates the one file that has been **PINNED**.

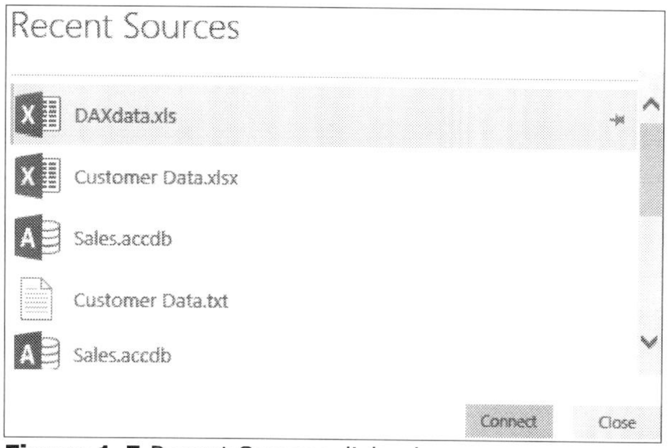

Figure 1-5 Recent Sources dialog box

Once you have saved report files, the most recent four, including pinned files (reports), will be displayed below the Recent Sources option on the splash screen. This is helpful when you need to open an existing file. By default, pinned files are displayed here first, whether or not they were recently used. If there is a file that you are not currently using, you can unpin it from this list.

Files that are displayed below the Recent Sources list have the shortcut menu shown in Figure 1-6. The options are explained in Chapter 2, Table 2-3.

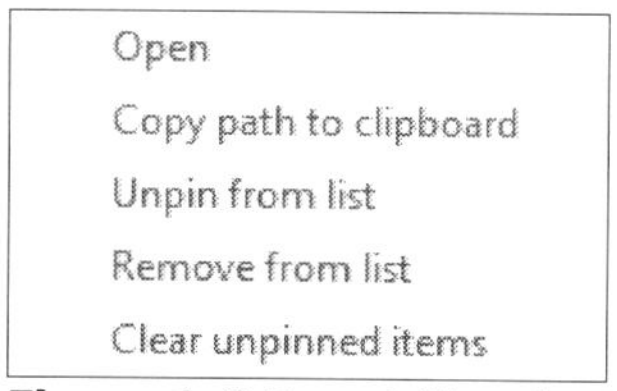

Figure 1-6 Recent files shortcut menu

The **OPEN OTHER REPORTS LINK**, on the splash screen, displays the last folder that you saved a report file to. This lets you select the file that you need.

Exercise 1.2: Create A Folder For Your Files

You will create and modify several files in this book. It is a good idea to store all of them in the same folder on your computer, so that you can find them easily. Many of the topics discussed in this book have step-by-step exercises. If you want to follow along, you need to download the practice files used in this book.

1. To obtain the files, send an email to powerquery@tolanapublishing.com. If you do not receive an email in a few minutes with the subject line Power Query Book Files, check the spam folder in your email software. When you receive the email, follow the steps below.

2. Open Windows Explorer ⇒ Right-click on the C drive ⇒ New ⇒ Folder. Type `Power Query Book` as the folder name. I will refer to this folder as **YOUR FOLDER** throughout this book.

3. From the web page listed in the email that you received, and download the zip file into your folder ⇒
   Once the zip file is downloaded, extract the files to your folder.

   Your folder structure should look like the one shown in Figure 1-7. You should also have files below these folders on the right side of Windows Explorer.

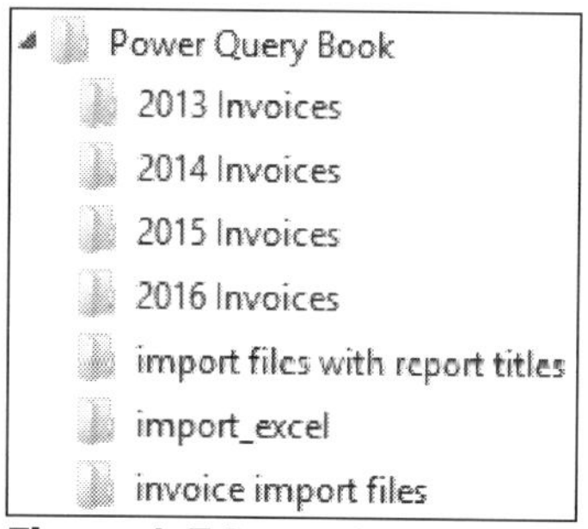

Figure 1-7 Power Query Book folder structure

> **Power Query Links.txt File**
> This file is in the zip file that you just downloaded. When you go through this book, there are links that you may need to type in. In case you do not want to type them in, you can copy and paste them from this file into your web browser. You're welcome! <smile>

Database Terminology

Below are key terms that you should understand about databases in order to work with Power BI Desktop efficiently.

Field A field contains one piece of information and is stored in a record. Examples of fields include customer name and order amount. A "column" in a Power Query table/query is the same as a field in a database.

Record A record has one or more fields. Each of the fields in a record are related. A record looks like a row of data in a spreadsheet. Power Query refers to records as rows.

Table A table is stored in a database and is a collection of records. Most databases have more than one table. Tables are linked on fields. Tables may remind you of a spreadsheet, because databases have rows and columns. Each table contains information about a specific topic. For example, a well designed Customers table would only contain information about customers. The Customers table would not contain information about products.

In Power Query, data stored on sheets in an Excel workbook, data stored in text files and other non database files are also considered to be tables.

Primary Key is a unique identifier for each row of data in the table. Primary keys are usually numeric and system generated, sequentially. They are usually used to create relationships (links) between tables.

Database A database is a collection of information that is stored in one or more tables.

Relational Database A relational database is a collection of **RELATED** information that is stored in one or more tables in the database.

Relationship A relationship is a connection between two tables. It is how two or more tables are joined (linked). Tables can be joined when they have at least one field in each table, that has the same value. Tables can have more than one relationship. For example, an invoice table can be joined to a products table because each invoice will have at least one item from the products table. The Invoice table can also be linked to the Customers table, because each invoice has a customer.

Data Concepts

Before you go any further, there are some terms that you need to understand to get a better idea of how Power BI Desktop can aid in the decision making process, display trends in data and much more. These terms will also help you start to understand how powerful Power BI Desktop is. These are terms that you may have heard before, but are not exactly sure what they mean. The goal of this section is to briefly explain them and their relationship to Power BI Desktop.

Aggregation Is a way to summarize data values or group data.

Dashboards The intended goal is to display large amounts of data in a clear, consolidated and meaningful way. Dashboards usually contain two or more visuals on the same page or screen. A dashboard should allow the person viewing it to see the information at a glance. Sadly, out in the workplace, you will see dashboards that have animation and gauges that make it hard to figure out what the data represents. Try not to join the group of people that create visualizations that are difficult to understand. <smile>

Data Analysis Expressions (DAX) Is a programming language that Power BI Desktop supports. It contains a collection of functions that are used to create formulas. These formulas are used to manipulate data that is stored in tables, in the data model. DAX formulas are created in the Data view. Power BI Desktop has over 200 DAX functions that you can use. Sum, Average, Count and Distinct Count are some of the functions. Unless all of the reports that you will create are very basic and do not need totals, at some point, you will have the need to use DAX. (1)

Data Refresh This feature is used to copy (re-import) the most recent version of data into the tables in Power BI Desktop, from the original data source.

Data Source A data source is what the data is stored in. Examples of data sources are databases, text files, OLAP cubes and spreadsheets.

Data Source Connection Contains instructions that Power BI Desktop uses to connect to a data source, so that data from the data source can be imported into Power BI Desktop.

M Language Is a programming language that the Query Editor (in Power BI Desktop) supports. Like DAX, M contains a collection of functions that are used to create formulas. These formulas are used to transform data that is stored in tables, in the data model. M formulas are created in the Query Editor. (1)

(1) In depth coverage of this language is beyond the scope of this book.

M vs DAX
M is the programming language used in the Query Editor to transform data. This language cannot reference fields in the data model. DAX is the programming language used on the Data and Report views to create calculated columns and measures. DAX can reference fields in the same table that the formula is created in, as well as, reference fields in other tables, in the data model.

M Formula Language Reference Guide
If you are interested in learning more about the M language, this web page is a good starting point. https://docs.microsoft.com/en-us/powerquery-m/power-query-m-reference

DAX Reference Guide
If you want to learn more about DAX, this link provides a starting point. https://docs.microsoft.com/en-us/dax/dax-function-reference. As luck would have it, I have written a book that you may find helpful, called Learning DAX For Power BI Desktop. The ISBN is 978-1-935208-42-6.

Power BI Desktop Terms

Below are some terms that are used in Power BI Desktop that you should understand.

.pbix This is the file extension for Power BI Desktop report files. This is the file type that is used most. It is the one that you import data into and create queries and reports in. It is often referred to as "the file" or "the report file".

.pbit This is the file extension for Power BI Desktop template files. This template file does not work like template files that you may have used in other software. For example, in some other software, if you make and save changes to the template file, you are given the option of updating any file that was created based on the template. The template file in Power BI Desktop, does not work like that.

Report is a series of pages (that have charts and tables) and data used in a .pbix file.

Visuals or **Visualizations** are items used to describe items on a report. Examples of reports are tables and charts.

Power BI Desktop Workspace

Figure 1-8 shows the Power BI Desktop workspace. Table 1-1 explains the illustrated options.

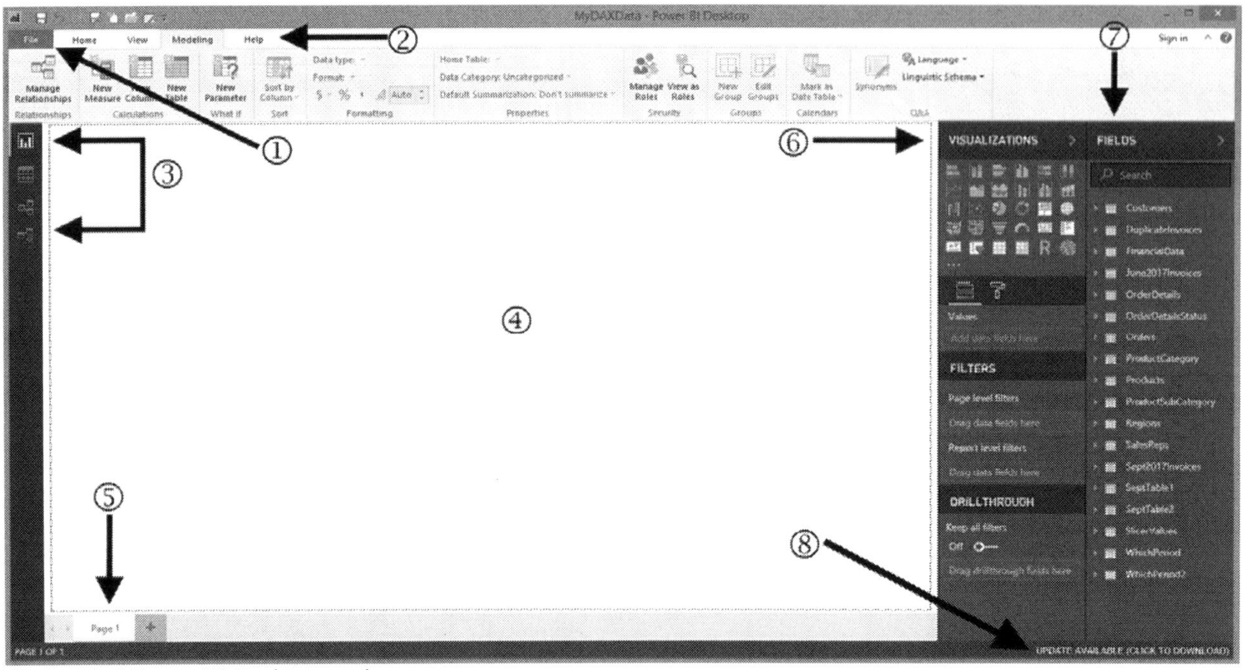

Figure 1-8 Power BI Desktop workspace

Option	Description
①	**FILE TAB** [See File Tab Options]
②	The **RIBBON** has options that are used to get and manage data and create reports. The options on the Modeling tab change, depending on the view that is selected.
③	The **VIEW** options are used to switch between the **REPORT VIEW**, **DATA VIEW**, **RELATIONSHIPS VIEW** and **MODELING VIEW**. [See Views]
④	The **CANVAS** (the white space) is used to create reports and dashboards.
⑤	The **PAGE OPTIONS** are used to view different pages in the report and add new pages to the report.
⑥	The **VISUALIZATIONS PANEL** has options to select a table or chart style to use to create and modify reports and dashboards. The options on the Fields tab (also known as the **FIELD WELL**), at the bottom of this panel change, based on the visualization that is selected. This panel is only available when the Report view is selected.
⑦	The **FIELDS PANEL** displays the tables and fields in the data model. This panel is available on the Data, Report and Modeling views. The fields are used to create reports.
⑧	**UPDATE NOTIFICATION** [See Getting Software Updates]

Table 1-1 Workspace options explained

File Tab Options

Figure 1-9 shows the options on the File tab.

The Import and Export options are explained below.

The **EXPORT TO PDF OPTION** is used to create a PDF file from the report pages in the file.

The **OPTIONS AND SETTINGS** option displays the menu on the right side of the figure. The **OPTIONS** option, opens the Options dialog box shown later in Figure 1-17.

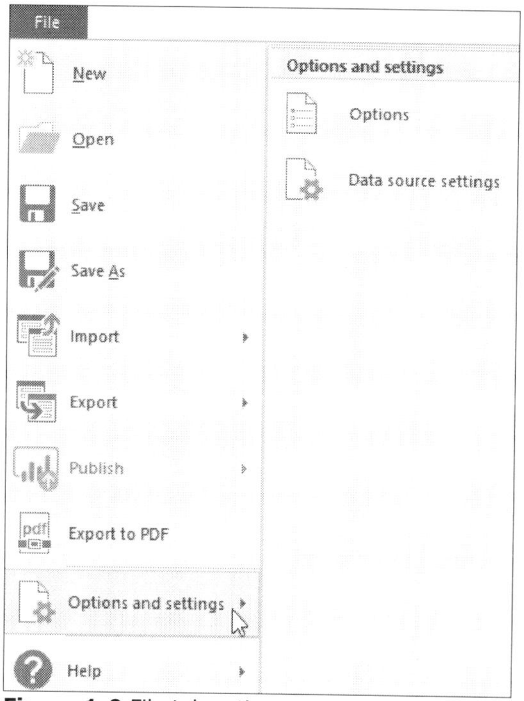

Figure 1-9 File tab options

Import Options

The right side of Figure 1-10 shows additional types of files that can be imported.

EXCEL WORKBOOK CONTENTS Select this option to import data models (including relationships, KPI's, measures and data categories that were created in Power Pivot), Power View reports, queries created in Power Query, linked tables and external data connections, from an Excel workbook.

This option will be helpful if you have created data models in Power Pivot or created visuals in Power View (in Excel), that you want to use in Power BI Desktop.

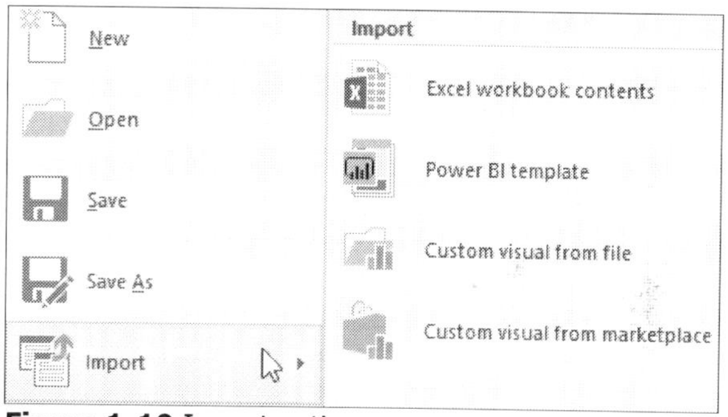

Figure 1-10 Import options

POWER BI TEMPLATE Select this option to open a **.PBIT** template file. Once opened, save the template file with a new (.pbix) file name. This option makes a copy of the template file (same as using File ⇒ Save As). It does not import the contents of the template file into the report file that you have open.

CUSTOM VISUAL FROM FILE Is used to import a custom visual (chart type) that you have downloaded. These are different chart styles then the ones on the Visualizations panel shown earlier in Figure 1-8. The links below will take you to the Custom Visuals home page, where you can look for chart types to download.

https://appsource.microsoft.com/en-us/marketplace/apps?product=power-bi-visuals or https://appsource.microsoft.com/en-us/marketplace/apps. On the left, in the Web Apps section, click on the **POWER BI VISUALS** link.

CUSTOM VISUAL FROM MARKETPLACE This option is used to download a custom visual that your organization has created. It requires a Power BI account, to access these files.

Export Option

The **POWER BI TEMPLATE** option is used to save the current report file (**.PBIX**) as a template (**.PBIT**) file. This is helpful if you have created a file that has data sources, relationships, DAX formulas, transformations or report layouts already set up, that you need to use as the basis for another report file. An example that comes to mind is creating a template file that has a date table, because many reports are date driven, and parameter fields for tables in the template.

Publish Option

The option shown in Figure 1-11 is used to copy the report file to a location where it can be used (shared) by other people. The option is only available when you have a file open.

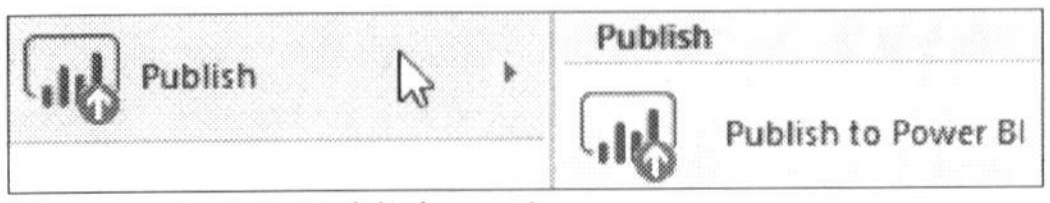

Figure 1-11 Publish options

PUBLISH TO POWER BI This option is used to upload the current file to PowerBI.com. Using this option is beyond the scope of this book.

> **Load vs Import Terminology**
> By default, Power BI Desktop uses the word **LOAD** to reference the process of copying data from one location to another. Other software packages use the word **IMPORT** to reference the same functionality. I use these terms interchangeably.

Views

There are four views, as described below.

The **REPORT VIEW** most resembles Power View, in terms of functionality, because it is used to create and view reports. This is the default view when Power BI Desktop is first opened.

The **DATA VIEW** most resembles Power Pivot in terms of functionality. It is used to manage the data model and create DAX formulas.

The **RELATIONSHIPS VIEW** most resembles the Diagram View in Power Pivot, in terms of functionality. It displays the tables in the data model in a graphical layout. It is used to create and manage relationships. Relationships can also be created and managed from the other views.

MODELING VIEW [See Chapter 3, Modeling View]

Getting Software Updates

Power BI Desktop is updated monthly. You will see the notification illustrated earlier in Figure 1-8, in the lower right corner of the window, when an update is available. Before you click on this link, save what you are working on. If you do not see this notification in 30-45 days, open the Options dialog box (See Figure 1-17) ⇒ Click on the **UPDATES** option in the Global section ⇒ Check the **DISPLAY UPDATE NOTIFICATIONS OPTION** ⇒ Click OK.

You will also see the message shown in Figure 1-12, on the taskbar. You can click on it to download the new update file.

Figure 1-12 Update message on the taskbar

Power BI Desktop Software Updates

Many software companies have changed to a faster update release schedule for some of their software titles. Many Microsoft products fall into this category. The core functionality of the software does not change frequently. A large portion of the updates are new features, modifications to existing functionality that was not working as expected (aka a bug fix) or a name change of an existing option.

One of my favorite features of Power BI Desktop is that an updated version is released monthly. For users, that is great. For authors that write books about the software, the frequent updating presents a problem. By the time you read this book, or any book on Power BI Desktop for that matter, some parts of the book will be out of date. Sadly, there isn't anything that I can do about this, other then what I am doing right now, and that is to be honest and up front about a situation that I cannot control.

Home Tab

The options on the tab shown in Figure 1-13, are used to import data, add objects to a report, create measures and columns, manage relationships and more.

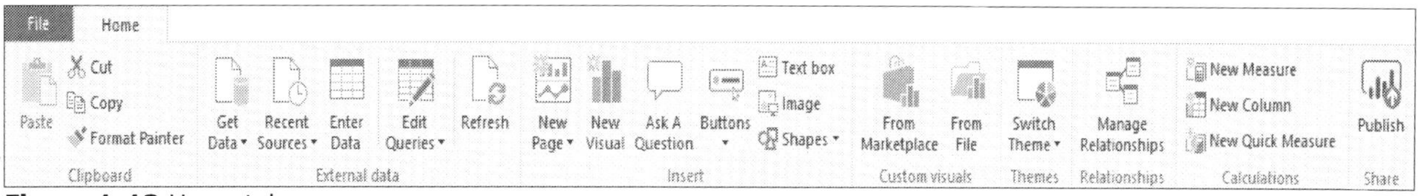

Figure 1-13 Home tab

External Data Group

The options in this group, shown above in Figure 1-13, are used to import data into the data model, create a new table, edit queries and parameters and refresh the data. [See Chapter 2, Table 2-1]

Relationships Group

The **MANAGE RELATIONSHIPS BUTTON** is used to create, edit and delete relationships between the tables. This button is only enabled when tables have been loaded into the data model.

Calculations Group

The options in this group are used to create columns and measures for the table that is selected. These buttons are used to create DAX formulas.

View Tab

The options shown in Figure 1-14 are only available from the Report view.

They are used to select options to display on the Report view.

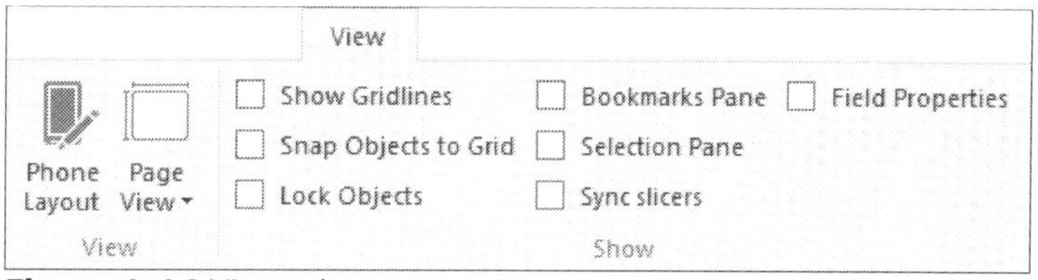

Figure 1-14 View tab

Modeling Tab

Some of the options shown in Figure 1-15, are the same as the ones on the Home tab. The majority of options on this tab are used to create DAX formulas and manage the data model. This tab is available on the Report and Data views.

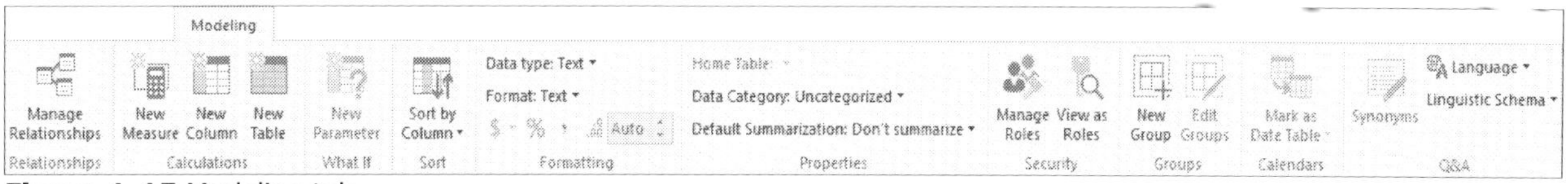

Figure 1-15 Modeling tab

Help Tab

The options on the tab shown in Figure 1-16, that I think you may find are the most helpful, are briefly discussed below.

The **POWER BI BLOG** is updated frequently. It has articles about all things Power BI Desktop, including free webinars on various topics and information about each monthly software update.

The **COMMUNITY BUTTON** is the forum for the Power BI tools, including Power BI Desktop (which is the forum that this button opens) and others like the Power BI Service. You can search for help and post questions.

The **SUBMIT AN IDEA OPTION** is used to submit a request for new functionality and read about existing requests.

Figure 1-16 Help tab

Options Dialog Box

This dialog box is used to customize the software by selecting the default options for Power BI Desktop, mainly Power Query, (the **GLOBAL** options), which are for all files. The **CURRENT FILE** options are only applied to the file that this dialog box was opened from.

From time to time, sections are added to the column on the left. So you may see sections on the left, that are not shown in Figure 1-17, below.

Global Options

As applicable, the options in this section are applied to every report file, that is created on the computer. That is because the Global options are saved on your computer.

Data Load Options

The options shown in Figure 1-17 are used to select the default options for loading data.

The **DATA CACHE MANAGEMENT OPTIONS** are used to select the maximum amount of hard drive space to allocate for copies of the query preview results that are stored on the computers hard drive. This feature makes it possible for the queries to load faster.

As shown in Figure 1-17, more than 9 MB has been used. This number grows each time you preview data in the Query Editor. Clear the cache when you are close to the maximum allowed amount.

If a copy or subset of the dataset is stored in the cache, that is what you are viewing, until the cache is cleared or you refresh the data. If you always want to use current data, make the **MAXIMUM ALLOWED** option a smaller number, like 32 MB, which is the smallest amount recognized. If that does not meet you needs, you will have to click the **CLEAR CACHE** button on a regular basis or raise the maximum allowed (MB).

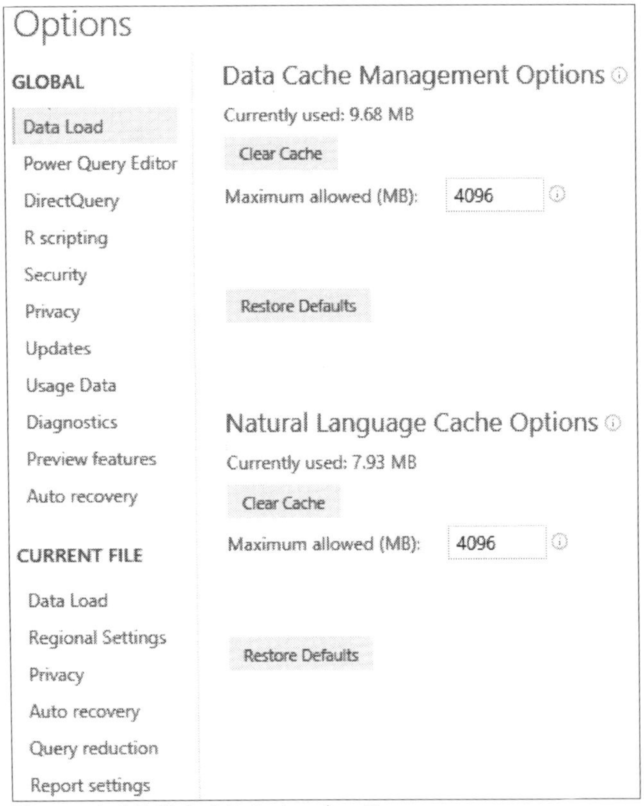

Figure 1-17 Global Data Load options

The **DIRECT QUERY OPTION** is used to select whether or not DAX measures are restricted when using the Direct Query options to connect to a data source. For more information see https://docs.microsoft.com/en-us/power-bi/desktop-use-directquery

The **R SCRIPTING OPTIONS** are used to select options so that R Scripts can be used in Power BI Desktop.

The **SECURITY OPTIONS** are used to select whether or not:

☑ Approval is needed to create to create native database queries or web previews.

☑ Data extensions that are not certified can be loaded.

☑ A warning should be displayed when a custom visual is added to a report.

Power Query Editor Options

The options shown in Figure 1-18 are used to select features that are enabled on the Power Query Editor. You can also select whether or not the option to create a new parameter is available on data source dialog boxes, like the Web connector [See Chapter 2, Figure 2-5] or on the Replace Values dialog box.

If you plan to create parameters, enabling the parameter option will be useful.

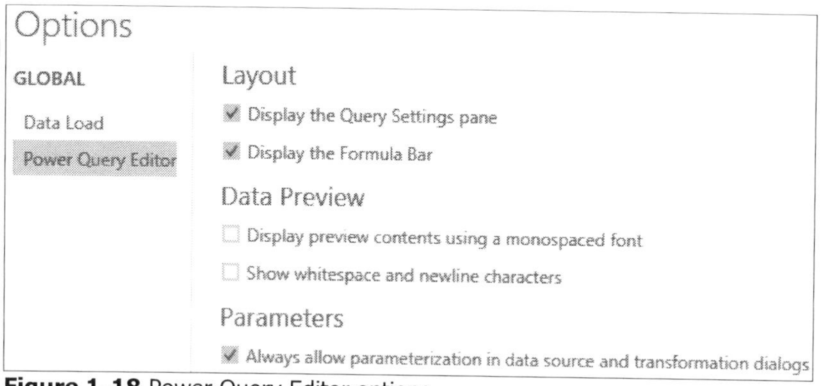

Figure 1-18 Power Query Editor options

Privacy Options

The global **PRIVACY LEVEL** options shown in Figure 1-19, are used to select whether or not the privacy level settings for each data source are used.

The **COMBINE DATA ... OPTION** is the default option.

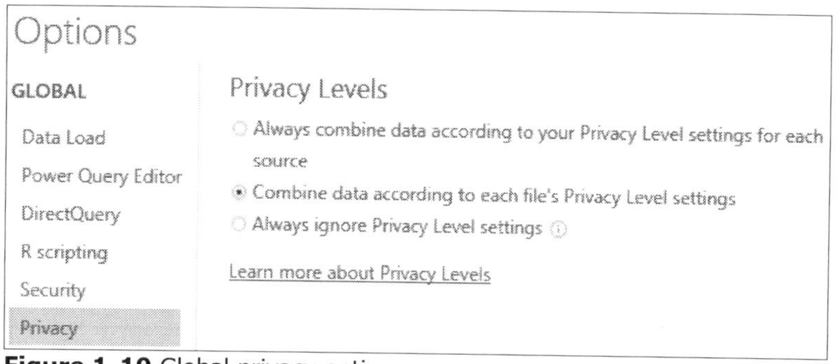

Figure 1-19 Global privacy options

The **UPDATES OPTION**, if checked, will display a message in Power BI Desktop, when an update for the software is available. [See the lower right corner of Figure 1-8 and Figure 1-12]

The **USAGE DATA OPTION**, if checked, will collect information about how you are using Power BI Desktop. The collected information is sent to Microsoft. Clear the option on this screen, if you want to opt out and not have your information sent to Microsoft.

The options on the **DIAGNOSTICS SCREEN**, if checked, will create a file that logs your actions in Power BI Desktop. This can be helpful if you are having issues with the software, because you can send the trace file to Microsoft, so that they can help resolve the problem. You can also enable the crash dump collection, which captures information when Power BI Desktop crashes. The screen also displays the version of Power BI Desktop that is installed.

The **PREVIEW FEATURES SCREEN**, shown in Figure 1-20, lists features that you can try out. The features on this screen can change monthly.

At some point, most of the features on this screen will be released and be a permanent part of the Power BI Desktop.

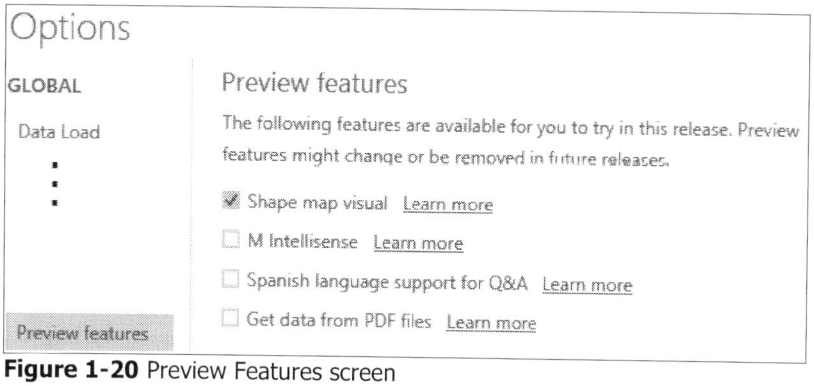

Figure 1-20 Preview Features screen

The first two **AUTO RECOVERY OPTIONS** shown in Figure 1-21, if enabled, will recover your files if Power BI Desktop crashes or if you close the software without saving changes that you made to any file that was open.

The **AUTO RECOVERY FILE LOCATION OPTION** can be changed. This is where the files are stored that can be recovered. I change this to a folder that I could easily find.

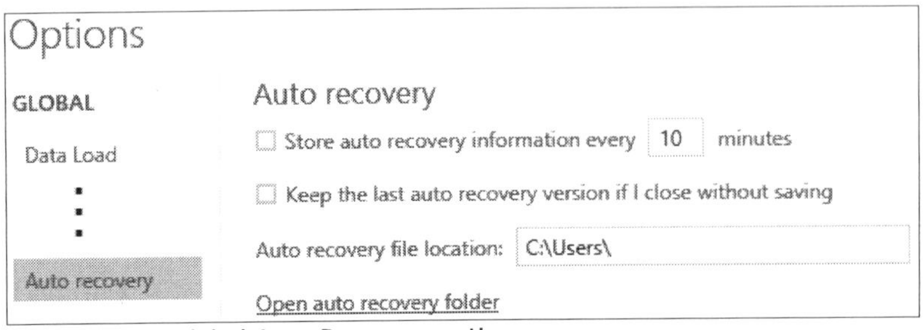

Figure 1-21 Global Auto Recovery options

When you open Power BI Desktop and you have files that can be recovered, you will see the **SHOW RECOVERED FILES** link on the splash screen, as shown in Figure 1-22.

Clicking on the link will display the files that can be recovered, on the dialog box shown in Figure 1-23.

If you want to recover a file shown, select it, then click the Open button to open the recovery file.

Figure 1-22 Recovered files link

If you click the Close button or click the X on the dialog box shown in Figure 1-23, you will see the dialog box shown in Figure 1-24. This lets you select whether or not you want to keep the file(s) that can be recovered and make a decision later about what to do with the files.

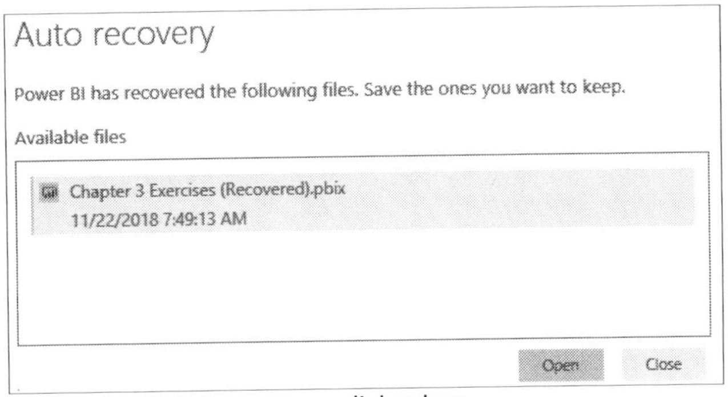

Figure 1-23 Auto recovery dialog box

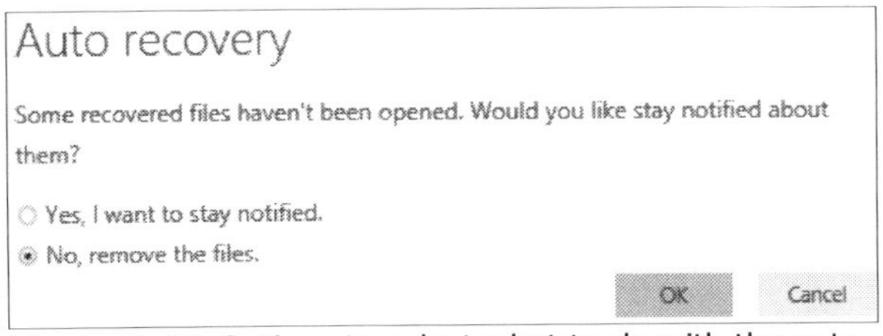

Figure 1-24 Options to select what to do with the auto recovery files

Current File Options

As its name suggests, options in this section are only saved in the file that the Options dialog box was opened from. They are not applied to all **.PBIX FILES** created on the computer, like the global options are. What is important to know is that these options override the corresponding global options, at the top of the Options dialog box.

> If you make changes in this section, you should save the file as soon as you have finished making the changes, so that they will be applied to the file.

Data Load Options

Figure 1-25 shows the current file options, which are explained below.

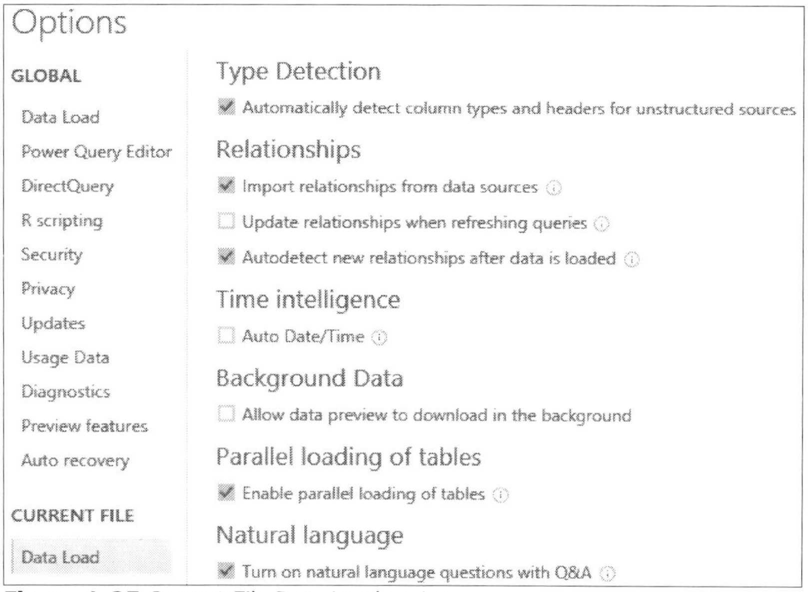

Figure 1-25 Current File Data Load options

① **TYPE DETECTION** [See How Type Detection Works]

② **RELATIONSHIPS** [See Relationships Options]

③ **TIME INTELLIGENCE** [See Time Intelligence Option]

④ **BACKGROUND DATA** By default, this option allows a preview of the data to be downloaded in the background, so that it can be previewed on the Navigator dialog box. Clearing the check mark reduces the amount of data that is processed, which increases performance.

⑤ **PARALLEL LOADING OF TABLES** Checking this option allows more than one table of data to be loaded into the data model, at the same time. Depending on the amount of data in the tables, the import can take longer to complete, when this option is checked. When I have tables that have millions of rows of data, I clear this option, so that they can be loaded individually.

⑥ **NATURAL LANGUAGE** Checking this option allows you to ask questions of the data in the file, using Q&A.

How Type Detection Works

This option is for the connectors in the **FILE** category on the Get Data dialog box. If this option is checked, each column of data imported from a data source in the File category is automatically converted to the correct data type. This means that changing the data type manually should not have to be done as much.

The feature that I like best is that before this option is applied, data in a CSV file that was imported, looked like the data shown in Figure 1-26, in the Query Editor. Yes, I know that applying the **USE FIRST ROW AS HEADER OPTION** would fix this, but one less step, is one less step, for us to do. <smile>

Additionally, when the Type Detection option is enabled, the same data is automatically displayed in the Query Editor, as shown in Figure 1-27. The formula at the top of the figure shows how some of the columns were transformed, which in this case, the transformation is selecting a data type for each column. Most of the time, the correct data type is selected, but it is a good idea to at least look at the formula. This is easier (for me), then clicking on each column in the query to view the data type. Being from the old school though, I do not enable this option because I prefer to change the data type myself.

	Column1	Column2	Column3	Column4	Column5	Column6
1	Order ID	Employee ID	Customer ID	Order Date	Shipped Date	Shipper ID
2	30	9	27	1/15/2006	1/22/2006	2
3	31	3	4	1/20/2006	1/22/2006	1
4	32	4	12	1/22/2006	1/22/2006	2

Figure 1-26 Imported CSV file without Type Detection enabled

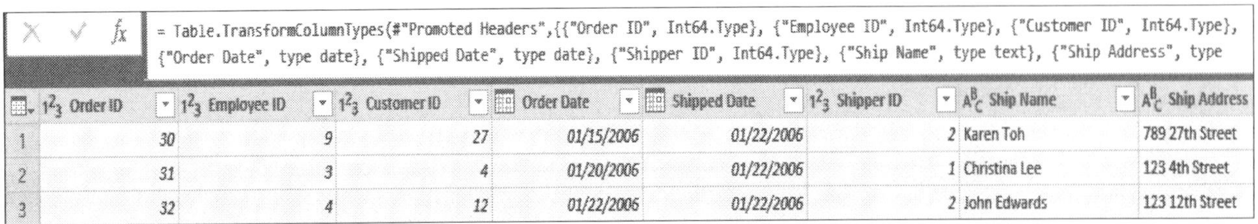
= Table.TransformColumnTypes(#"Promoted Headers",{{"Order ID", Int64.Type}, {"Employee ID", Int64.Type}, {"Customer ID", Int64.Type}, {"Order Date", type date}, {"Shipped Date", type date}, {"Shipper ID", Int64.Type}, {"Ship Name", type text}, {"Ship Address", type

	Order ID	Employee ID	Customer ID	Order Date	Shipped Date	Shipper ID	Ship Name	Ship Address
1	30	9	27	01/15/2006	01/22/2006	2	Karen Toh	789 27th Street
2	31	3	4	01/20/2006	01/22/2006	1	Christina Lee	123 4th Street
3	32	4	12	01/22/2006	01/22/2006	2	John Edwards	123 12th Street

Figure 1-27 Imported CSV file with Type Detection enabled

Some of the exercises in this book will say to delete X number of rows from the top of the table or to promote the first row as headers. Before you complete that step, look at the data on your computer. Selecting the Automatically detect column types . . option, will automatically promote rows to be headers. For example, if the instruction says to delete the first two rows and your second row from the top is actual data, only delete one row. If the instruction says to promote the first row to headers and the header columns on your computer are correct, skip that instruction and go to the next one.

Relationships Options

The options in this section are designed to auto detect relationships from data that is imported from a database. The options are explained below.

① **IMPORT RELATIONSHIPS FROM DATA SOURCES** Check this option if you want relationships that have been created in the data source (tables in a database) to be included when the data is imported. This option is implemented before the data is imported.

② **UPDATE RELATIONSHIPS WHEN REFRESHING QUERIES** Check this option if you want relationships to be checked for and updated each time you refresh the data. If you manually created relationships in Power BI Desktop for the same tables, it is possible that they will be removed, if this option is checked. Most of the time, you will probably want to check this option, unless you have created a lot of relationships manually.

③ **AUTO DETECT NEW RELATIONSHIPS AFTER DATA IS LOADED** Check this option if you want to check for relationships after the data is loaded in the data model. This is helpful if new tables are loaded to the data model, as there may be a relationship with tables already in the data model. When that is the case, the relationships will automatically be created.

Time Intelligence Option

If checked, the **AUTO DATE/TIME OPTION** is used to automatically create a hidden date table for each field that has a Date or Date/Time data type. You should uncheck this option, if the data model has a date table.

These hidden tables emulate **TIME INTELLIGENCE** behavior. I suspect that this functionality is for people that do not want to learn about time intelligence, in particular date tables. From what I can tell, if this option is enabled, the size of the data model grows. Instead of the data model only having one date table, which is all that is really needed, the data model will have several date tables.

Regional Settings Option

The **LOCALE** option, shown in Figure 1-28, is used to select regional settings for Power BI Desktop to use. The options in the drop-down list contain the regions and countries.

The region selected will be used to format dates, times, numbers and text data, when it is imported. The option selected here is the default for all of the data imported into the file.

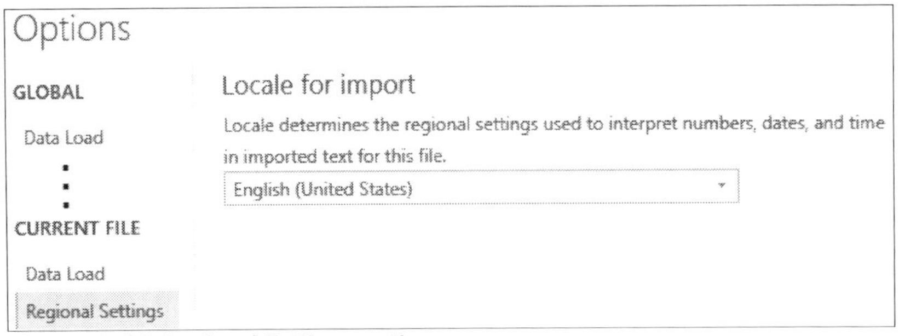

Figure 1-28 Regional Settings option

If you need to override this setting for specific columns, you can, on the Query Editor after the data is loaded. [See Chapter 4, Change Type With Locale Options]

Windows System Options
Figures 1-29 and 1-30 show you some of the Windows system settings that you can change, if they are the cause of the date or numeric data not being displayed as needed. Keep in mind that changing these system setting, affects **ALL** software on your computer that use them, not just Power BI Desktop.

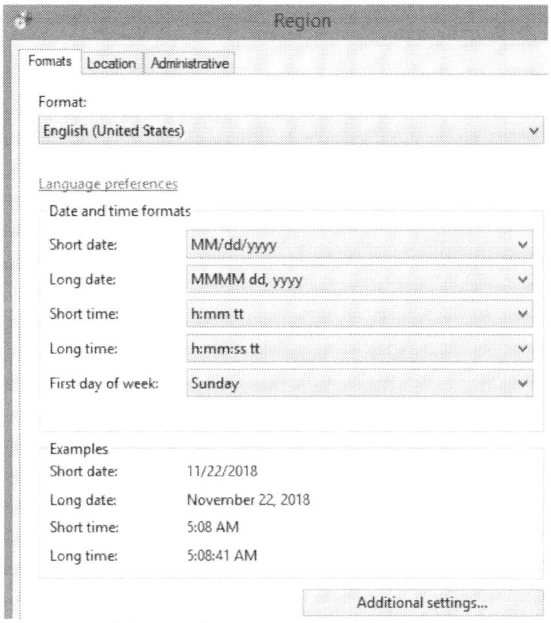

Figure 1-29 Date format options

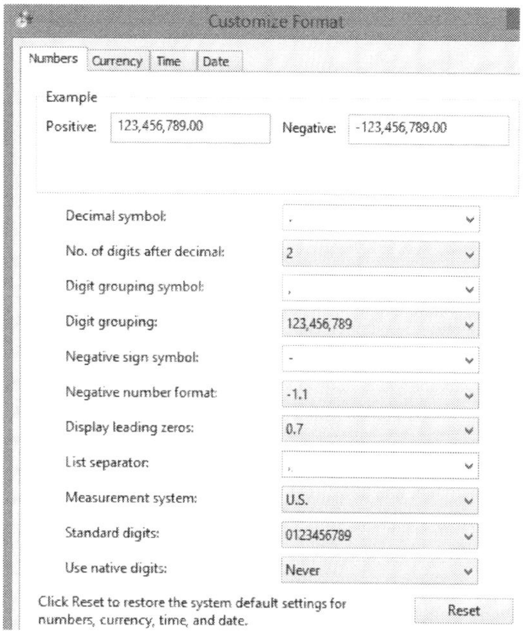

Figure 1-30 Number format options

How To Display The Date And Number Format Options Shown Above
In Windows 8.1, open the Control Panel and select **REGION**, to display the options shown above in Figure 1-29. Click the **ADDITIONAL SETTING BUTTON**, shown in Figure 1-29, to display the dialog box shown in Figure 1-30. Notice that negative numbers will be displayed with a minus sign. The other option is to display negative numbers in parenthesis. The choice is yours.

Privacy Options

Figure 1-31 shows the options that can be used to make loading data faster, by bypassing security.

The **PRIVACY LEVELS** options are used to select whether or not the firewall and privacy settings are ignored, when you combine data from more than one source.

A reason people use this option is to improve the queries performance, even though the option can make the data less secure.

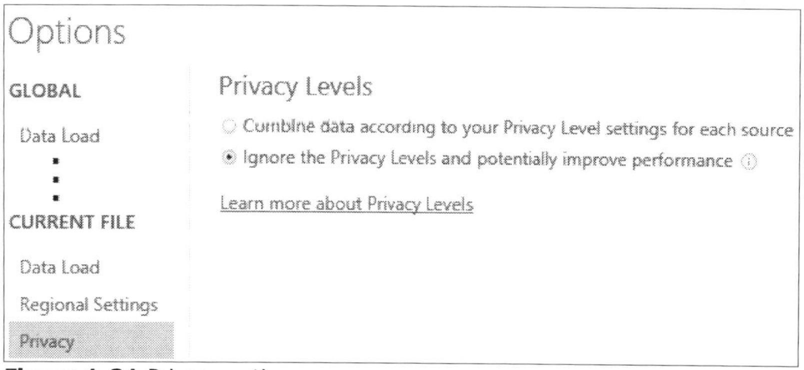

Figure 1-31 Privacy options

The **AUTO RECOVERY OPTION** shown in Figure 1-32 is used to disable the global auto recovery options, covered earlier in this chapter, for the current report file.

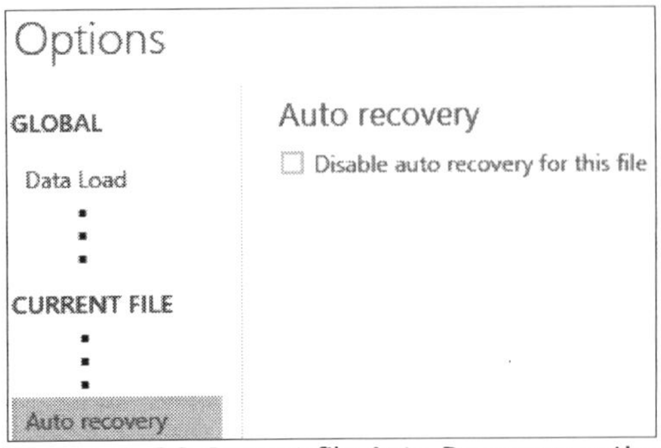

Figure 1-32 Current file Auto Recovery option

Query Reduction

The options shown in Figure 1-33 are used when you are using a really large or really slow data source in a Direct Query connection.

When using Direct Query, some actions can take a long time to respond. The options on this screen are used to send fewer queries. If an Apply button option is selected an Apply button is added to the report. Doing this means that regardless of how many selections you make, no queries will be sent until the corresponding Apply button is clicked.

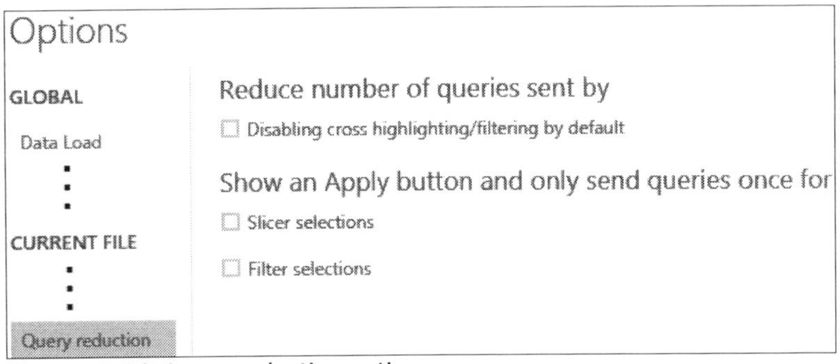

Figure 1-33 Query reduction options

Report Settings

The options shown in Figure 1-34 are used to customize reports that you create.

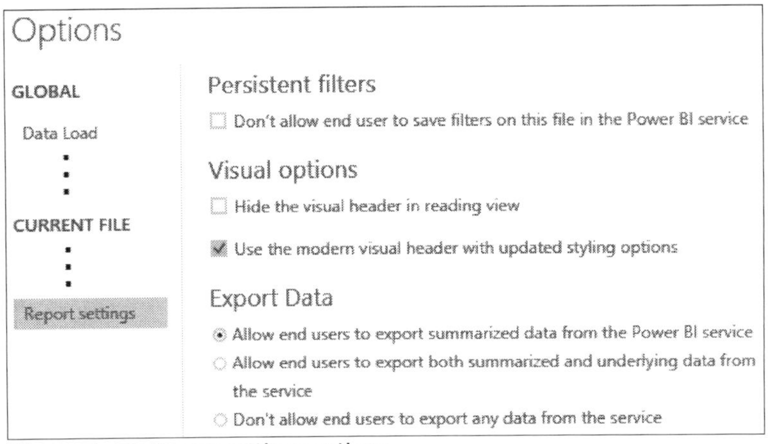

Figure 1-34 Report settings options

Data Source Settings

Selecting the **DATA SOURCE SETTINGS OPTION** on the File tab, displays the options shown in Figure 1-35. This dialog box displays a list of the recent data sources that you have used. This information is stored (cached) on your computer. Having this information cached means that you do not have to recreate the connection (as in you can skip the "Get Data" option and just select the data source that you need), each time you need to import data from another table in the data source.

The options on this dialog box are used to manage and configure settings for all data sources that you have connected to, either in the current file or since you have been using Power BI Desktop.

Data source locations, privacy levels, credentials and more can be changed. The data source location of the selected file can be changed for all queries at the same time. Examples would be a database that requires you to logon to gain access to it or the location of the data source file has changed.

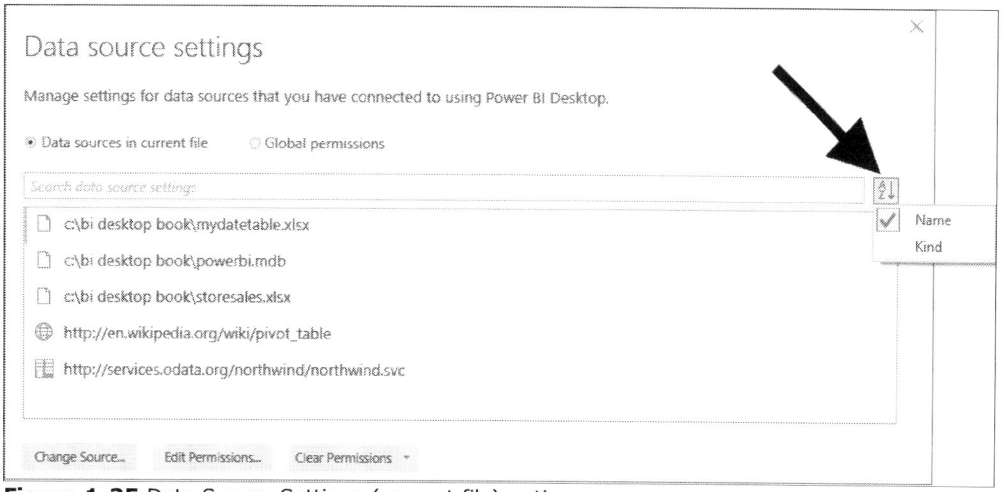

Figure 1-35 Data Source Settings (current file) options

Select the **DATA SOURCES IN CURRENT FILE OPTION** to only display data sources that are used in the current file.

The list of data sources can be sorted by **NAME** (the default) or by **KIND** (the data sources are grouped by the data source type), by selecting the option on the Sort button, illustrated above in Figure 1-35.

When selecting privacy options, keep the following in mind: The privacy options shown earlier in Figure 1-31, are used to protect company data, when it is merged or combined with non company or external data. By default, when you attempt to combine company and external data, you will be prompted to select a data privacy level. If you only use company data, selecting the **IGNORE THE PRIVACY LEVELS AND POTENTIALLY IMPROVE PERFORMANCE** option, shown earlier in Figure 1-31, will let you ignore the privacy functionality in Power BI Desktop. I have read posts on a forum that stated that when the privacy options are disabled, queries run faster.

Connecting to a SQL Server database, displays the options shown in Figure 1-36.

Select the **USE MY CURRENT CREDENTIALS** option if you want to use your Windows credentials, to connect to the data source.

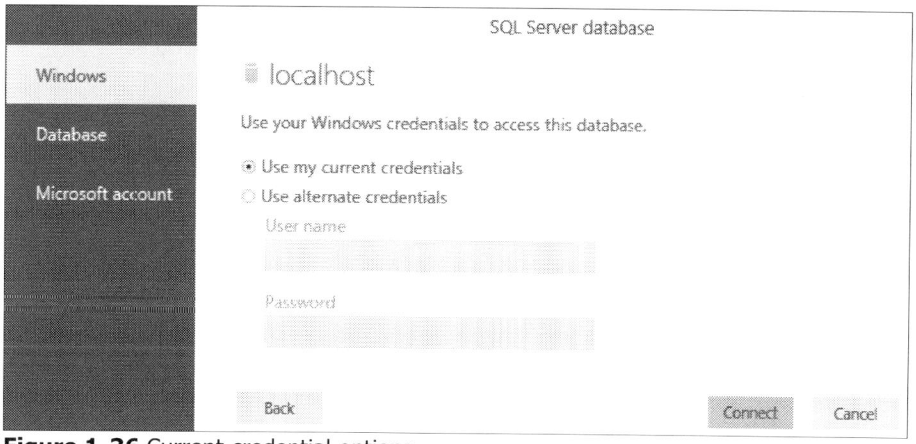

Figure 1-36 Current credential options

Managing Your Credentials

Maybe it's just me, but I think that how credentials work is a well kept secret. I figured it out the hard way. Some of the data source options require you to login. Once you enter your login information for a data source, it is saved, so that you do not have to log into the data source again.

This login information (which some refer to as authentication) is saved in an encrypted file on your computers hard drive, not in the report file, as I originally thought. This is great if your file will be used by someone else, because your personal information is not saved in the file. Not so great if you use the file on another computer. PS and by the way, that is how I found out. <smile>

When the report file is opened on another computer, Power BI Desktop searches for the encrypted file, when you select a data source that requires a user name and/or password. If this file is found, it is used. If the encrypted file is not found, you or the person using the report file, will be prompted to login.

The encrypted file is for all of the files that you create in Power BI Desktop on the computer. Each user has their own encrypted file on the computer. If you get a new computer, you can copy the file to the new computer.

The location of this file (in Windows 8.1) is: C:\users\username\AppData\Local\Microsoft\Power BI Desktop\user.zip. If you do not see the user.zip file in this location, search for it on the hard drive that you used to create the report file.

Exercise 1.3: Change Some Of The Default Options

Like all other software, Power BI Desktop has default options, that may or may not have the settings that you need. This exercise will show you how to change the settings for the exercises in this book.

1. Open Power BI Desktop ⇒ File tab ⇒ Options and Settings ⇒ Options ⇒ Current File section ⇒ Data Load.

2. Clear the check mark for the following options, as illustrated in Figure 1-37.

   ☑ Auto detect new relationships after data is loaded
   ☑ Auto Date/Time

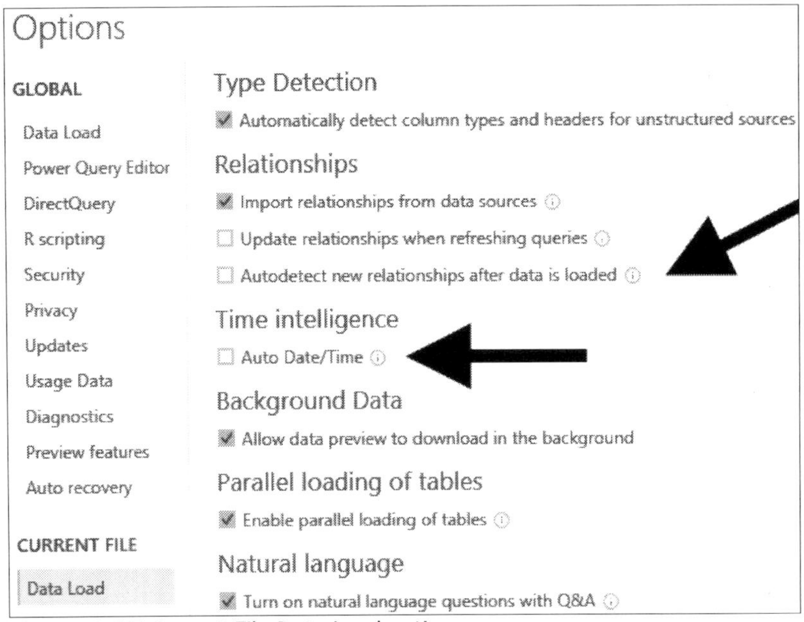

Figure 1-37 Current File Data Load options

3. The preview options checked in Figure 1-38 are covered in this book. If you see any of the options on your screen, check them now.

   If you do not see them, it means that they are out of preview mode and are in production.

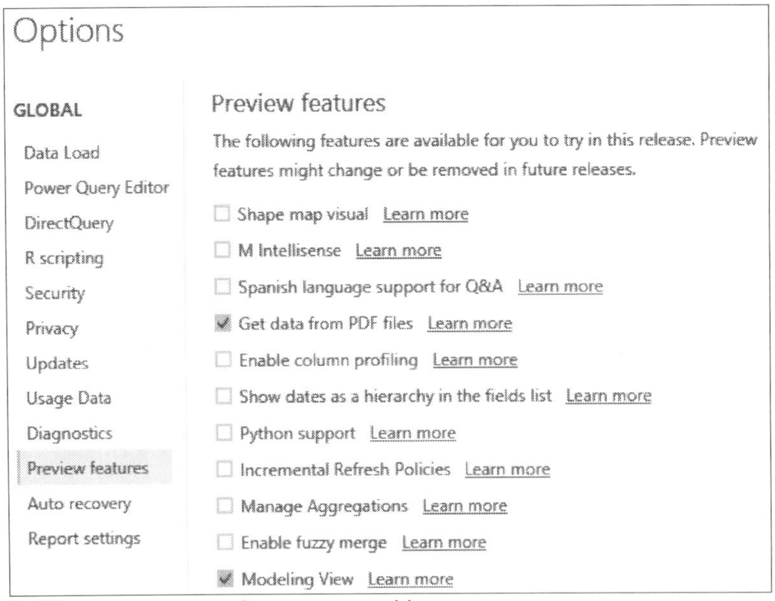

Figure 1-38 Preview features to enable

4. Click OK ⇒
   If prompted to restart your computer, click the X in the upper right corner of the dialog box, shown in Figure 1-39.

   Both dialog boxes will close, but the options that you checked, are still checked.

   Otherwise, Click OK.

   Leave the file open to use in the next chapter.

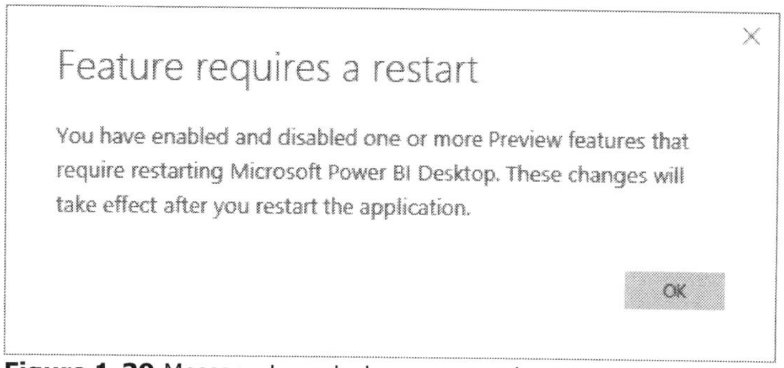

Figure 1-39 Message to restart your computer

> Options that you select in the **CURRENT FILE** section of the Options dialog box, are only applied to the file that you have open. This means that when you create another **.PBIX** file and you want some or all of the same options enabled or disabled, you have to select them again, in the Current File section. My workaround is to enable or disable the options that I need an save the file without any data. When I need to create a new .pbix file, I open this file (which I cleverly named My pbix template <smile>) and save it with a new name. For me, this is easier then trying to remember which options to check and uncheck.

Customize The Quick Access Toolbar

Throughout this book you will create a lot of report files and save existing report files with a new name. You may find it easier and faster to have options for these "File saving" tasks on the Quick Access Toolbar. The steps below show you how to add the Save options to the toolbar, shown earlier in Figure 1-2. Customizing the Quick Access Toolbar in Power BI Desktop is not required to complete the exercises in this book.

> The Undo and Redo buttons on the Quick Access Toolbar only work from the Report view. You can also use CTRL+Z (undo) and CTRL+Y (redo).

> **Quick Access Toolbar**
> Currently, there is no way to change the order of the buttons on this toolbar.

By default, your toolbar should have the Save button. The steps below show you how to add the Save As button to the toolbar.

1. Display the File tab.

2. Right-click on the Save As option ⇒
   On the shortcut menu shown in Figure 1-40, select the Add to Quick Access Toolbar option.

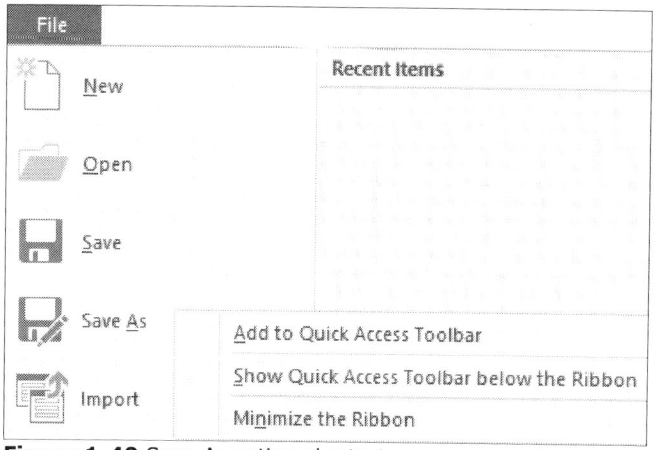

Figure 1-40 Save As option shortcut menu

Summary

This chapter provided a high level overview of Power BI Desktop. Specific features of the software were covered, in preparation for the rest of the book. The next chapter covers loading data. The goal is to get you familiar with where options are and to demonstrate how to get data from a variety of data sources and load it into Power BI Desktop.

Concepts and terminology that will help you become familiar with Power BI Desktop were also covered in this chapter. Hopefully, you downloaded the practice files, so that you can dive right in to the next chapter. I think that once you start using this software, you will start to see the potential of what it has to offer.

What Is Power BI?

At some point, if you haven't already, you will see a reference to "Power BI". Power BI is a collection of connectors, apps and more that are used to connect to the Power BI Service (in the cloud). You can think of Power BI as the cloud version of Power BI Desktop, with some additional functionality. This topic is beyond the scope of this book. For more information, you can see https://docs.microsoft.com/en-us/power-bi/power-bi-overview.

Power BI Free vs Power BI Pro Accounts

Power BI Desktop is used to import and transform data, as well as create reports. If you want to share the files that you create with other Power BI Desktop users, you will need a Power BI account to upload/publish the file to powerbi.com. The biggest differences between the free and paid Power BI accounts is that the free account only allows you to use the unsecure public sharing option. The free account cannot export a Power BI Desktop file to PowerPoint and cannot use the Analyze in Excel functionality.

LOADING DATA INTO THE DATA MODEL

In this chapter you will learn about the following:

- ☑ Data sources that Power BI Desktop supports
- ☑ Many of the options in the External Data section on the Home tab
- ☑ Loading (getting) data from a variety of file types

CHAPTER 2

Importing Data

Without data, Power BI Desktop is useless. The most used way to get data into Power BI Desktop is to import it. Small amounts of data can be pasted in. The options on the **GET DATA BUTTON** and **GET DATA DIALOG BOX** are used to import data that can be transformed and used to perform data analysis, usually for some type of decision making.

You can search for (which is referred to as **DATA DISCOVERY**) the data that you need. Data can be imported (which Power BI Desktop refers to as **LOADING DATA**) from a variety of sources and locations, including the web, text files and databases. Even though each Power BI Desktop file, only has one data model, data from various sources can be loaded into the same data model. Data can also be imported from corporate data sources, including big data (like Hadoop) and even social media data sources.

Once you have the data in Power BI Desktop, you can query it to reduce the number of rows and columns (also known as **CLEANSING THE DATA**). The columns of data can be rearranged in Power Query, to best meet your needs. Being able to **MASH UP DATA** is helpful when you need to slice and dice data to create charts and other types of visualizations. Cleaning data is not a requirement to loading data into Power BI Desktop. If the data that you will use, is already clean, you can start creating reports and dashboards as soon as the data is loaded. You can also clean the data after it has been loaded into the data model.

If you have used options in the **GET EXTERNAL DATA**, **CONNECTIONS** or **RELATIONSHIPS** sections on the Data tab in Excel, you will be familiar with the Get Data button functionality in Power BI Desktop.

If you use Power BI Desktop for any length of time, you will see that new connectors are added on a regular basis and existing connectors will be enhanced. To import data, a connector (which is the front end interface to creating a **CONNECTION STRING**), is used to get data from a data source.

Getting Data

DATA DISCOVERY, as it is sometimes called, is a component of Business Intelligence. It focuses on finding the data needed for both graphical and visual analysis, instead of text based reports (like reports that are created using tools like Microsoft SQL Server Reporting Services and SAP Crystal Reports). This chapter covers how to connect to and get data from some of the data sources supported by Power BI Desktop.

What Happens To The Data Now?

This chapter and Chapter 4 to the end of the book, covers discovering data, then transforming it by using sorting and filtering techniques, as well as, creating calculated columns and applying aggregations in the Query Editor. You also have to decide whether to keep (load) the data or discard it and any changes that you may have made to the data. When connecting to a data source, you can immediately load the data to the data model, or use the Edit button, to load the data into memory. The **EDIT QUERIES BUTTON** is used to view and transform the data, to decide whether or not you want to keep it and load it into the data model.

External Data Options

The options shown in Figure 2-1 are on the Home tab. They are used to bring data into Power BI Desktop and manage it. The options are explained in Table 2-1.

The other options on the Home tab are mainly used to create reports.

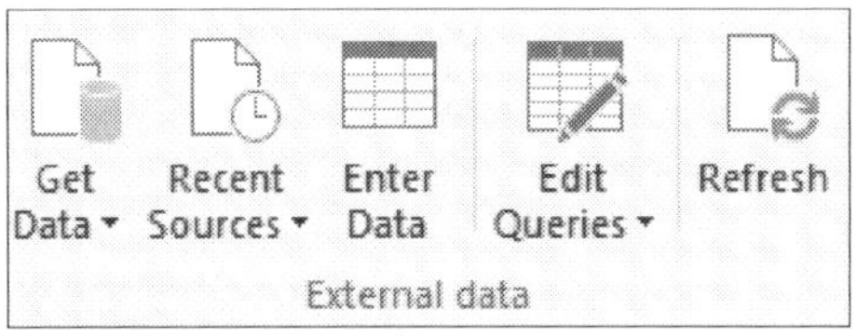

Figure 2-1 External Data options

Clicking on the top half of a button that has an arrow, (where the icon is, above the words on the button) automatically selects the first option on the drop-down list. For example, look at the Get Data button, shown above in Figure 2-1. If you click on the top half of this button, the Excel option would be displayed and selected on the Get Data dialog box, because it is the first option on the drop-down list, as shown in Figure 2-2. Clicking on the icon on the Edit Queries button, opens the Power Query Editor.

Button	Description
Get Data	[See Get Data Button Options]
Recent Sources	[See Recent Sources Button Option]
Enter Data	Is used to create a new table by pasting in the data or by typing the data in the table.
Edit Queries	Clicking on the arrow, on this button, displays a shortcut menu with the following options: The **EDIT QUERIES OPTION** opens the Query Editor. The **DATA SOURCE SETTINGS OPTION** opens a dialog box with the same name, that was covered in the previous chapter. The **EDIT PARAMETERS OPTION** is used to view the current parameter values or modify them. This option is only enabled if a parameter has already been created in the file. The **EDIT VARIABLE OPTION** is used to view and modify the current cube values. It is only enabled when the file has a formula that has a variable in it.
Refresh	Reloads the data from the data source for each table in the file.

Table 2-1 External Data options explained

Get Data Button Options

Data from multiple sources can be imported into the database (called the **DATA MODEL**) that is part of and stored in a Power BI Desktop (**.PBIX**) file. You may see the terms "internal data model" and "data model" used interchangeably. They are one in the same.

Figure 2-2 shows the options on the Get Data button. They are the most common data sources. The options on this button are used to select the type of data that you want to import. Each of these options has what is known as a **CONNECTOR**, which contains instructions on how to import data from a specific data source. Table 2-2 explains the data source categories. The categories make it easier to find the data source that you are looking for, if it is not on the Get Data button drop-down list, because the options are not in alphabetical order, in any category.

The **MORE OPTION**, at the bottom of Figure 2-2, displays the dialog box shown in Figure 2-3.

The **ALL OPTION**, in Figure 2-3, displays all of the data source options. Once you select an option on the Get Data dialog box, click the **CONNECT BUTTON**.

The word **(BETA)** after a data source type (as illustrated in Figure 2-2), means that the data source is in the testing phase, but you can use it now. Eventually, the beta options will be permanently integrated into the software.

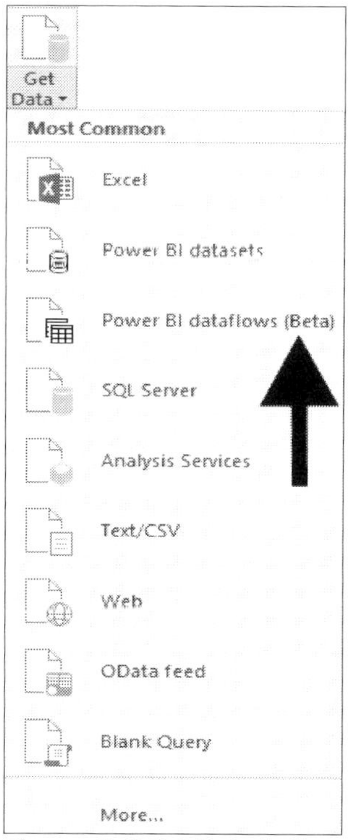

Figure 2-2 Get Data button options

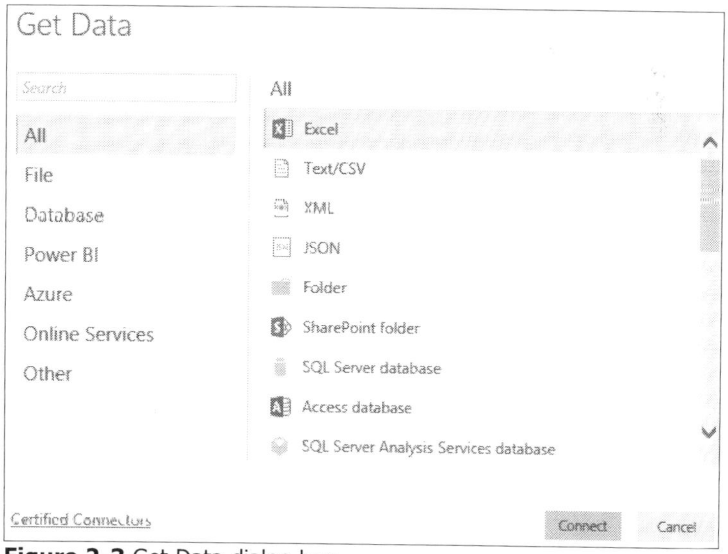

Figure 2-3 Get Data dialog box

When opening a new file, you can click on the **GET DATA LINK** on the splash screen to open the Get Data dialog box. [See Chapter 1, Figure 1-4]

Another Way To Find The Data Source
You can also type in the name of the data source type (SQL, Mail Chimp, etc) in the Search field at the top of the Get Data dialog box, to find the data source type that you are looking for.

Category	Is Used To Connect To And Import Data From . . .
File	Excel, CSV, XML, JSON and Text files. Metadata can also be imported.
Database	Relational databases.
Power BI	Power BI datasets or **DATA FLOWS**, which come from a live connection to the data source.
Azure	An Azure data source.
Online Services	Databases that are stored online.
Other	A variety of data sources, including data feeds, a web page, Hadoop and R Script.

Table 2-2 Data source categories explained

My Data Source Is Not Listed. What Should I Do?
If the data source that you want to use is not listed, you can try the **ODBC** or **OLE DB** connectors. Select one of these options if your data source has an ODBC or OLE DB driver. The latter comes pre-installed with Windows. If this does not work, search the Power BI Desktop forum to see if a solution has been posted for your data source. If not, post a question in the forum.

Recent Sources Button Option

This option displays a list of files and servers that you have already connected to and probably imported data from.

The **MORE OPTION** (at the bottom of the Recent Sources button list), displays the dialog box shown in Figure 2-4. You can select a file from this list to load data from, into the current file.

When connected, the Text and CSV file data sources will open the dialog box, shown later in Figure 2-20. Database and spreadsheet data sources are displayed in the Navigator dialog box (shown later in Figure 2-9), so that you can select the tables, in the database or file, that you want to import.

In an Excel file, each sheet/tab is recognized as a table in Power BI Desktop.

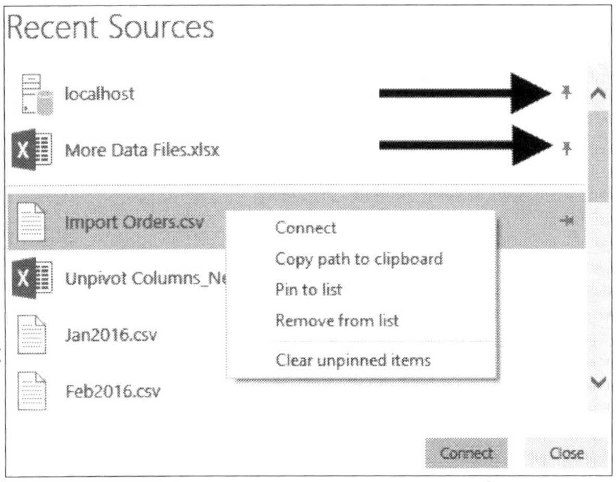

Figure 2-4 Recent Sources list with pinned files

Right-clicking on a file in the list, displays the shortcut menu shown in Figure 2-4. The options on the shortcut menu are explained in Table 2-3.

In addition to storing a list of at least the last 30 data sources (it is probably more, but that is how many data sources are in my Recent Sources list right now, while I am writing this <smile>), your login information for the data sources in the Recent Sources list is also maintained.

Option	Is Used To . . .
Connect	Add the selected data source to the current file.
Copy path to clipboard	Copy the path (location) of the data source so that it can be pasted some place else.
Pin to list	Attach the selected data source to the top of the Recent Sources list, by clicking the push pins, illustrated above, at the top of Figure 2-4.
Remove from list	Remove the selected data source from the Recent Sources list.

Table 2-3 Recent Sources list shortcut menu options explained

Option	Is Used To . . .
Clear unpinned items	Remove the items on the Recent Sources list that are not pinned. I personally do not see the point in removing an item unless you have no plans to use the connection anytime soon. Also, keep in mind that removing an item from this list, removes it from all files created in Power BI Desktop, not just the current file.

Table 2-3 Recent Sources list shortcut menu options explained (Continued)

Web Connector

This connector is used to retrieve data from a web site. It requires you to type in the web site address of the page that has data formatted in an HTML table or any HTML data, that you want to extract. You can also select or create a parameter that will retrieve data from the web page, that you select in the parameter.

Figure 2-5 shows the advanced options that are available to import data from a web page. If you are going to type or paste the URL in, you can use the **BASIC OPTIONS**.

Holding the mouse pointer at the end of the URL parts field will display the ellipsis button shown on the right side of the figure. Click on this button to display the shortcut menu shown in the figure.

Select **DELETE** to remove the option as part of the URL.

Select **MOVE UP/MOVE DOWN** to change the order of the parts of the URL.

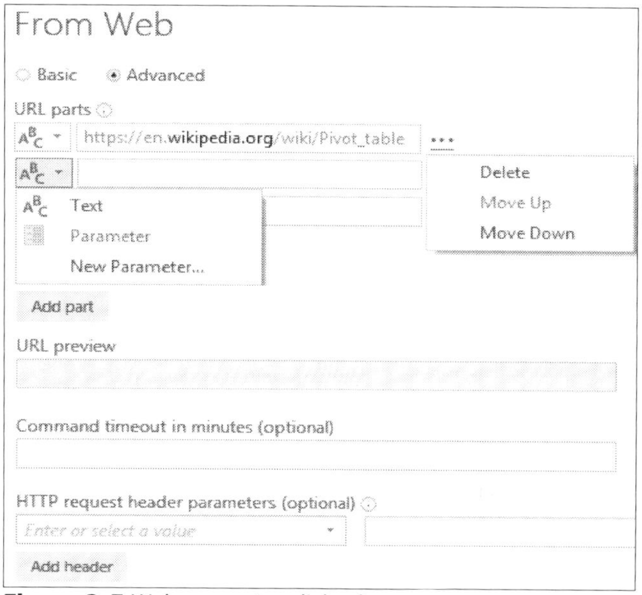

Figure 2-5 Web connector dialog box

The **URL OPTIONS** drop-down list (the button with ABC on it) is used to select where the URL is. The options are explained below.

☑ Select **TEXT** if you want to type in the web page. This is the default option.

☑ Select **PARAMETER** if you want to use an existing parameter field to select the web site to use. (1)

☑ Select **NEW PARAMETER** if you need to create a new parameter, that will be used to select the website from. (1)

(1) A parameter field would be useful if there are several web pages that you need to get data from, or you just do not want to have to type in the web page address more than once. For example, you need to be able to import statistics for three basketball teams. The web page for each team would be listed in the parameter.

The **ADD PART BUTTON** adds another field that is used to enter another part of the URL.

The **URL PREVIEW FIELD** displays all of the values from the URL parts that were used.

The **COMMAND TIMEOUT IN MINUTES OPTION** is used to enter the amount of time to wait for the web page to be displayed, before the connection times out.

Import Exercise Tips
Below are some tips that hopefully will make completing the exercises a bit easier.

① Unless specified otherwise, at the beginning of each exercise in this chapter, open a new report file. (File menu ⇒ New, or click the **NEW** button on the Quick Access toolbar)
② The options to select a data source are on the Get Data button, shown earlier in Figure 2-2. If the file type that you need is not shown in Figure 2-2, select the More option, at the bottom of the list, to view all of the data source file types.
③ After you select the type of file that you want to import data from on the Get Data dialog box, click the **CONNECT BUTTON**, shown earlier at the bottom of Figure 2-3. Then select the file that you want to import data from.
④ When you see the instruction "Close and Apply the changes", it means to click the **CLOSE & APPLY** button ⇒ Close & Apply option, in the Query Editor, unless stated otherwise.
⑤ If you do not like to type, you can save the files that you create using the exercise number (E2.1, for example) as the file name, instead of typing the entire file name. I use long file names to help explain the task covered in the exercise.

Exercise 2.1: Import Data From A Web Site

The URL in step 2 is in the Power Query links.txt file, in the zip file, that you downloaded in Chapter 1, in case you do not want to type it in.

1. Get Data button ⇒ **WEB** option.

2. On the Basic or Advanced screen, type `http://en.wikipedia.org/wiki/pivot_table` in the URL field, as shown above in Figure 2-5 ⇒ Click OK. The Navigator dialog box shown below in Figure 2-6, will open.

Navigator Dialog Box

After you connect to a lot of the data source options, you will see the Navigator dialog box. This dialog box is used to select the tables from the data source that you need. You can also preview the data.

The dialog box shown in Figure 2-6 displays the HTML tables that were detected in the data source, because this part of the exercise is using the **WEB CONNECTOR**. Slightly different options are displayed on the right side of the Navigator dialog box, depending on the connector that is being used.

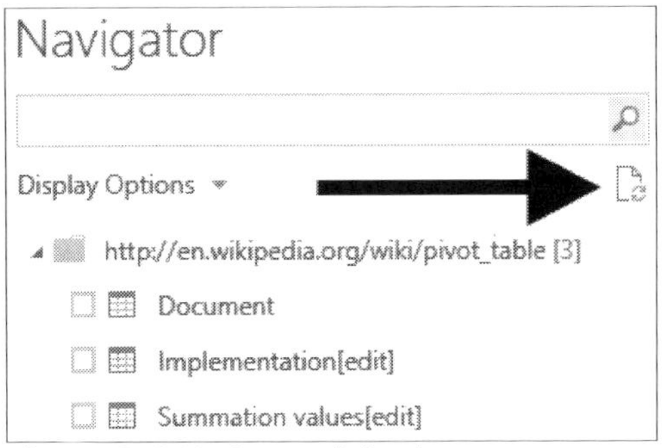

Figure 2-6 Navigator dialog box

Power BI Desktop displays data sets that it recognizes and believes that can be imported. One feature that I think is cool about the Navigator dialog box is that regardless of the format that the data is saved in, it looks the same on the right side of this dialog box.

The **REFRESH** button (the sheet of paper icon, illustrated in Figure 2-6) is used to update the data from the data source.

This dialog box can be used as a **DATA DISCOVERY TOOL** because it displays some of the data before it is loaded. Keep in mind that the tables retrieved can change, especially when getting data from a web site. This dialog box appears for most data sources. It does not appear when the following data source file types are used: CSV, TXT, XML and **METADATA FILES.**

Click on a table name in the list on the left side of the Navigator dialog box to display the data. The check boxes are used to select the tables that you want to import. A query is created for each table that you select.

The exercises in this book do not connect to corporate databases. On your own, if you need to connect to corporate databases, you will often see a list of databases on the Navigator dialog box first. When that is the case, select the database that you need, then select the tables. You will probably need authorization to connect to and view corporate databases.

Display Options

The options shown in Figure 2-7 are used to select whether or not preview data is displayed on the right side of the Navigator dialog box.

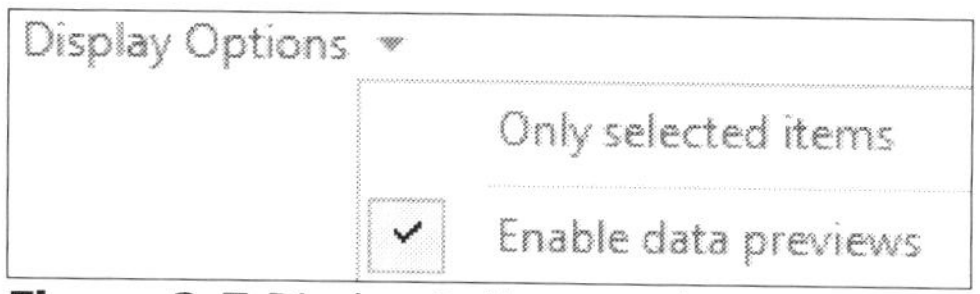

Figure 2-7 Display Options on the Navigator dialog box

Check the **ONLY SELECTED ITEMS OPTION** to display tables that you have checked. The tables that are not checked in the list on the left, are hidden.

If checked, the **ENABLE DATA PREVIEWS OPTION** allows data from the selected table to be displayed on the right side of the Navigator dialog box, as shown below in Figure 2-9.

> **Column Name Conflicts**
> If you have a table that has columns with the same name except for the case (for example, Orders and orders), you do not have to rename one of them before importing the table, unless you want to. That is because the import process will add ".1" after one of the column names, as illustrated in Figure 2-8.

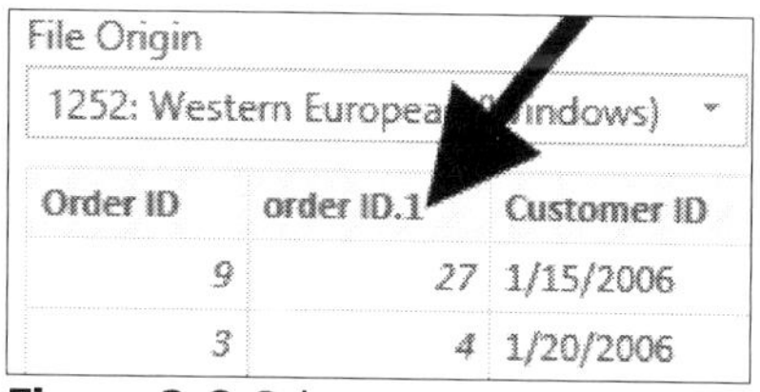

Figure 2-8 Column name conflict resolution

> **Resizing The Navigator Dialog Box**
> What may not be obvious is that this dialog box can be resized. Dragging the line, illustrated below in Figure 2-9, changes the size of the left and right panels. Dragging the lower right corner of the dialog box is used to make the dialog box smaller or larger.

The Navigator dialog box options for the **WEB CONNECTOR** are displayed in Figure 2-9. The options are explained below.

The tables displayed on the Navigator dialog box have a shortcut menu. Right-click on a table to display the shortcut menu shown in Figure 2-9. The Load and Edit buttons at the bottom of the dialog box, are enabled when a table is selected (has a check mark next to it).

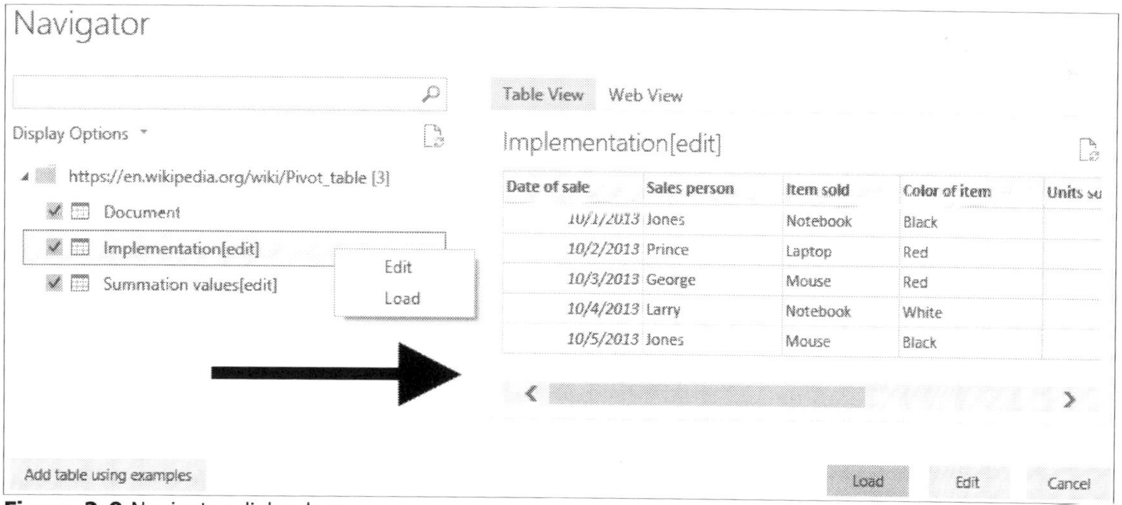

Figure 2-9 Navigator dialog box

The **EDIT OPTION** (on the shortcut menu on the left of the figure) and **EDIT BUTTON** (in the lower right corner of the figure) creates a query for the data, then displays the data in the Query Editor. This gives you the opportunity to view more of the data and transform it before it is loaded to the data model. This can be helpful if you are not familiar with the data or if the dataset has millions of rows of data.

The **LOAD OPTION** (on the shortcut menu) and the **LOAD BUTTON** automatically loads the data into the data model. Once loaded, you can open the Query Editor.

The **TABLE VIEW TAB** displays the data, as shown above in Figure 2-9. This is the default view. (2)

The **WEB VIEW BUTTON** displays the web page. You can scroll down the page to view the tables that are on the page, as shown in Figure 2-10. In the figure, you can see the data in the table in a format that is easy to understand. (2)

This button is helpful because when you see tables that do not have a descriptive name, you don't know what type of data they contain.

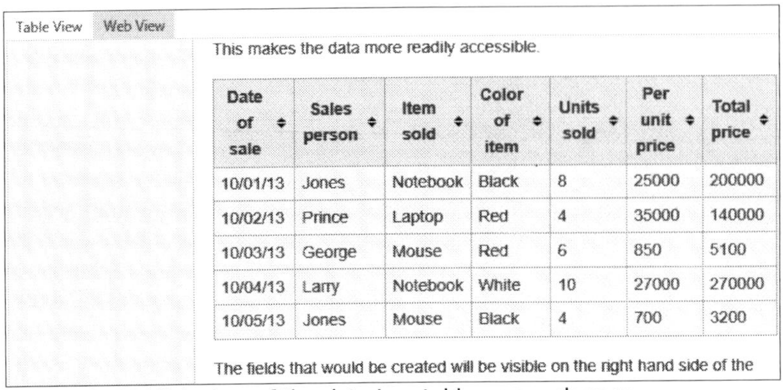

Date of sale	Sales person	Item sold	Color of item	Units sold	Per unit price	Total price
10/01/13	Jones	Notebook	Black	8	25000	200000
10/02/13	Prince	Laptop	Red	4	35000	140000
10/03/13	George	Mouse	Red	6	850	5100
10/04/13	Larry	Notebook	White	10	27000	270000
10/05/13	Jones	Mouse	Black	4	700	3200

Figure 2-10 Web view of the data in a table on a web page

The **ADD TABLE USING EXAMPLES BUTTON**, shown earlier in the lower left corner of Figure 2-9, is available when the data source is a web page. (2)

Clicking this button displays the dialog box shown in Figure 2-11, which is used to view the web page and type in sample values (in the column at the bottom of the figure) of the type of data that you want to extract. This option is helpful when the web page does not have a table that looks like the one shown above in Figure 2-10 or when the data that you want to extract, is not in a table.

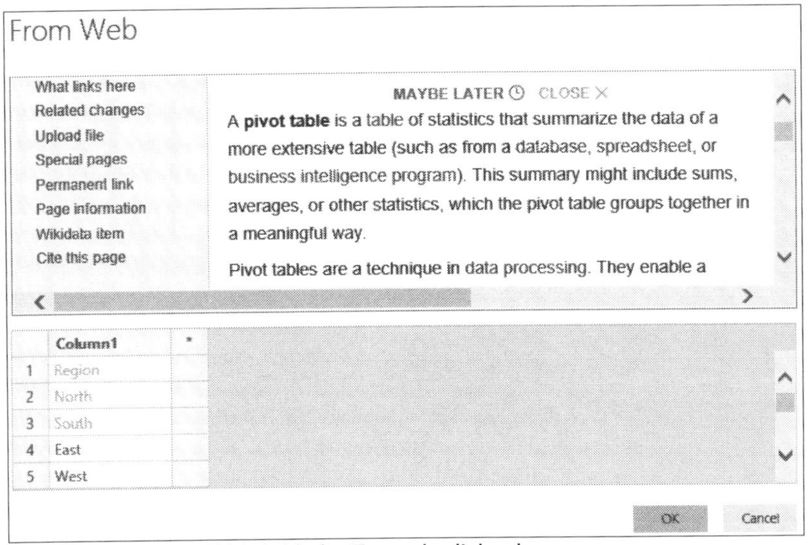

Figure 2-11 From Web table by Example dialog box

The example pattern data that you type in, is how Power Query figures out what data to extract. You will probably have to type in two or more data patterns for each column that you want to extract.

This option works the same as the **COLUMN FROM EXAMPLES OPTION** (on the Add Column tab) in the Query Editor.

(2) This option is only available when the data is on a web page.

3. Check all three tables, shown earlier on the left side of Figure 2-9 ⇒ Click the Edit button. You should see three queries in the Query Editor.

4. In the Query Editor, click the Save button on the Quick Access Toolbar ⇒
   On the dialog box shown in Figure 2-12, click the **APPLY LATER BUTTON**.

   The Apply and Apply Later buttons are explained in Chapter 4. [See tip box above Figure 4-2]

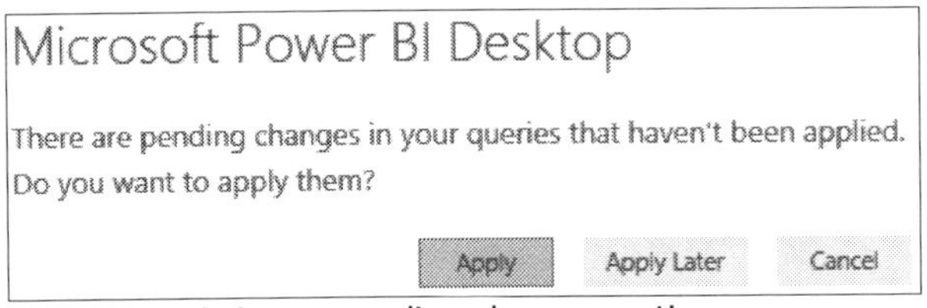

Figure 2-12 Query pending changes options

5. On the Save As dialog box, navigate to and select your folder ⇒ Save the file as `E2.1 Web and Excel data` ⇒ Minimize the Query Editor window.

> **Data Source Shortcut Menu**
> It should not come as a surprise that the data source has it's own shortcut menu, similar to the one for tables, shown below in Figure 2-13. The Edit and Load options on the data source shortcut menu, have different functionality. These options are applied to all of the tables in the data source. The Load and Edit buttons on the Navigator dialog box are for the selected tables.

Navigator Dialog Box Data Source Shortcut Menu

Right-clicking on the data source file name displays the shortcut menu shown in Figure 2-13.

The **EDIT OPTION** displays information about each table (in the data source) in the Query Editor, as shown in Figure 2-14. This is used to view more of the data and perform transformations, if needed, to help decide if the data is what you need.

The **LOAD OPTION** loads the data in each table that is selected, into the data model.

The **REFRESH OPTION** re-imports the data from the data source.

If you want to view the data in a table shown in Figure 2-14, that has not been loaded, click on the word "Table", in the Data column, for the table that you want to see.

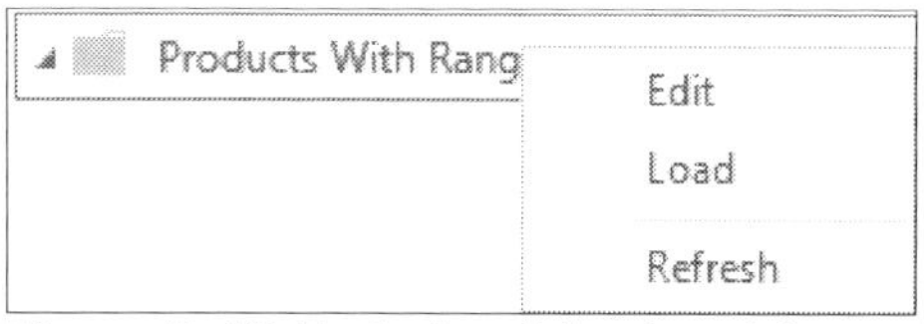

Figure 2-13 Navigator dialog box data source shortcut menu

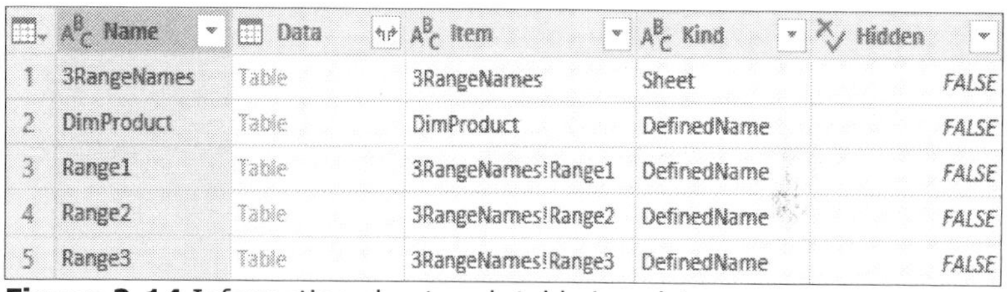

	Name	Data	Item	Kind	Hidden
1	3RangeNames	Table	3RangeNames	Sheet	FALSE
2	DimProduct	Table	DimProduct	DefinedName	FALSE
3	Range1	Table	3RangeNames!Range1	DefinedName	FALSE
4	Range2	Table	3RangeNames!Range2	DefinedName	FALSE
5	Range3	Table	3RangeNames!Range3	DefinedName	FALSE

Figure 2-14 Information about each table in a data source

File Connector Options

The **EXCEL OPTION** is used to get data (that is not in the data model of the workbook) from an Excel workbook. Excel files from version 97 and higher can be imported. In addition to data on worksheets in the workbook, **NAMED TABLES**, **NAMED RANGES** and **DYNAMIC NAMED RANGES**, can also be imported. They will be displayed on the Navigator dialog box, just like sheets (tabs of data) are.

.xls and .xlsx Excel files have automatic **COLUMN TYPE DETECTION** enabled during the import process. This means that Excel files are treated more like tables in a database, during the import process. This is a good thing because more of the data types that are automatically selected, will be correct.

Filters that are applied to data in an Excel file are ignored when the data is imported. The filter criteria is not imported, so it will have to be set up in the Query Editor, if it is still needed.

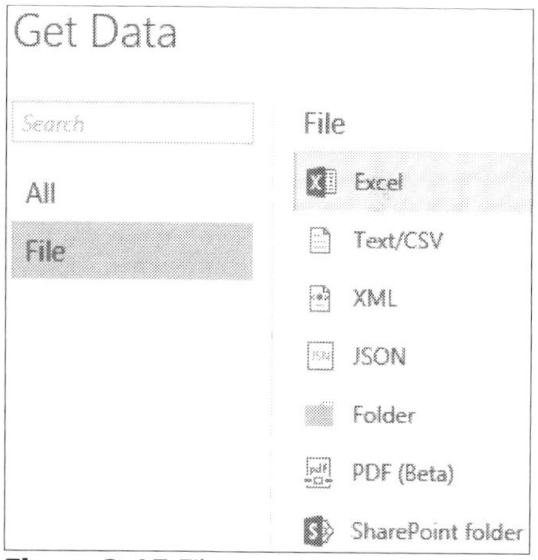

Figure 2-15 File connector options

The Text/CSV, XML, and JSON options, shown above in Figure 2-15, are used to import data from different types of text files. These options are explained in this chapter, in the exercise that they are covered in.

The **FOLDER CONNECTOR OPTION** is used to import multiple files (that are in the same folder) at one time and combine (append), the data in the files, into one table.

Import Data From Excel

In this part of the exercise, you will import data that is on a worksheet, that has not been converted to an Excel table. The data will be loaded to the data model.

1. Get Data button ⇒ Excel ⇒

   On the Open dialog box, select the More Data Files workbook.

   You should see the worksheets shown in Figure 2-16 ⇒

   Check the 02 Products table.

   In Excel, each sheet counts as at least one table, on the Navigator dialog box. One sheet can have more than one table defined.

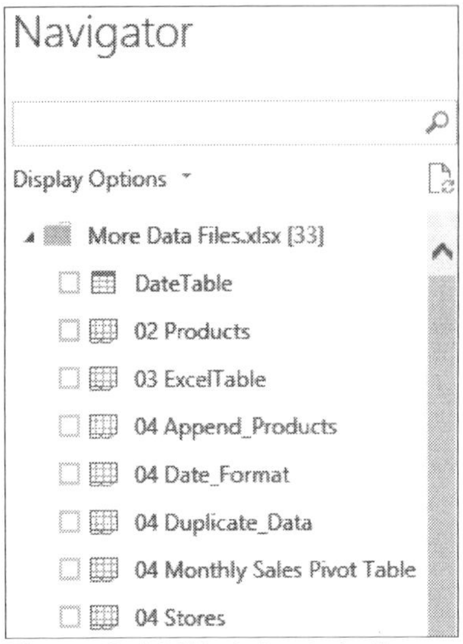

Figure 2-16 Worksheets in the workbook

> **Empty Worksheets**
> If you scroll down the list of tables shown above in Figure 2-16, you will see is a worksheet named "Sheet 1". If you click on a worksheet in the Navigator dialog box that does not have any data, you will see a message indicating that the table is empty. Clear the check mark for empty sheet before importing the data. There is no value in importing empty worksheets. It would be helpful if the number of rows was displayed next to each table or sheet, to help make it easier to know whether or not it contains data.

2. Click the Load button. The Products table will be loaded into the data model.

3. Save the changes to the report file ⇒ When prompted to apply the pending changes, click Apply. The tables from the web site will be loaded into the data model ⇒ Close the Query Editor.

> **Automating Importing Sheets In A Workbook**
> In the exercise that you just completed, when you imported data from a workbook, you were instructed to select some or all of the sheets to import, on the Navigator dialog box. That import option, imported each sheet individually and created a query for each sheet. Doing that is fine, when the data on each sheet should not be appended, as long as you know for sure that in the future, new sheets will not be added to the workbook, that you may need to import.
>
> If you know or think that more sheets will be added to a workbook in the future, that you will need to import, on the Navigator dialog box, do not select (check) individual sheets in the Excel file. Instead, right-click on the workbook name and select Edit. Doing this will automatically select and import any new sheets that are added to the workbook and create a query for each sheet, when you refresh the data in the query. This is better then having to figure out when or if new sheets were added to the workbook. If new sheets are added and you did not right-click on the Excel file name, you would have to modify the query by adding the new worksheet(s) manually. This is probably not something that you would want to be responsible for doing. <smile> If you have the need to import and append multiple sheets from a workbook, see Chapter 9, Exercise 9.3.

Importing Data Using Named Ranges

This option is also known as a **NAMED SET**. A named range is a pre-selected section of a worksheet. Named ranges are often created when there is a need to only print or import part of the data on a worksheet. An example would be that you only needed to import data for two years, but the spreadsheet has six years of data. You would create a named range or two, for the two years of data that you need to import.

Figure 2-17 shows the named ranges in the workbook that will be used in the next exercise.

As you will see, each named range will be displayed as a table in the Navigator dialog box.

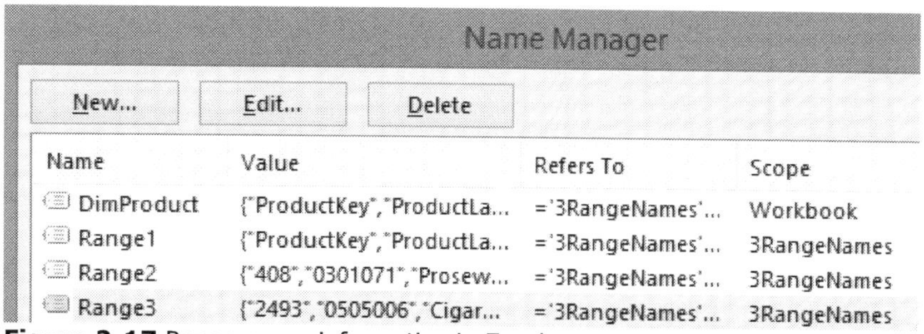

Figure 2-17 Range name information in Excel

Named Range Tips
① Make sure that the named ranges that you plan to import, include column headings, otherwise, no headings will be imported.
② When using a named range to import data, by default, the query name will be the name of the named range. Once imported, you can rename the query/table.

Exercise 2.2: Import Data From Multiple Sources Into The Same Data Model

The way spreadsheets can be set up varies. Some have multiple tables on one worksheet, while others have ranges set up. In this exercise, you will see a variety of worksheet layouts that can be imported.

Import Data Using Named Ranges

In this part of the exercise, you will import data that will be accessed by a named range.

1. Get Data button ⇒ Excel ⇒ Products With Range Names workbook.

2. You should see the tables shown in Figure 2-18.

   Notice that the icon next to the range name tables (the last three in the list) is different from the 3 Range Names table. The different icons let you know that they are not a true table, or in the case of a workbook file, they are not on individual worksheets, like the 3 Range Name option is.

   Check all of the tables ⇒ Edit button ⇒
   Close and apply the changes ⇒
   Save the file as `E2.2 Import from multiple workbooks` ⇒
   Leave the file open to complete the next part of this exercise.

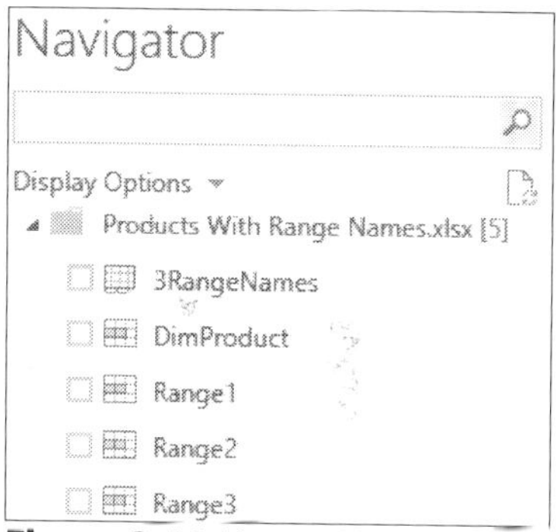

Figure 2-18 Named Range tables

   The 3 Range Names table contains all of the data. The three range tables, each contain a portion of the data in the 3 Range Names table.

Import Multiple Tables From One Sheet

In this part of the exercise you will import data from a different workbook, into the same data model, as the previous part of this exercise.

1. Get Data button ⇒ Excel ⇒ More Data Files workbook ⇒ Check the 03 Excel table ⇒ Edit button. Notice that only one table was loaded. There are actually three tables on the Excel table worksheet, in the workbook, as shown in Figure 2-19.

Customers

Customer ID	Last Name	First Name	City	State
1	Bedecs	Anna	Seattle	WA
2	Gratacos Solsona	Antonio	Boston	MA
3	Axen	Thomas	Los Angeles	CA
4	Lee	Christina	New York	NY
5	O'Donnell	Martin	Minneapolis	MN
6	Pérez-Olaeta	Francisco	Milwaukee	WI
7	Xie	Ming-Yang	Boise	ID
8	Andersen	Elizabeth	Portland	OR
9	Mortensen	Sven	Salt Lake City	UT
10	Wacker	Roland	Chicago	IL
11	Krschne	Peter	Miami	FL
12	Edwards	John	Las Vegas	NV
13	Ludick	Andre	Memphis	TN
14	Grilo	Carlos	Denver	CO
15	Kupkova	Helena	Honolulu	HI
16	Goldschmidt	Daniel	San Francisco	CA
17	Bagel	Jean Philippe	Seattle	WA
18	Autier Miconi	Catherine	Boston	MA
19	Eggerer	Alexander	Los Angeles	CA

Order Header

Order ID	Customer	Order Date	Shipped Date	Payment Type
30	1	01/15/2006	01/22/2006	Check
31	4	01/20/2006	01/22/2006	Credit Card
32	12	01/22/2006	01/22/2006	Credit Card
33	8	01/30/2006	01/31/2006	Credit Card
34	4	02/06/2006	02/07/2006	Check
35	12	02/10/2006	02/12/2006	Check
36	3	02/23/2006	02/25/2006	Cash
37	17	03/06/2006	03/09/2006	Credit Card
38	5	03/10/2006	03/11/2006	Check
39	8	03/22/2006	03/24/2006	Check
40	10	03/24/2006	03/24/2006	Credit Card
42	9	03/24/2006	04/07/2006	Check
43	11	03/24/2006	04/07/2006	Credit Card
45	18	04/07/2006	04/07/2006	Credit Card
46	9	04/05/2006	04/05/2006	Check
47	13	04/08/2006	04/08/2006	Credit Card
48	8	04/05/2006	04/05/2006	Check

Order Details

ID	Order ID	Product ID	Quantity	Unit Price
27	30	34	100	14.00
28	47	80	30	3.50
29	31	7	10	30.00
30	31	51	10	53.00
31	48	80	10	3.50
32	32	1	15	18.00
33	44	43	20	46.00
34	33	19	30	9.20
35	34	19	20	9.20
36	35	48	10	12.75
37	36	41	200	9.65
38	37	8	17	40.00
39	38	43	300	46.00
40	39	48	100	12.75
41	40	81	200	2.99
42	41	43	300	46.00
43	45	6	10	25.00
44	46	4	10	22.00
45	42	19	10	9.20
46	43	80	20	3.50
47	43	81	50	2.99

Figure 2-19 Tables on the 03 Excel sheet

2. Apply the changes and save the file.

Text/CSV File Connector

The dialog box shown in Figure 2-20 is displayed (instead of the Navigator dialog box) when a .txt, .csv or **.PRN FILE** is being imported. The three drop-down lists are used to select import options, as needed. A custom delimiter can be created.

The **DATA TYPE DETECTION FIELD OPTION** is used to select how many rows of data are used to determine the data type, for each column. The default is the first 200 rows, but the entire data set can be used to determine the data type, if necessary.

The **DO NOT DETECT DATA TYPES OPTION** (in the Data Type Detection drop-down list) turns off data type detection. Select this option when you want to select the data types yourself on the Data view or in the Query Editor.

The preview data displayed in Figure 2-20, can change based on the options that you select, in the Delimiter drop-down list. This dialog box, like the Navigator dialog box, will let you see the data before it is loaded.

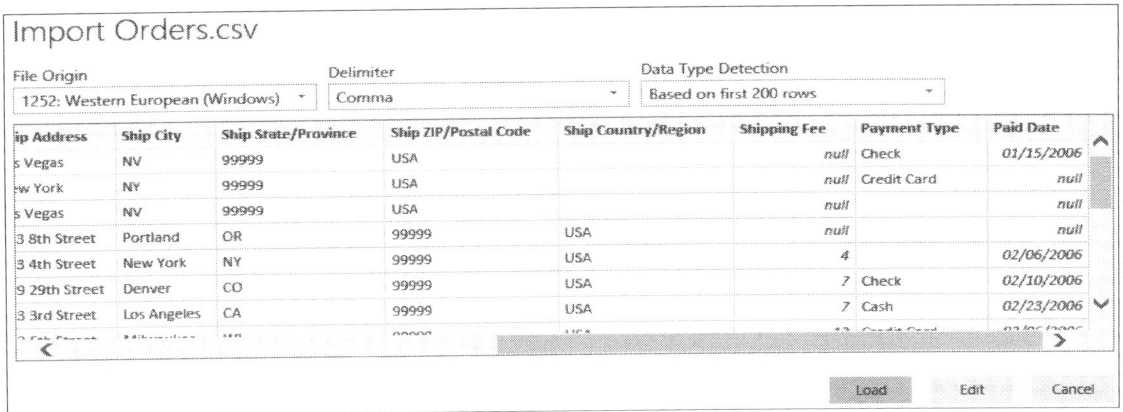

Figurer 2-20 Text and CSV file connector options

The **DELIMITER FIXED WIDTH OPTION**, shown in Figure 2-21, is used to list the positions to split the data into columns, if needed. Replace the default fixed width, with the length of the fields in the file that you are using.

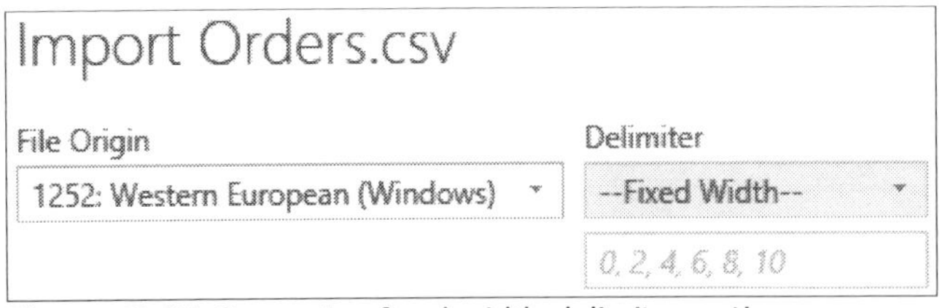

Figure 2-21 Connector fixed width delimiter options

CSV File Tips
To use a CSV file, it must meet certain criteria, in addition to having the CSV file extension. On your own, if you are having trouble loading a CSV file, open the file in Note Pad or another text editor and confirm the following:

① The file does not have anything other than a header row and the rows of data. If used, the header row has to be the first row in the file.
② If column headings are used, the first row must contain a heading for every field. The remaining rows (the rows with data) can have fewer fields then the first row, but not more fields. For example, most addresses have a zip code field, but there are a few records that do not. The first row must have a zip code field heading.
③ Commas or double quotes need to separate each field.
④ Each row must end with a line feed or carriage return (the equivalent of pressing Enter).

Exercise 2.3: Import Data From Different Types Of Text Files

CSV, XML, TXT and JSON files are different types of text files. CSV and TXT files should only contain data for one table. XML files can contain data for more than one table. In this exercise you will load data from all of these file types into one file (the data model).

Import Data From A CSV File

CSV files are text files because they do not contain any formatting, even though they are usually saved in Excel. This file type is most often created as an export file from a database or a spreadsheet, especially when moving data between systems or applications.

Having the ability to import data into Power BI Desktop from CSV files opens up a lot of possibilities, especially if you do not have direct access to data that is stored in an enterprise system. You can get the IT department to export the data from an enterprise system and save it in a CSV file for you.

1. Get Data button ⇒ Text/CSV ⇒ Select the Import Orders.csv file ⇒ On the dialog box shown earlier in Figure 2-20, click the Edit button.

2. On the right side of the Query Editor, change the query name from Import Orders to `Orders`, as illustrated in Figure 2-22.

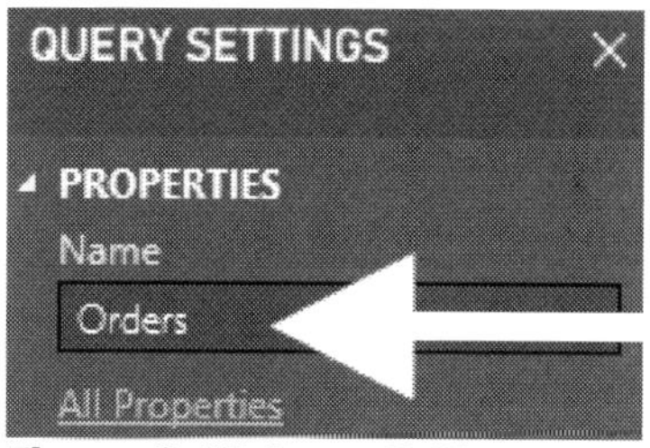

Figure 2-22 Query Settings

3. Apply the changes ⇒ Save the file as `E2.3 Import using text file data sources`. Leave the file open to complete the rest of this exercise.

Using CSV Files That Have A Different Number Of Columns

The concept of a CSV file that has rows of data with a different number of columns, is known as a **JAGGED CSV FILE**.

Most of the time, the CSV files that you use have the same number of columns of data for each row. As shown earlier in Figure 2-20, some of the cells do not have data. Also notice that the same type of data is not the same for every row. For example, the first three rows have a zip code in the Ship Date column. This indicates one of two things: Either those rows have a delimiter problem, or those rows are missing data. Figure 2-23 shows the last three columns from the CSV file that you just imported.

The **TEXT/CSV CONNECTOR** also supports files, where each row does not have data in all of the of columns, as shown in Figure 2-24. You do not have to do anything different for CSV files that fall into this category. The null values and empty cells indicate that there is no data in the cell. The columns data type determines whether null values or empty cells are added to fields that do not have any data.

$1^2{}_3$ Shipping Fee	$A^B{}_C$ Payment Type	Paid Date
200	Check	01/15/2006
5	Credit Card	01/20/2006
5	Credit Card	01/22/2006
50	Credit Card	01/30/2006
4	Check	02/06/2006
7	Check	02/10/2006
7	Cash	02/23/2006

Figure 2-23 Imported data with each row having the same number of columns

$1^2{}_3$ Shipping Fee	$A^B{}_C$ Payment Type	Paid Date
5	Check	03/22/2006
9	Credit Card	03/24/2006
0		null
0		null
0		null
0		null
40	Credit Card	04/07/2006

Figure 2-24 CSV file with a different number of columns

Import Data From An XML File

XML stands for **EXTENSIBLE MARKUP LANGUAGE**.

XML produces a text file, as shown in Figure 2-25. It is used to send formatted data between systems or applications.

In this type of text file, the data is enclosed (wrapped) in tags. These tags are what allows the data in XML files to be displayed on the web. Keep in mind that there are different types of XML files.

Some XML files can have more than one table. When that is the case, each table (dataset) will be displayed in the Navigator dialog box.

```
<?xml version="1.0" encoding="utf-8"?>
<xml>
  <Months>
    <MonthID>1</MonthID>
    <MonthName>January</MonthName>
  </Months>
  <Months>
    <MonthID>2</MonthID>
    <MonthName>February</MonthName>
  </Months>
  <Months>
    <MonthID>3</MonthID>
```

Figure 2-25 XML file

Check the table(s) that you need from the XML file, to load them. In this respect, an XML file works like an Excel workbook that has more than one table of data.

> **Adding A Data Source From The Query Editor**
> If you need to import data and have the Query Editor displayed, open the **NEW SOURCE BUTTON** drop-down list. It works the same as the **GET DATA BUTTON** in Power BI Desktop.

1. Get Data button ⇒ More option ⇒ XML ⇒ Connect button ⇒ MonthsXMLTable.xml file.
2. Load the Months table to the query.

> **Text File Tips**
> One way to know that there is a problem with a text file is that all of the fields have been imported into one column, when displayed in the Query Editor. In Chapter 7, you will learn how the **TRIM** and **CLEAN FUNCTIONS** are used to help separate the columns and data that are imported as one large column. To use a text file in Power BI Desktop, the file must meet certain criteria in addition to having the TXT file extension. On your own, if you are having trouble importing the data in a text file, open the file in Note Pad and confirm the following:
>
> ① The file does not have anything other than a header row and the rows of data. If used, the header row has to be the first row in the file.
> ② The separator between fields is valid.
> ③ When each row does not have the same number of fields the data will not line up properly, as shown in Figure 2-26. Notice in the first three rows that the Customer ID field has dates. This lets you know that these rows are missing either the Order ID or Employee ID field. The data should be modified before it is imported.

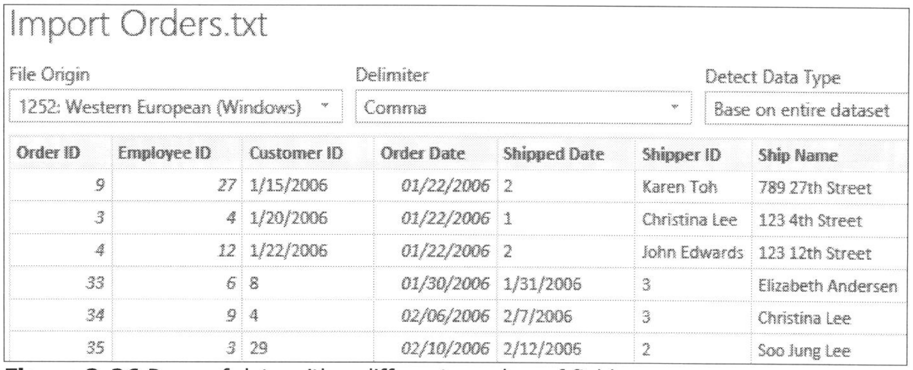

Order ID	Employee ID	Customer ID	Order Date	Shipped Date	Shipper ID	Ship Name
9	27	1/15/2006	01/22/2006	2	Karen Toh	789 27th Street
3	4	1/20/2006	01/22/2006	1	Christina Lee	123 4th Street
4	12	1/22/2006	01/22/2006	2	John Edwards	123 12th Street
33	6	8	01/30/2006	1/31/2006	3	Elizabeth Andersen
34	9	4	02/06/2006	2/7/2006	3	Christina Lee
35	3	29	02/10/2006	2/12/2006	2	Soo Jung Lee

Figure 2-26 Rows of data with a different number of fields

Import Data From A Text File

Text (TXT) files do not have any formatting like bold, italic or font size. To be used in Power BI Desktop, this file type has to have rows of data, as shown in Figure 2-27. Each row of data has fields (columns). An advantage of text files is that they can handle millions of rows of data. The fields are usually separated by commas. While the comma is the most used separator for text files, other separators like **QUOTES**, can also be used as a separator. Another type of file that can be imported using the Text import option, is text files with the **.TAB EXTENSION**.

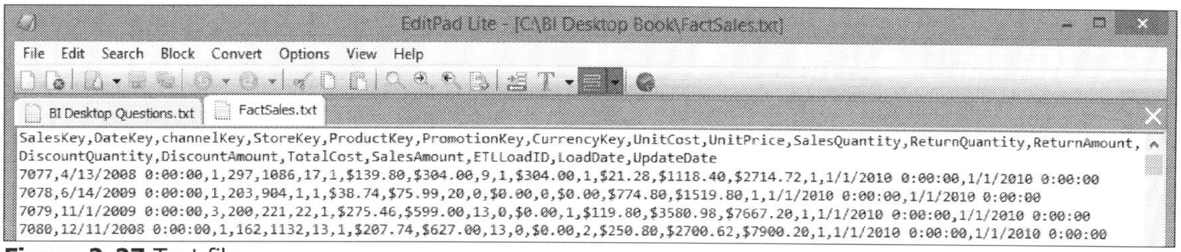


```
SalesKey,DateKey,channelKey,StoreKey,ProductKey,PromotionKey,CurrencyKey,UnitCost,UnitPrice,SalesQuantity,ReturnQuantity,ReturnAmount,
DiscountQuantity,DiscountAmount,TotalCost,SalesAmount,ETLLoadID,LoadDate,UpdateDate
7077,4/13/2008 0:00:00,1,297,1086,17,1,$139.80,$304.00,9,1,$304.00,1,$21.28,$1118.40,$2714.72,1,1/1/2010 0:00:00,1/1/2010 0:00:00
7078,6/14/2009 0:00:00,1,203,904,1,1,$38.74,$75.99,20,0,$0.00,0,$0.00,$774.80,$1519.80,1,1/1/2010 0:00:00,1/1/2010 0:00:00
7079,11/1/2009 0:00:00,3,200,221,22,1,$275.46,$599.00,13,0,$0.00,1,$119.80,$3580.98,$7667.20,1,1/1/2010 0:00:00,1/1/2010 0:00:00
7080,12/11/2008 0:00:00,1,162,1132,13,1,$207.74,$627.00,13,0,$0.00,2,$250.80,$2700.62,$7900.20,1,1/1/2010 0:00:00,1/1/2010 0:00:00
```

Figure 2-27 Text file

1. Get Data button ⇒ Text/CSV ⇒ FactSales.txt file (This file has over 2 million rows of data) ⇒ Click the Edit button. If you used the New Source button in the Query Editor to select the file, click OK.

2. Change the Query Name to `FactSalesTxt` ⇒ Apply and save the changes. This will take longer then the previous saves, because you are loading over 2 million rows of data, into the data model.

> **Renaming A Table**
> You do not have to use the Query Editor to rename a table (query). In Power BI Desktop, right-click on the table name in the Fields panel ⇒ Select Rename, as shown in Figure 2-28 ⇒ Type in the new name and press Enter.

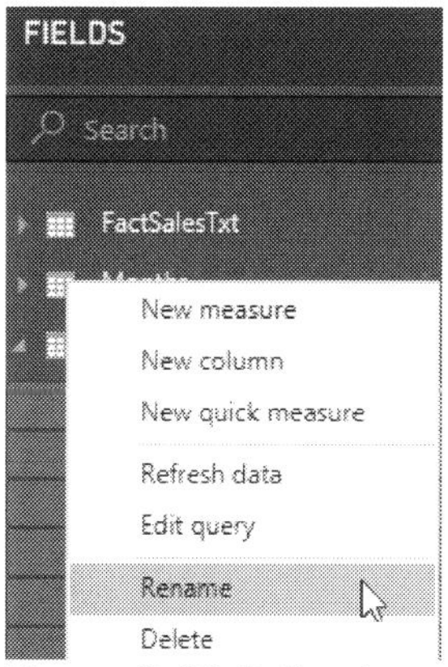

Figure 2-28 Option to rename a table on the Fields panel

Import Data From A JSON File

JSON stands for **JAVASCRIPT OBJECT NOTATION.**

JSON is a programming language used for simple data structures. It is often used instead of XML because it requires fewer tags. Figure 2-29 shows the JSON file that you will import in this part of the exercise.

```
{
   "firstName": "Jane",
   "lastName": "Smith",
   "age": 25,
   "address":
   {
       "StreetAddress": "21 3rd Avenue",
       "City": "New York",
       "State": "NY",
       "ZipCode": "10021"
   },
   "PhoneNumber":
   [
       {
         "type": "home",
         "number": "212 555-1234"
       },
       {
         "type": "fax",
         "number": "646 555-2345"
```

Figure 2-29 JSON file

1. Get Data button ⇒ More option ⇒ JSON ⇒ Select the CustomerForm.json file.

2. On the Query Editor, type `JSON` in front of the query name, in the Query Settings panel. You should see the contents of the file, as shown in Figure 2-30 ⇒ Save the changes to the file. You will also see a new tab. The **RECORD TOOLS CONVERT TAB** and the **RECORD** and **LIST DATA TYPES** are covered in Chapter 6.

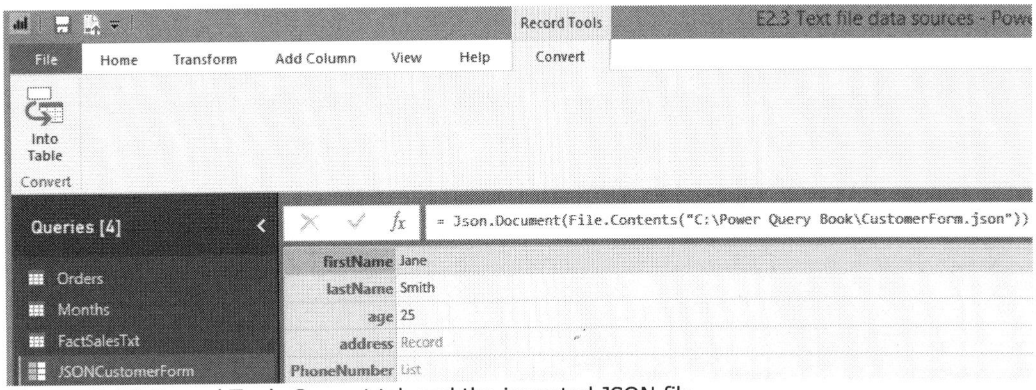

Figure 2-30 Record Tools Convert tab and the imported JSON file

Connect To A PDF File

So far in this chapter, you have learned how to connect to several options in the File section of the Get Data dialog box. One that you may find helpful is the PDF option. If you do not see this option, as shown earlier in Figure 2-15, open the Options dialog box and check the Get data from PDF files option, on the Preview features screen. You will be prompted to restart Power BI Desktop. Do so.

The **PDF CONNECTOR** works the same as others that you have used. You can try it by using the PDF Data File.pdf file that is in your folder.

The file has four tables and four pages, as shown in Figure 2-31. At the time this book went to print, this preview feature did not have an option to select a range (a start and end page) of pages in the PDF file to import.

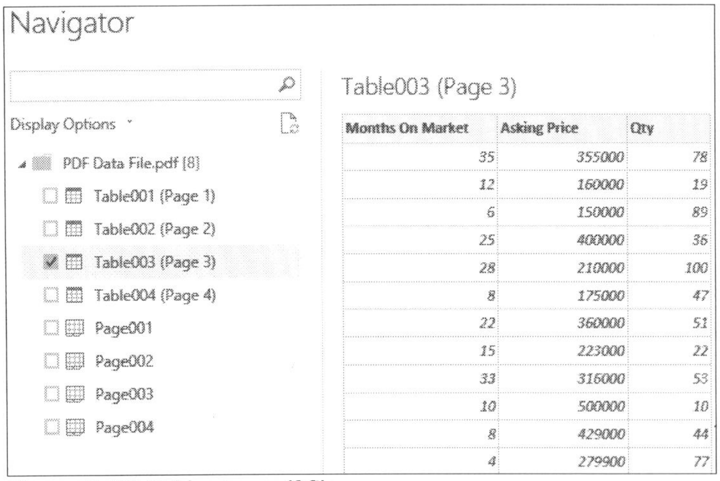

Months On Market	Asking Price	Qty
35	355000	78
12	160000	19
6	150000	89
25	400000	36
28	210000	100
8	175000	47
22	360000	51
15	223000	22
33	316000	53
10	500000	10
8	429000	44
4	279900	77

Figure 2-31 Tables in a pdf file

You can check the specific pages on this dialog box or modify the formula for the Source step in the Query Editor, to include the range of pages, as shown in Figure 2-32.

```
= Pdf.Tables(File.Contents("C:\Power Query Book\PDF Data File.pdf"), [StartPage=2, EndPage=4])
```

Figure 2-32 Modified formula for the Source step that specifies the page range to import from the PDF file

Database Connector Options

Figure 2-33 shows some of the types of database that you can import data from. This section explains some of the database options shown in the figure.

SQL Server Database is a scalable data warehouse solution that is capable of storing hundreds of terabytes of data.

Oracle, IBM DB2, and Sybase are all enterprise level relational database management systems, owned by different companies.

Many data sources require that connectors (also known as drivers or providers) be installed. You will see a message like the one shown below in Figure 2-34, when that is the case.

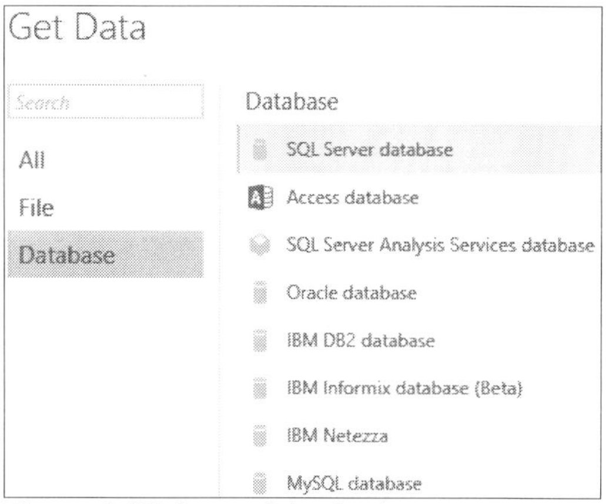

Figure 2-33 Some of the database connector options

The **LEARN MORE LINK** shown on Figure 2-34, will let you know what needs to be installed. If you need to connect to one of these types of databases, you have to get and install the drivers from the company, if you do not already have the driver installed on your computer.

Keep in mind that many of the databases shown in the figure, will require you to get permission from someone in IT, just to get a logon account.

Many of these databases use the connection options shown in Figure 2-35. In addition to using an **SQL STATEMENT** to get the data to import, a call to a **STORED PROCEDURE** can be used in the SQL Statement field.

To connect to OLAP (Online Analytical Processing) cubes, select the SQL Server Analysis Services database option.

The **DIRECT QUERY OPTION**, shown in Figure 2-35, is used to connect to a live data source. This option does not load data to the data model. While using a Direct Query connection means reports will display the most current data, without ever having to refresh the data, keep the following in mind:

① This connection type is slower then using data in the data model because the data is not stored on your computer. That is because the data is constantly being updated at the source.
② If you need to publish the data (that you connect to, using this connection option) to Power BI, you will have to install one of the Gateway tools.

The **NAVIGATE USING FULL HIERARCHY OPTION** shown in Figure 2-35, is used to see schema information with the Navigation hierarchy.

Relationships
Power BI Desktop does not automatically recognize or use relationships that are created between tables in a database. The relationships can be loaded to the data model, if the **IMPORT RELATIONSHIPS OPTION** is selected on the Options dialog box.

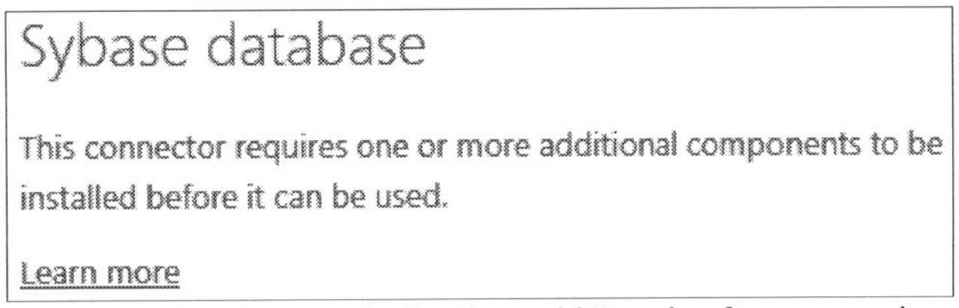

Figure 2-34 Message indicating additional software needs to be installed

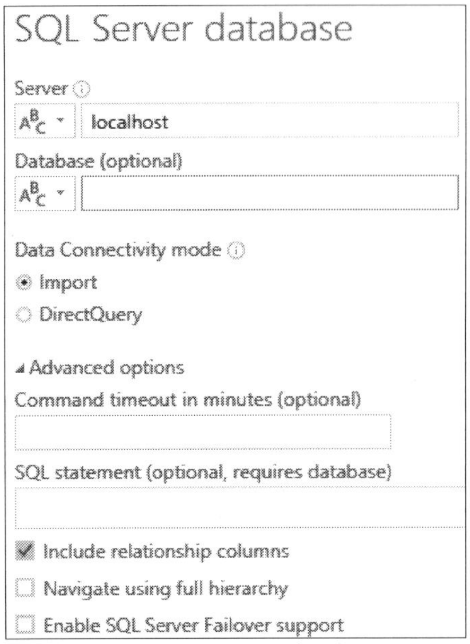

Figure 2-35 SQL Server database connector options

When you connect to a server and do not specify a database, as shown above in Figure 2-35, you will probably see more than one database, as shown in Figure 2-36.

Display the table(s) for the database that you want to use, then check the tables that you want to use.

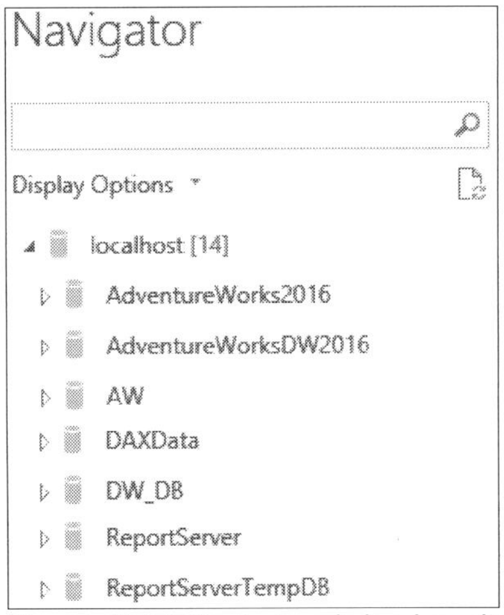

Figure 2-36 Navigator dialog box displaying multiple databases

Exercise 2.4: Use A Microsoft Access Database As The Data Source

In this exercise, you will learn how to connect to and load data from an Access database.

1. Get Data button ⇒ More ⇒ Access database ⇒ My Orders database.

2. On the Navigator dialog box, check the following tables: Customers, Customers Extended, Order Details, Order Price Totals, Orders and Products ⇒ Click the Load button.

3. Save the file as `E2.4 My Orders database`.

Microsoft Access Import Tip
Access views can also be imported. Currently, there is no way to distinguish a table from a view on the Navigator dialog box for Access databases, unless the table name indicates that it is a view. It is best to use a view, if one exists, for the data that you need. The reason is because views usually have fewer columns of data and often, the data in a view has been cleaned.

Load Data From Another Source

If you need data from other sources, you can load the data now. In this part of the exercise, you will load data from a workbook into the same query.

1. Load all of the 04 tables and the Products table, in the More Data Files workbook, into the E2.4 file.

Both of the data sources that you loaded data from in this exercise, have a table named Products. While Power BI Desktop can handle this, it will be confusing for us mere mortals, so we will rename one of the Product queries.

2. In the Query Editor (Home tab ⇒ Edit Queries button ⇒ Edit Queries), rename the Products (2) query to `New Products`.

3. Click on the 04 Monthly Sales Pivot Table query ⇒ If the first row has the column headings, Home tab ⇒ Use First Row As Headers button ⇒ Use First Row As Headers option.

4. Save and apply the changes.

How To Pin A File To The Recent Items List

The file that you just created, will be the starting point for many of the exercises in this book. You may want to pin it on the Recent Items list (on the File tab), shown in Figure 2-37, so that you can get to it quickly.

To pin a file, click on the icon illustrated in the figure.

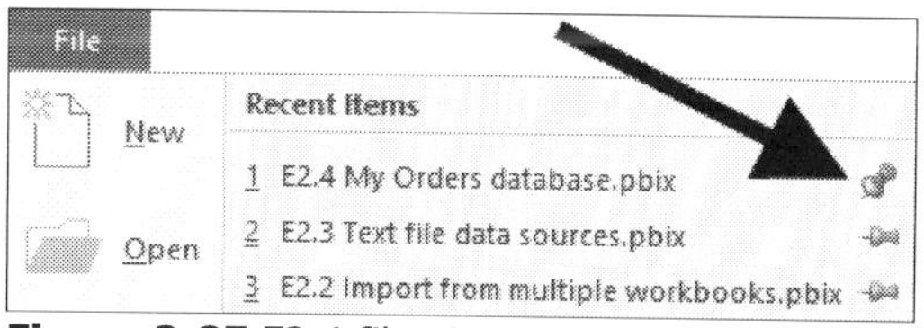

Figure 2-37 E2.4 file pinned to the Recent Items list

> When a file is pinned on the Recent Items list, it is also pinned on the splash screen automatically, and vice versa. [See Chapter 1, Figure 1-4]

Selecting Related Tables

You will see the **SELECT RELATED TABLES BUTTON** shown at the bottom of Figure 2-38, when a relational database is selected as the data source and at least one table has been checked to be imported. This includes databases that use an **ODBC** or **OLE DB CONNECTION**.

Clicking this button will search the relationships in the database to see if there are any tables that have a relationship created for the selected table. If so, the related tables will automatically be checked.

If you are not familiar with the selected tables or do not need them, you can view the data and decide whether or not you want to import any of the related tables.

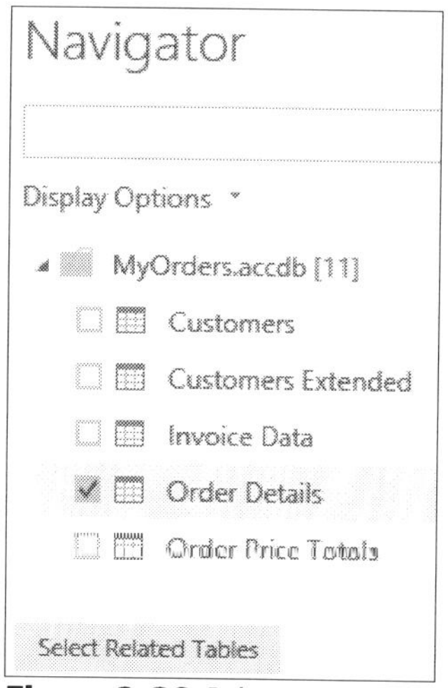

Figure 2-38 Select Related Tables button

Power BI Connector Options

The options shown in Figure 2-39, are used to create a **LIVE CONNECTION** to a dataset or data flow, on the Power BI Service. To use these connectors, you need a Power BI account, which was discussed at the end of Chapter 1.

These connectors are helpful when other people need to work on the same data model. Once the data model is published to the Power BI Service, other people can use it to create reports.

A **DATA FLOW** is a collection of data (similar to tables) that is created in app workspaces in the Power BI Service. Once created, a data flow is used to create datasets and reports.

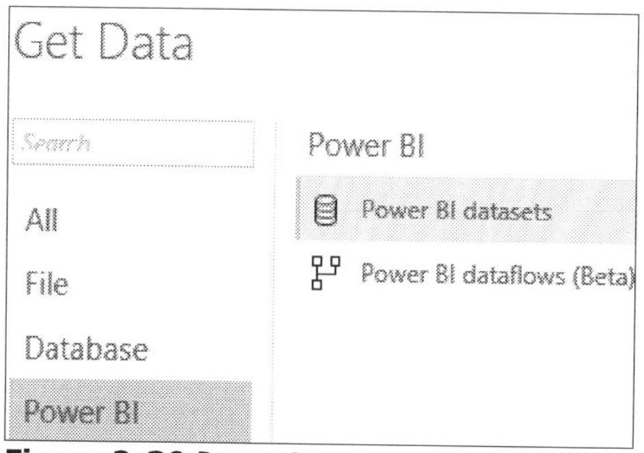

Figure 2-39 Power BI connector options

Azure Options

Figure 2-40 shows some of the Azure data source options. "Azure" is Microsoft's cloud version of SQL databases.

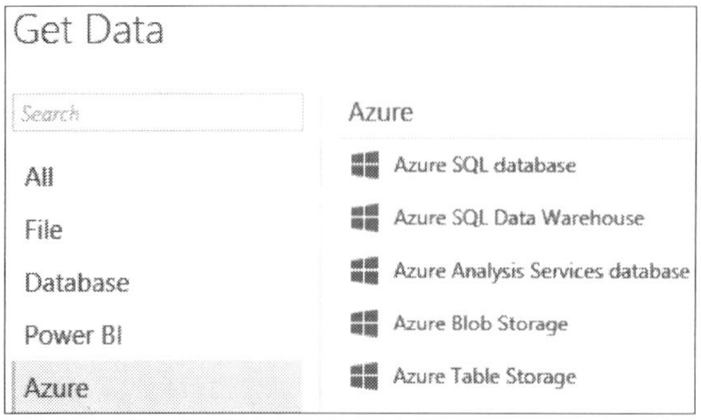

Figure 2-40 Azure connector options

Other (Data Source) Connector Options

In addition to the data source connectors that have been covered so far, the data source options shown in Figure 2-41 are also available.

The **BLANK QUERY OPTION** (shown at the bottom of Figure 2-41) opens the Query Editor. This option is used to create a script using the **M LANGUAGE**, which will be used to import the data.

The ODBC and OLE DB connectors are considered generic because they are used to connect to a variety of data sources.

The **ODBC CONNECTOR** is used to import data from any third-party driver, by selecting it in the DSN (Data Source Name) drop-down list, from the ones already set up on your computer, as shown in Figure 2-42.

The options in the Data Source Name drop-down list can vary from computer to computer. Select (None) in the Data Source Name drop-down list, to create a connection string that does not rely on an existing DSN.

This dialog box can also be used to create or add connection string information, as well as, connect to database types that are not listed in the Database or Azure sections on the Get Data dialog box.

Examples of databases that can use this connector are IBM Netezza, DynamoDB and Hive. As shown, an SQL statement (query) can be created.

If the driver that you need is not listed in the DSN drop-down list, you can download and install it.

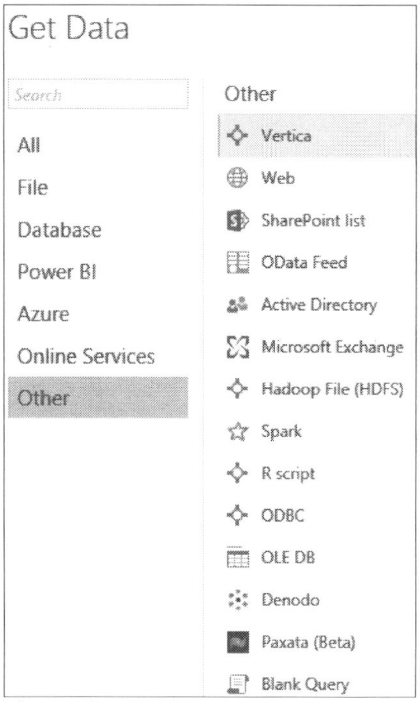

Figure 2-41 Other data source connector options

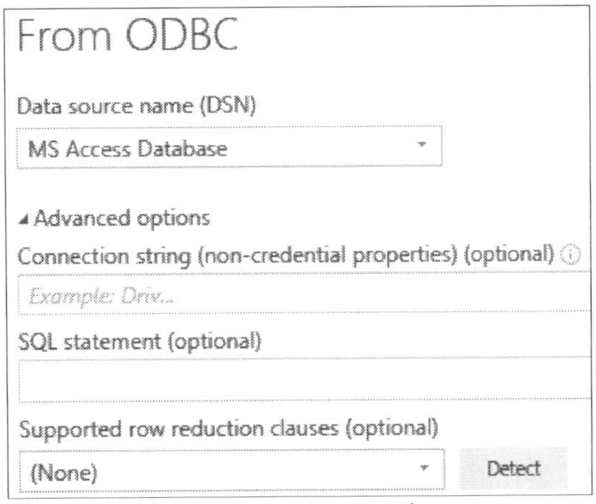

Figure 2-42 ODBC connector options

In addition to the ODBC connector, the **OLE DB CONNECTOR** also uses third-party drivers and supports SQL statements to connect to a data source, as shown in Figure 2-43.

This connector is used to specify a **CONNECTION STRING** or an SQL statement to connect to a data source.

The **BUILD BUTTON** opens a dialog box that has a list of drivers that are already installed on your computer.

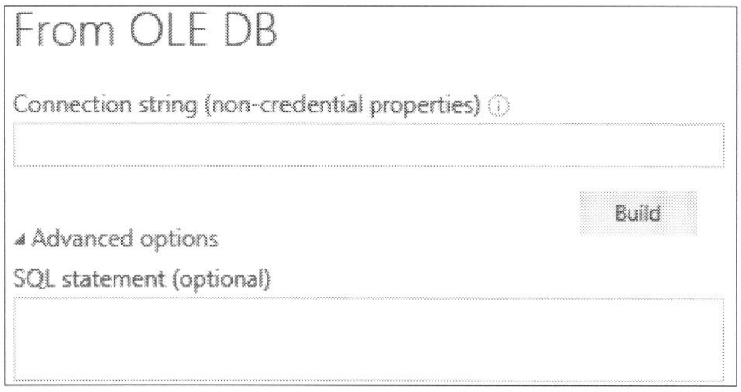

Figure 2-43 OLE DB connector options

Data Feeds

Earlier in this chapter, you read that data feeds can be used as a data source. If you have seen the icon shown in Figure 2-44 on a web site and clicked on it, you were subscribing to a data feed.

Figure 2-44 Data Feed icon

A data feed is a way to exchange data. They provide the data via web services. To connect to a web service, type in the web site address of the web service. Data feeds allow you to receive updates when the data on the web site changes.

Using Data Feeds As The Data Source

Select this option when the data that you need to import is on a web site or corporate intranet. A data feed is an **XML DATA STREAM** that is created from an online source. This data stream is sent to a document or application.

Figure 2-45 shows the OData Feed connector options.

The **INCLUDE OPEN TYPE COLUMNS OPTION** is used to indicate that there are columns of data that have dynamic properties that you want to import. Check this option when you need to import extra data properties or extra navigation properties.

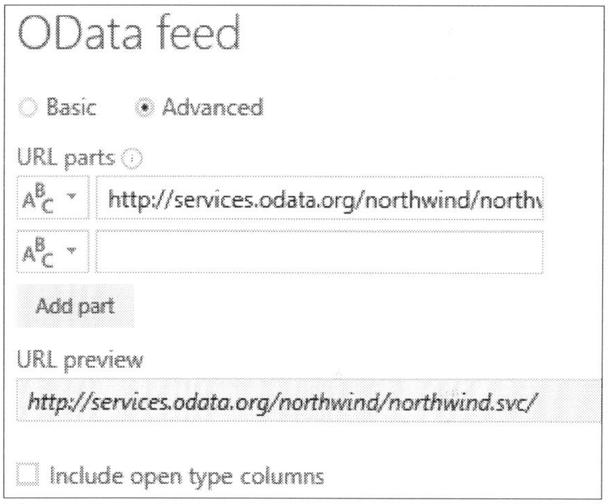

Figure 2-45 OData Feed connector options

Exercise 2.5: Import Data From An OData Data Feed

In this exercise you will learn how to import data from a public data feed.

1. Get Data button ⇒ OData Feed.

2. In the **URL** field, type `http://services.odata.org/northwind/northwind.svc/`, as shown above in Figure 2-45 ⇒ Click OK.

You should see the tables shown in Figure 2-46.

You will see more tables then those shown in the figure.

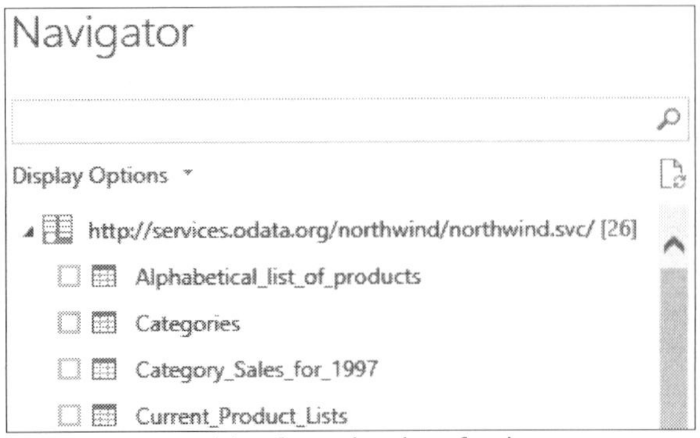

Figure 2-46 Tables from the data feed

3. Select some of the tables ⇒ Click the Load button ⇒ Save the file as `E2.5 Import from an OData feed`.

Excel Workbook Contents Import Option

This import option is used to import the data in the Power Pivot data model, in an Excel workbook. This includes queries, measures, calculated columns and reports created in Power View. Connections to external data sources that were created in Power Pivot are also imported.

Import Limitations
There are some features of the Power Pivot data model in an Excel workbook, that can't be imported, including the following:
☑ Power View Scatter charts that have a Play Axis, Theme or drill-down functionality.
☑ Named Ranges that were created using the From Table option in Power Query in Excel.
For more information, see https://docs.microsoft.com/en-us/power-bi/desktop-import-excel-workbooks
Over time, I suspect that some, if not all of these limitations will be removed.

Exercise 2.6: Import Data From A Power Pivot Data Model

So far, all of the exercises that demonstrated importing Excel data, have used data on worksheets in the workbook. Data can also be imported from the data model in an Excel workbook. In this exercise, you will import data from the Power Pivot data model in an Excel workbook.

1. In a new file ⇒ File tab ⇒ Import ⇒ **EXCEL WORKBOOK CONTENTS.**

2. Select the dm_orders workbook ⇒ On the Import Excel Workbook Contents dialog box, click Start. The data and objects in the data model will be imported.

3. When finished, you will see the dialog box shown in Figure 2-47. You have to scroll down to see all of the content categories shown in the figure ⇒ Click Close.

   If you open the Query Editor, you will see that the tables from the data model in Excel were imported and converted to queries.

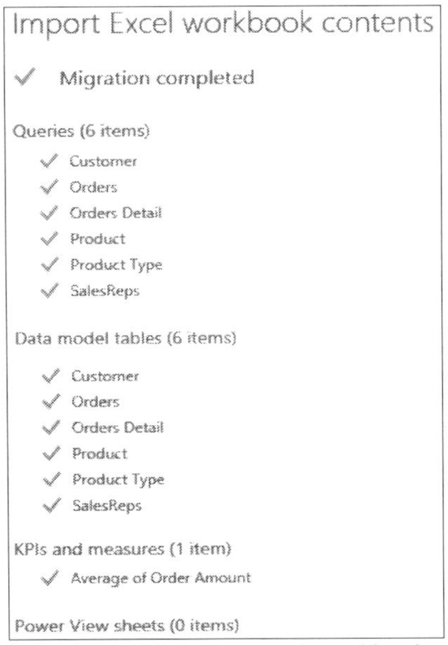

Figure 2-47 Import Excel Workbook Contents results

4. Apply the changes ⇒ Save the file as `E2.6 Imported from a Power Pivot data model.`

How To Copy Data To An External File

While this chapter focused on loading data into Power BI Desktop, the options listed below are used to copy data in a query, in Power BI Desktop, to an external file, like a spreadsheet.

① Copy table option (in the Data View) [See Chapter 3, Table 3-1]
② Copy entire table option [See Chapter 4, Table 4-1]
③ Copy entire list option [See Chapter 4, Table 4-7]

Summary

This chapter covered finding (discovering) and loading data from a variety of data source types, including data from the web. As you saw, some data source types allow you to preview the data in the Navigator dialog box, and other data sources like JSON files, automatically bypass viewing data in the Navigator dialog box and immediately display the data in the Query Editor.

While the import exercises in this book work as expected, out in the real world, this may not always be the case, with some of the data that you need to import. Take your time to work through the issue.

Regardless of how the data can be viewed, it does not have to be loaded to the data model first. The goal of this chapter is to get you acquainted with the external data options on the Home tab, especially the options on the Get Data button, because they are how you import data.

Yes, I know that there wasn't a lot of exciting topics in this chapter. Chapter 4 will formally introduce the Query Editor and show you some techniques for cleaning data and getting the data ready to create reports.

My Import Data Advice

The best advice that I can give you is **Do Not Import Data That You Will Not Use**. Keep in mind that the import can fail if your computer does not have enough RAM to support the amount of data requested for the import. The second best piece of advice that I have is to rename tables after they are imported, so that they are meaningful, when needed.

Sadly, the Get Data import option does not have functionality to let you delete specific columns or rows that are not needed, before opening Power Query (aka the Power Query Editor) to clean the data. This means that you have to import all of the fields and rows in a table, then use the Query Editor, to filter out the fields and rows that you do not need.

USING THE DATA AND RELATIONSHIPS VIEWS

After completing this chapter you will have a better understanding of the following:

- ☑ The options on the Data view
- ☑ Data view Modeling tab options
- ☑ Understand relationships and how to create them
- ☑ Know how to use the Relationships view
- ☑ Relationships view Modeling tab options
- ☑ Know what the data model is and it's role in Power BI Desktop

CHAPTER 3

Overview

While importing and transforming data using the Query Editor is the primary focus of this book, you will probably have the need to use the Data and Relationships views, as part of transforming data, especially if you will be creating reports. This chapter provides a brief overview of these views. As you will see, creating relationships between tables is easier and more efficient than merging data from one table into another table.

If the data that you are using comes from a database, it is possible that you will not need to use the Query Editor. Keep in mind that the purpose of using the Query Editor, is to get the data ready to create reports.

Data View

As it's name suggests, this view is used to see the data (similar to viewing data in the Query Editor). One difference is that the Data view is used to view data after it has been loaded into the data model. The other difference is that the Data view displays all of the rows of data. If you recall, in Chapter 2, Exercise 2.3, you imported a text file that had over 2 million rows of data.

In the Query Editor, you cannot see all of the rows in this table. In the Data view, you can view all 2 plus million rows if you want to, as shown in Figure 3-1.

Figure 3-1 Total number of rows in the Fact Sales table

This view is primarily used to manage the data model, which includes formatting data. Some of the other features are the same as ones in the Query Editor.

In addition to being able to see millions of rows of data and create relationships and hierarchies, (calculated) column and measure formulas can be created using DAX, which may be a main reason to use this view. This view is an additional way to get the data ready to create reports. Figure 3-2 shows the Data view and its Modeling tab. The options are explained below.

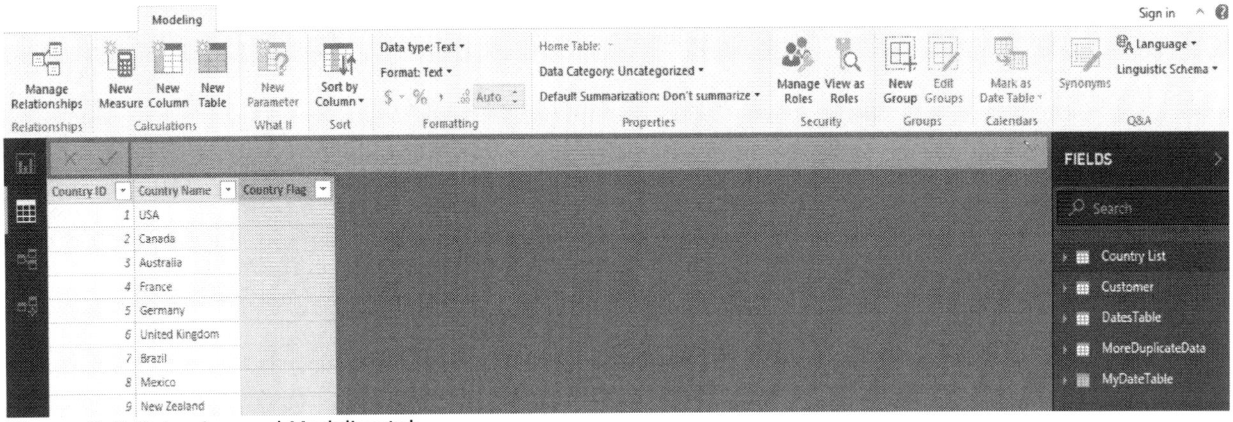

Figure 3-2 Data view and Modeling tab

> **Resizing Columns In A Table**
> The columns in a table on the Data view, can be resized the same way that they are resized in Excel. Drag the vertical line after the column name in the direction that you want to resize the column to.

> **Importing Comment And Note Fields**
> At some point, you will come across a table or file that has a comment or note field. You should not import these fields, unless absolutely necessary, because this type of field will take up unnecessary space in the data model. This field type also prohibits the engine behind the data model from doing the job that it was intended to do, in terms of compressing the data.

Column Shortcut Menu

The shortcut menu shown in Figure 3-3 is available for each column of data, like the ones shown above in Figure 3-2. The options are explained in Table 3-1.

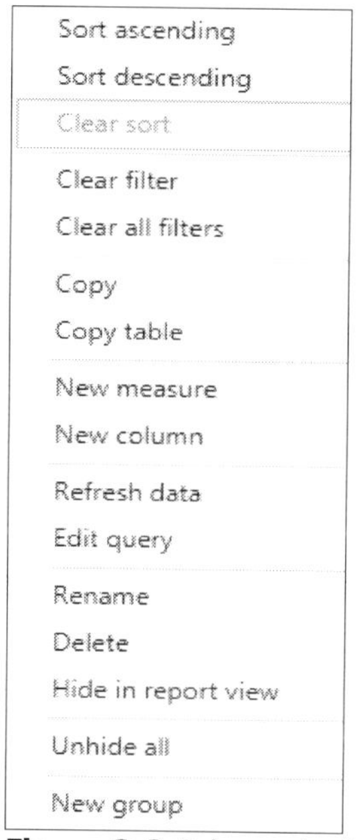

Figure 3-3 Column shortcut menu

Option	Is Used To . . .
Sort Ascending	Sort the data in the table in ascending (A to Z or 1 to 9) order, based on the values in the field. (1)
Sort Descending	Sort the data in the table in descending (Z to A or 9 to 1) order, based on the values in the field. (1)
Clear Sort	Remove the sort that was applied.
Clear Filter	Remove the filter from the selected column.
Clear All Filters	Remove all filters in the table.
Copy	Copy the column of data. (2)
Copy Table	Copy the entire table. (2)
New Measure	Create a formula that aggregates the values in a column. (3) (4)
New Column	Is used to create a calculated column in the current table. (3) (4)
Refresh Data	Update (re-import) the data in the table.
Edit Query	Open the Query Editor and display the data in the table.
Rename	Change the name of the column.
Delete	Delete the column from the table.
Hide in report view	Keep the selected column from being displayed in the Report view. When this option is applied, the column is grayed out and a check mark is added to the shortcut menu for the column. [See Table 3-4]
Unhide All	Display all columns that have the Hide in report view option applied.
New Group	Create groups. [See Creating Groups]

Table 3-1 Column shortcut menu options explained

(1) Only one column in the table can be sorted on at a time.
(2) The column or table that is copied, can be pasted in an external file, like a spreadsheet.
(3) This option enables the formula bar, above the table of data.
(4) This option uses DAX to create the formula.

Creating Groups

Groups are created when you want to define how data is grouped and displayed on a report.

Figure 3-4 shows the Groups dialog box. It is used to create new groups, based on the values in a column and modify existing groups.

If the group is created using a numeric or date field, you can use the **BINNING OPTIONS**, shown in Figure 3-5, to create the size (range) of the groups.

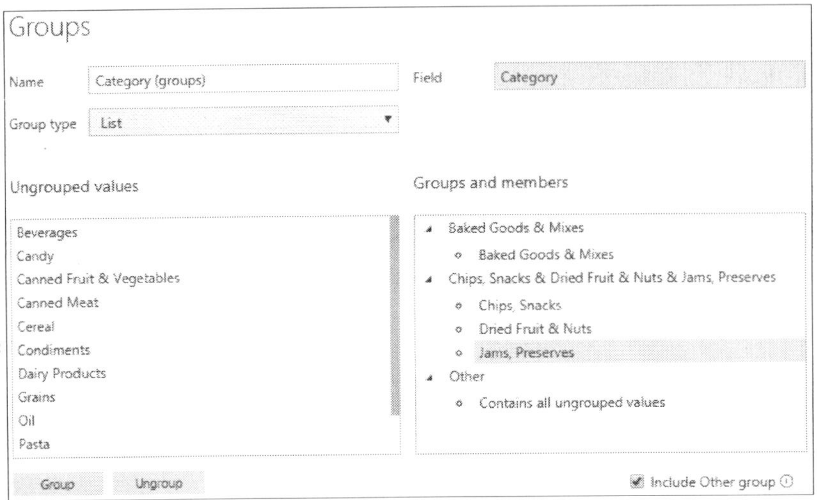

Figure 3-4 Groups dialog box options for a text field

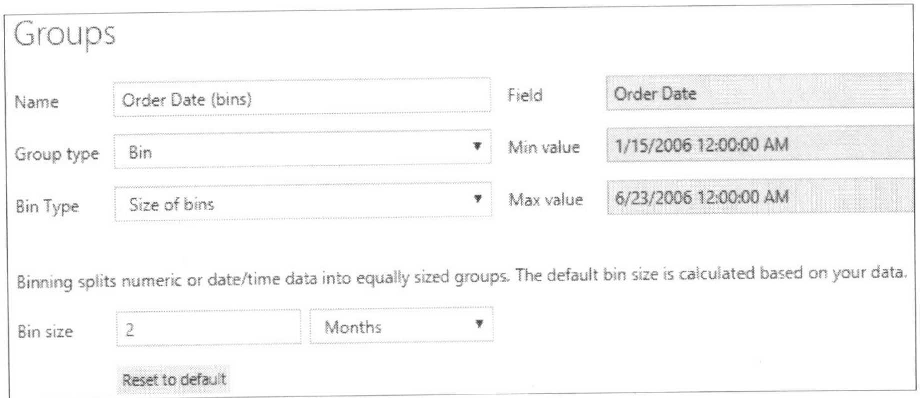

Figure 3-5 Groups dialog box options for a date field

Fields Panel

This panel is on the right side of the Data view, as shown earlier in Figure 3-2. It contains all of the queries (tables) and fields like the Query Editor has. The table name and column name shortcut menus have a subset of options that the Column shortcut menu, shown earlier in Figure 3-3 has.

To access the shortcut menu for a table, right-click on the table name or hold the mouse pointer to the right of the table name and click the ellipsis button after the table or field name.

Modeling Tab

This tab was shown earlier at the top of Figure 3-2. The options are explained in Table 3-2.

Option	Description
Manage Relationships	[See Figure 3-19]
New Measure	[See Table 3-1]
New Column	[See Table 3-1]
New Table	Is used to create a table by typing in the values or pasting the data in.
New Parameter	Is used to create a What-If parameter for a report.
Sort By Column	Is used to select the column to sort another column by.
Data Type	Is used to change the data type of the selected column. The data type options are the same as the ones in the Query Editor.

Table 3-2 Data view Modeling tab options explained

Option	Description
Format	The options vary, depending on the data type, that is selected. The options are used to change how the data in the column is displayed. Figure 3-6 shows some of the date/time format options.
Currency format	Displays the options shown in Figure 3-7, which are used to display the value in a specific currency format.
Percentage format	Displays the data in percent format.
Thousands separator	Adds commas to a numeric value, as needed.
Decimal places	Increases or decreases the number of decimal places. The **AUTO OPTION** defaults to the number of decimal places that the data in the column currently has.
Home Table	This option is enabled when a measure field is selected. It is used to select a table to move the measure to.
Data Category	Is used to select a category for the selected column. As needed, these category options are used to better define the data in a table.
Default Summarization	Is used to select how the column should be aggregated (summarized), by default, when creating a visualization.
Manage Roles	[See Figure 3-16]
View Roles	[See Figure 3-16]
New Group	[See Creating Groups, earlier in this chapter]
Edit Groups	Is used to edit a group. To enable this option, click on a group column. The Groups dialog box shown earlier in Figure 3-5 will open.
Mark as Date Table	This option is enabled when a table that has a date field is selected on the Fields panel. It is used to designate a table that some DAX functions need, to process a formula that uses dates.
Synonyms	[See Figure 3-16]

Table 3-2 Data view Modeling tab options explained (Continued)

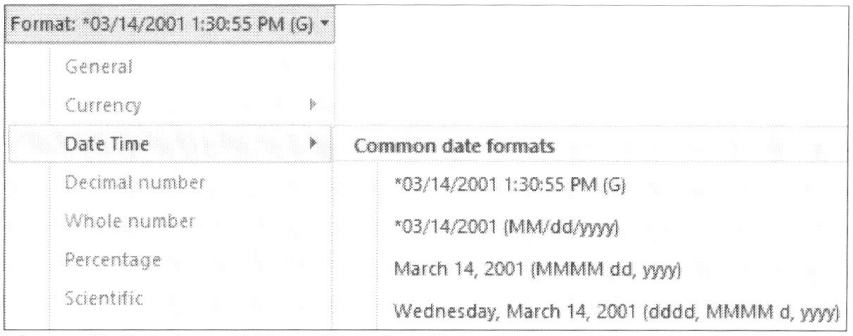

Figure 3-6 Date and Time format options

Figure 3-7 Currency format options

Data View vs Query Editor

While it may not seem like these tools have any significant differences, this section explains the biggest differences that I have observed.

① The Data view only displays data in the data model. The Query Editor displays tables in the data model and tables that have been imported, but not loaded into the data model.
② DAX formulas are created in the Data view. The Query Editor uses the M language to create formulas.
③ The Data view displays all of the data in each table. The Query Editor displays a maximum of 999 rows per table.
④ Relationships can be created and modified in the Data view, in addition to the Relationships view. This usually eliminates the need to merge columns of data in one table into another table or eliminates the need to create a new table that adds data from two or more existing tables. Both of these scenarios are done in the Query Editor and duplicate data, which makes the report file larger than it has to be.

My recommendation is if the task can be done in the Data view, use that option instead of doing it in the Query Editor.

> When a table or column is renamed, from anywhere in Power BI Desktop, it is renamed throughout the report file, which includes the Query Editor.

What Is A Data Model?

This topic was briefly discussed earlier in Chapter 1, but it needs further discussion, because it is a key component of using Power BI Desktop. A data model is a way to create a relational database, if you will, inside a Power BI Desktop report file. The Power Pivot data model in Excel, that was used in Chapter 2, Exercise 2.6, is another example of a data model. When using Power BI Desktop, imported tables are added (loaded) to the data model. So yes, you have already created a data model.

A data model is a collection of tables and their relationships. Relationships allow data from different tables to be used to create one report. This is possible without having to use the **VLOOKUP FUNCTION** in Excel or the Merge options in the Query Editor. Figure 3-8 shows tables in a data model.

While the data in a data model can come from being directly imported into the data model or from queries in the Query Editor, it is not a requirement, because the data can also be added to the model by creating tables, using the **ENTER DATA OPTION**. Data can also be imported from the data model in Excel workbooks. Keep in mind, that each Power BI Desktop report file can only have one data model database.

In my opinion, the biggest benefit of putting data in the data model is that the data model can support millions of rows of data, which is often needed for analysis, while an Excel worksheet has a maximum of 1,048,576 rows. Another benefit of the data model is that calculations are processed faster because the data in a data model is loaded into the computers memory (RAM). Other benefits of using a data model include:

1. Saves disk space because an efficient data compression algorithm is used to store data.
2. Supports complex calculations.
3. Data models support KPI's and hierarchies.

When viewed, a data model contains tables with lines between them that point to the field (in the table) that they have in common. These lines represent the relationships between the tables. Figure 3-8, displays a data model that includes the Orders, Order Details, Customer, Order Subtotals and Employee tables and their relationships.

Data modeling is an important concept to understand because even though the relationships that are imported with tables from a database are saved in the data model, relationships are not automatically created from data that is imported from other file types, like spreadsheets and text files.

What Is The Star Schema?

Now that you have created a data model and have a better understanding of them, it is time to clearly define what the data model will be used for. If in the real world, the data model created in this book would be used for analyzing and reporting on data. The three schema types for data models are:

1. **STAR** Has one level of **CHILD TABLES**.
2. **SNOWFLAKE** Can have multiple levels of child tables. Some people say that this schema can cause performance issues because of the increased number of relationships. My advice is to try it and see for yourself. It may also be the only option, depending on the tables that are needed to create the data model.
3. **CONSTELLATION** Is used when there is more than one fact table.

A **FACT TABLE** is the parent or **PRIMARY TABLE** in the data model. My personal favorite is the Star schema because it handles large datasets. That, and it is easy to understand. <smile> Most of the time though, the tables in a data model requires using the Snowflake schema.

The fact table usually has some or all of the following characteristics:

1. It has measurable data, meaning that the data will answer a question. For example, the Orders table has an order amount field, which would be used to answer, which five states have the most sales.
2. Other tables are linked to it. The fact table usually has the most ID fields.
3. It has one or more date fields, which confirm when something happened, like when the order was placed or the date of each basketball game.
4. Fact tables often have more of rows of data, then any other table in the data model. A date table is not included when determining which table is the fact table, because a date table does not contain data that will be analyzed.

The primary table is surrounded by the other tables in the data model, forming, you guessed it, a star, as shown in Figure 3-8. This is also known as **DIMENSIONAL MODELING** because it describes the logical way that data should be structured, to obtain the best performance.

The Orders table is the fact table in this figure. It is not a requirement to arrange the tables in this layout, in the Relationships view. If you use the Relationships view to create or view relationships, the layout of the tables is not what is important. What is important is that the relationships that are created are correct.

On your own, if you are not sure which table is the fact table, create the relationships for the tables and see which table has the most relationships. More than likely, the table with the most relationships to other tables is the fact table.

The other tables (known as the **DIMENSION TABLES**, **LOOKUP TABLES** or **CHILD TABLES**) in the schema contain supporting data, if you will, that provide additional information about a field in the fact table. For example, in Figure 3-8, the Customer table contains information on who placed each order. The Order Details table contains the items for each order. Notice that each dimension table is linked to the fact table and none of the dimension tables are linked to each other.

Dimension tables can be linked to each other. An example would be adding a Products table to the schema shown in the figure.

It would be linked to the Order Details table, using the Product ID field. That would allow the product name to be displayed on the report.

If the schema rules were strictly followed, adding a relationship to the Products table would make the Star schema shown in Figure 3-8, a Snowflake schema, because the Products table does not have a direct relationship with the Orders **FACT TABLE**.

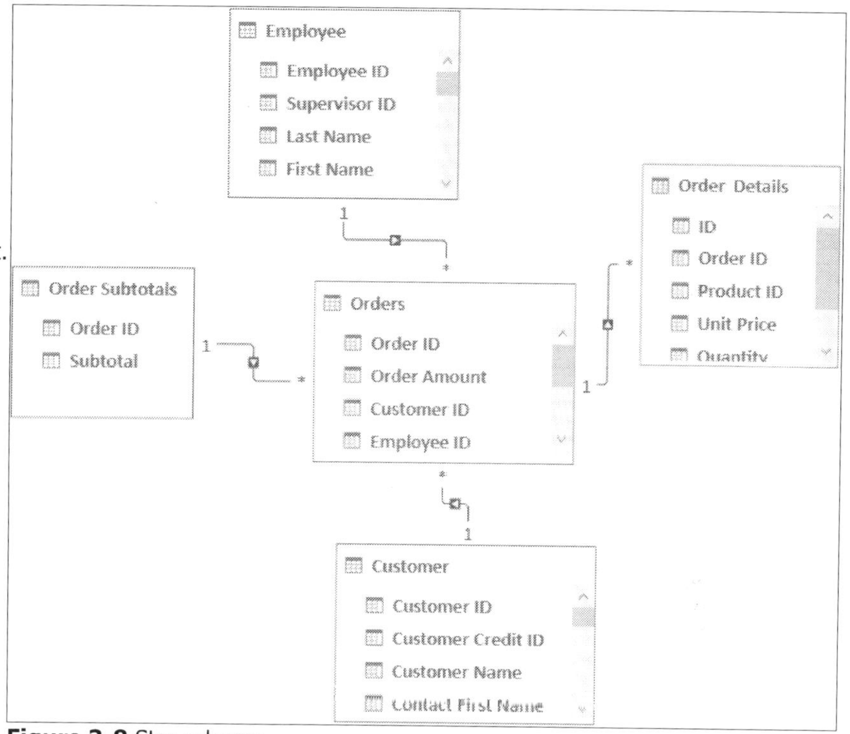

Figure 3-8 Star schema

What Is Normalization?

There are two normalization strategies, as explained below. The **PIVOT** and **UNPIVOT TRANSFORMATIONS** that are covered in Chapter 10, can help with the normalization process.

① **DENORMALIZATION** is the process of combining several tables (usually small tables) into one big table. While this causes the new table to have redundant data, it is done on purpose, because it allows the queries to process faster against the other table(s) in the data model.

② **NORMALIZATION** is the process of removing redundancy in the data model. It works the opposite of denormalization. It takes a large table and turns it into two or more smaller tables. If a value occurs more than once in a column, it is only saved once in the table. The other occurrences of the value in the column are replaced with a reference to the first occurrence of the value.

For example, in a customers table, the same zip code will often appear more than once in the zip code column. The first occurrence of the zip code is saved. The remaining occurrences of the same zip code are replaced with a pointer to the first location in the column that has the zip code.

Using The Data And Relationships Views

After the tables have been imported into the data model, you have to determine if the tables are set up to run in the most efficient way. This is known as **NORMALIZING THE DATA MODEL**. This process organizes the data to make querying it more efficient. This includes tasks like verifying that the data in a table only has one value per column (for example, the first and last name should be in two columns) and that all of the columns in a table are related (meaning the customer zip code should not be in the products table). As much as possible, I fix items like these before the data is imported. The goal of normalization is to ensure that other then key fields, the same data is not stored in more than one table.

Supported Data Types In The Data Model

The data model supports the data types listed in the first column in Table 3-3. The first column in the table is how the data model "classifies" data. The second column in the table, is how DAX classifies data.

Once imported, each column in the table must have a specific data type and all values in the column have to be the same data type. If all of the data in a column is not defined as text and does not have the same data type, you will see an error that the column is not defined as the Text data type.

The data model does not support all of the data types that some databases use. This means that some columns of data may not be displayed and that they may not be imported.

While some databases support more than one variation of a data type listed in the first column in the table, the data model does not. If the original data type for the field is similar to one in the table, it will be mapped to a data type in the first column in Table 3-3. This may or may not be what you want.

Data Model Data Type	DAX Data Type	Description
Text	String	Usually contains character text. Dates and numbers can be stored in this data type. They will be represented as text in this data type. If all of the data in a column cannot be converted to any of the other data types in this table, the column defaults to the text data type, but you can change the data type.
Decimal Number	Decimal number (64-bit)	Positive and negative numbers, with or without a decimal point. Zero is also a decimal number.
Whole Number	Integer (64-bit)	Positive and negative numbers, without a decimal point.
Date	Date/time	DAX only supports dates on or after January 1, 1900.
Currency	Currency	Currency values are imported into the currency format that the computer is set to use. This could produce different or unexpected results, from one computer to another. There is a maximum of four decimal places.
True/False	Boolean	A true or false value.
(Not available)	Blank	In DAX, this data type replaces SQL null values. The BLANK function can be used to create a blank and the ISBLANK function is used to test for blank values.
(Not available)	BLOB (Binary Large Object)	This data type stores an image file or a link to the location of the image file. This data type can only be displayed. It cannot be used in a DAX formula.

Table 3-3 Data model and DAX supported data types explained

Data Type Tips

① If all of the data in a column cannot be converted to any of the other data types in Table 3-3, the column defaults to the **ANY DATA TYPE**, that is covered in Chapter 6.

② It is a good idea to check the data type of the fields (in particular, fields that have dates or numeric values) after the import, as data that "looks" like it is a certain data type, may not actually be defined as that. If all of the values in a field are not the same type, for example, a field of numeric values that has been defined as text, should have the data type changed in the table, if the field will be used in a formula or used to create a relationship. The fields data type can be checked in the Data view or in the Query Editor.

Importing Data From A Database

Importing data from tables in a database is a popular way to add data to the data model. In addition to tables, some databases can use SQL queries to add data to the data model. Views and stored procedures are other ways to import data from a database. Queries, views and stored procedures usually retrieve a subset of the data that is in the tables in the database, instead of retrieving all of the fields and records, in all of the tables in the database.

For example, there could be a view that only retrieves orders from specific states. **UNLIKE TABLES, QUERIES, VIEWS AND STORED PROCEDURES DO NOT STORE DATA.** They contain code that specifies which records in the tables should be retrieved or in the case of the data model, which records should be imported. If you find that you are using the same criteria over and over to retrieve records or you are always applying the same filters to the same data, each time that you import the data, you can create an SQL query (to use on the dialog box for the database connector) that has all of the options that you need. Using a query, view or stored procedure will save you time when importing data from a database because you do not have to manually select the criteria in the Query Editor. Views and stored procedures are discussed in more detail in the next few sections.

Views

Views are usually created by a Database Administrator (DBA), or someone that has administrator rights to the database. Views allow one to gather data from a variety of tables and combine the data into a "view". This makes it easier for end users to access just the data that they need. Views are useful if you use the sorting and data selection (filter) options in the data model.

A view is a **RECORDSET** (the result) of a query. Views usually display a subset of the data in a data source. Views are stored in the database and are like tables, but they do not have the physical characteristics of a table. For example, records cannot be added to or deleted from a view. Fields cannot be added to a view unless the view is modified to include more fields. The field length cannot be changed in a view, like it can in a table.

Instead of selecting all of the tables when importing data into the data model, select the view in the database instead. If you do not have access to do this at the database level, you will need a DBA to create the view for you.

Tables vs Views

When possible, using views is preferred over using tables to import data from a database. There are some differences between importing tables and views, as described below.

① Tables already have relationships that the data model in Power BI Desktop recognizes, when the tables are imported.
② In views, the tables have already been joined for you, so you may not need to create relationships, unless you need to use a date table.
③ If the view has all of the fields you need, for several reports, there will probably be no need to create relationships for the view.
④ Views usually have cleaner data because the data has been filtered and only includes the fields that are needed.

Views vs Queries In Power Query

The **MERGE QUERIES TRANSFORMATION** in the Query Editor creates the equivalent of a view. Merging queries requires more steps. The benefits that views have over the Merge Queries transformation include the following.

☑ Views are created at the database level and are imported like any table in the database. Once imported into Power Query, views will probably not need many, if any transformations.
☑ Unless you are a DBA, you probably will not have to create the views.
☑ The more the data can be cleaned and transformed before it is imported into Power Query, the easier it is to maintain the data in Power Query.
☑ The more data cleansing and transformations that are created in Power Query, the greater the risk of having data refresh errors and causing the data model to run slow because of all of the processing.
☑ Using the Merge Queries option, duplicates data by copying columns of data in one table to another table. While views display data, they do not actually store any data. Views are like a virtual table.

Stored Procedures

Stored Procedures contain queries that are more complex then views, but less complex than commands.

The majority of the time, stored procedures are created by a DBA or programmer. Figure 3-9 shows the views and stored procedures in a database.

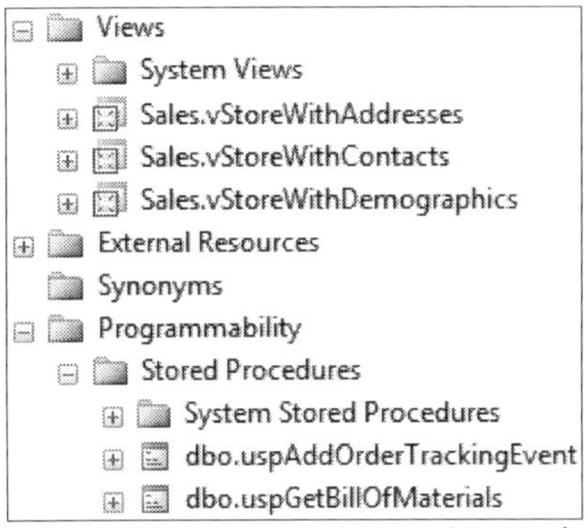

Figure 3-9 Views and Stored Procedures in a database

What Is A Relationship?

In order to be able to use the tables in a data model together, to create a report, or create formulas that need fields in different tables, there has to be a connection between the tables. The actual connection is called a **LINK**. The lines between the tables shown earlier in Figure 3-8 are the visual representation of the links that I am referring to.
The result of a link between tables is called a **RELATIONSHIP**. The ability to create relationships to join tables and use the data from multiple tables to create one formula or one report, may be the number one reason that the data model exists.

Relationships are created between a column of data that two tables have in common. Relationships between tables allow for a higher level of analysis, because columns of data from different tables can be used together. Data in one table can be filtered by data in another table, which provides even more flexibility and control over the data that is displayed on a report.

Relational Databases

The reason that tables can have relationships created between them is because there is at least one column in each table, that has the same related data, thus the term "Relational Databases". Yes, this is a complicated topic and there are a lot of books on the concepts associated with relational databases and how to create them, so I won't bore you with all of the details, but please hear me out and don't skip this section. Creating relationships is a concept that is necessary to understand. Creating relationships in a data model and creating relationships in a database is the same.

While databases are not the primary focus of this chapter, it is important that you understand a little more than the fundamentals. My goal is to explain, as painless as possible, how all of the components fit together. <smile>
The reason that you need to understand this database concept is because it is the foundation of why you are creating a data model in the first place. And that is to allow users access to the data in a way that they need it and will use it. If you have never created a database, or have very little experience creating them, the next few sections in this chapter will be your crash course in databases and relationships. Figures 3-10 and 3-11 illustrate the layout of two tables, in a database.

Orders			
Order ID	Order Date	Order Amount	Cust ID
1000	1/2/2015	$263.99	48
1001	1/2/2015	$322.45	57
1002	1/3/2015	$196.00	3
1003	1/4/2015	$124.99	48

← Table Name
← Field Names
← Records

Figure 3-10 Orders table

Order Details		
Order ID	Product ID	Quantity
1000	43	4
1000	76	2
1001	76	3
1001	10	2
1003	10	1
1004	25	3

← Table Name
← Field Names
← Records

Figure 3-11 Order Details table

Primary Key Fields

Primary key fields and ID fields are terms that are used interchangeably. I prefer to use the term ID field because primary key fields in databases often have "ID" as part of the field name. Recently though, I have seen the word "Key" at the end of a field name to signify that the field is a primary key field.

ID is short for identification. It is jargon that the computer programming community uses to know whether or not a field was created to be used to link one table to another table.

Primary key fields or the field used to reference the row, is usually the first column in a table.

The tables in the database that you use in the this book, to create a relationship, have at least one ID field. Hopefully, you will find that this is also true out in the real world. The reason that ID fields are used, is because by design, they provide a way for each record in the table to have a unique way to be identified. A **FOREIGN KEY** points back to a primary key in a related table. An example of a foreign key is the Cust ID field in the Orders table, shown above in Figure 3-10. The Cust ID field is the primary field in the Customers table. It is used to create a relationship with the Customers table.

I have taught several database classes and almost without fail, this topic causes a lot of confusion. For some reason, people want to create links on string (text) fields. Please don't do that for tables in databases. It can cause you problems and should be avoided. It is a bad table design choice. However, if you have a dataset that uses text fields as primary key fields, creating relationships for tables in the data model on text fields is acceptable, in particular, for data that is not imported from a database.

If you needed to create a report that displays all of the orders and what items were on each order, you would need a way to link the Orders and Order Details tables, shown above. Think of creating relationships as having the ability to combine two or more tables "virtually" and being able to display the result of this "virtual linking" on a report. The virtual relationship linking discussed in this chapter refers to the process of joining two tables based on data in a column, that the tables have in common.

In Figures 3-10 and 3-11 above, the common ID field is the Order ID field. If you look at the data in the Order Details table, you will see that some records have the same Order ID number. That's okay. This means that some orders have more than one item. Each record in the Order Details table represents one item that was ordered. If you were to "virtually" join the data in these two tables, the **VIRTUAL TABLE** would look like the one shown in Figure 3-12.

This "virtual" join is what happens when tables are **LINKED** (have a relationship). If all of this data was stored in one table instead of two, at the very minimum, all of the fields in the Orders table would be repeated for every record that is in the Order Details table.

Orders				Order Details		
Order ID	Order Date	Order Amount	Cust ID	Order ID	Product ID	Quantity
1000	01/02/2015	$263.99	48	1000	43	4
1000	01/02/2015	$263.99	48	1000	76	2
1001	01/02/2015	$322.45	57	1001	76	3
1001	01/02/2015	$322.45	57	1001	10	2
1002	01/03/2015	$196.00	3			
1003	01/04/2015	$124.99	48	1003	10	1
				1004	25	3

Figure 3-12 Virtually joined tables

Virtually joined tables represent the concept of merging queries, that is covered in Chapter 8. The difference is that merging queries places a copy of the selected fields into the first table selected on the Merge dialog box or into a new query. The problem with merging queries is that the same data is stored in multiple tables.

Repetition of data is why this information is stored in two tables in a database, instead of one. In this example, an additional row would be added to the Orders table for each row in the Order Details table. It is poor table design to have the same information (other than fields that are used to join tables) stored in more than one table.

Usually if you see a record in the Order Details table, like Order ID 1004, shown above in Figure 3-12, or any **CHILD TABLE** that is in a **PARENT-CHILD RELATIONSHIP**, there is a problem (usually with referential integrity not being enabled, or enabled incorrectly) with the data, in at least one of the tables because all of the records in the child table should have at least one matching record in the parent table. Parent tables are used to get data from a **CHILD TABLE**, also known as a **LOOKUP TABLE**. In this scenario, the record for Order ID 1004, in the Order Details table, would not be retrieved or shown on a report, with the parent-child relationship.

Understanding Relationships In Power BI Desktop

An ID field in the Orders table is how you find the matching record (known as a **ONE-TO-ONE RELATIONSHIP**) or matching records (known as a **ONE-TO-MANY RELATIONSHIP**, which is the most popular type of relationship) in another table. These are the two most common types of relationships. The **MANY-TO-MANY RELATIONSHIP** is a third type of relationship. It is not used as much as the other two relationship types.

A relationship between tables may appear to work in the reverse of what you may be use to. They work in a **MANY-TO-ONE RELATIONSHIP** because the table at the top of the Create Relationship dialog box, is the "many" table and the second table, is the "one" table. The good thing though, is that you can create relationships traditionally, with the "one" table at the top and the "many" table at the bottom. Fortunately, if you create a relationship between tables that Power BI Desktop wants in the opposite direction, you will see a warning message.

> **Many-To-Many Relationships**
> The many-to-many relationship functionality is available when tables are joined using the Many-to-Many **CARDINALITY** option. [See Figure 3-23] This relationship type does not require that the column being used to create the relationship have unique values in one of the tables. This means that if in the past, you had to import an additional table that had the unique values or import the same table twice, you no longer have to do that. Instead, select the Many-To-Many cardinality option.

What Is Cardinality?

Lookup tables usually have values in the primary key field that are repeated. This type of table is the "Many" side of a relationship. The primary table usually has values that are not repeated in the primary key field. This type of table is the "One" side of a relationship. This concept of primary and lookup tables is also known as the **CARDINALITY** of a relationship. Cardinality is the term used to classify the type of relationship that two tables have.

How Relationships Work

More than likely, the business requirements for the data model will require data from more than one table. For example, reports that display the equivalent of a Product List report will probably only use one table, so there is no linking required. For reports that require data from two or more tables, the tables need to be linked by creating a relationship between them.

When you need to view or modify existing relationships, you can do so by opening the Manage Relationships dialog box, shown later in Figure 3-19. Even though some of the time, the relationships that you need are automatically created for you during the import process, it is important to understand what is going on behind the scenes, as they say. The best way to understand the basic concept of creating relationships between tables, especially if you are not familiar with the data, is to take the time to view at least some of the data in the tables that need to have a relationship created.

Figures 3-13 and 3-14 show the records in the Employee and Employee Addresses tables. The field that these tables have in common is the Employee ID field. This would be the primary key field used to create a relationship between these two tables.

Employee

Employee ID	Supervisor ID	Last Name	First Name	Position	Birth Date	Hire Date
1	5	Davolio	Nancy	Sales Representative	12/8/1972	3/29/1991
2		Fuller	Andrew	Vice President, Sales	2/19/1969	7/12/1991
3	5	Leverling	Janet	Sales Representative	8/30/1971	2/27/1991
4	5	Peacock	Margaret	Sales Representative	9/19/1973	3/30/1992
5	2	Buchanan	Steven	Sales Manager	3/4/1975	9/13/1992
6	5	Suyama	Michael	Sales Representative	7/2/1963	9/13/1992

Figure 3-13 Employee table

Employee Addresses

Employee ID	Address1	Address2	City	Region	Country	Postal Code
1	507 - 20th Ave. E.		Port Moody	BC	Canada	V3D 4F6
2	908 W. Capital Way	Suite 100	Coquitlam	BC	Canada	V3H4J7
3	722 Moss Bay Blvd.		Vancouver	BC	Canada	V6M 8S9
4	4110 Old Redmond Rd.		Richmond	BC	Canada	V5S 6H7
5	14 Garrett Hill		London		UK	SW1 8JR
6	Coventry House		London		UK	EC2 7JR

Figure 3-14 Employee Addresses table

Depending on the table structure, tables can have more than one field that they can be linked on. An example of this would be the Order Details table. This table has an ID field that would be used to link it to the Orders table. There is also a Product ID field in the Order Details table, that would be used to retrieve the Product Name from another table (the Products table) to display on the report, instead of displaying the Product ID number. Displaying the product name is more meaningful then displaying the Product ID field, which contains a number. If you are asking why the Product Name is not stored in the Order Details table, there are three reasons that I can think of, as explained below.

① The ID field takes up less space then the Product Name field, thereby keeping the size of the Order Details table (and any other table that would store the Product Name field instead of the Product ID field) smaller.
② If a product name has to be changed for any reason, it only has to be changed once, in the Products table. Every report that the Product Name field is displayed on, would automatically be updated with the revised product name, the next time the data for the report is refreshed. If the product name was stored in the Order Details table, every record in the Order Details table that had that product name would have to be changed, as well as, any other table that stored the product name. That would be a lot of extra work (for you) and increase the chance for having inaccurate data.
③ Without a Products table, there would be no place to add new products.

Keep in mind that if the relationships are incorrect, the data displayed on visualizations that are created from the tables with incorrect relationships, will not display the correct data or may not display any data.

Recursive Join

In addition to the inner and outer join types, there is another join type called **RECURSIVE JOIN**. (This join type is also known as a **SELF-JOIN**.) This join type is not always obvious when looking at the table structure. A recursive join occurs when the same data is stored in two different fields (usually primary key fields) in the same table. This is not the same as a parent/child (also known as a master/detail) relationship, because this type of relationship does not require two tables to create the link, like the Orders and Order Details tables do. No link is required to use this join type.

An example of a recursive join is in the table shown earlier in Figure 3-13. The Supervisor ID field in the table contains the Employee ID of another record in the same table. This is because supervisors are also employees. As shown, four employees have the number 5 in the Supervisor ID field. This is because they all have the same supervisor, Steven Buchanan, whose Employee ID, is number 5.

Recursive joins are often used to create **HIERARCHICAL REPORTS**. An example of this type of report would be a report that displays a list of managers and the people in their department, as discussed above.

Relationships View

Figure 3-15 shows the Relationships view. It displays the tables, columns and relationships in the data model. (This data model is from Exercise 2.4.) As you can see, not all tables have a relationship. That may not be a problem if the tables that do not have a relationship are either going to be used to create a list report, not going to be used to create a report or that a field in the table was merged into a table that will be used to create a report. When data is imported from a database, some, if not all of the relationships are created, as long as you have the correct relationship options selected on the Options dialog box.

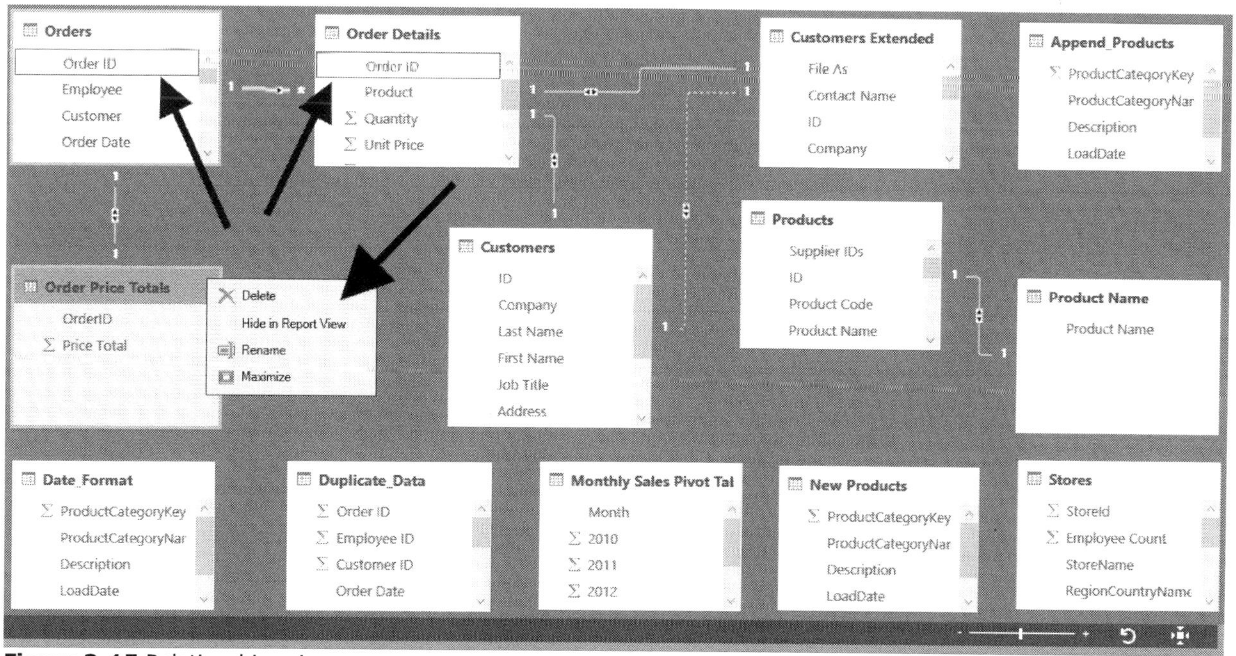

Figure 3-15 Relationships view

The **MAXIMIZE OPTION** shown above in Figure 3-15, on the shortcut menu, is used to display all of the fields in the table. This option is also available when you hold the mouse pointer to the right of the table name. When a table is maximized, this option changes to **RESTORE**.

If you want to see the details of a relationship or edit a relationship, double-click on the line between the tables. You will see the Edit Relationship dialog box. This dialog box looks like and has the same options as the Create Relationship dialog box. [See Figure 3-22]

It can be difficult to tell which fields are used to link the tables. The easy way to tell is to click on the line between the tables. The field in each table that is used as the link, will have a border around it, as illustrated in the upper left corner of Figure 3-15. The other option is to click the **MANAGE RELATIONSHIPS BUTTON** on the Home tab.

Status Bar Options

In the lower right corner of Figure 3-15 are three options that are used to change the appearance of the Relationships view. The options (from left to right) are explained below.

The **ZOOM SLIDER** is used to increase or decrease the size of the tables displayed in the window. In addition to this option, you can use drag and drop to rearrange where the tables are displayed.

The **RESET LAYOUT BUTTON** restores the previous layout of the view.

The **FIT TO SCREEN BUTTON** resizes the tables so that they are all displayed in the current window size.

Rearranging The Tables
If you rearrange the tables on this view, the new layout is saved when you save the report file.

Table Shortcut Menu

The Order Price Totals table in Figure 3-15, shows the shortcut menu. To display this menu, right-click near the table name. The options are explained in Table 3-4.

Option	Description
Delete	Deletes the table from the data model. There is no Undo option for this feature. If you make a mistake and need the table, you can import it again or if it is not too late, close the report file and not save the changes to it, then reopen it. (5)
Hide in report view	Prevents the table from being displayed in the Report view. This means that the table cannot be used to create a report. The table is grayed out in the Relationships view. The table is also grayed out on the Data view, but has all of the functionality that tables have on that view. (5)
Rename	Renames the table. This change is made throughout the data model automatically. (5)
Maximize	Displays the table longer and hides the other tables. Press the ESC key to return to the Relationships view. If you hold the mouse pointer to the right of the table name, there is a button that will also maximize the table.

Table 3-4 Table shortcut menu options explained

(5) This option is also available for each field.

Hiding vs Deleting Columns Tips
Below are some tips and guidelines that you may find helpful in deciding whether to hide or delete a column.
① If a column is deleted from a table, the data in the column is no longer available in Power BI Desktop.
② Before deleting a column, make sure that it is not a column that is needed to create a relationship with another table. When in doubt about deleting a column, hide it instead.
③ Hiding a column prevents it from being displayed in the Report view.
④ Hide columns that are used to create a relationship. The reason to consider doing this is because these fields are rarely displayed on a report because the numeric values in key fields, provide no value to anyone reading the report.
⑤ As you have seen, many tables that you imported have a lot of fields. On the Report view, having to sift through all of the fields on the Fields panel can take a lot of time. If you know that some fields will not be used, hide them if you do not want to delete them.

Modeling Tab

Figure 3-16 shows the options on the Modeling tab. The options are explained below.

The **MANAGE ROLES BUTTON** displays the dialog box shown in Figure 3-18. This tool is used to create and edit security options for the report file.

The **VIEW AS ROLES BUTTON** is used to view the data that each user or security role (group) has access to.

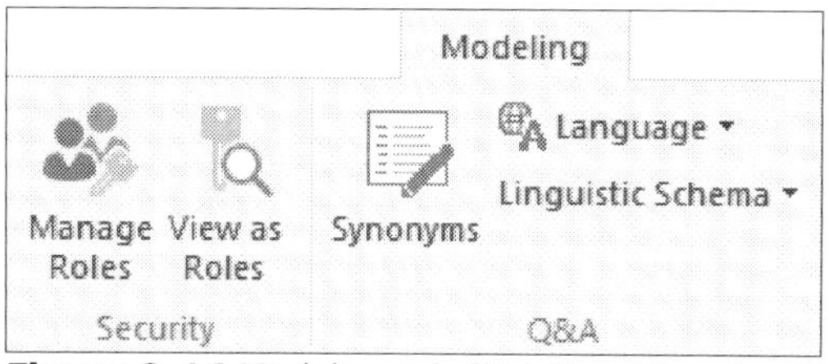

Figure 3-16 Modeling tab (Relationships view)

The options in the Q&A section are used with Power BI's **Q&A NATURAL LANGUAGE** feature.

The **SYNONYMS BUTTON** shown above in Figure 3-16, displays the panel shown in Figure 3-17.

This panel is used to enter words or phrases for a table that have the same or similar meaning. Click the Synonyms button again, to close the panel.

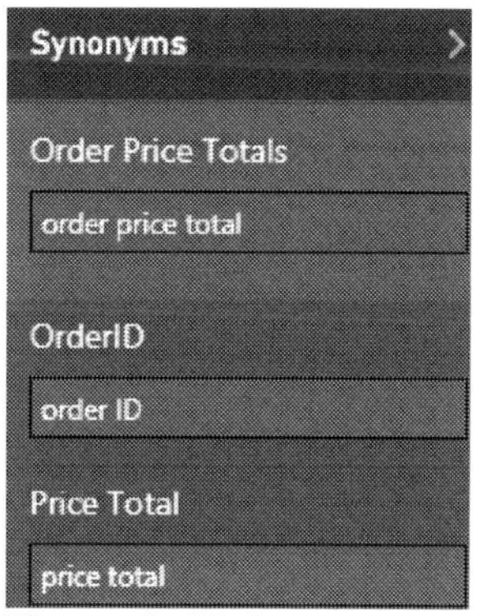

Figure 3-17 Synonyms panel

ROW LEVEL SECURITY can be created on this dialog box by:

① Creating a DAX expression to filter the data that can be viewed in Power BI Desktop.
② Creating a role.
③ Assign a DAX expression to the role.

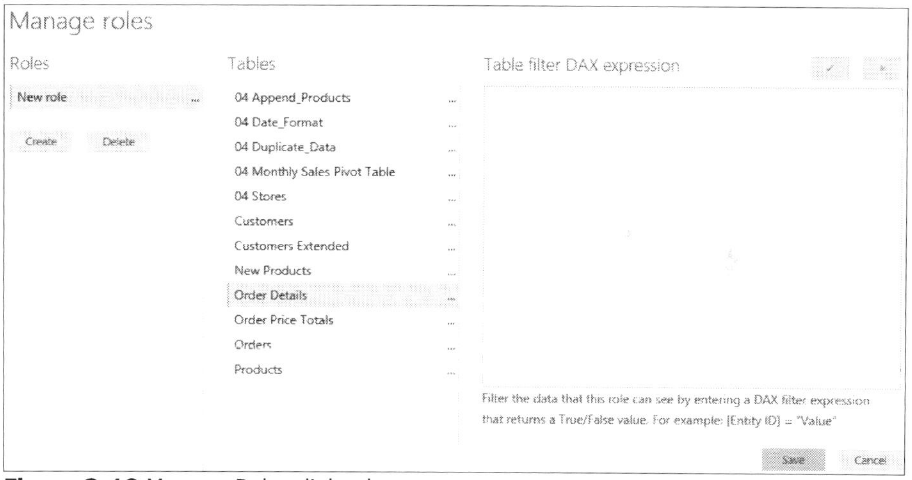

Figure 3-18 Manage Roles dialog box

Manually Creating Relationships

To create a relationship on the Relationships view, click on the primary key field in the primary table of the relationship, that you want to create, and drag the mouse pointer to the matching field in the child table, then release the mouse button. The field names in both tables do not have to be the same, to create a relationship.

While you can create relationships starting with the secondary table, it is possible that you will not retrieve all of the records from the primary table. For example, in Figure 3-10 shown earlier, Order ID 1002 would not be displayed because the Order Details table does not have any matching records. Granted, that is a data problem (often because referential integrity was not enforced), but I prefer to display bad data like this on a report, so that hopefully someone, that uses the report, will see the bad data and fix it.

Exercise 3.1: Create Relationships

In this exercise, you will learn how to create relationships in a data model.

1. Save the E2.4 file as `E3.1 Create relationships`.
2. Display the Relationships view.
3. Right-click on each of the lines between the tables and select Delete. You may have to scroll to the right to see all of the tables. You are doing this, so that you can recreate them.
4. Drag the Order ID field in the Orders table to the Order ID field in the Order Price Totals table.
5. Drag the Order ID field in the Order Details table to the Order ID field in the Orders table. This will create a many-to-one relationship, which you will edit and change to a one-to-many relationship, later in this exercise. The next section shows you another way to create relationships.

Manage Relationships

The dialog box shown in Figure 3-19 is used to create, edit and delete relationships.

I tend to create relationships manually, then view them on this dialog box and make any changes that are needed.

The **ACTIVE OPTION** indicates whether or not the relationship is currently being used.

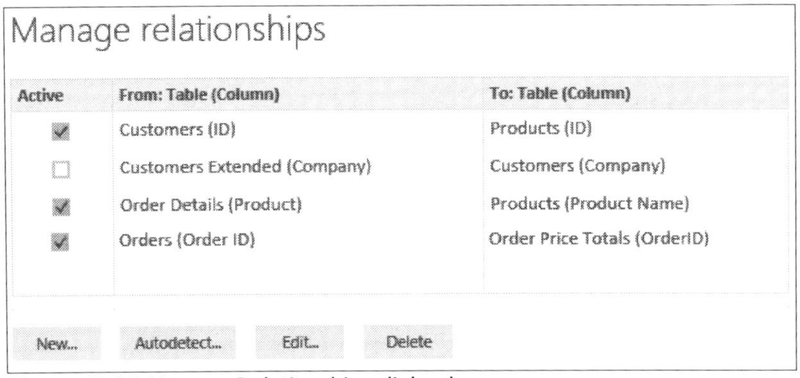

Figure 3-19 Manage Relationships dialog box

Use The Auto Detect Option

The **AUTODETECT BUTTON**, shown above in Figure 3-19, will check to see if there are any relationships that can be created. If relationships are found, they are created. Keep in mind that just because a relationship is automatically created when using this button, doesn't mean that the Active box for the relationship is automatically checked, or that the relationship is needed.

1. Home tab ⇒ Manage Relationships button. You should see the two relationships that you created in the previous part of this exercise, on the Manage Relationships dialog box.
2. Click the **AUTO DETECT BUTTON**. You should see the message shown in Figure 3-20.

   This feature lets you know how many relationships were found ⇒ Click the Close button.

Figure 3-20 Auto detect relationship results

Delete Relationships

The previous part of this exercise automatically created relationships. In this part of the exercise, the relationships created by the Auto detect feature will be deleted. The **DELETE BUTTON** deletes the selected relationship.

1. Delete all of the relationships except the one for the Orders and Order Price Totals tables and the Order Details and Orders table.

Create A New Relationship

In this part of the exercise, you will create a one-to-many relationship. The **NEW BUTTON** is used to create a relationship.

1. On the Manage Relationships dialog box, click the New button.

2. Open the first drop-down list and select the Orders table.

3. Open the next drop-down list and select the Order Details table. You should see the message shown in Figure 3-21. It lets you know that you are creating a relationship between tables that already have a relationship.

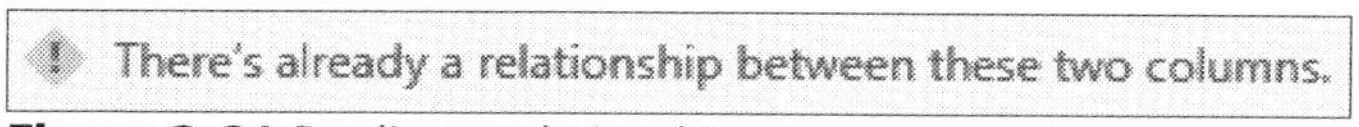

Figure 3-21 Duplicate relationships message

4. Open the first table drop-down list and select the Customers table ⇒ Select the Orders table in the next drop-down list.

5. As you can see, a relationship was not automatically detected. The good news is that like creating a merge, you can click on the column in each table to use, to create a relationship (the link between the tables).

   In the Customers table, click on the Company column ⇒

   In the Orders table, click on the Customer column. You should have the options shown in Figure 3-22 ⇒

   Click OK.

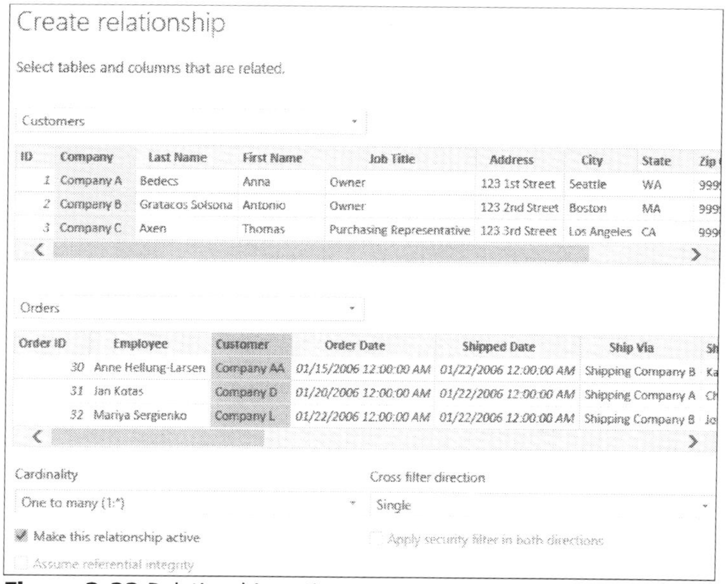

Figure 3-22 Relationship options

Create Relationship Dialog Box Options

The options discussed in this section also apply to the **EDIT RELATIONSHIP DIALOG BOX**.

The **CARDINALITY OPTIONS**, shown in Figure 3-23, are used to select the type of relationship to create between the tables. These are the same relationship options that were covered earlier in this chapter. If you select an option that is not appropriate for the tables and columns selected to create the relationship, you will see the message shown in Figure 3-24, or one similar.

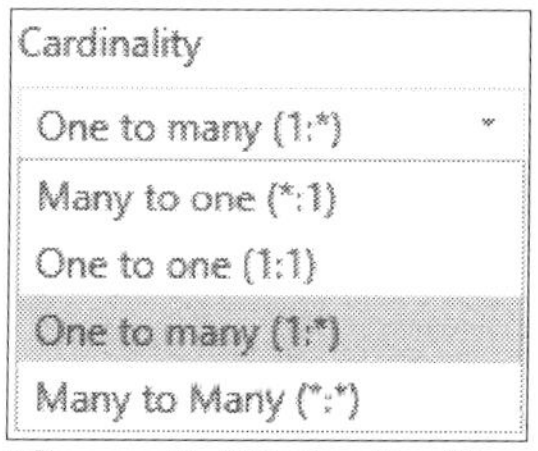

Figure 3-23 Cardinality options

Figure 3-24 Cardinality warning message

The **CROSS FILTER DIRECTION OPTIONS**, shown in Figure 3-25, are used to select which table the relationship (filter) should be applied to.

SINGLE OPTION This option means that the fact table can be filtered by the lookup table, but not the other way around. For example, the Orders table can be filtered by the Dates table, but the Dates table cannot be filtered by the Orders table.

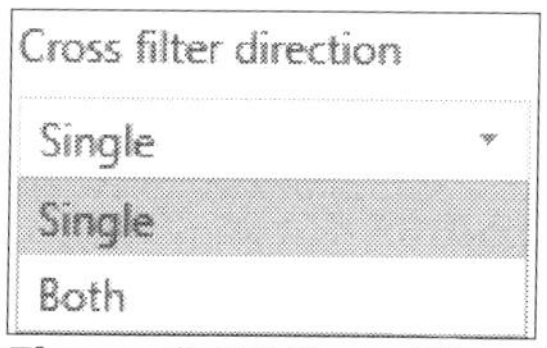

Figure 3-25 Cross filter direction options

The **BOTH OPTION** applies the filter to either table, which filters the data in the other table. This option is referred to as a **MANY-TO-MANY RELATIONSHIP**. An example of when to select this option is when you need a count of an item by date. In the Orders table, you would use the Order Date field. In the Item table (maybe a products table) you would use the Item number. In the example just explained, there are many items sold on the same date and the same item is sold on many dates.

The **MAKE THIS RELATIONSHIP ACTIVE OPTION** is used to select whether or not the relationship should be applied to the tables. A pair of tables can have more than one relationship, but only one relationship can be active at a time, when using the same field to link the tables. Relationships that are not active are often used with the **USERELATIONSHIP** DAX function. This function allows you to override the active relationship between the pair of tables and use a relationship that is not active between the pair of tables.

The **ASSUME REFERENTIAL INTEGRITY OPTION** is only enabled when using a Direct Query connection. Referential integrity is a concept used to ensure that relationships between tables are consistent. This means that both tables must have the same keys. This prevents records from being added to the child table using a key field that does not already exist in the primary table.

For example, Figure 3-11 shown earlier, shows the foreign key 1004. If referential integrity had been applied to these tables in the data source, this record could not have been created. If at some point, there was a corresponding record in the Orders table, shown in Figure 3-10 and it was deleted, any corresponding records in the Order Details table would have been deleted at the same time, if referential integrity was enabled.

Edit An Existing Relationship

The **EDIT BUTTON** is used to view or change an existing relationship. Earlier in this exercise, you created a many-to-one relationship between the Orders and Order Details table. In this part of the exercise, you will change the relationship to a one-to-many relationship.

1. On the Manage Relationships dialog box, click on the relationship that has the Order Details table.
2. Click the Edit button to open the Edit Relationship dialog box.
3. Change the Order Details table to the Orders table in the first drop-down list ⇒ Select the Order Details table in the next drop-down list. The Cardinality field should have the One-To-Many option selected ⇒ Click OK ⇒ Click Close.
4. Save the changes to the file.

Disclaimer: At the time that this book went to print, the Modeling view was a preview option. It is very possible that by the time you are reading this book, that this view has replaced the Relationships view, covered earlier in this chapter.

Modeling View

The **MODELING VIEW** shown in Figure 3-26, is used to take data models that have a lot of tables and make them more manageable by creating diagram layouts that only have a few tables on each layout. For example, you could put all customer tables on one layout and all manufacturing and product tables on a different layout.

This view can manage hundreds of tables. This view comes with the **ALL TABLES VIEW**, which displays all of the tables and relationships, just like the Relationships view, discussed earlier in this chapter.

You can also view and modify properties of a table or field on the **PROPERTIES PANEL**, shown on the right side of the figure. As shown at the bottom of the figure, two layouts, Customers and Sales have been created. What I like is that you can apply settings to multiple tables or fields at the same time. When you select two or more tables or fields, the options on the Properties panel change and only display properties that can be changed for all of the selected fields or tables. If you do not see this view, enable the Modeling View option on the Preview features screen on the Options dialog box.

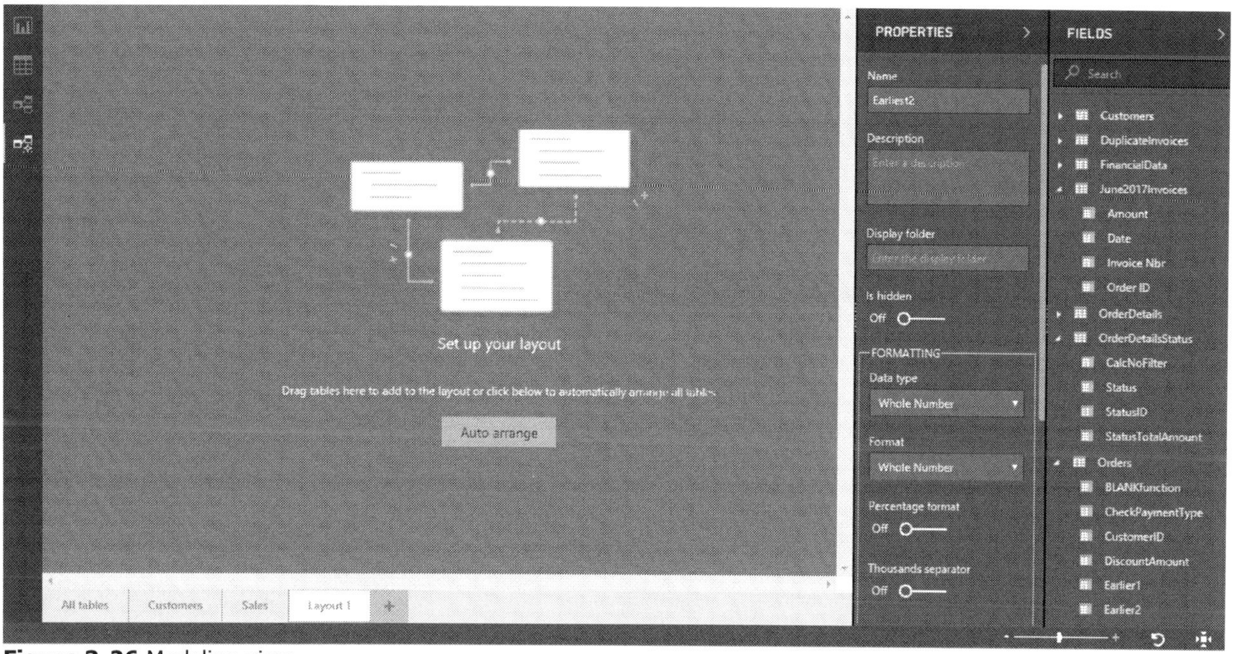

Figure 3-26 Modeling view

To create a layout, click the Yellow plus sign + button. There are two ways to add tables to a layout, as discussed below.

① Click the **AUTO ARRANGE BUTTON** shown above in Figure 3-26. This adds all of the tables in the data model to the layout.
② Drag a table from the Fields panel to the layout.

You can delete any tables that you do not want in the layout, by clicking on the ellipsis button in the upper right corner of the table or by right-clicking on the table and selecting **REMOVE FROM DIAGRAM**, as shown in Figure 3-27.

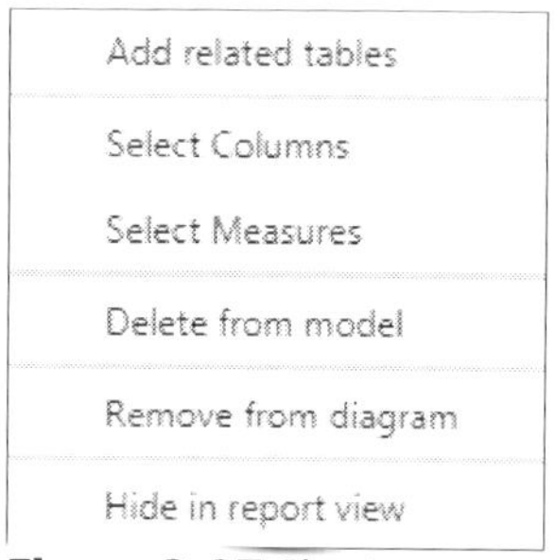

Figure 3-27 Shortcut menu for a table in the layout

Emulating The Merge Queries Transformation

In Chapter 8, Exercise 8.1, I discuss how creating relationships is easier then using the Merge Queries transformation. The steps below are the equivalent of using the Merge Queries transformation. If you want to follow along, after you complete Exercise 8.1, come back here and use that file.

1. Display the Modeling view ⇒ Click the plus sign button.

2. Drag the Order Details and Products tables to the canvas.

3. Click on the Product ID column in the Order Details table and drag it to the same column in the Products table.

A link will be created between the tables, as shown in Figure 3-28. The three steps above, accomplish the same result as the steps in the Merge The Product Name Column Into The Order Details Table and the Add The Lookup Column sections, in Exercise 8.1.

The tables in Figure 3-28, are the data model, if you will, for this portion those sections of the exercise.

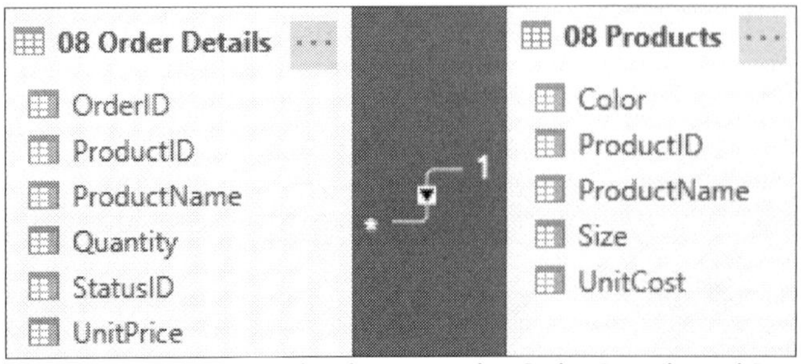

Figure 3-28 Relationship between the Order Details and Products tables

If you need to modify or view the relationships, double-click on the line between the tables to open the dialog box shown in Figure 3-29.

As you can see, it resembles the Merge dialog box. Notice that the column that the tables are linked on, is highlighted.

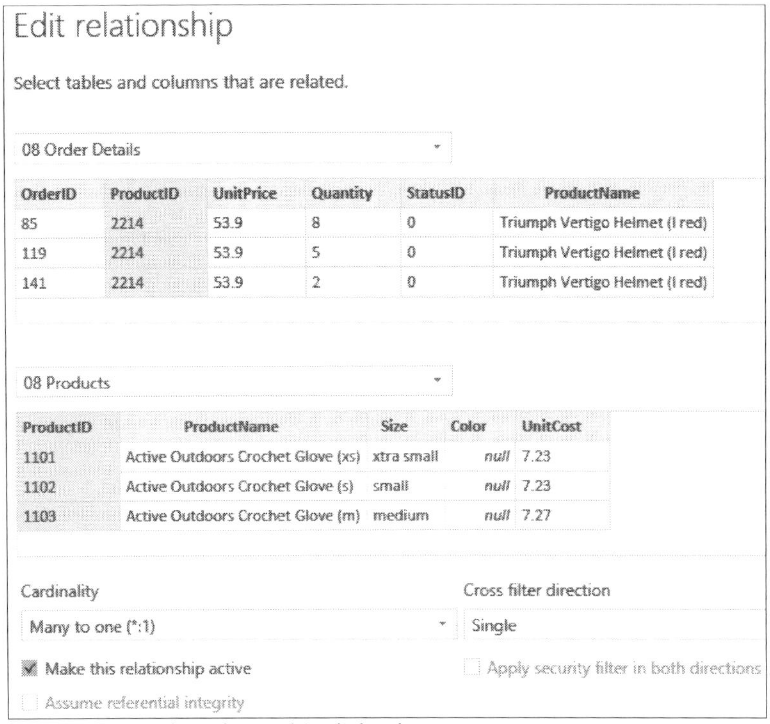

Figure 3-29 Edit Relationship dialog box

Summary

This chapter covered the options on the Data view, including the Modeling tab options. The options on the Data view, are preparation for creating DAX formulas and reports.

Using relationships to link data instead of merging data from one table to another is the most important topic to understand in this chapter, in my opinion. Not only are relationships easier and faster to create, they are also easier to maintain and are less prone to causing errors. Relationships do not add redundant data to the data model, like merging data does. On your own, if you have trouble creating relationships between tables, it is usually for one of the following reasons:

① At least one table is missing a primary or foreign key.
② Another table needs to be imported.

The Relationship view was also covered. You learned how to create, edit and auto detect relationships. The data model was covered to hopefully provide a better understanding of the data and what is required to be able to create the reports that you need.

The data model schema options were covered. The **STAR SCHEMA** was discussed as being the easiest schema to understand, in terms of the data model. As you saw, there are two types of tables, as discussed below.

① The **PRIMARY TABLE** is also known as the "fact", "parent" or "transaction table". Usually, primary tables have a lot of rows, when compared to child tables. Primary tables also tend to have fewer columns then child tables. Primary tables have the data that needs to be analyzed. This table type has a key field for each table that it needs to get additional data from, to create the report. These key fields are the ones used to link to the child tables.

② The **CHILD TABLE** is also known as the "dimension" or "lookup table". This table type is used to look up an item that is being reported on. For example, when displaying orders, it is helpful to display customer information for the order. The customer information has to be looked up, as it is not stored in the Orders table. Child tables have at least one row for each unique value in the parent table. Usually, only one field is used to make each row of data, unique.

One exception that comes to mind is an order or sales detail table. This table contains one row for each item on each order. This means that if one order contains five items, the detail table has five rows for the same order. Each of the five rows, in the detail table, has the same Order ID number. The detail table sometimes has another field that has a unique value for each row in the detail table. This field (with the unique value) is not the field that is linked on, in the scenario just described.

GETTING STARTED WITH THE QUERY EDITOR

In this chapter you will learn about the Query Editor. This includes learning about the interface and types of data shaping options that are available.

CHAPTER 4

Query Editor Overview

In Chapter 2, you learned how to connect to and import data from a variety of data sources. Once you have found the data that you need to create reports, you may find that some or all of the data needs to be cleaned or modified. This is what the Query Editor was designed to handle.

The official name of the Query Editor is **POWER QUERY EDITOR**. In the beginning, the name was Query Editor. At some point, it was renamed to Power Query Editor, but I suspect that I am not the only person that still calls it Query Editor.

The primary goal of this chapter is to show and explain some of the functionality that the Query Editor has. Without knowing what is available and where the options are, you will spend a lot of time looking for the right options for the transformations that you need to create. So while, this chapter may not have the wow factor, it is important. The rest of this book covers the transformation options in more detail.

As you will see, the Query Editor does not have any formatting options like bold or selecting a font. That type of formatting is done when the report is created in the Report view. You will also see that many of the options on the toolbars are also on more than one shortcut menu. The Query Editors role is to get the data ready to be used to create reports.

Power BI Desktop refers to this process as **TRANSFORMING DATA** or **TRANSFORMATIONS**. Examples of transformations are excluding and removing rows or columns of data, merging and creating new columns of data, as well as appending data in two or more tables. This transformation process can be done before the data is loaded into the data model (by selecting the Edit button on the Navigator dialog box). Transforming data can also be done after the data is in the data model. It is really up to you. The Query Editor is the tool that is used to accomplish the tasks listed below, plus a whole lot more, including the following.

- ☑ Filter records
- ☑ Merge and append data from different tables
- ☑ Rename, reorder or delete columns

If all of the data that you will use on your own, comes from databases and you will not have a need to clean the data or the data cleansing is the DBA's responsibility <lucky you, smile>, you may not have as much of a need to use the Query Editor. On the other hand, if you have data that comes from CSV, text, web pages or multiple spreadsheets, the Query Editor may quickly become your friend. <smile>

If any of the following tasks even vaguely resembles how you currently get data ready to create reports, the Query Editor will make your life easier.

① Copy and paste data between sheets or workbooks.
② Use data on hidden sheets in an Excel workbook and use VLOOKUP to combine data.
③ Spend hours cleaning data in Excel.
④ The data is in columns, but you need it in rows.
⑤ Create macros to try and automate the tasks listed above.

The reason that the Query Editor will make your life easier is because you can accomplish each of the tasks listed above, usually with a few mouse clicks and you do not have to write code to do it. As you will see, the Query Editor has a lot of options that you can use to modify data. I realize that the number of options can be overwhelming, especially if you are just getting stared. This is why I devoted this chapter, primarily to explaining a large number of options that are available in the Query Editor. I tried to structure the exercises to cover options that I think people will use the most. Most of the options are probably not as complicated to use, as you may be thinking.

What Is The Query Editor Designed To Do?

It is used to discover (find), search, connect to, filter, view, append and merge data sets, without being forced to load the data into the data model first. The Query Editor makes it easy to get data into the right format and clean it. The selected data can be loaded to the data model so that it can be analyzed using several tools including the other components in Power BI Desktop, Power BI and even Excel. In some respects, the Query Editor is like Print Preview, because you can see the data before making the decision to use it to create a visualization. [See What Is ETL?]

The section below discusses what the Query Editor brings to the table. It is designed to do all of the following:

☑ **DATA DISCOVERY** This is the process of finding the data sources that possibly have the data needed to create visualizations. The data can be a public or private data source.

☑ **DATA MODIFICATION** In Power BI Desktop, this is referred to as **TRANSFORMING** the data. This is the process of filtering, cleaning (changing the formatting from all lower case to all upper case, for example) and changing the structure of the table. When needed, data from one table can be added to another table, even if the tables come from different file types. For example, you have a list of all of the basketball games for the season on a spreadsheet and the stats for each game are on different web pages. You could import the data in the table on each web page into a query in Power BI Desktop, then add the stats for each game to your table of games.

☑ **LOADING DATA** This feature loads the data into the data model. This process copies the data from where it is, to the data model.

Another reason to take a look at the Query Editor is if you currently use or know that you are just around the corner from having to use or learn to use (but don't want to), Excel formulas or functions, like **VLOOKUP** or **VISUAL BASIC FOR APPLICATIONS (VBA)**, to transform your data. The Query Editor takes nothing away from these tools, because in some instances, they are more powerful. Being powerful though, does come with a higher and longer learning curve. And if you already know SQL, you can use SQL queries in the Query Editor.

If you have had or are currently having difficulty getting data from a data source or are having to write SQL formulas to get data, also give the Query Editor a try, because it does make "getting" the data easy. For the most part, writing SQL, DAX (in the Data view) or M code is optional because they extend what the Query Editor offers. Hopefully, you will be pleasantly surprised with what can be achieved in the Query Editor alone.

What probably is not obvious is that the Query Editor works like a macro. Behind the scenes (of the Query Editor interface), options that you select to get data, as well as, the steps that are created in the Query Editor to transform the data, are recorded and saved in what the Query Editor calls a query. This "query" will remind you of an Excel table. This query is created in the M language. Like a macro that you can create in Excel, the steps created and saved in the query (in the Query Editor), can be used over and over. The steps can also be reordered or changed easily.

What Is ETL?

The process of selecting data, loading data, rearranging or deleting columns, joining columns from different tables and creating calculated fields are all part of getting the data ready to be analyzed. The IT world refers to this process as **EXTRACT TRANSFORM LOAD** (ETL for short). Yes, the Query Editor is an ETL tool. Many Excel users have been completing these tasks manually for years, without knowing what its called.

It is very possible that you will need to repeat many of the ETL steps several times to get the data the way that you need it. It took me hours and hours to create some of the practice files and exercises for this book. I remember spending six hours creating and loading data into a database, then realized that I had some fields in the wrong table. ETL tools provide the functionality discussed below.

Extract

This is the process of selecting a data source (or as many data sources as needed) and extracting a subset of the data in each data source. Power BI Desktop supports many data sources and new connectors are currently created on a regular basis, as you learned in Chapter 2.

Transform

Transformation shapes and cleans the extracted data. This is the process of changing the data by using one, some or all of the following data enhancement techniques:

① **DATA INTEGRATION** Appending, joining and grouping data are examples of integration.

② **DATA CLEANSING** Deleting rows or columns of data that are not needed. Other examples of data cleansing include formatting, which includes changing the data type, or filtering data.

③ **DATA ENRICHMENT** Usually refers to adding new data. Adding a new column by combining data from other columns or creating a calculated field, are examples of data enrichment. If the data will be loaded to the data model, many of the data enrichment tasks, are best accomplished using the Data view, in my opinion.

Load

Load takes the dataset from the transform process (the changes) and copies the data, including the changes to the data model.

Understanding The "Query" In Power BI Desktop

This may be the most important concept or component of the Query Editor to understand. Queries, like the data model, are stored in the report .pbix file. Unlike the data model, which is one per file, in theory, there can be an unlimited number of queries in the report file. Just like tables can be joined, so can queries. A query in Power BI Desktop, is the equivalent of a table in a database, which is why in this environment, the terms, table and query are used interchangeably.

What Is A Query?

In Power BI Desktop, in addition to storing the data, a query contains a list of instructions (called **STEPS**), in a specific order, that get (imports the data) and transforms data. Usually, this data will be used to create a report. Think of a query in Power BI Desktop, like a macro (because it has the same functionality), where the instructions (steps) are processed in the order that you specify. Queries have at least one step, named **SOURCE**. It is the step that imports the data into Power BI Desktop. Usually, there is more than one step in a query.

Each step generates code using the **M LANGUAGE**, which is a language that is used to create and enhance the transformations. It is case sensitive. In addition to using this language in Power Query in Power BI Desktop, it can also be used in Power Query in Excel. Behind the scenes, the Query Editor generates M code for the steps that you add to the query. Learning the M language, in detail, is beyond the scope of this book.

The data source always creates the first step of a query. The options that you select and save in the Query Editor are added to the query. The query contains instructions for how the data needs to be manipulated. A Power BI Desktop report file can have more than one query, because each table or file that is imported, has its own query, as well as, tables that you create using the **ENTER DATA BUTTON**.

The Query Editor

As covered in Chapter 1, the Query Editor has a lot of sections. The window shown in Figure 4-1 is primarily used to transform the data, but data can also be imported from the Query Editor window. I guess you could say that this is where the magic happens in Power BI Desktop. <smile> In addition to the numbered sections, there are five tabs (File, Home, Transform, Add Column and View), that have options to complete the transformation tasks. The Ribbon section, covered later in this chapter, provides an overview of the tabs. The options on the tabs are explained in different chapters. The numbered sections in Figure 4-1, are explained below.

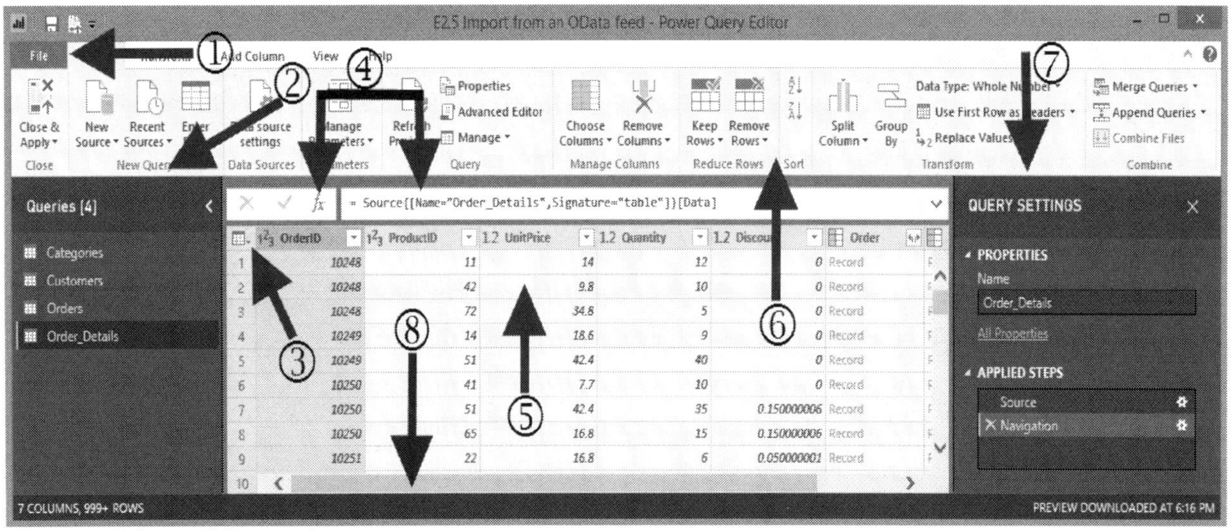

Figure 4-1 Query Editor workspace

① **FILE TAB** [See File Tab Options]

② The **QUERIES PANEL** is similar to the Navigator dialog box, because it displays the queries (tables) that are in the report file. The difference is that in the Query Editor, the panel is collapsible, by clicking the arrow to the right of the number of queries. This panel is used to switch between queries without having to close and reopen the Query Editor. You can create new queries that are based on an existing query by duplicating or creating a reference to an existing query. The order that the queries are displayed in, can also be changed. The shortcut menus for this panel are covered later in this chapter.

③ The **TABLE BUTTON** displays the shortcut menu shown later in Figure 4-5. [See Table (Button) Shortcut Menu]

④ The **FORMULA BAR** is used to create and edit the formula that each transformation (**M LANGUAGE FORMULA**) creates for each step in the query. The **FX BUTTON** adds a custom step, that is used to create an M formula. View tab ⇒ Checking the Formula bar option, enables the formula bar. The formula created by the transformation usually does not need to be modified, but there are instances where it will.

⑤ The **RESULTS SECTION** (which is also called the **GRID**, **PREVIEW SECTION** or **DATA WINDOW**) displays the data up to and including the selected step in the Query Settings panel. Selecting different steps on the Query Setting panel, displays the data after the transformation for that step has processed the data. Keep in mind that all of the rows in the data source may not be displayed. As you will see, this section has a lot of shortcut menus.

⑥ The **RIBBON** (which many, including yours truly, still call the **TOOLBAR**) contains the options to transform the data. Making changes to the data is what creates the steps and formulas in the query.

⑦ **QUERY SETTINGS PANEL** [See Query Settings Panel]

⑧ The **STATUS BAR** displays the number of columns and rows in the selected query. The far right side of the status bar displays the date that the data was imported into Power BI Desktop, or was last refreshed. If you enabled the option to be notified when a new version of Power BI Desktop is available, you will see a message here, letting you know.

Opening The Query Editor

There are several ways to open the Query Editor, as listed below. These options start from the Power BI Desktop window.

① Home tab ⇒ Edit Queries button ⇒ Edit Queries

② Home tab ⇒ Click on the top half of the Edit Queries button

③ Navigator dialog box ⇒ Select a table ⇒ Click the Edit button

④ Navigator dialog box ⇒ Right-click on a table ⇒ Select Edit

⑤ Data view ⇒ Right-click on a column heading ⇒ Edit Query

⑥ Data view ⇒ Right-click on a table in the Fields panel ⇒ Edit Query

⑦ Report view ⇒ Right-click on a table in the Fields panel ⇒ Edit Query

Saving Changes In The Query Editor
There are two ways that **PENDING CHANGES** can be saved: Now or Later. If you want to apply the pending changes and save the report file, at the same time, click the Save button on the Query Editors Quick Access toolbar. If there are pending changes when the Save button is clicked, you will see the dialog box shown in Figure 4-2. Click the **APPLY BUTTON**, to apply the pending changes and save the file now. Click the **APPLY LATER BUTTON** to keep the pending changes, but not save them now.

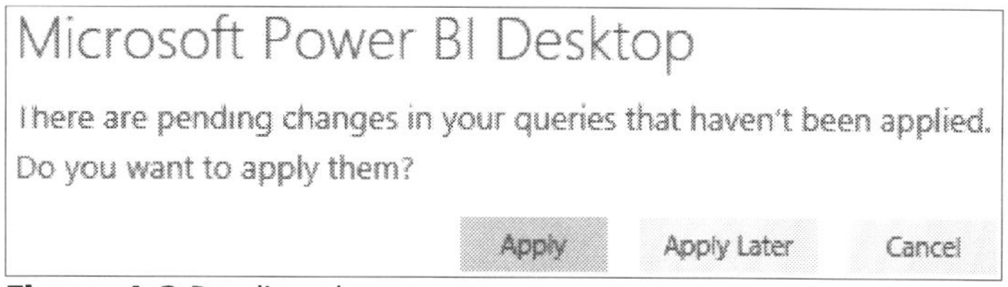

Figure 4-2 Pending changes message

Queries Panel Icons

The queries have different icons, as shown in Figure 4-3.

Imported data has an icon that looks like a spreadsheet.

Parameters and queries created using the **BLANK QUERY OPTION**, have the icon shown next to Query 3 in the figure.

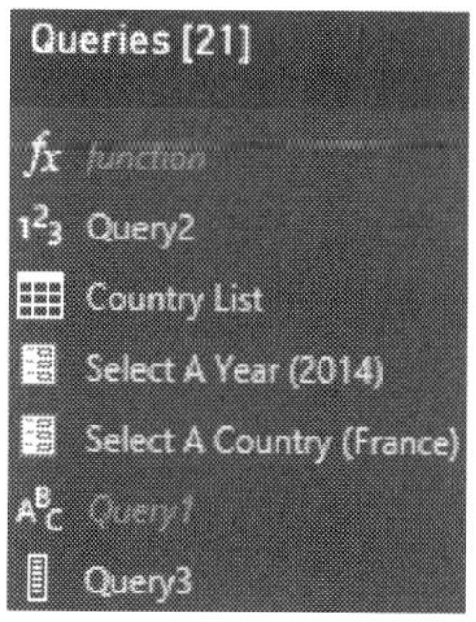

Figure 4-3 Queries panel

> **Query Editor Row Limit**
> The Query Editor will only display a maximum of 999 rows per table. When this is the case, "999+ Rows" will be displayed in the lower left corner of the status bar, as shown earlier in Figure 4-1. Keep this in mind if you need to copy data to another source, like a spreadsheet, because you will only be copying 999 rows maximum. If you need to copy 1,000 rows or more, use the Data view to copy the data.

> **Undoing A Transformation**
> While the Query Editor has a lot of options, it does not have an "undo" option. To undo a transformation, delete the corresponding step in the Query Settings panel.

The Query Editor Ribbon

As mentioned earlier, the ribbon has five tabs. They are explained below. Except for the File tab, the other tabs are covered in more detail in later chapters.

HOME TAB This tab has the most used transformations and options to connect to and load data, create and manage parameters. The option to refresh data is also on this tab.

TRANSFORM TAB The majority of transformations on this tab, replace the data in the selected column. The options that are enabled, depends on the data type of the column that is selected.

ADD COLUMN TAB The transformations on this tab are used to create new columns of data in the query. The new columns are stored in the data model. The new columns are **NOT** added to the data source. While most of the transformations on this tab have the same functionality as those with the same name on the Transform tab, the following options are more advanced and are covered in more detail through this book: **COLUMN FROM EXAMPLES**, **CUSTOM COLUMN**, **INVOKE CUSTOM FUNCTION** and **CONDITIONAL COLUMN**.

VIEW TAB The options on this tab are primarily used to customize the Query Editor.

File Tab Options

Figure 4-4 shows the options on the File tab. The options unique to the Query Editor, are explained below.

CLOSE & APPLY [See Close & Apply Options, Figure 4-41]

CLOSE Closes the Query Editor without applying the pending changes to the query.

OPTIONS AND SETTINGS Displays the options shown on the right side of the figure. It is helpful having these options in the Query Editor, so that you do not have to switch between the Power BI Desktop window and the Query Editor, to change options on these dialog boxes. An example is changing the location of a data source.

OPTIONS Opens the Options dialog box.
[See Chapter 1, Figure 1-17]

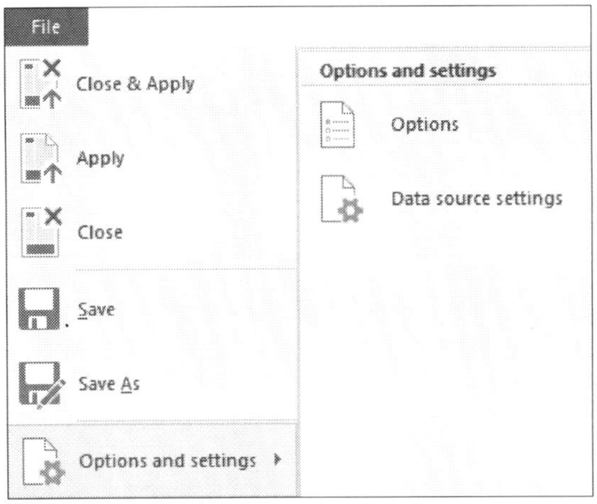

Figure 4-4 File tab

DATA SOURCE SETTINGS Opens the Data Source Settings dialog box. [See Chapter 1, Figure 1-35]

Table (Button) Shortcut Menu

As shown earlier in Figure 4-1, this button is above the Row Number column, in the Results section. The options on the menu shown in Figure 4-5 are used to customize the data and are applied to the entire table. Many of the options on this shortcut menu are also on the Home tab.

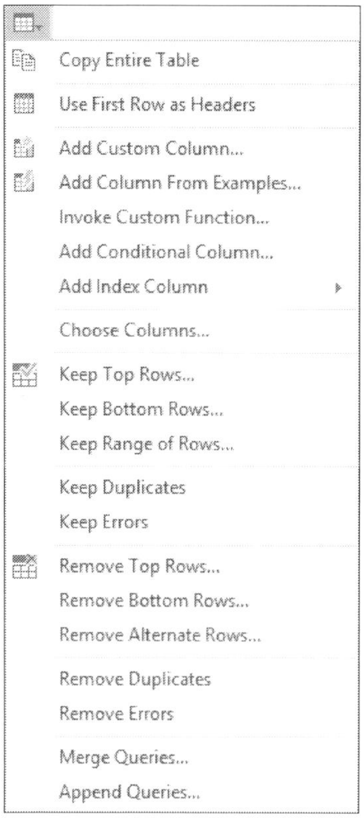

Figure 4-5 Table (button) shortcut menu

Option	Description
Copy Entire Table	Is used to copy the data in the query to a file, like a worksheet in Excel or a text file.
Use First Row As Headers	[See Use First Row As Headers Transformation]
Add Custom Column	[See Chapter 5, Custom Column Options]
Add Column From Examples	Is used to create a column of data, based on the example data that you type in.
Invoke Custom Function	[See Invoke Custom Function]
Add Conditional Column	[See Chapter 7, Conditional Columns]
Add Index Column	[See Chapter 5, Index Column Options]
Choose Columns	(1)
Keep Top Rows	(2)
Keep Bottom Rows	(2)
Keep Range of Rows	(2)
Keep Duplicates	(2)
Keep Errors	(2)
Remove Top Rows	(2)
Remove Bottom Rows	(2)
Remove Alternate Rows	(2)
Remove Duplicates	(2)
Remove Errors	Removes rows that have an error in any cell in the row. The Remove Errors option on the Remove Rows button, works differently. [See Figure 4-49]
Merge Queries	(1)
Append Queries	(1)

Table 4-1 Table (button) shortcut menu options explained

(1) [See Merge Queries And Append Queries Buttons]
(2) [See Keep Rows And Remove Rows Transformation Options]

Invoke Custom Function

Selecting this option displays the dialog box shown in Figure 4-6. The options are used to select a custom function that has already been created in the file.

The input arguments can be static values or a reference to other columns in the current query.

Once the options are selected on this dialog box, the custom function is invoked (run) on the current query.

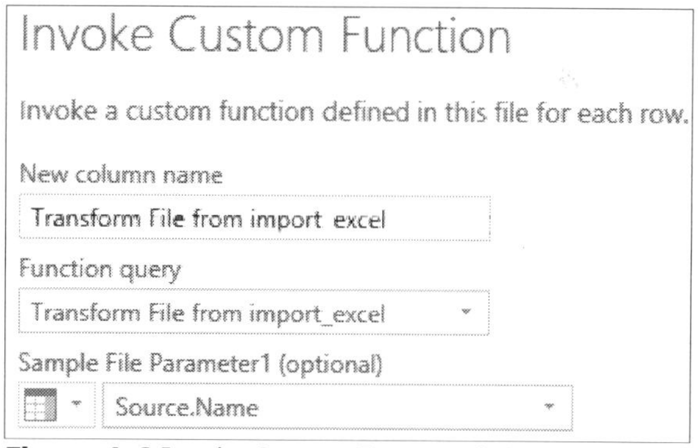

Figure 4-6 Invoke Custom Function dialog box

Query Shortcut Menu

Right-clicking on a query in the Queries panel displays the shortcut menu shown in Figure 4-7. The options are explained in Table 4-2.

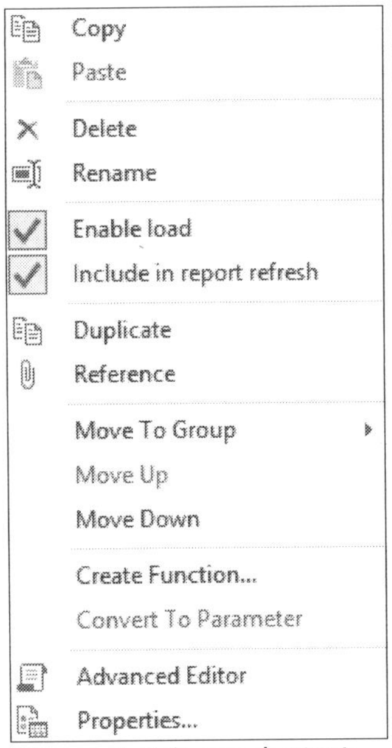

Figure 4-7 Query shortcut menu

Option	Description
Copy	Copies the code for the query, so that it can be used for another query. Once selected, the Paste option is enabled.
Paste	Adds a copy of the query to the current file or another file.
Delete	Deletes the selected query.
Rename	Is used the change the name of the query. Double-clicking on the query name or clicking on the query name and pressing F2, can also be used to rename a query.
Enable load	Loads the data in the query into the data model. (3)
Include in report refresh	If checked, the data in the query will be refreshed when the Refresh All option is selected. [See Figure 4-45] (3)
Duplicate	(4)
Reference	(4)
Move To Group	[See Move To Group Option]
Move Up	Moves the selected query up one row in the group. (5)
Move Down	Moves the selected query down one row in the group. (5)
Create Function	Is used to create a function from the selected query, whether or not it references a parameter. A link is created between the original query and the new generated function. This allows you to modify the original query and have the changes passed to the new function that was created, without having to modify the new functions formula.
Convert To Parameter	This option is only enabled when a query is selected that does not reference a parameter. When selected, the query will be converted to a parameter.
Convert To Query	This option is only displayed when a parameter query is selected. Selecting this option will change the parameter query to a regular query.
Advanced Editor	[See Chapter 6, Advanced Editor]
Properties	Is used to add a description or note to the query.

Table 4-2 Query shortcut menu options explained

(3) Clicking on this option also enables/disables the corresponding option on the Query Properties dialog box. [See Figure 4-25]
(4) [See Using A Query As A Data Source]
(5) This option cannot be used to move queries to another group.

Queries Panel (Blank Space) Shortcut Menu

Right-clicking on a blank space on the Queries panel displays the shortcut menu shown in Figure 4-8.

The options are explained in Table 4-3.

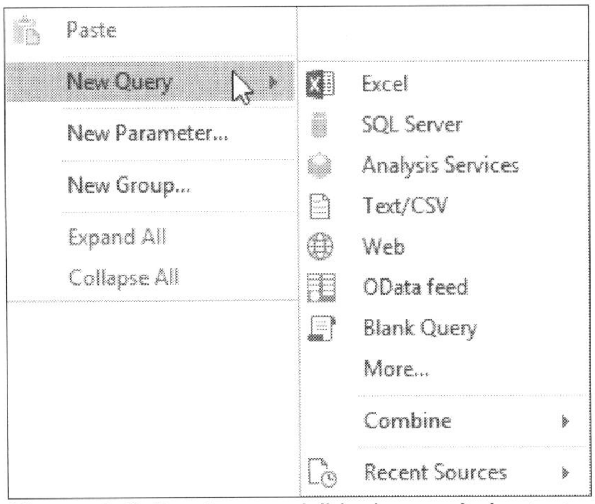

Figure 4-8 Queries panel (blank space) shortcut menu

Option	Description
Paste	Places a copy of the query (that is in the clipboard) into the Queries panel.
New Query	Is used to import data by creating a new query. The import options are the same as the Get Data options covered in Chapter 2.
New Parameter	[See Chapter 9, Parameters]
New Group	[See Table 4-4]
Expand All	[See Table 4-4]
Collapse All	[See Table 4-4]

Table 4-3 Queries panel (blank space) shortcut menu options explained

Query Naming Convention
Function names like DATE and UPPERCASE, are reserved words and should not be used as a query name.

Renaming A Column
While you have the option to rename a column to whatever you want, within reason, there should be some consideration for the people that will use the reports and dashboards that you create. They need to understand the column name.

On the Reports view, you do have the option of displaying a different name for the columns, without having to rename the column in the table.

Another consideration is if you are going to use the **Q&A NATURAL LANGUAGE OPTION**, with the reports that you create in Power BI Desktop. This option works best when the column names can be recognized as synonyms.

Using A Query As A Data Source

There are two ways to use an existing query as the data source for another query, as explained below. Both options can be accessed from the shortcut menu (when a query is selected) on the Queries panel and the **MANAGE BUTTON** on the Home tab.

DUPLICATE Creates a copy of the selected query, then displays the data in the Query Editor. The copy can be used to make changes to the data and leave the existing query unchanged. There is no link if you will, between the original query and the duplicated query. Changes made in the original query do not affect the duplicated query.

REFERENCE This option also creates a copy of the query. The difference is that this option uses the output (the structure of the data, as it is, on the last applied step) of the original query. This option is often selected when a query that has a lot of data, needs to be divided into smaller queries. Doing this can make the data easier to maintain. The other difference between this option and the Duplicate option is that **THIS QUERY IS LINKED TO THE ORIGINAL QUERY**. This link is called a **QUERY DEPENDENCY**. This means that changes made to the original query can cause queries that reference it, to no longer work as intended. Dependencies are covered in more detail in Chapter 6.

One use for creating a query using the Reference option is when you need to create two or more reports that are based on the same query. For example, in the original query, you could create the majority of transformations, except the filter transformations. Then create a reference query for a report that needs the data filters on the Country column for report A, then create another reference query from the original query and create filters for the Order Amount in a specific range, and a filter for specific order years, for report B.

The transformations that both reference queries need, would be made in the original query. These changes are then automatically filtered down to each reference query.

Keep in mind when using the Reference option as the base table to create a new query, that it uses the last step in the original query. That means that any query that is based on the original query can change when steps are added or deleted in the original query.

Move To Group Option

This option is used to create groups (folders) for the queries and move the queries to a group, to organize them. It provides a way to display selected queries together. Figure 4-9 shows eight queries, that are in one of three groups.

This technique is useful if several queries have something in common, like a group for each department that needs reports or a group of queries that have the same data source. For example, the queries in Group A, could use tables in database A and the queries in Group B use data from the web.

The **OTHER QUERIES** group, shown in the figure, is automatically created, after you create the first group in the file. By default, this group contains all of the queries, until you move them to another group.

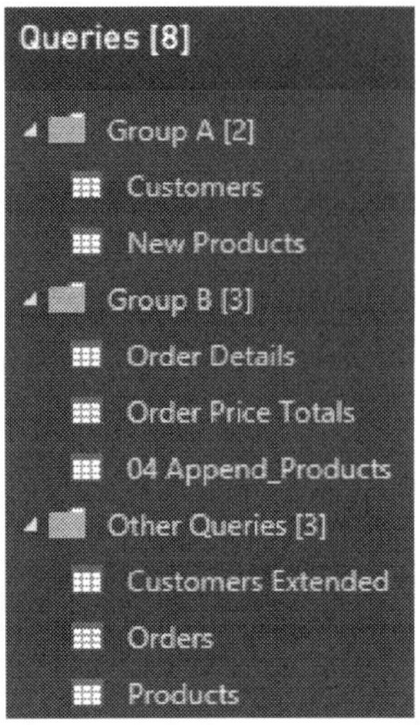

Figure 4-9 Groups created for the queries

> **Queries Panel Tip**
> In addition to creating groups to place queries in, you can also rearrange the order that the queries are displayed in, on the Queries panel shown above in Figure 4-9, by using drop and drag to move the query to where you want it.

Group Name Shortcut Menu

Groups have their own shortcut menu, as shown in Figure 4-10. The options are explained in Table 4-4.

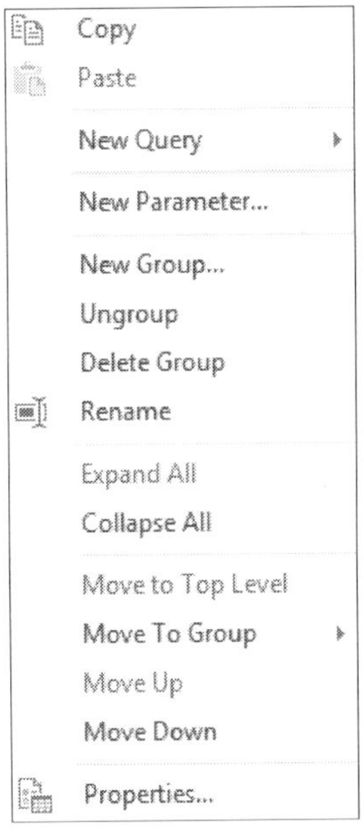

Figure 4-10 Group name shortcut menu

Option	Description
Copy	Places a copy of the group and all items in it, into the clipboard. (6)
Paste	Pastes the copied group in the clipboard and all queries in it, into another location on the Queries panel. (6)
New Query	[See Table 4-3] (6)
New Parameter	[See Chapter 9, Parameters] (6)
New Group	Displays the dialog box shown in Figure 4-11. The options are used to create a subgroup for the group that this option was selected from.
Ungroup	Deletes the selected group and moves the queries in the group to the Other Queries group, unless the group being deleted has a sub group. If there is a sub group, the sub group is promoted to a group and the queries that were in the original group are moved to the promoted group.
Delete Group	Deletes the selected group and queries in the group. (6)
Rename	Is used to rename the group. (6)
Expand All	Displays all of the queries in the Queries panel. (6)
Collapse All	Hides all of the queries in the Queries panel. (6)
Move to Top Level	This option is enabled on a sub group, on the Queries panel. Selecting this option makes the sub group a group. (7)
Move To Group	Moves the group to another group and becomes a sub group. The **NEW GROUP OPTION** creates a group, a level above the selected group.
Move Up	Moves the selected group up, above the previous group. (7)
Move Down	Moves the selected group down, below the next group. (7)
Properties	Displays the Group Properties options, which are the same as the New Group options, shown in Figure 4-11. You can change the name of the group, on this dialog box.

Table 4-4 Group name shortcut menu options explained

(6) This option is also on the "Other Queries" group shortcut menu.
(7) The queries in the group are also moved.

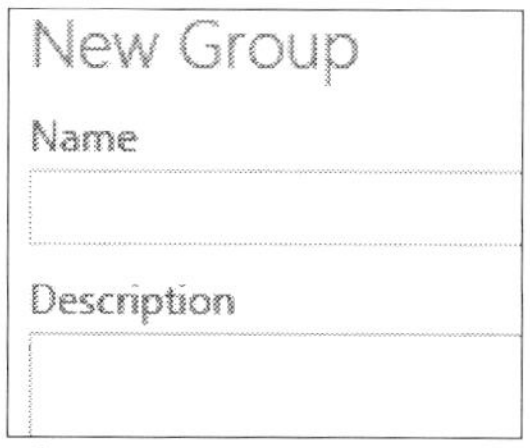

Figure 4-11 New Group dialog box

Column Shortcut Menu

The options shown in Figure 4-12 are used to transform (change) the data.

This shortcut menu is available when you right-click on one column header. Keep in mind that these options are applied to all of the data in the column, not just a specific cell.

Many of these options are also available on the Query Editor ribbon (toolbar).

If you need to transform a single cell of data, use the cell shortcut menu options covered later in this chapter.

If multiple columns are selected, you will only see options on the shortcut menu that can be applied to all of the selected columns, as shown in Figure 4-13.

The options that are available on either shortcut menu, depend on the data type of the selected columns.

The options on both shortcut menus are explained in Table 4-5.

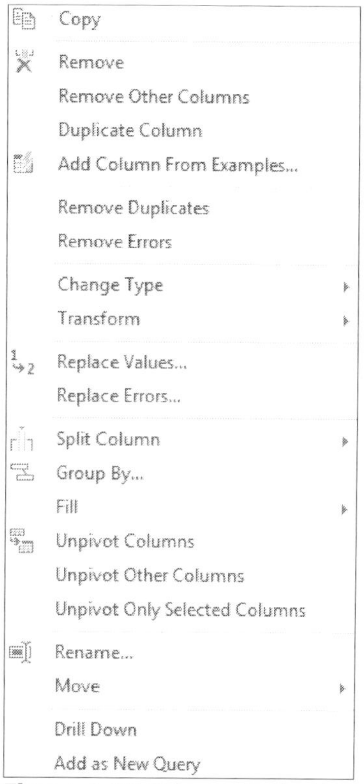

Figure 4-12 Column shortcut menu

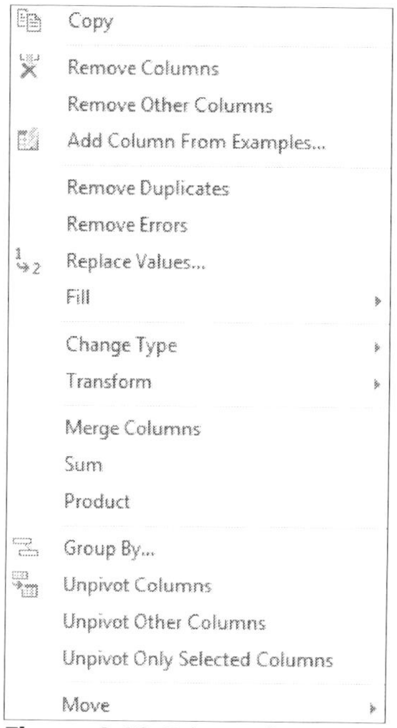

Figure 4-13 Column shortcut menu when multiple columns are selected

Option	Description
Copy	Is used to copy the data in the selected column to a file, like a worksheet in Excel.
Remove	[See Remove Columns Options] (8)
Remove Columns	[See Remove Columns Options] (8)
Remove Other Columns	[See Remove Columns Options] (8)
Duplicate Column	Creates a copy of the column of data and places the new column at the end of the table.
Add Column From Examples	[See Table 4-1]
Remove Duplicates	[See Keep Rows And Remove Rows Transformation Options] (8)
Remove Errors	Deletes rows that have a data error in the column, that this option is applied to. (8)
Change Type	[See Change Type Option] (8)
Transform	[See Transform Option] (8)
Replace Values	[See Replace Values] (8)
Replace Errors	Opens the Replace Errors dialog box. It is used to enter the value that will replace the errors (the values that are not correct) in the selected column(s).
Split Column	This option is only available for a text data field. If you need to split a column that has a different data type, use the Split Column option on the Home tab. [See Split Column Options]

Table 4-5 Column shortcut menu options explained

Option	Description
Group By	[See Group By Transformation Options] (8)
Fill	[See Chapter 6, Using The Fill Option] (8)
Unpivot Columns	[See Chapter 10, Unpivoting Data] (8)
Unpivot Other Columns	[See Chapter 10, Unpivoting Data] (8)
Unpivot Only Selected Columns	[See Chapter 10, Unpivoting Data] (8)
Rename	Is used to change the column heading name, in the table. Keep in mind that by default, the column name is what is displayed on the visuals that you create, as well as formulas that use the column. You can display a different name for the column on a visual.
Move	[See Chapter 6, Move Button Options] (8)
Drill Down	Adds a step to the query that changes the view to only display the data in the selected column. This option is mostly used with columns that have metadata that has embedded information.
Add as New Query	[See Add As New Query Option]
Merge Columns	[See Chapter 6, Table 6-1] (8)
Sum	Adds the values in the selected columns and places the result in a new column named **ADDITION**. This option works the same as the **ADD FUNCTION**. (9)
Product	Multiples the values in the selected columns and places the result in a new column named **MULTIPLICATION**. This option works the same as the **MULTIPLY FUNCTION** with two columns selected. (9)

Table 4-5 Column shortcut menu options explained (Continued)

(8) This option can be applied to multiple columns at the same time.
(9) This option is only available when two or more columns with a numeric data type are selected. At the time this book went to print, the option on the shortcut menu did not create a calculation. It created a column with binary data. Instead, use the corresponding option on the Add Column tab ⇒ Standard button. Use the Add option to replace Sum. Use the Multiply option to replace Product.

Change Type Option

This option works the same as the Data Type option on the Home tab. It is used to change the data type of the selected column.

The difference is that the Change Type option, also has the **USING LOCALE OPTION**, shown at the bottom of Figure 4-14. This option opens the dialog box shown in Figure 4-15.

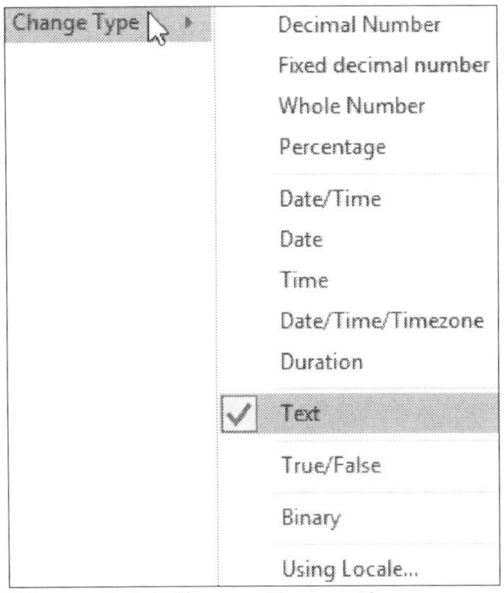

Figure 4-14 Change Type options

Change Type With Locale Options

The options shown in Figure 4-15 are used to override the Current File Locale options on the Options dialog box, for the selected column.

This is helpful when the other Change Type options shown above in Figure 4-14, do not display the data the way that you need it displayed.

When you select a data type other then the one currently applied to the column, the **SAMPLE INPUT VALUES** section will be displayed, as shown at the bottom of the figure. This allows you to see formats that the data in the column will be changed to.

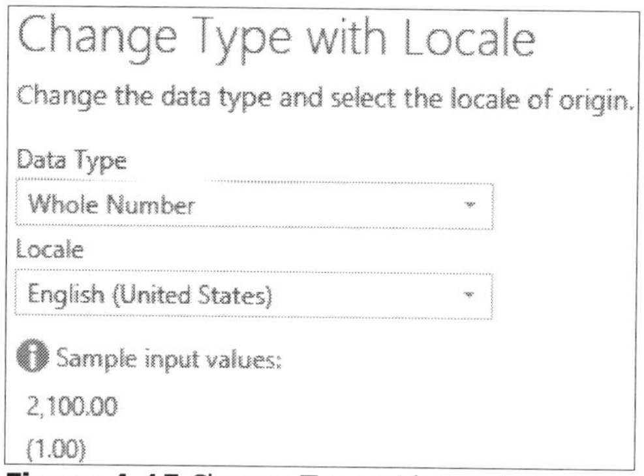

Figure 4-15 Change Type with Locale options

The locale options can be applied to one column or all columns in the query at the same time, by selecting the columns that you want to apply the data type to, before opening this dialog box.

The **DATA TYPE** drop-down list contains all of the data types that Power BI Desktop supports.

The **LOCALE** drop-down list contains a list of world-wide regional formatting settings.

You may have the need to change how dates are displayed. As shown earlier in Figure 4-14, there are several date formats that you can select from. If the imported date field is not in the format that you need, select the format that you need from this list.

The Locale option is also important if you use data from countries other then your own, because date and numeric data is often formatted differently. For example, if the imported date field has time zone information and you do not need to display it, select the Date or Date/Time data type. Before applying the Change Type with Locale options, I check to see if the column already has a Changed Type step (in the Query Settings panel). If it does, I delete it.

One reason that importing dates can be problematic is because not all software that we use, uses the same standard. For example, dates in the US are formatted as MM/DD/YYYY and in Europe, dates are formatted as DD/MM/YYYY. The Locale option is only applied when importing and transforming data in Power BI Desktop.

Transform Option

This option provides shortcuts to some of the more popular transform formatting options. The options are used to change the appearance of the value.

Figure 4-16 shows the text data type transform options. Applying the Uppercase option to the Ship Name field in the Orders table, formats and displays the values, as shown in Figure 4-17.

Figure 4-18 shows the date/time data type transform options. Figure 4-19 shows the **DAY OF WEEK FUNCTION** applied to the Order Date field. Zero equals Sunday.

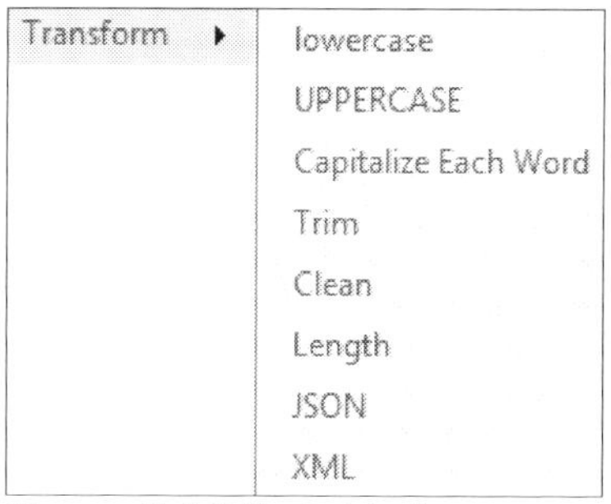

Figure 4-16 Text data type transform options

Figure 4-17 Uppercase function applied

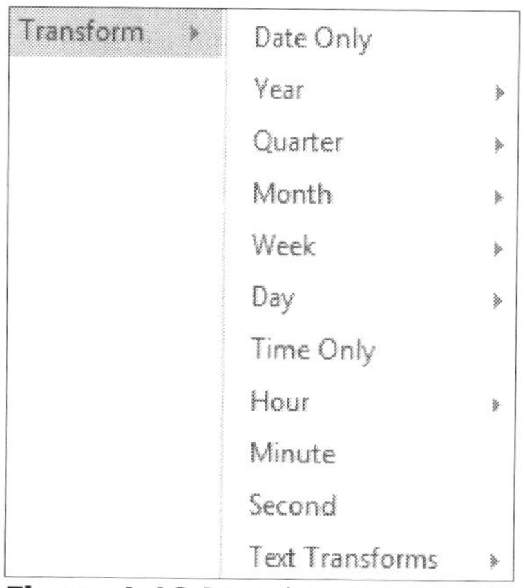

Figure 4-18 Date data type transform options

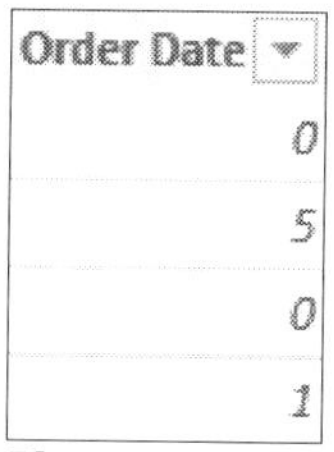

Figure 4-19 Day of week transform function applied

Add As New Query Option

This option is used to create a new query. The query is created from the selected column or a single cell.

The contents of the new query contains the values in the column or cell. Figure 4-20 shows a new query created from the Product Name column.

The name of the new query is the column name used to create the query. All of the steps, up to and including the one selected when the Add As New Query option is applied, is also copied to the new query. There is no dependency on the original query.

If the new query is created from a column, you will see the tab shown in Figure 4-20, at the top of the Query Editor.

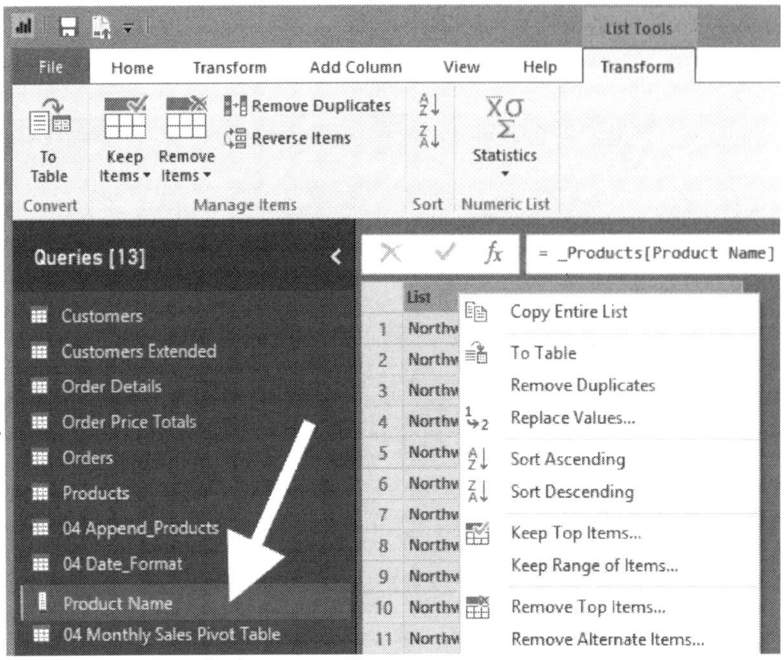

Figure 4-20 New (list) query options

Right-clicking on the **LIST** column heading displays the shortcut menu, shown in the lower right corner of Figure 4-20.

The options on the **LIST TOOLS TRANSFORM TAB** are used to create a list from the values in an existing column and convert the column to a table.

> A **LIST QUERY** is most often created to use as values for a parameter. [See Chapter 9, Exercise 9.6, Create The List Query section]

List Tools Transform Tab Options

The List Tools Transform tab options are explained in Table 4-6.

Option	Description
To Table	[See To Table Options]
Keep Items	(10)
Remove Items	(10)
Remove Duplicates	(10)
Reverse Items	[See Chapter 6, Table 6-1 Reverse Rows]
Sort	[See Table 4-11]
Statistics	[See Chapter 6, Table 6-1]

Table 4-6 List Tools Transform tab options explained

(10) [See Keep Rows And Remove Rows Transformation Options]

To Table Options

The **TO TABLE** button, shown earlier at the top of Figure 4-20, is used to convert the list (the column) of data, to a table (query), by using the options shown in Figure 4-21.

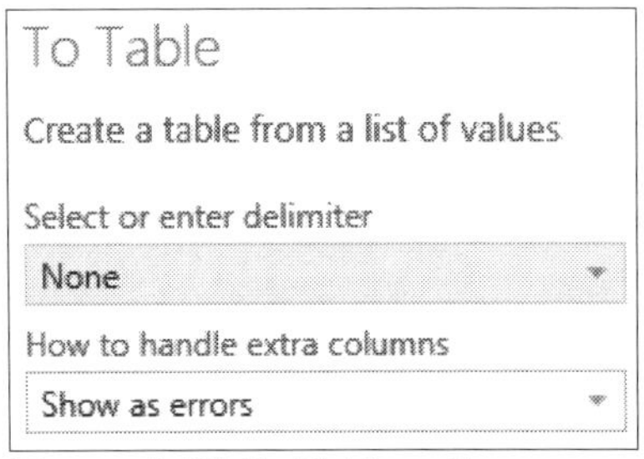

Figure 4-21 To Table options

List Column Shortcut Menu Options

The options on the shortcut menu shown earlier in Figure 4-20, are explained below in Table 4-7.

Option	Description
Copy Entire List	Copies the data in the List column to the clipboard, so that it can be pasted someplace else, like in a spreadsheet.
To Table	[See To Table Options, above]
Remove Duplicates	(11)
Replace Values	[See Replace Values]
Sort Ascending	Sorts the values in the list in low to high order.
Sort Descending	Sorts the values in the list in high to low order.
Keep Top Items	(11)
Keep Range of Items	(11)
Remove Top Items	(11)
Remove Alternate Items	(11)

Table 4-7 List column shortcut menu options explained

(11) [See Keep Rows And Remove Rows Transformation Options]

Cell Shortcut Menu (From Using The Add As New Query Option)

Figure 4-22 shows the shortcut menu for a cell, created from using the Add As New Query option, like the query shown earlier in Figure 4-20.
The options are explained in Table 4-8.

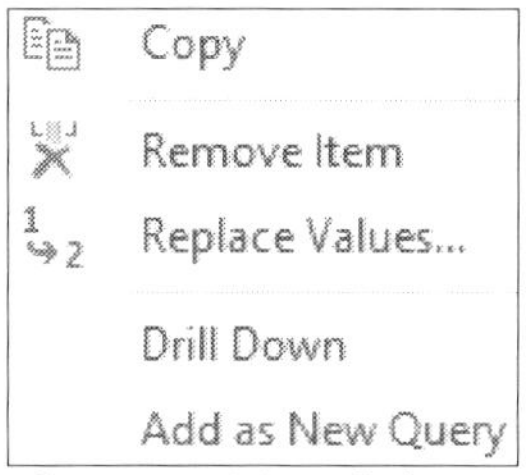

Figure 4-22 Cell shortcut menu (Add As New Query option)

Option	Description
Copy	Is used to copy the value in the cell, then paste the value into a field on the Replace Values dialog box or to a file, like a spreadsheet.
Remove Item	Deletes the row from the list.
Replace Values	[See Replace Values]
Drill Down	Adds a step to the query that changes the view to only display the data in the selected cell.
Add as New Query	Creates a new query from the selected cell.

Table 4-8 Cell shortcut menu options explained (from using the Add As New Query option)

Cell Shortcut Menu

Right-clicking on a cell in the grid displays the shortcut menu shown in Figure 4-23, for a text field. The name of the Filters option at the top of the menu, changes to match the type of data in the cell.

These options are only applied to the selected cell. They are explained in Table 4-9.

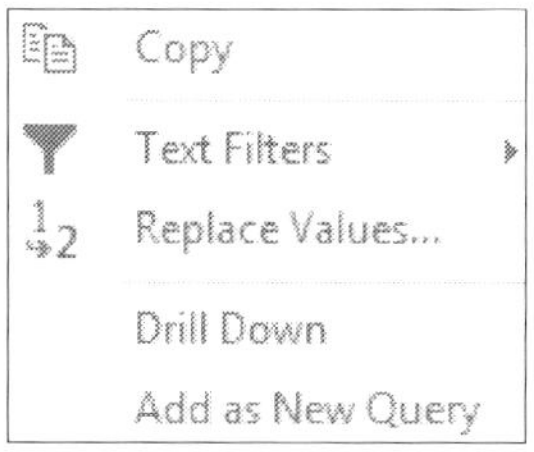

Figure 4-23 Cell shortcut menu

Option	Description
Copy	[See Table 4-8]
Filters	This option displays the filter options. The difference between the filter options on the column shortcut menu and the options on this shortcut menu, is that the options for the cell do not open the Filter Rows dialog box. Instead, the filter options for the cell are automatically created and applied to the data in the grid, based on the value in the cell that was right-clicked on, to open the cell shortcut menu. Once created, you can open the Filter Rows dialog box by clicking on the cog wheel button for the Filtered Rows step on the Query Settings panel. [See Chapter 5, Tables 5-1, 5-2 and 5-3]
Replace Values	[See Replace Values]
Drill Down	[See Table 4-8]
Add as New Query	[See Add As New Query Option]

Table 4-9 Cell shortcut menu options explained

Column Data Type Shortcut Menu

The icon to the left of the column heading indicates the **DATA TYPE** of the column, as illustrated in Figure 4-24.

Clicking the icon displays the shortcut menu shown in the figure. The options are used to change the data type or **LOCALE** for the column.

Notice that the icons next to the column headings are also on the shortcut menu. The options are explained in Chapter 6, Table 6-2.

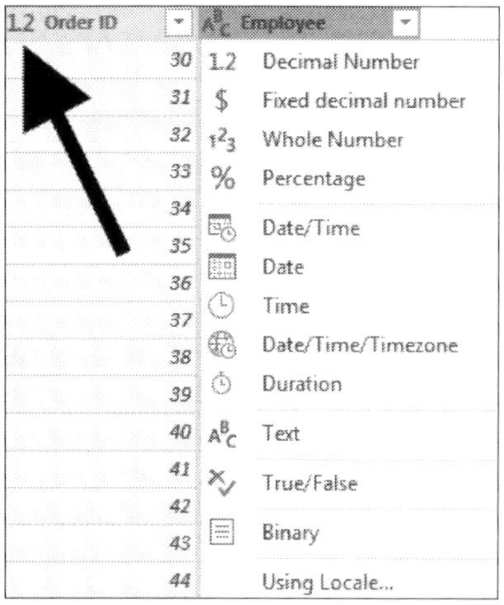

Figure 4-24 Column data type shortcut menu

Query Properties Dialog Box

The options shown in Figure 4-25 are explained below.

The **NAME** field is used to rename the query.

The **DESCRIPTION** field can be used to explain what the query does, especially the applied steps.

The **ENABLE LOAD TO REPORT OPTION** is used to select whether or not the data in the query is loaded to the data model.

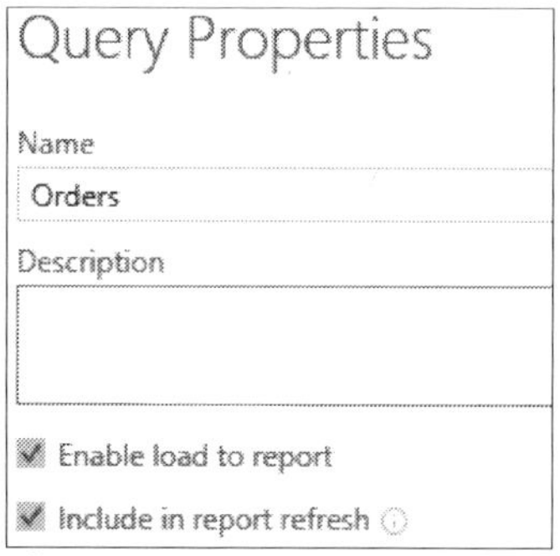

Figure 4-25 Query Properties dialog box

If a query is only used because some columns will be merged into another query, you may not want to keep loading that query into the data model. Not loading a query prevents it from being displayed in the Fields panel, in the Report view. This may be a good thing if the report file has a lot of tables.

Keep in mind that doing this will remove the table from the data model, but not from the Query Editor.

> When the **ENABLE LOAD TO REPORT OPTION** is not checked, the query will be displayed in italic text on the Queries panel. This makes it easier to know which queries are loaded and which ones are not. Query 1 shown earlier in Figure 4-3, is an example of a query that does not have this option enabled.

The **INCLUDE IN REPORT REFRESH OPTION** is used to select whether or not the data in the query should be refreshed when the Refresh button is clicked in the Power BI Desktop workspace. This option is only enabled if the Enable load to report option is checked. This means that only data in the data model can be refreshed.

If the enable options are checked here, they will also be checked on the Queries shortcut menu [See Figure 4-7].

Loading Data
If either of the following is true, the data is not initially loaded into the data model.
① The **EDIT BUTTON** on the Navigator dialog box is clicked.
② The Enable load to report option shown above in Figure 4-25, is not checked.

If the data has not been loaded to the data model, it is still able to be used and saved in the report file. Not loading the data, but having access to it, allows for more "discovery" because you can use all of the Query Editor features, as if the data was loaded into the data model.

Often, tables that will be used as lookup tables, to add data to a different table are not loaded, because only specific fields are needed. Tables that fall into this scenario can be deleted, once the data has been added to another table.

Queries that are not loaded into the data model cannot be used to create a visual (table, chart, etc). Queries that have not been loaded are not displayed in the Report, Data or Relationships view.

Query Settings Panel

The panel shown in Figure 4-26 displays information about the selected query, including the name and steps.

Each table displayed in the Queries panel has its own set of query settings. They are used to modify the selected query, including the order that the transformations for the query are completed in.

Clicking on the X in front of the step name, will delete the step.

NAME This is the name of the query. The default name is the table name, but it can be changed. Usually, when the name is changed, it is changed to something descriptive. I find it easier to change the query name here, then renaming the query on the Queries panel or on the Query Properties dialog box.

ALL PROPERTIES Clicking on this link displays the dialog box shown above in Figure 4-25.

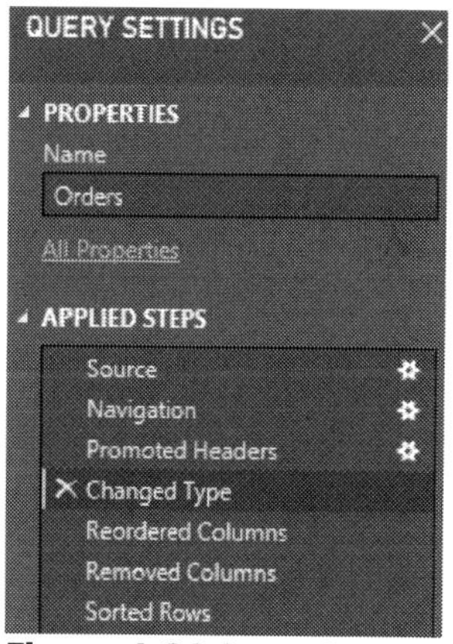

Figure 4-26 Query Settings panel

Applied Steps

This section is on the Query Settings panel. It contains an entry (a step) for each action (modification) that is made to the query.

The default name of a step is the function name.

What Is A Step?

A step is an action that helps transform the data. During the import process, other steps in addition to the Source and Navigation steps can be created. More steps are created when you clean the data or add columns of data to a query.

Each option on the toolbar and shortcut menus, creates a step that is also displayed in the **APPLIED STEPS** section of the Query Settings panel. A step is created for each action that you take. This includes deleting a column and rearranging the order of columns. Keep in mind that the data will change in each step, based on the instructions for the step. Each step will display the data slightly differently, which is what should happen.

What you will come to appreciate about the steps (the M code) is that they are run automatically, each time the data is refreshed. This means that you do not have to reapply the steps manually.

For the most part, each step is one instruction, like load the data or format a column of data. Change the format of a date field, would be another step. Sorting the data would be another step. By default, these steps are displayed in the Applied Steps section of the Query Settings panel, shown above in Figure 4-26, in the order that they are created in. The order of the steps can be changed. Make sure that the last step displays the data that will be used to create visualizations. The data displayed in the last step is also what will be loaded into the data model.

By default, new steps are added to the end of the Applied Steps section. If a step other then the last one is selected and a new step is created, it is placed after the selected step and not at the end of the steps.

There are two categories of instructions (steps), as explained below:

① **SHAPING THE DATA** Instructions in this category remove data (rows and columns) that is not needed, filter data and rename columns. Creating calculated columns and splitting data in existing columns, is also classified as shaping the data.

② **DATA TRANSFORMATION** Instructions in this category are used to change the appearance of the data, including rounding numbers, changing the case of text and extracting part of the data in a field. These tasks are also known as "modifying data".

Applied Steps Shortcut Menu

The options shown in Figure 4-27 are available when you right-click on a step.

The options are used to edit the selected step. They are explained in Table 4-10.

Changing The Order Of The Applied Steps
In addition to using the Move Up/Move Down options shown in Figure 4-27, to change the order of the query steps, you can change the order of the steps by using drop and drag.

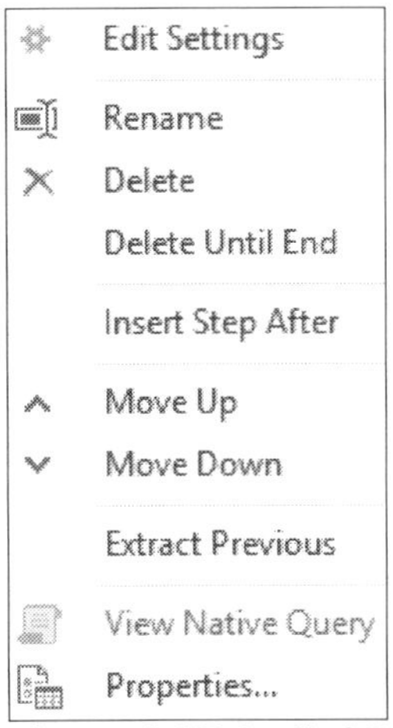

Figure 4-27 Applied Steps shortcut menu

Option	Description
Edit Settings	This option is only enabled for steps that have the icon. [See Applied Steps Options]
Rename	Is used to rename the step. Renaming a step is optional, but it is helpful because you can provide a better description of what the step does. I only rename a step that I think that I will have the need to modify at some point in the future. Doing this makes it easier for me to find the right step.
Delete	(12)
Delete Until End	(12) Also deletes all steps below it, in the Applied Steps list.
Insert Step After	Is used to add a step after the one that is selected.
Move Up	Moves the selected step up once. (13)
Move Down	Moves the selected step down once. (13)
Extract Previous	[See Extract Previous Option]
View Native Query	[See View Native Query Option]
Properties	Opens the **STEP PROPERTIES DIALOG BOX**, which has the same options as the New Group dialog box. [See Figure 4-11] This is helpful if you want to document what the step does or why you created the step. The information entered on the dialog box will be displayed as a tooltip when the mouse pointer is held over the step, as shown in Figure 4-28.

Table 4-10 Applied Steps shortcut menu options explained

(12) Deletes the selected step. The data is put back to the way it was before this step changed the data. Selecting this option displays the message shown in Figure 4-29. Click the Delete button if you want to remove the step.

(13) Using this option changes the order that the steps in the query will be processed in. Changing the order means that it is possible that the data can change in a way that you are not expecting it to change. This option can be used more than once, to move the same step.

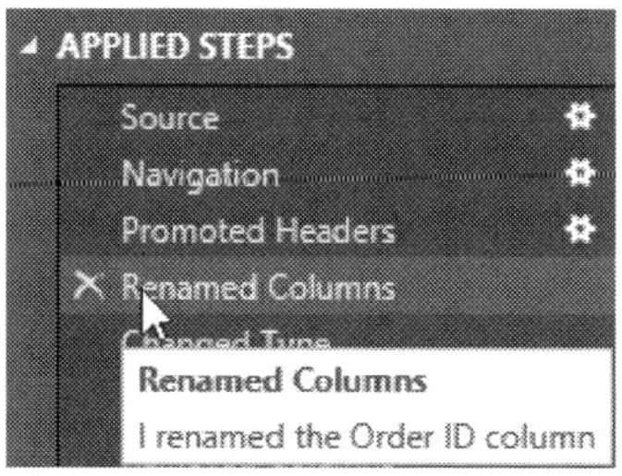

Figure 4-28 Step properties description displayed as a tooltip

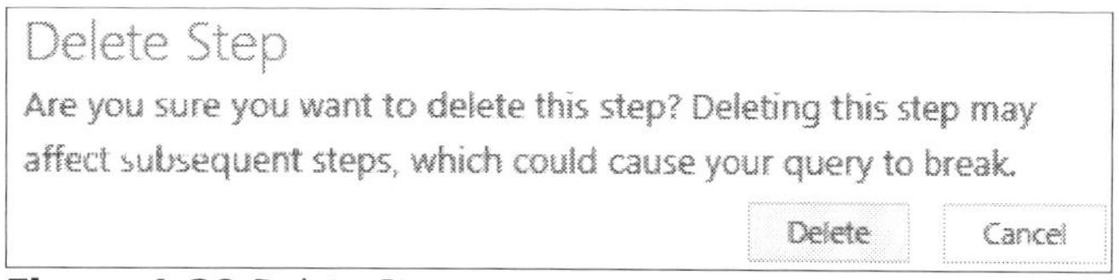

Figure 4-29 Delete Step message

Extract Previous Option

The Extract Previous option, shown earlier in Figure 4-27, displays the dialog box shown in Figure 4-30. This option is used to create a new query using the steps above the one selected, when this dialog box was opened. The steps above are deleted from the current query and placed in the new query. The Source step is copied to the new query, but not deleted from the current query.

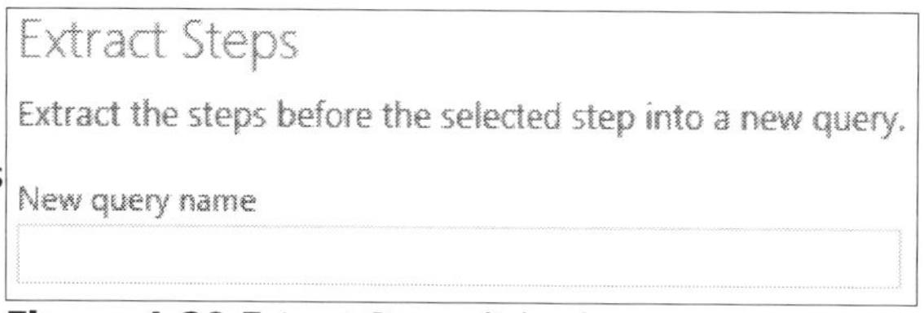

Figure 4-30 Extract Steps dialog box

View Native Query Option

This option is enabled on steps that have a symbol (the **COG WHEEL ICON**), as shown earlier in Figure 4-28. Figure 4-31 shows the code used to select the fields from the data source and any filters that were created in the Query Editor. The **WHERE CLAUSE** (on the last line) contains the options that were selected to filter the data that is displayed in the query. The code cannot be edited on this dialog box.

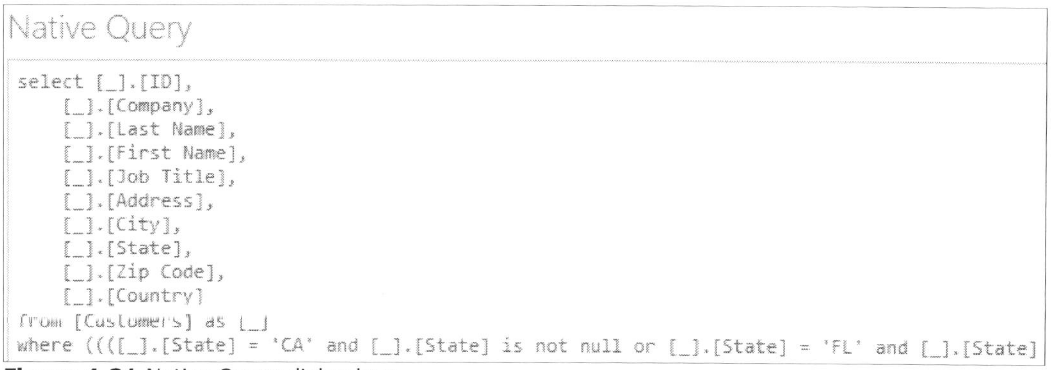

Figure 4-31 Native Query dialog box

Applied Steps Options

As shown earlier in Figure 4-28, some of the steps have an icon to the right of the step name. Steps that have this icon have a dialog box. This dialog box is also how you can change the import options for the step, if needed. The icon means that the values in the step can be changed in one of the following ways:

① Selecting the Edit Settings option, shown earlier in Figure 4-27.
② Clicking on the cog wheel icon.
③ Double-clicking on the step. The corresponding dialog box opens and displays the options that were selected to create the step.

Applied Steps Tips
① Most of the time, each action that you take, adds a step to the Applied Steps list. The exception that I noticed is when you perform the same action (remove or change the data type for example) two or more times consecutively (on the same or a different column), the actions are all added to the same step. The way that you know this, is to click on the step and view the formula, in the formula bar.
② At the end of some step names, you may see a number. The number is a counter of how many times the same action/transformation has been used in the query. If you rename a step, the counter number is no longer applied.
③ What I think is cool about the Applied Steps list is that you can click on any step to display the data as it was after the selected step was applied.

The Source, Navigation, Changed Type and Promoted Headers steps are the steps that you will see often. They are explained below.

Source Step

Queries always have a step named **SOURCE**. This step contains the import information about the data source for the query. Figure 4-32 shows the import options for an Excel file. The options displayed vary, depending on the data source type. For example, Figure 4-33 shows the import options for a CSV file.

The options on a source step dialog box are used to change the data source options. This is helpful if the path or data source name changes. You can make the change here and not have to switch to the Power BI Desktop window, to make the changes.

If the query has a database as the data source, clicking on the Source step displays a list of tables and views in the database, as shown in Figure 4-34. Notice that the formula bar displays the data source, path and file name. You can change the information in the formula bar, as needed. Figure 4-35 shows the import options for an Access database.

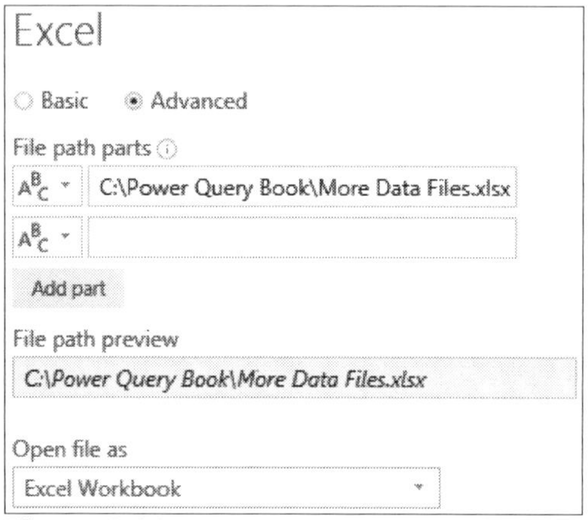

Figure 4-32 Source step import options for an Excel file (in Advanced mode)

Source Step
This step is always the first step. It cannot be renamed or moved, like the other steps can.

Connectors

Connecting to data is the first step to being able to transform data and ultimately create reports. Without data, you cannot do much in Power BI Desktop. As you will see, there are a lot of connectors and the list is continuously updated and added to. The next few sections cover some of the popular connectors. Others are covered in later chapters.

Comma-Separated Values Connector

The options shown in Figure 4-33 are for importing a CSV file.

By default, the delimiter character is automatically detected. If necessary, you can change or customize the delimiter character on this dialog box.

The **BROWSE BUTTON** opens the folder that the file is in.

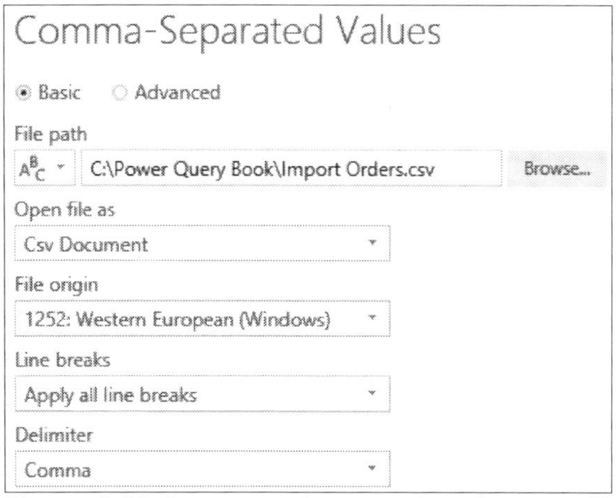

Figure 4-33 Source step import options for a CSV file

Changing The Locale In The Query Editor

Chapter 1 covered the Locale option, on the Options dialog box, and it was also covered earlier in this chapter. For CSV files, there is another way to change the Locale. On the dialog box for the Source step, open the **FILE ORIGIN** drop-down list, shown above in Figure 4-33 and select the Locale that you want the data interpreted as.

SQL Server Database Connector

It is probably no surprise what database this connector is for. <smile> The list of tables on the left side of Figure 4-34 are all of the tables in the database. The right side of the figure shows the connector options. While you can type in a specific server name, notice that I typed **LOCALHOST** instead of the server name. I use this as a shortcut, because all of the SQL databases that I use are on the same server, on my laptop.

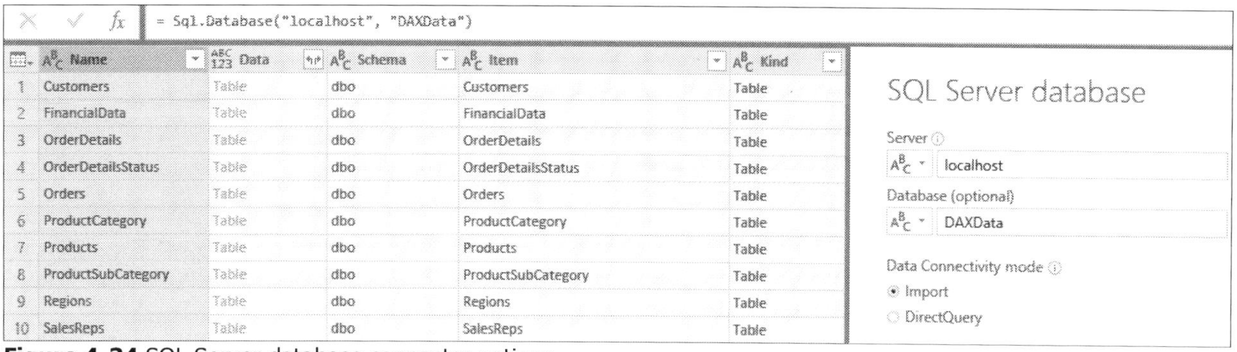

Figure 4-34 SQL Server database connector options

Access Database Connector

As shown in Figure 4-35, a list of tables is displayed in the Query Editor, when you do not select specific tables and select the Edit option on the shortcut menu, for the database file name on Navigator dialog box.

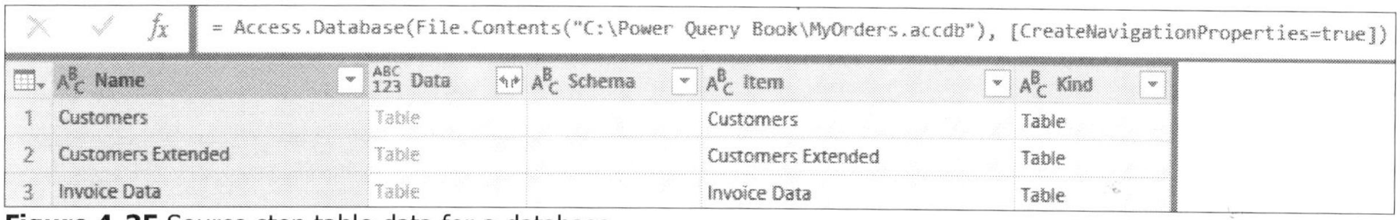

Figure 4-35 Source step table data for a database

Check the **INCLUDE RELATIONSHIP COLUMNS OPTION**, shown in Figure 4-36, when you need to have related tables automatically selected to be imported.

I don't see where this option adds any value for Access databases because you can use the Selected Tables button on the Navigator dialog box, when you first import the data. This option may be useful for other types of databases, but I haven't tested that.

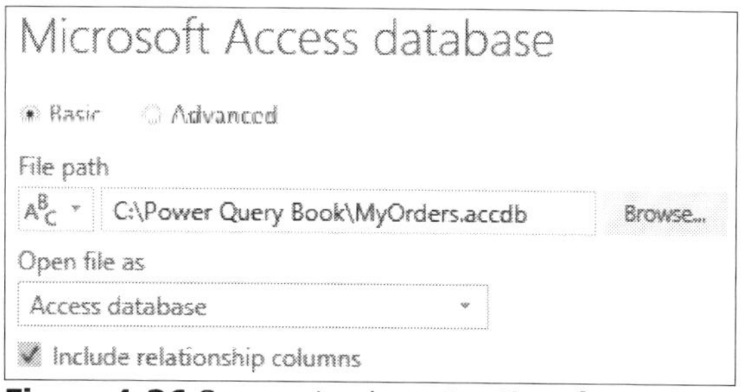

Figure 4-36 Source step import options for an Access database

Navigation Step

The Navigation step is only available for data sources that use the Navigator dialog box during the import process.

When available, this is the second step in the Applied Steps list. Right-clicking on the **NAVIGATION** step and selecting Edit Settings, displays the options shown in Figure 4-37. This option displays all of the tables and views (called **RESOURCES**) in the data source, for the selected query. This window is used to select a different table to view.

Keep in mind that all of the resources shown in the Navigation window, may not have been imported (meaning that there is no query for it in the data model). Even if the table that you want to view has not been imported, you will still be able to view the data, just not from here. At one point in the past, you could view tables from here.

If you want to view data from a table that has not been loaded, click on the Source step. You will see a table similar to the one shown earlier in Figure 4-34 ⇒ Click on the word "Table", (in the Data column) next to the table that has the data that you want to view. At the bottom of the window, you will see the data for the table that you selected.

Having this option in the Query Editor, just allows all of the tables and views in the data source to be viewed. For example, the Date Table shown in Figure 4-37 was not imported in Exercise 2.4. Selecting the table here, will allow you to view the data in it.

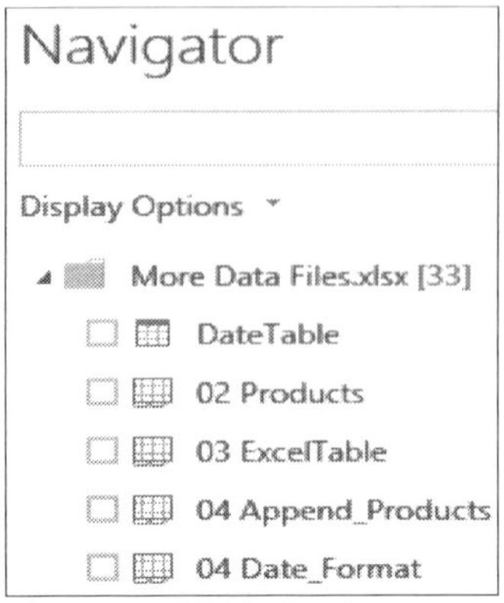

Figure 4-37 Navigation step options

> **Changed Type Step**
> The **CHANGED TYPE STEP** that is sometimes automatically created during the initial load, should be deleted. The Automatic detection of data types option, on the Options dialog box, should be unchecked for each file. One or both of these options can cause errors when the data is refreshed. Instead, you should change the data types when needed, manually.
>
> When this step is automatically created when you load data into Power Query, it can be problematic when you refresh the data. In my experience, the error that is generated when the data is refreshed, is when the data source is an Excel or text file. The Changed Type step problem is covered in more detail in Chapter 9.

Promoted Headers Step

You may see the Promoted Headers step, shown earlier in Figure 4-26, when a file type in the Get Data button ⇒ File section, is used as the data source.

When you first display a query and see this step, it means that during the import, the first row had data that was not consistent with the rest of the data in the table and the import process concluded that the first row must be header information. When that is the case, the first row of data is changed (promoted). This changes the data in the first row to the column headings for the table. This saves you from having to do this manually, once the data is displayed in the Query Editor. You will also see this step, when you manually select to have the first row used as the headers for the query.

The **TYPE DETECTION** option on the Options dialog box (Current File ⇒ Data Load screen), determines whether or not you see the Promoted Headers step, when data is first imported. If this option is checked, you probably will not see the Promoted Headers step, unless you apply it manually.

Modifying Steps

How you modify a step depends on how it was created. If the step that you want to modify has the **EDIT SETTINGS** option enabled on the Applied Steps shortcut menu, you can modify the step from there. If the Edit Settings option is not enabled, you have to use the corresponding option on a tab in the Query Editor or modify the formula for the step.

> **Modify A Step**
> What may not be obvious is that if you click on an existing step, for example, the Renamed Columns step and rename another column, even though you see the Insert Step message, the column will be renamed and the change will be added to the existing Renamed Columns step, instead of a new step being created.
>
> To me, adding to an existing step makes it much easier to know, all of the same type of changes that were made to the query. If there is only one Changed Type step and one Renamed Columns step, you know where to look for that type of change. This is also helpful if you need to change the order of the steps, because it is fewer steps to reorder and you do not have to check to see if you are moving the right step (that there is more than one of).

Deleting Steps

Deleting steps can produce unexpected outcomes for the steps below the step that you are deleting. When an error occurs, the icon for the query changes, in the Queries panel, and the data is replaced by an error message, as shown on the right side of Figure 4-38.

Figure 4-38 Error from deleting a step

Try To Avoid Deletion Errors

Often, the steps that cause an error when deleted, are dependent on a prior step. While there is no rule on the order that steps should be created in, I have fewer problems when I complete tasks in the order listed below.

① Use the Close & Apply option a few times during the data transformation process, as this option applies the query changes up to that point.
② Delete columns that are not needed.
③ Promote and/or rename column headers.
④ Filter out records that are not needed.
⑤ Change the data type, as needed.

After these tasks are completed, I apply and close again, especially before creating new columns and cleaning the data. Then, I save the changes. Think about it. If you create formulas, then insert a step to delete a column (above the formula step), used in the formula, the formula would stop working and the word "Error" would be displayed in the column.

Home Tab

Figure 4-39 shows the options on the Home tab in the Query Editor. The options are explained in Table 4-11.

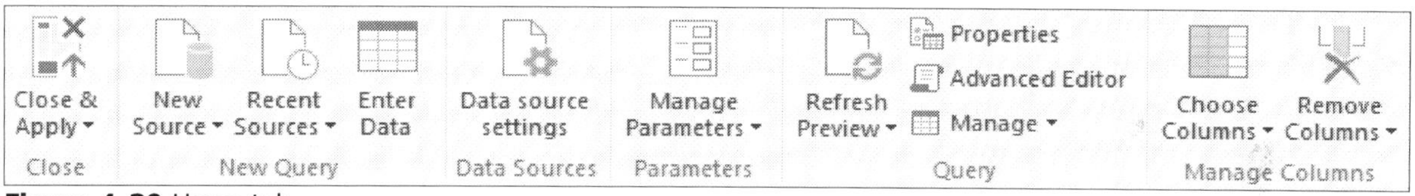

Figure 4-39 Home tab

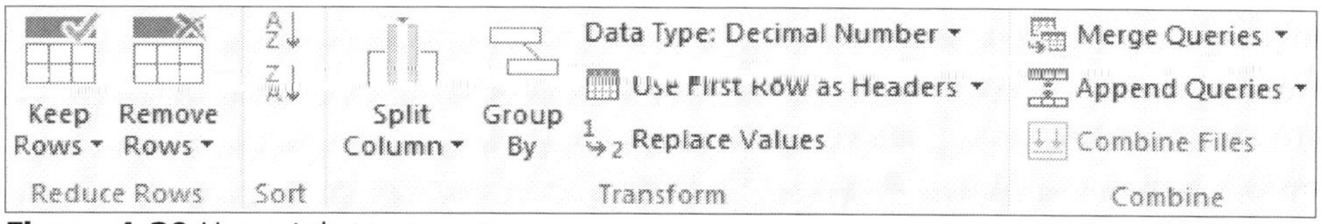

Figure 4-39 Home tab (Continued)

Option	Description
Close & Apply	[See Close & Apply Options]
New Source	[See New Source Options]
Recent Sources	[See Chapter 2, Recent Sources Button Option]
Enter Data	[See Chapter 2, Table 2-1]
Data Source Settings	[See Chapter 1, Data Source Settings]
Manage Parameters	[See Chapter 9, Manage Parameters]
Refresh Preview	[See Refresh Preview Options]
Properties	[See Figure 4-27]
Advanced Editor	[See Chapter 6, Advanced Editor]
Manage	[See Manage Button Options]

Table 4-11 Home tab options explained

Option	Description
Choose Columns	Displays all of the columns in the query, as shown in Figure 4-40. Remove the check mark for the column(s) that you want removed from the query. This button also has the **GO TO COLUMN OPTION**, which is helpful if the query has a lot of columns. You can select the column that you need and it will be highlighted in the table.
Remove Columns	[See Remove Columns Options]
Keep Rows	[See Keep Rows And Remove Rows Transformation Options]
Remove Rows	[See Keep Rows And Remove Rows Transformation Options]
Sort	The buttons sort in ascending, descending, low to high or high to low order, based on the values in the column that is selected, prior to selecting this option.
Split Column	[See Split Column Options]
Group By	[See Group By Options]
Data Type	Is used to change the data type for the selected column.
Use First Row As Headers	[See Use First Row As Headers Transformation]
Replace Values	[See Replace Values]
Merge Queries	[See Merge Queries And Append Queries Buttons]
Append Queries	[See Merge Queries And Append Queries Buttons]
Combine Files	[See Combine Files Button]

Table 4-11 Home tab options explained (Continued)

Choose Columns Dialog Box

The **SORT BY** options, on the right side of Figure 4-40, are used to change the order that the columns are displayed in.

NATURAL ORDER is the default sort option and displays the columns in the order that they are in the table.

The **NAME** option sorts the column names in alphabetical order.

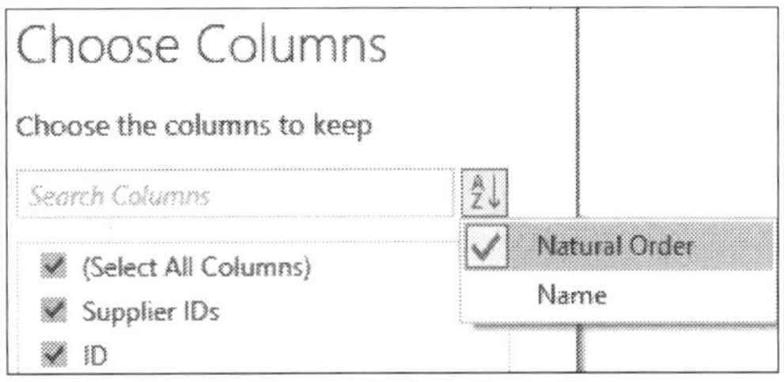

Figure 4-40 Choose Columns options

Close & Apply Options

The options shown in Figure 4-41 are used to select what to do with the (pending) changes made in the Query Editor.

The **CLOSE & APPLY** option saves the changes to the query, then closes the Query Editor and loads the data, based on the changes.

The **APPLY** option applies the changes and leaves the Query Editor open.

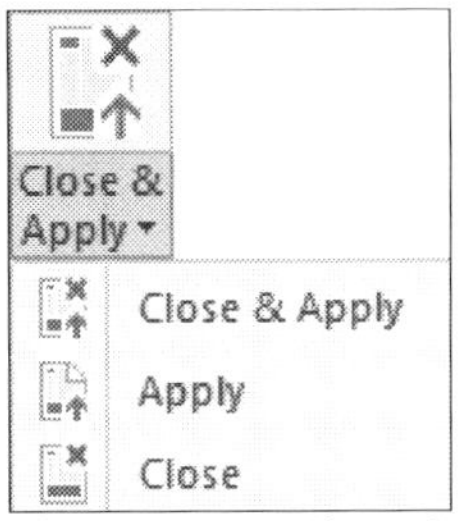

Figure 4-41 Close & Apply button options

Select the **CLOSE** option when you do not want to apply the pending changes to the data model now. The Query Editor window will close. The changes are not removed. You will see the message shown in Figure 4-42 in the Power BI Desktop workspace as a reminder, that there are **PENDING CHANGES**. When you save the report file, you will see the message shown in Figure 4-43. You can apply the changes now or later.

Clicking the Apply Later button, on the dialog box shown earlier in Figure 4-2, saves the pending changes when the file is saved, but does not apply them. This means that when you reopen the report file, the changes that have not been applied are still there and the message shown in Figure 4-42, is still displayed.

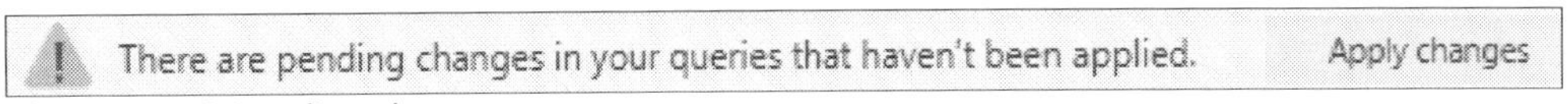

Figure 4-42 Pending changes message

How To Get Rid Of The Pending Changes
When you close the Query Editor without applying the pending changes, you will see the message shown above in Figure 4-42. You also see this message when you save the report file if the changes have not been applied. If you do not want to save the pending changes, click the X in the upper right corner of the Query Editor ⇒ Select Not Now ⇒ Click the X on the Power BI Desktop window. You will see the message shown in Figure 4-43 ⇒ Click the **DON'T SAVE** button. The file will close and all pending changes (made after the last time pending changes were applied) will be removed from the file. The next time that you open the report file you will not see the message shown above in Figure 4-42, letting you know that there are pending changes.

Just be sure when clicking the Don't Save button that you haven't made changes that you want to keep. After I have made a few changes that I want to keep, I apply them and save the file. That way when I make a change that I do not want, using this solution is not a problem.

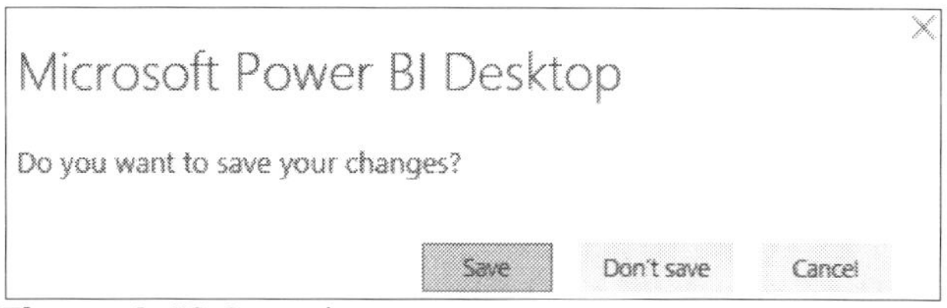

Figure 4-43 Save changes message

New Source Options

The options shown in Figure 4-44 are used to select the data source type for a file that you want to import data from.

These options work the same as the options on the Get Data button and dialog box.

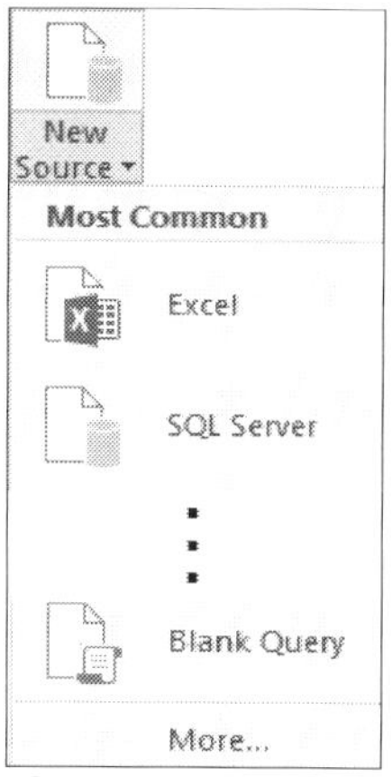

Figure 4-44 New Source button options

Refresh Preview Options

The options shown in Figure 4-45 are used to select which queries are refreshed.

REFRESH PREVIEW Refreshes the selected query.

REFRESH ALL Refreshes all of the queries on the Queries panel, that have the Enable refresh query option selected.

CANCEL REFRESH Is used to stop the refresh that is in progress.

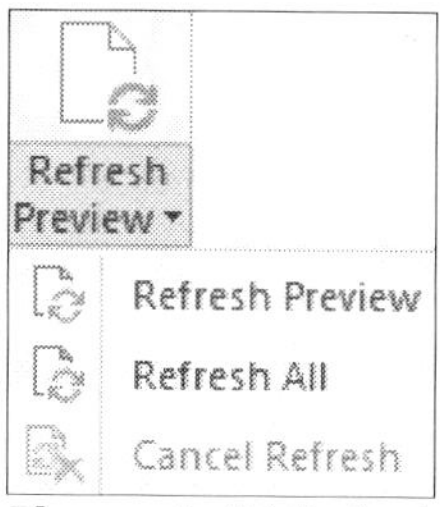

Figure 4-45 Refresh Preview button options

Manage Button Options

The options shown in Figure 4-46 are used to modify the selected query.

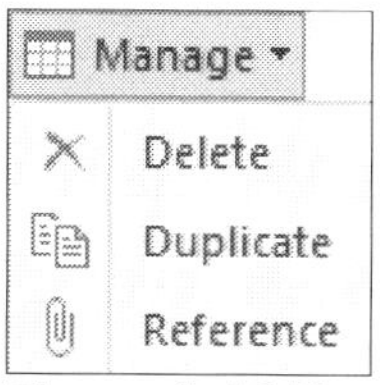

Figure 4-46 Manage button options

Remove Columns Options

The remove options are shown in Figure 4-47.

REMOVE COLUMNS Deletes the selected columns.

REMOVE OTHER COLUMNS Deletes all of the columns, except the ones that are selected.

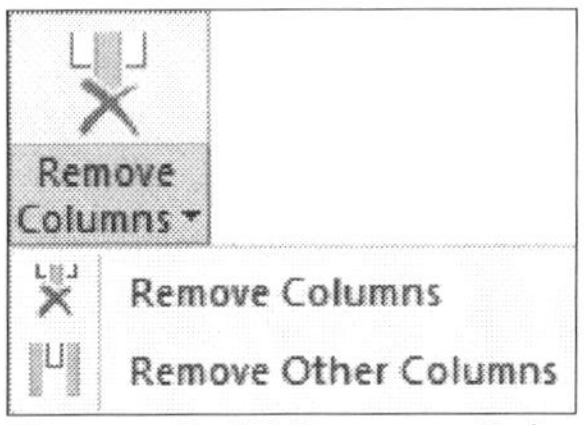

Figure 4-47 Remove Columns button options

Keep Rows And Remove Rows Transformation Options

The **KEEP ROWS** options shown in Figure 4-48, are used to select which rows to keep in the query. Rows that are not kept are deleted from the query.

The **KEEP DUPLICATES** option shown in Figure 4-48, will only keep records that have duplicate values, based on the column(s) that you select. This option is helpful when you need to clean the source data because you can work from the records that this transformation creates.

The **KEEP ERRORS** option will only keep rows of data that have an error. (14)

The **REMOVE ROWS** options shown in Figure 4-49, are used to remove rows from the query. These options are used to keep or delete records, based on the value of **N**. The rows that are selected are removed from the query. They are not deleted from the data source. The next time data is refreshed, removed rows will not be re-imported. If you are already familiar with **TOP N FUNCTIONALITY**, you will be familiar with these options.

The **REMOVE TOP ROWS** and **REMOVE BOTTOM ROWS** options, display the dialog box shown in Figure 4-50. The dialog box is used to select the number of rows (from the top or bottom of the data displayed in the query) to keep.

Use the **KEEP TOP ROWS** option if you need to display the rows that have one of the top N values in the selected column. To do this, sort the column that has the data that will determine which rows to keep, in ascending or descending order, then use the Keep Top Rows option and type the number of rows (like 10 for the top 10 rows), to keep in the field.

The **KEEP RANGE OF ROWS** options shown in Figure 4-51, are used to select the range of rows of data to keep. The number entered in the First row field equals the first row in the table to keep. The number entered in the Number of rows field equals how many rows, in total, you want to keep.

The **REMOVE ALTERNATE ROWS** options shown in Figure 4-52, are used to select the starting point and pattern for how rows will be removed from the query. The values shown in the figure will remove rows as follows: Rows 5 to 15 will be deleted. The next two rows will be saved. This process is repeated until the end of the table is reached.

The **REMOVE BLANK ROWS** option deletes any blank rows in the table.

The **REMOVE ERRORS** option deletes rows that have an error, based on the column that is selected. Use this option with caution because you can remove rows of data that should be kept. (14)

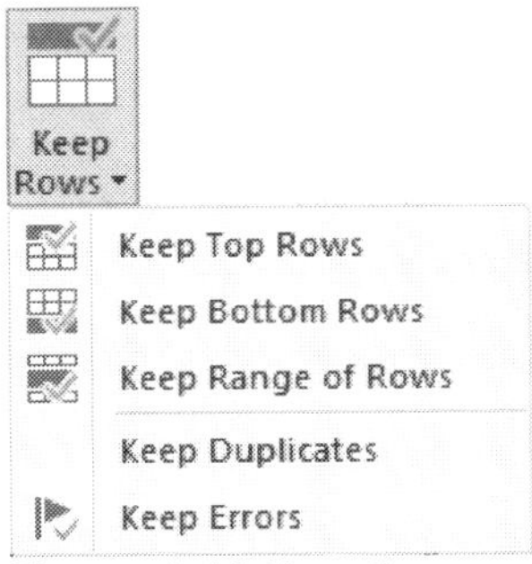

Figure 4-48 Keep Rows button options

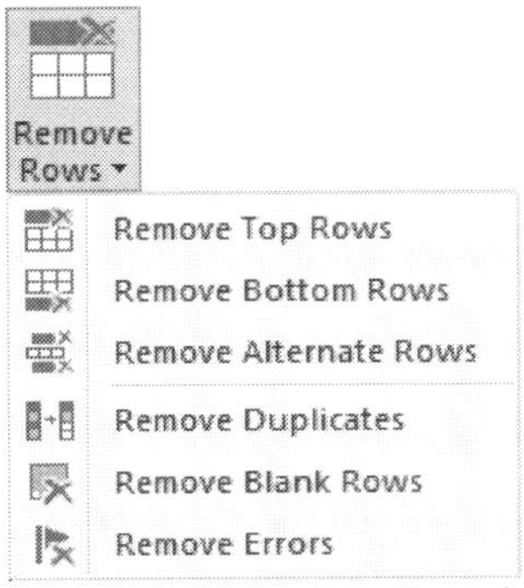

Figure 4-49 Remove Rows button options

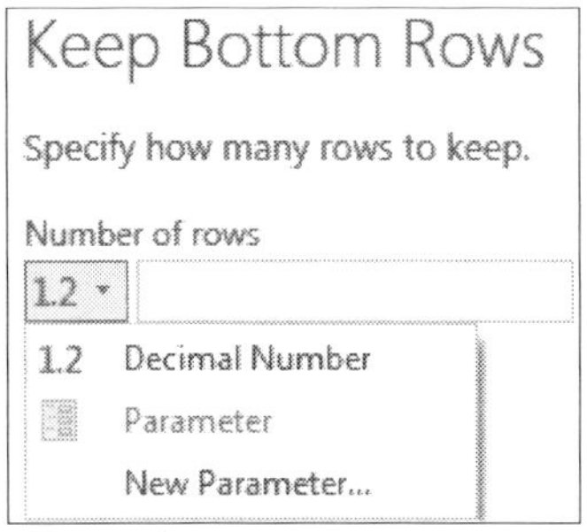

Figure 4-50 Keep Bottom Rows dialog box

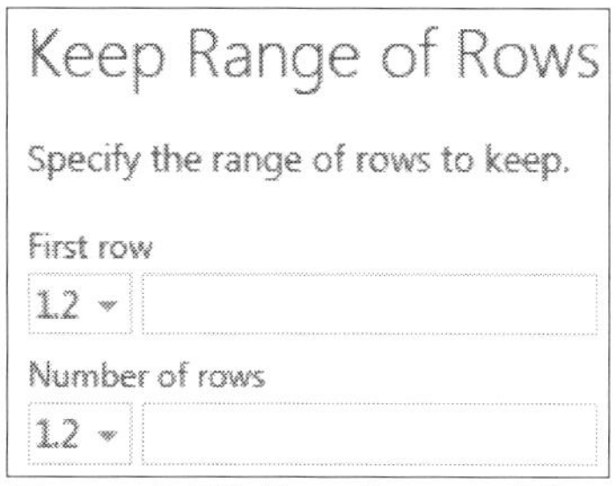

Figure 4-51 Keep Range of Rows options

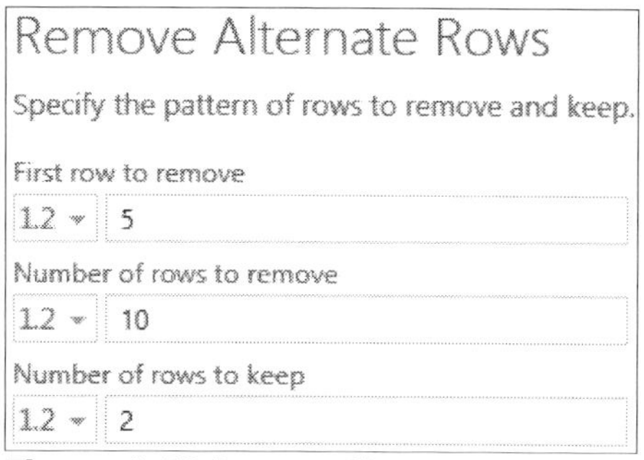

Figure 4-52 Remove Alternate Rows options

The **REMOVE DUPLICATES** option is used to delete duplicate records. If you want to remove duplicate rows of data, you have to select enough columns in the table to make the rows that you want to delete, duplicate. Often, in addition to selecting criteria to use to determine what makes records duplicate, looking at some of the data will help you select the correct criteria. Most of the time, at least two columns should be used as criteria to select duplicate records. For example, Figure 4-53 shows a table that will have duplicate rows deleted, based on the values in two columns. (14)

If multiple columns are selected (like the Order ID and Quantity) and the Remove Duplicates option is applied, rows 3, 5, 9 and 10 would be deleted because each of these rows have the same value as the record above it, in those columns. Row 13 would not be deleted because the Quantity column does not have the same value as row 12.

The Query Editor is **CASE SENSITIVE** when checking for duplicate values.

I don't know if I can stress enough, how important it is to remove duplicate records. Having duplicate records, distorts the totals (values) that are created and displayed on a report. This will cause the wrong conclusion or decisions to be made.

	1²3 ID	1.2 Order ID	1.2 Quantity	$ Unit Price
1	1	1	1	41.9
2	2	1002	3	33.9
3	3	1002	3	1652.8599
4	4	1003	3	48.51
5	5	1003	3	13.78
6	6	1004	3	274.35
7	7	1005	2	14.5
8	8	1006	1	16.5
9	9	1006	1	33.9
10	10	1006	1	14.5
11	11	1007	3	16.5
12	12	1008	2	726.61
13	13	1008	1	431.87

Figure 4-53 Query that has duplicate rows of data

(14) This option is based on the columns that are selected, before this option is applied.

Exercise Tips

① I rearranged the order that some columns (in a table) appear in, in some figures, to make it easier to understand the result of a transformation.

② While not a requirement, you should save the file after each exercise. Some of the transformations require a lot of processing power and can cause Power BI Desktop to crash, if you computer runs low on RAM. That way, should Power BI Desktop freeze or crash for any reason, you will not loose every transformation that was created, up to that point. Doing this is optional.

Exercise 4.1: Use The Remove Columns And Rows Transformations

In this exercise, you will learn some ways to reduce the amount of data that is loaded in the query.

1. In a new file, import (load) all of the 05 tables in the More Data Files workbook.

2. Query Editor ⇒ Click on the Products query ⇒ Change the query name to `ModifyRowsAndColumns`. The next three parts of the exercise use this query.

Use The Choose Columns Transformation

1. Home tab ⇒ Choose Columns button ⇒ Choose Columns.

2. On the Choose Columns dialog box, clear the check mark for the Discontinued column ⇒ Click OK.

Use The Remove Columns Transformation

1. Click on the Reorder Level column, in the query.

2. Home tab ⇒ **REMOVE COLUMNS BUTTON** ⇒ Remove Columns.
   As you see, the Choose Columns and Remove Columns options can be used to remove columns from the query.

Use The Remove Errors Transformation

1. Home tab ⇒ Remove Rows button ⇒ Remove Errors.

   You should have the Applied Steps shown in Figure 4-54.

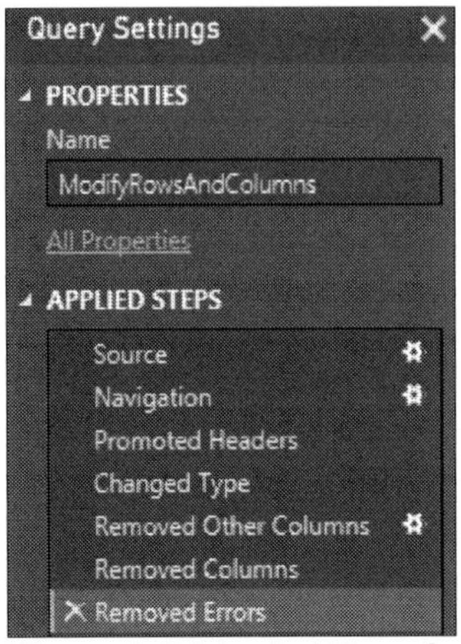

Figure 4-54 Applied Steps for Exercise 4.1

2. Save the file as `E4.1 Remove columns and rows` ⇒ When prompted, apply the changes.
   Leave the file open to complete the rest of the exercise.

Use The Remove Bottom Rows Transformation

In this part of the exercise, you will learn how to remove the last 50 rows of data in a table.

1. Display the Modify Rows and Columns query ⇒ Click on the Removed Columns step in the **APPLIED STEPS** section on the Query Settings panel.

2. Remove Rows button ⇒ Remove Bottom Rows ⇒

   On the window shown in Figure 4-55, click Insert.

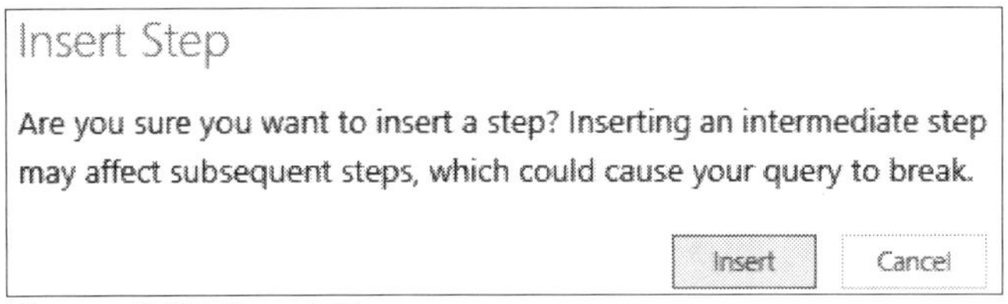

Figure 4-55 Insert Step message

The message wants to confirm that you really want to add a step between existing steps and to let you know that inserting a step can change the how the steps below it, are applied. Prior to starting this part of the exercise, you would not see this message. If you wanted to move this step, you could use the Move Up and Move Down options in the Applied Steps shortcut menu.

3. On the Remove Bottom Rows dialog box, type `50`. There should now be 27 rows in the query ⇒ Close the Query Editor without applying the changes ⇒ Save the file.

Exercise 4.2: Remove Duplicate Records

1. Save the E2.4 file as `E4.2 Remove duplicate records.`

2. Select the Duplicate_Data query in the Query Editor. Notice that there are 26 records (rows).

3. Home tab ⇒ Remove Rows button ⇒ Remove Duplicates. There should only be 20 records now.
   Do you have any idea what rows were deleted and if they are truly duplicates?

By default, the first column in the query is used to determine whether or not there are duplicate rows of data. Most of the time, you will probably want to use more than one column to determine if the rows are duplicate. At this point in the process, I would like to be able to view the records that were are selected to be deleted, to make sure that they are duplicate.

Sorting On Multiple Columns

It is possible to sort on multiple columns. The thing to remember is that the columns have to be sorted on, back to back. This will combine the sorts into one step. Follow the steps below when you need to sort on multiple columns.

1. Click on the first column that you want to sort on ⇒ Home tab ⇒ Click the Sort Ascending or Sort Descending button.

2. Click on the next column that you want to sort on ⇒ Home tab ⇒ Click the Sort Ascending or Sort Descending button.

3. Repeat step 2 for each column that you want to sort on.

When finished, each column will have a number after the column header, as illustrated in Figure 4-56. The formula for the **SORTED ROWS** step should have all of the columns that you sorted on, as shown in Figure 4-57. If not, clear the sort and start over.

The sort numbers and buttons only appear when the Sorted Rows step is selected on the Query Settings panel.

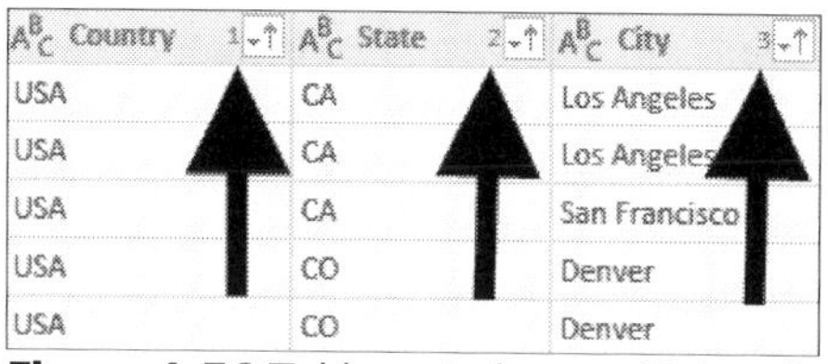

Figure 4-56 Table sorted on multiple columns

```
= Table.Sort(#"Reordered Columns",{{"Country", Order.Ascending}, {"State", Order.Ascending}, {"City", Order.Ascending}})
```
Figure 4-57 Sorted Rows step formula

Split Column Options

The options shown in Figure 4-58 are used to split the data in a column, into two or more columns.

The options are explained below.

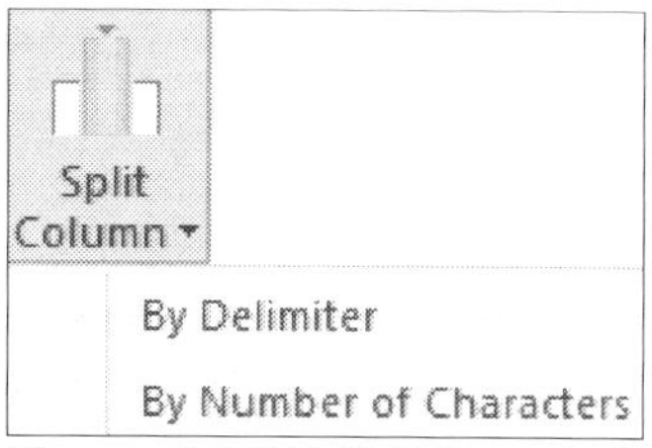

Figure 4-58 Split Column button options

By Delimiter Options

Figure 4-59 shows the **BY DELIMITER** options. The options change, depending on the delimiter character that is selected. The delimiter field is automatically populated (selected) with a delimiter, that is based on the text pattern when Power BI Desktop previews that data.

Figure 4-60 shows the delimiter options that you can select, if you need to change the default option that was selected.

The **CUSTOM DELIMITER OPTION** is used to enter something other then the options shown in Figure 4-60, to select what character should be used to separate the columns. The option that comes to mind of when to use the Custom option is the pipe | character (The pipe character is to the right of the right bracket key, on my keyboard).

Select the **LEFT-MOST DELIMITER OPTION** when the column should only be split once, at the first occurrence of the delimiter.

Select the **RIGHT-MOST DELIMITER OPTION** when the column should only be split once, at the last occurrence of the delimiter.

Select the **EACH OCCURRENCE OF THE DELIMITER OPTION** when the column should be split each time the delimiter is in the column.

The **ADVANCED OPTIONS** change, based on the Split option that is selected. You can select to split the column into more columns or into rows. (15)

The **QUOTE CHARACTER OPTION** is used to select whether or not you want to use the CSV quote style (" "). Comma delimited is also supported.

Selecting the **SPLIT USING SPECIAL CHARACTERS OPTION** enables the **INSERT SPECIAL CHARACTER** drop-down list (shown at the bottom of Figure 4-59). It has additional special characters that can be used, as the character to determine where to split the data.

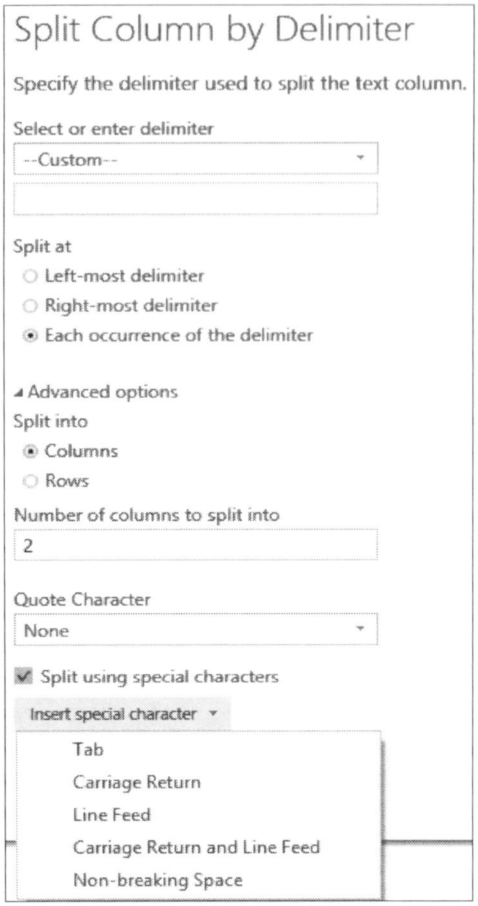

Figure 4-59 By Delimiter options

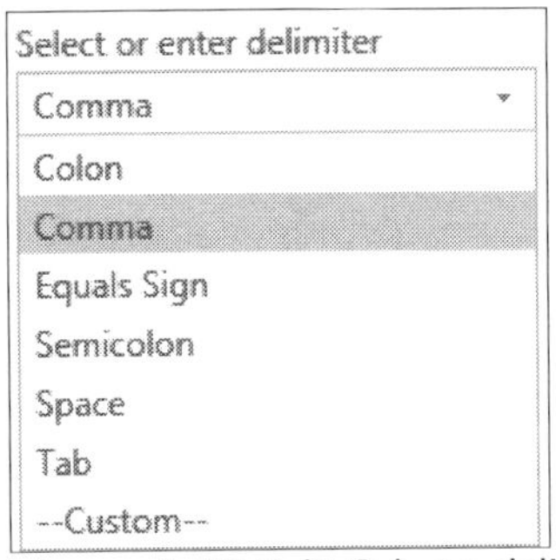

Figure 4-60 Split Column delimiter options

The options selected in Figure 4-61, change the data in the Ship Name column, to the columns shown in Figure 4-62.

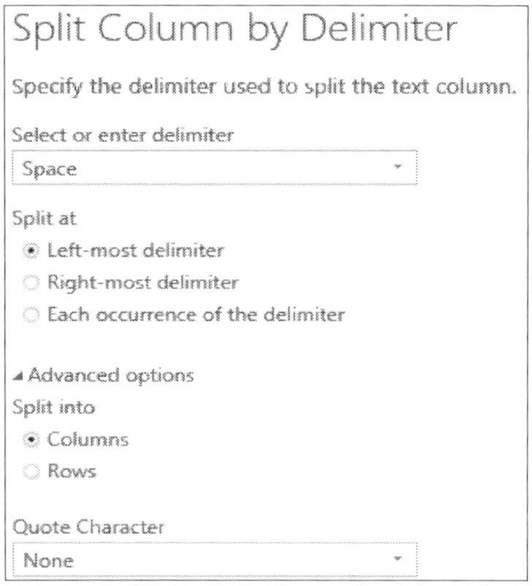

Figure 4-61 By Delimiter options to split the Ship Name column

	Customer ID	Ship Name.1	Ship Name.2
1	27	Karen	Toh
2	4	Christina	Lee
3	12	John	Edwards
4	8	Elizabeth	Andersen

Figure 4-62 Split column by delimiter option applied to a text column

The options shown in Figure 4-63 will change a date column, to the columns shown in Figure 4-64. The options that are pre-selected when you open the Split Column by Delimiter dialog box are based on what Power Query recognizes about the column selected before the dialog box is opened. For example, the Split at each occurrence option was pre-selected, because Power Query detected that the slash delimited is in the date field at least twice, as shown in Figure 4-63. Power Query also detected that the Order Date column could be split into three columns, as shown by the value in the Number of columns to split into field.

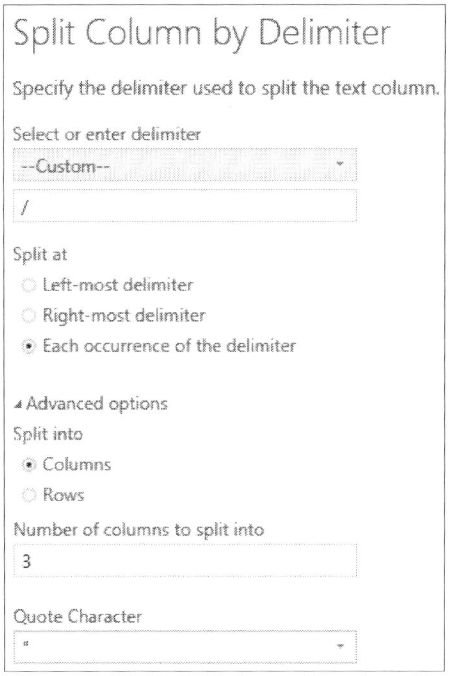

Figure 4-63 By Delimiter options to split a date column

	Order Date.1	Order Date.2	Order Date.3
1	1	15	2006
2	1	20	2006
3	1	22	2006
4	1	30	2006

Figure 4-64 Split column by delimiter option applied to a date column

By Number Of Characters Options

Figure 4-65 shows the **BY NUMBER OF CHARACTERS** transformation options.

I think the intended use of these options is to only to split columns that have a text data type, even though they can be used to split columns with other data types.

The options are designed to split a column into at least two columns where the data is the same length. (15)

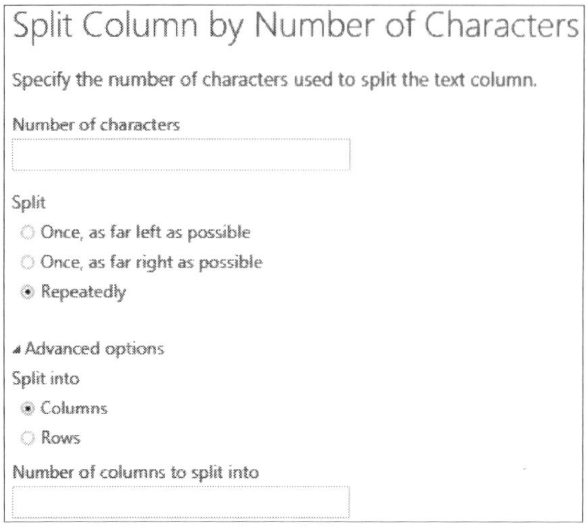

Figure 4-65 By Number of Characters options

(15) The **SPLIT INTO OPTIONS** are used to split the data into columns (the default) or rows. The options shown in Figure 4-66 will transform the Order Dates shown in Figure 4-67, to the format shown in Figure 4-68. There are now three rows for each order date.

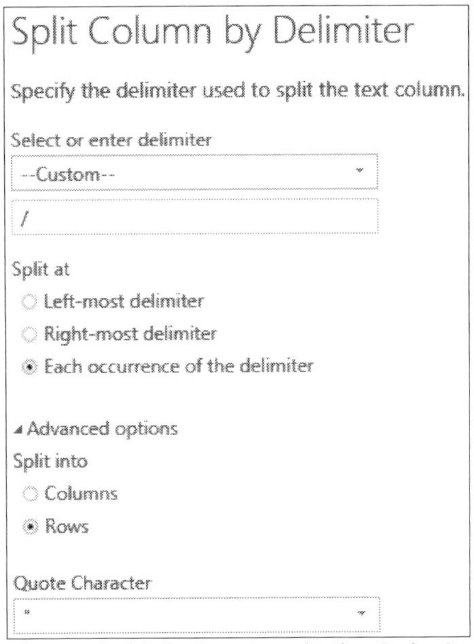

Figure 4-66 Options to split the Order Date into rows

	Order ID	Employee	Customer	Order Date
1	30	Anne Hellung-Larsen	Company AA	01/15/2006
2	31	Jan Kotas	Company D	01/20/2006
3	32	Mariya Sergienko	Company L	01/22/2006

Figure 4-67 Rows before the split option was applied

	Order ID	Employee	Customer	Order Date
1	30	Anne Hellung-Larsen	Company AA	1
2	30	Anne Hellung-Larsen	Company AA	15
3	30	Anne Hellung-Larsen	Company AA	2006
4	31	Jan Kotas	Company D	1
5	31	Jan Kotas	Company D	20
6	31	Jan Kotas	Company D	2006

Figure 4-68 Split into rows option applied

Most of the time when there are a fixed number of delimiters, selecting the **SPLIT INTO COLUMNS OPTION** works best. When the number of delimiters is unknown, select the **SPLIT INTO ROWS OPTION**, is often the best option.

Sometimes splitting a column into new columns seems to work . . . right up to the point when you try and create a report. That is when you realize that the data really needs to be split into rows. The Split into rows option is covered in more detail in Chapter 11.

Group By Transformation Options

The options shown in Figure 4-69 are used, for lack of a better word, to create a pivot table and aggregate (summarize) the data in a table. This is also known as an **AGGREGATE VIEW**. As shown at the top of the figure, there are two options available to group data by: Basic and Advanced. The good thing is that you can switch between the two modes, while creating the transformation.

The **GROUP BY OPTION** changes the structure of the query because it puts the rows of data into groups.

The rows in the query are rolled up into one of the Group by categories (fields), at the top of the dialog box, so that the aggregations at the bottom of the dialog box, can be applied.

For example, the options shown in Figure 4-69 summarize the data shown in Figure 4-70, to display the data in the layout shown in Figure 4-71.

The options shown in Figure 4-69 group the data in the query, by customer (Customer ID field). A count of the orders shipped to each customer is also calculated.

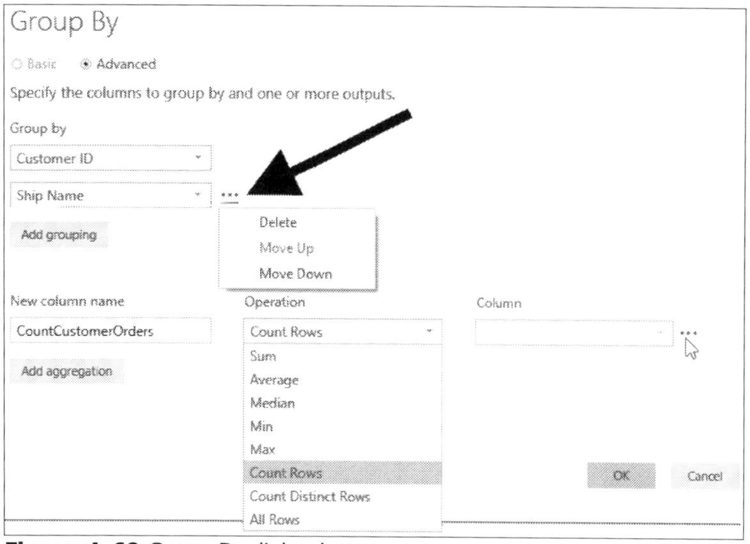

Figure 4-69 Group By dialog box

The top section of the Group By dialog box is used to select columns that you want to create groups for. The columns not used in the Group By section are not initially displayed in the query.

You can select the columns to group by before you open this dialog box. The order that you select them in does not matter. When selecting columns before opening the dialog box, they will be displayed in the order that they appear in the query, from left to right.

When clicked, the **... ELLIPSIS BUTTON** to the right of a Group By and Column fields, displays options to delete or move the selected field up or down, as illustrated above in Figure 4-69.

The **ADD GROUPING BUTTON** is used to add another field to the Group by section.

The bottom section of the dialog box is used to create the aggregate column(s). These new columns will appear to the right of the group by fields in the query, as shown in Figure 4-71.

The **NEW COLUMN NAME FIELD** is used to type in the name for the aggregate column that will be created, to display a total (summary) for the group(s) at the top of the dialog box.

The **ADD AGGREGATION BUTTON** is used to add a row to create another calculation.

The **OPERATION** drop down list contains the types of summary totals (**AGGREGATE FUNCTIONS**) that can be created, as shown above in Figure 4-69. The options in this drop-down list are explained in Table 4-12. This drop-down list also has a **ROW OPERATION**.

The **COLUMN** drop-down list contains all of the fields in the query. Select the field that should be used in the calculation.

```
= Table.PromoteHeaders(Source, [PromoteAllScalars=true])
```

	Order ID	Employee ID	Customer ID	Order Date	Shipped Date	Shipper ID	Ship Name
1	30	9	27	1/15/2006	1/22/2006	2	Karen Toh
2	31	3	4	1/20/2006	1/22/2006	1	Christina Lee
3	32	4	12	1/22/2006	1/22/2006	2	John Edwards
4	33	6	8	1/30/2006	1/31/2006	3	Elizabeth Andersen
5	34	9	4	2/6/2006	2/7/2006	3	Christina Lee
6	35	3	29	2/10/2006	2/12/2006	2	Soo Jung Lee
7	36	4	3	2/23/2006	2/25/2006	2	Thomas Axen

Figure 4-70 Data without the group by options applied

= Table.Sort(#"Grouped Rows",{{"Customer ID", Order.Ascending}})

	Customer ID	Ship Name	CountCustomerOrders
1	1	Anna Bedecs	2
2	3	Thomas Axen	3
3	4	Christina Lee	5
4	6	Francisco P,rez-Olaeta	6
5	7	Ming-Yang Xie	2
6	8	Elizabeth Andersen	6

Figure 4-71 Data with the group by options shown earlier in Figure 4-69 applied

Group By Functions

Function	Description
Sum	Adds the values in the column to get a total. (16)
Average	Calculates the average of the values. (16)
Median	Returns the middle value. (16)
Min	Returns the lowest value. (16)
Max	Returns the highest value. (16)
Count Rows	This operation is displayed by default, when the dialog box is first opened. It can be changed. It returns the number of rows in the query. (17)
Count Distinct Rows	Returns the number of rows that have a unique value in the selected column. (17)
All Rows	Creates a new column in the current query that has the **TABLE DATA TYPE**. The table displays the columns from the query. It is used to select additional columns that can be displayed in the query. This is how you can add columns that would not be displayed in the query, because they were not used on the Group By dialog box. (17)

Table 4-12 Group By functions explained

(16) This operation is an **AGGREGATE FUNCTION**. The values come from the Column field in the same row on the Group By dialog box.
(17) This option is known as a **ROW OPERATION**. It does not use the Column field on the Group by dialog box.

The options shown in Figure 4-72 create the table shown in Figure 4-73.

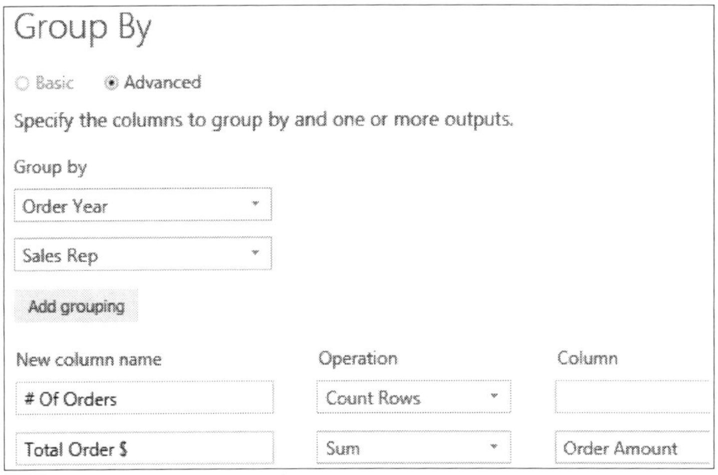

Figure 4-72 Group By options

	Order Year	Sales Rep	# Of Orders	Total Order $
1	2013	Justin Brid	14	12821.37
2	2013	Xavier Martin	10	13386.07
3	2013	Margaret Peacock	18	23878.33
4	2013	Albert Hellstern	15	41820.13
5	2013	Steven Buchanan	7	9932.2

Figure 4-73 Query based on the options shown above in Figure 4-72

Use First Row As Headers Transformation

When the data being imported is from a database, this option is automatically applied to the data. The Use First Row As Headers button displays the options shown in Figure 4-74. If the data in the query looks like the data shown in Figure 4-75, selecting the **USE FIRST ROW AS HEADERS** option replaces the current column headings (Column 1, Column 2, etc) with the values in the first row of data, as shown in Figure 4-76. This transformation is the front end to the Promote Headers function. Selecting the **USE HEADERS AS FIRST ROW** option, moves the header row down, so that it becomes the first row of data.

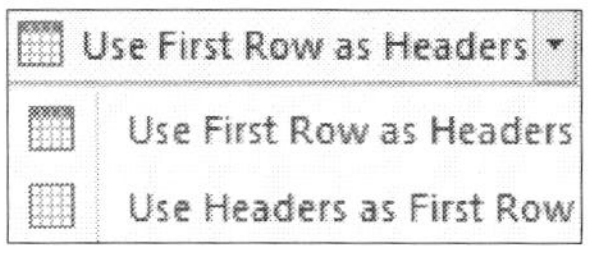

Figure 4-74 Use First Row As Headers button options

	ABC 123 Column1	ABC 123 Column2	ABC 123 Column3	ABC 123 Column4
1	ProductID	ProductName	CategoryID	QuantityPerUnit
2	1	Chai	1	10 boxes x 20 bags
3	2	Chang	1	24 - 12 oz bottles
4	3	Aniseed Syrup	2	12 - 550 ml bottles

Figure 4-75 Data without column headings

	1²3 ProductID	A^B_C ProductName	1²3 CategoryID	A^B_C QuantityPerUnit
1	1	Chai	1	10 boxes x 20 bags
2	2	Chang	1	24 - 12 oz bottles
3	3	Aniseed Syrup	2	12 - 550 ml bottles
4	4	Chef Anton's Cajun Seasoning	2	48 - 6 oz jars

Figure 4-76 Data with the Use First Row As Headers option applied

What may not be obvious is that when this transformation is used, in addition to it creating new headings, it also changes the data types, as needed. As shown earlier in Figure 4-75, the current column headings (Column 1, Column 2, etc) all have the Text data type. After the Use First Row as Headers option is applied, the data type of the first and third columns in Figure 4-76, have been changed to the Whole Number data type.

> The **REPLACE VALUES BUTTON** has two options: Replace Values (the default) and Replace Errors. If you need to apply the **REPLACE ERRORS** transformation to a column, see Chapter 6, Replace Errors.

Replace Values

This transformation will remind you of the search and replace functionality that is available in other software, because it works the same way. It is used to replace the value in the selected column(s), using the options shown in Figure 4-77.

This transformation can also be used to fill in fields that do not have data. The two types of blank fields are empty fields (which usually have the Text data type) and **NULL VALUES** (which have a numeric data type).

While it is not a requirement that all cells have data, it can present problems if there are too many empty cells. This is particularly true for numeric fields that are used in calculations.

Allowing null values in numeric fields means that you will have to test for null values before each calculation, because formulas can fail if a numeric field is empty. It is better to replace null values in numeric fields that will be used in a calculation, with a zero.

The Advanced options shown in the figure are used to customize the value in the Replace With field.

If checked, the **MATCH ENTIRE CELL CONTENTS OPTION** will only replace the current value, if the current value is all that is in the cell.

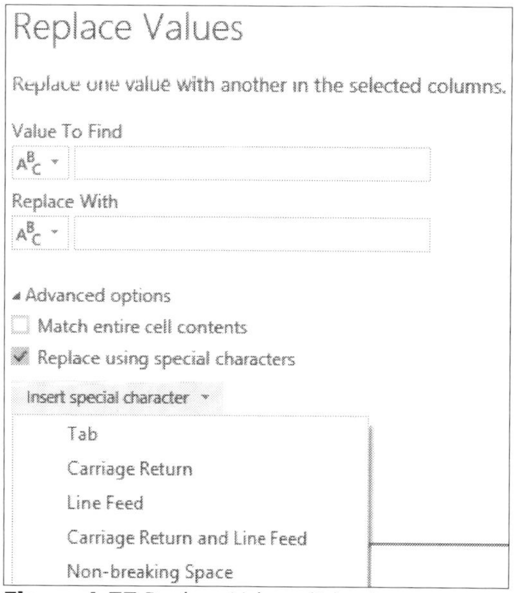

Figure 4-77 Replace Values dialog box

Selecting the **REPLACE USING SPECIAL CHARACTERS OPTION** enables the **INSERT SPECIAL CHARACTER BUTTON**. This button has the additional special characters shown in the figure, that can be searched for. These options can also be used as replacement characters.

To select a special character to use in the Value To Find or Replace With field with, click in the field, then click on the special character that you want to use. This allows special characters to be searched for or used to replace the value in the cell.

Replace Values Tips

① This transformation only works with columns that have the Text data type. If you need to use it with date or numeric data type columns, you can try changing the data type to text, use the Replace Values options, then change the data type back to what it was.

② The **COPY OPTION FOR CELLS** [See Figure 4-23] can be used with this dialog box.

③ If you want to delete a value in a column and not replace it with anything (meaning you want the cell to be blank), leave the Replace With field empty.

④ The options on the Replace Values dialog box, search for every occurrence of the text entered in the Values To Find field. By default, it does not check to see if the value being searched for, is all that is in the cell, unless the Match entire cell contents option is checked.

⑤ If you want to replace empty cells with a null value, leave the Value To Find field empty and type `null` in the Replace With field.

Merge Queries And Append Queries Buttons

These buttons have two options, as shown in Figure 4-78. The options are explained below.

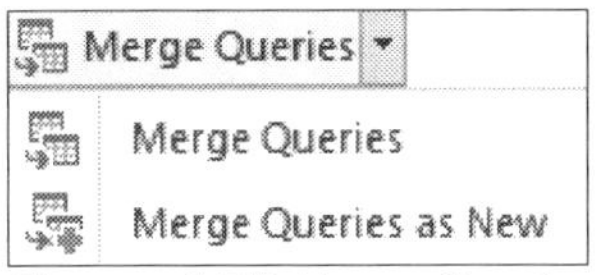

Figure 4-78 Merge Queries options

The **MERGE QUERIES OPTION** adds columns from one query to the selected query. A column to link the queries on is required.

The **MERGE QUERIES AS NEW OPTION** creates a new query by combining the data in the two queries that you select. Once the tables are merged, you can delete the columns from either table, that you do not need. (18)

The **APPEND QUERIES OPTION** adds all of the rows in one or more tables to the bottom of the selected query.

The **APPEND QUERIES AS NEW OPTION** creates a new query by appending the data in two or more tables that you select. (18)

(18) This option leaves both of the original queries (tables) intact.

Combine Files Button

This button is enabled for columns that have the word **BINARY** in the cells. Columns set to binary that have a null value will not work. This option is used to append the data from multiple files into one table. For example, this option will combine (append) the data in several CSV files (in the same folder) into one file. This button is used in Chapter 9, Exercise 9.1.

Customize The Quick Access Toolbar

Just like the Power BI Desktop workspace has a Quick Access Toolbar, so does the Query Editor. If there are options on any of the tabs in the Query Editor that you know that you will use a lot, you can add them to the Quick Access toolbar, by following the steps below.

1. Right-click on the button (on one of the tabs) that you want to add to the Quick Access Toolbar.

2. Select the Add to Quick Access Toolbar option, illustrated in Figure 4-79.

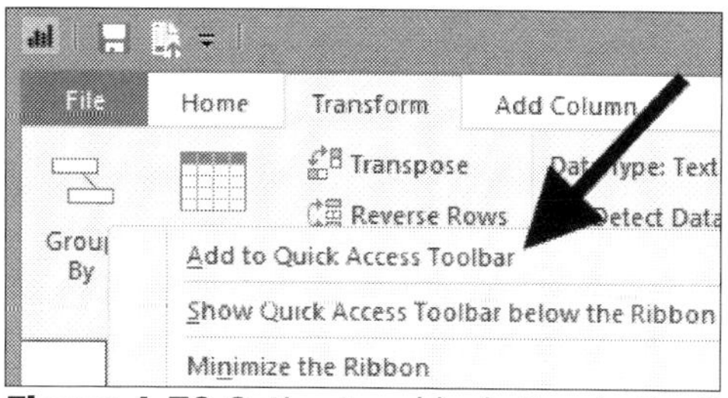

Figure 4-79 Option to add a button to the Quick Access Toolbar illustrated

How Old Is The Data Displayed In The Query Editor?

The Query Editor will display a message, like the one illustrated in Figure 4-80, once the data is more than 24 hours old.

The message lets you know approximately how old the data is, based on when it was imported or last refreshed.

Click the **REFRESH** button if you want to refresh the data.

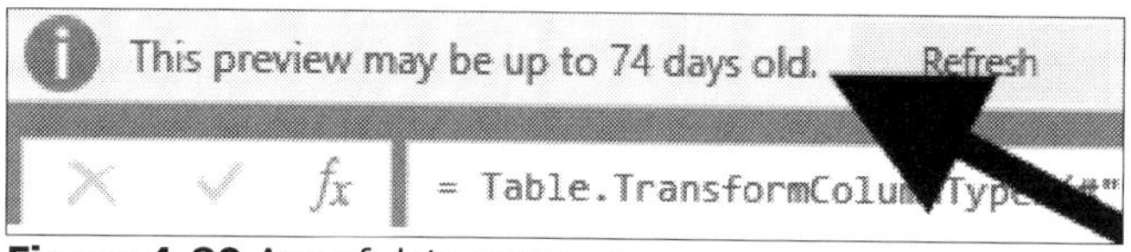

Figure 4-80 Age of data message

Exercise 4.3: Loading A List Of Tables

In Chapter 2, you imported a few tables from an Access database. Databases can have a lot of tables and views, sometimes hundreds. I don't know about you, but I can't remember that many table names. The good news is that you do not have to remember the table names. A list of the tables and views, is part of the database import process. Even better, once the list of tables and views is imported or a connection is created, you can view the data in the tables and views. This process (storing a list of tables and/or views) is known as storing **METADATA** about the database.

1. In a new file ⇒ Get Data button ⇒ More ⇒ Access database ⇒ Select the My Orders database.

2. Right-click on the database name, on the Navigator dialog box and select Edit, as shown in Figure 4-81.

   The Query Editor will open and display a query that has the metadata for all of the tables and views in the database, as shown in Figure 4-82.

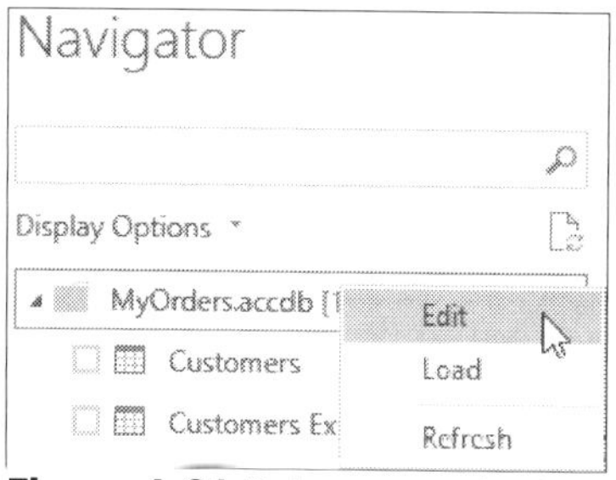

Figure 4-81 Data source shortcut menu

Use The Metadata Query To View Data

1. Rename the My Orders accdb query to `My Orders database tables`.

2. Right-click on a Table link, in the **DATA COLUMN**. You will see the shortcut menu shown in Figure 4-82.

Figure 4-82 Database metadata in the Query Editor

The options on the shortcut menu are explained in Table 4-13, at the end of this exercise.

3. In the Data column, click to the right of the **TABLE LINK**, of the table or view that you want to see the data of.

   In the grid below the table, you will be able to view some of the data, as shown at the bottom of Figure 4-83.

   To make the grid larger, place the mouse pointer above the grid, as illustrated in the figure, and drag the bar up.

   To close the grid, click on a blank space in the query.

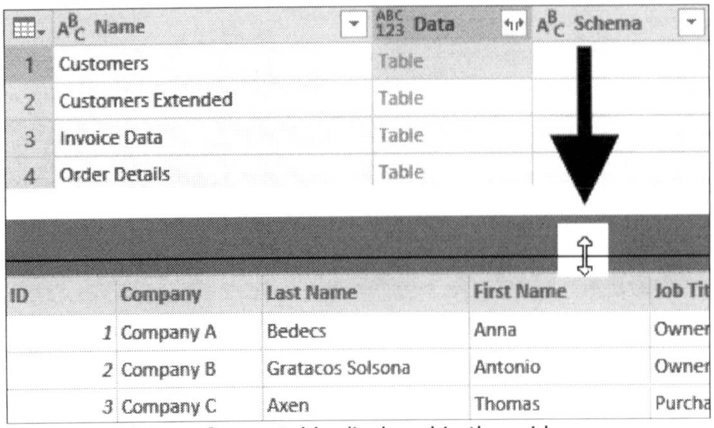

Figure 4-83 Data from a table displayed in the grid

4. Save the file as `E4.3 List of tables`.

Data Column Shortcut Menu Options

Option	Description
Copy	Nothing is copied because the Table link displays the data in the table.
Drill Down	Displays the data for the table or view.
Add as New Query	Creates a query for the selected table or view.

Table 4-13 Data column shortcut menu options explained

Summary

This chapter introduced you to the Query Editor and explained the transformations on the Home tab. The exercises showed you how to use some of the most popular transformations on the Home tab. Hopefully, you are thinking about how to use the transformations with your own data.

My Views On The Query Editor

① I think the Query Editor should be used with the Data view, not instead of.

② As much as possible, keep the Query Editor formulas to a minimum. Formulas that you create in the Query Editor should be to transform data, opposed to creating calculated columns of data.

③ It is better to create a measure or calculated column in the Data view because measures automatically adjust to accommodate filter and slicer selections. This makes measures dynamic.

④ It has been reported that the Query Editor calculations (custom columns) can run slow or increase the data model size significantly. I tested this by recreating DAX formulas using the M language in the Query Editor and the query took a long time to process the data.

⑤ Merged queries in the Query Editor (aka a **FLATTENED TABLE**), that are loaded into the data model are not the best option, because the data model was designed to use data from multiple tables, to create a chart or report, meaning that the lookup data should not be in the same table, as the main data.

⑥ **M FORMULAS** are only recalculated when the data is refreshed.

Don't Be Overwhelmed I understand that the concept of data cleansing can be a bit much to grasp at first. After viewing your data, make a short list by table of the changes that need to be made. If you break down the process into smaller groups of tasks, it will be easier to accomplish all of the tasks. Below is an example of how to group the list of changes that you write down. Start with the changes in your list that fit into Task 1 below, then move to your changes that fit into Task 2 and so on. While the topics listed in the tasks below do not cover every change that may be on your list, you will be well on your way.

Think of it in terms of remodeling a house. Task 1 is cleaning the house, by getting rid of what you don't want or need. Tasks 2 and 3 is fixing each room in the house. Task 4 is adding new rooms, if needed.

Task 1: Delete rows and columns that are not needed, delete duplicate records.

Task 2: Rename columns, filter data if necessary, reorder the columns.

Task 3: Change the data type, modify the data by filling in empty cells if possible, remove or add formatting of numeric values, confirm that date fields have the data type that you need.

Task 4: Merge or append data, add calculated columns, group data.

While creating reports is beyond the scope of this book, on your own, once you have finished transforming the data, the best way to determine if you have made all of the necessary changes, is to create a report. To test the data, you do not have to add all of the formatting to the test report. If you can add the fields that you need to each section of the Visualizations panel on the Report view, to create the type of report that you need and the data looks correct, there is a very good chance that you have completed all of the necessary transformations.

If there are totals that a report needs, that cannot be created in the Query Editor with the built-in aggregations, or on the Report View, you may have to learn DAX to create the calculations.

My 2 Cents On The Load Data vs Edit Data Options

If you know that the tables that you select will be used to create a report, select the Load option. If you are not sure, even after viewing some of the data on the Navigator or Combine Files dialog box, select the Edit button. I just don't want you to get hung up trying to decide which option to select, because you can delete any table that has been loaded into the data model, whenever you decide to. I always load the tables, just to be consistent. <smile>

Learning To Create Transformations

While I have not seen this, it is possible that you could create a data model that does not need any transformations, to be able to create the reports that are needed. If you are still reading this chapter, it means that you know that on your own, you will need to create at least a few transformations for reporting needs.

For some, learning to create transformations can be intimidating. **LEARNING TO CREATE TRANSFORMATIONS REQUIRES TIME, PATIENCE, DEDICATION AND ATTENTION TO DETAIL**. The reality is that you will make some mistakes along the way. One mistake that many people make is trying to run before they crawl, if you know what I mean. While the exercises and examples in this book, do not require you to understand the raw data that is used to create the transformations, on your own, you will find it easier to know which transformation(s) to use, if you understand the data that you are using.

The way to learn about transformations is by creating them. Just reading what the transformations do and looking at the figures in this book, really won't cut it. That is because on your own, you will not have a foundation to draw from, to know whether or not a transformation produces the values that you are expecting. Just because a transformation does not generate an error, does not mean that it is providing the right values.

I am not saying this to be mean. I just know what it takes to learn Power Query. Completing the exercises, will let you get a feel for what it is like to create the transformations that you need, on your own.

Hopefully, knowing that creating transformations cannot hurt "live data", by making a copy of the data and using the copy to create and test your transformations on, will put you at ease.

If you think that I created all of the transformation examples and exercises in this book correctly on the first try, you are sadly mistaken. <smile> Sometimes, just getting the syntax right for some formulas, can stop you for 10 plus minutes. If you have a fear of making mistakes, this is the time to let go of the fear, because the fear will prevent you from learning.

It is also normal to initially get confused on what to do next. Even though you may not understand why you are being instructed to do something, the steps in each exercise will allow you to achieve the expected result. This is how you will begin to build a foundation for creating transformations on your own.

CREATING FILTERS, CUSTOM COLUMNS AND FORMULAS

In this chapter you will learn how to complete the following tasks, using the Query Editor:

- ☑ Create different types of filters
- ☑ Create custom columns
- ☑ Create calculations
- ☑ Use the IF function

CHAPTER 5

Using Filters

Filters have several uses, including the following:

① To select records that should be displayed on a report.

② To select records that have incorrect data.

③ To find records that need to be updated or records that need to be deleted.

Filter Options

In the previous chapter you saw some of the filter options that are available in the Query Editor. The filter options are like the ones Excel and Power Pivot.

Clicking the arrow button at the end of a column header in the Query Editor, displays filter options like the ones shown in Figure 5-1.

These options are used to change the order that records are displayed in or reduce the number of records that are displayed in the query.

The **REMOVE EMPTY OPTION**, filters out (does not display) rows that have an empty or null value in the column.

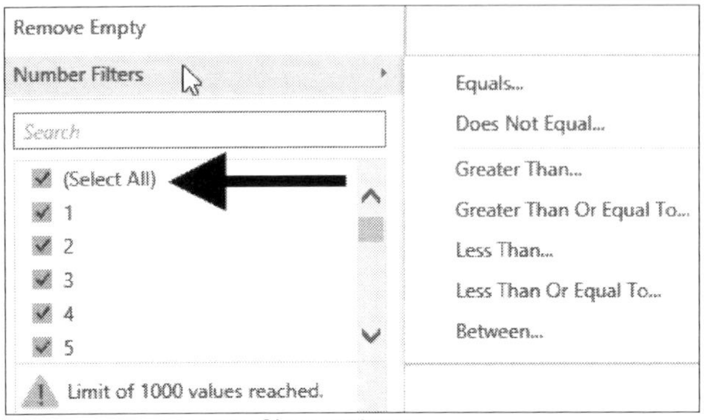

Figure 5-1 Numeric filter options

What you will find is that there are two ways to filter data in the Query Editor, as explained below.

① By selecting one or more values at the bottom of a filter shortcut menu, like the one shown above, on the left side of Figure 5-1.

② By creating filter criteria, as shown later in Figure 5-4.

The **LIMIT OF 1000 VALUES REACHED** message, shown above in Figure 5-1 or the **LIST MAY BE INCOMPLETE** message, shown in Figure 5-2, indicates that all of the values in the column are not displayed in the list. By default, the Query Editor displays the first 1,000 unique values in the column.

Clicking the **LOAD MORE LINK**, shown in Figure 5-2, loads the next 1,000 unique values in the column.

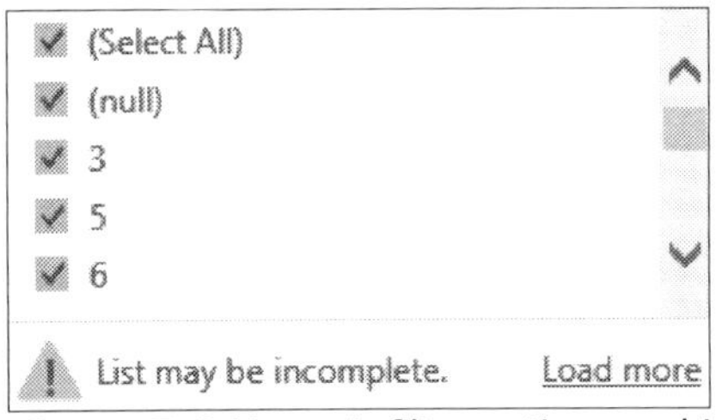

Figure 5-2 Numeric filter options and List incomplete message

Using The (Select All), (Null) And (Blank) Filter Options

By default, the (Select All) and (Null) options are checked, as illustrated earlier in Figure 5-1.

When checked, the **(SELECT ALL)** option causes all of the options below it to also be checked. If you clear this option, the check mark for all of the options below it are also cleared. This is helpful when you only want to use a few of the options to filter the data, because you can select them one by one.

The **(NULL)** option shown in Figure 5-2, indicates that there are null values in the column. Clear this option when you do not want rows with a null value, in the selected column, to be displayed. Null values are in numeric fields.

The **(BLANK)** option shown in Figure 5-3, indicates that there are rows of data that do not have a value in the selected field. You will see this option for text fields.

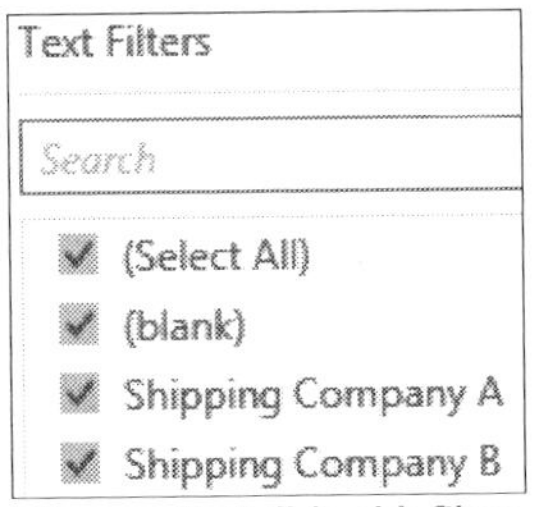

Figure 5-3 (blank) filter option

Creating Filters
While there is definitely a need to create filters, keep in mind that filters, like all other transformations, are created for the purpose of creating reports. If all of the reports that will be created, that are based on the query that the filter is being created for, need the data filtered, then you will not run into a problem. On my own, instead of trying to anticipate what future reporting needs will be, I create one query for each report. This gives me the freedom to tailor the query specifically for one report.

Basic Filter Criteria

Selecting one of the filter options on the right side of Figure 5-1, opens the dialog box shown in Figure 5-4. The filter option that you select, is displayed in the first drop-down list on the dialog box. Select the other filter options that will display the data that you need.

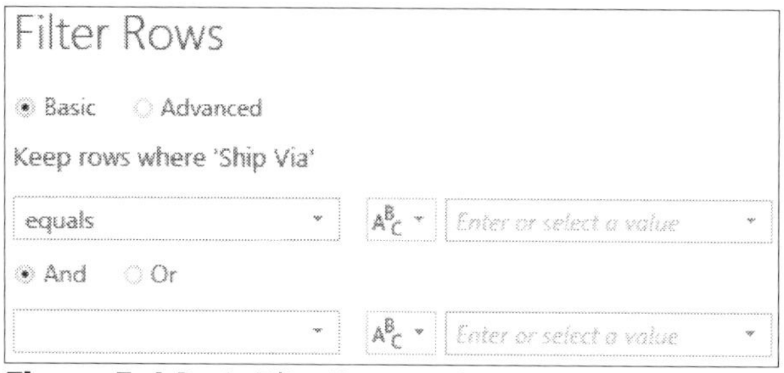

Figure 5-4 Basic Filter Rows options

The AND and OR operators are used to create two or more conditions to filter on. Basic filter criteria (as shown in Figure 5-4), only allows one of these operators to be used. If you need to use both, select the Advanced option.

Select **AND** when the data must meet both filter conditions. This reduces the rows of data that will be displayed. Select **OR** when the data only needs to meet one of the filter conditions to be displayed. This increases the number of rows of data that will be displayed, because the data only needs to meet one of the filter conditions. The Advanced Filter Rows options are covered later in this chapter.

Using The Filter Rows Transformation
Use the dialog box shown above in Figure 5-4, when selecting values from the field, shown earlier, on the left side of Figure 5-1, will not handle your needs. All of the options (on the right side of Figure 5-1) open the Filter Rows dialog box, just like selecting the Custom Filter option, (shown below at the bottom of Figure 5-5). The difference is that if an operator is selected before opening the Filter Rows dialog box, the operator is displayed on the dialog box. You can select a different operator once the dialog box is open.

Filter Data In The Query Editor

In addition to reducing the number of rows of data that are added to the data model, filtering data is also helpful when you want to analyze the data before adding it to the data model.

Figure 5-5 shows the filter functions for date fields.

The date and time functions use the computers current date and time, as part of the formula. If the formula evaluates to True, meaning the date in the field meets the criteria, the record is selected.

CUSTOM FILTER Select this option when the other filter options on the shortcut menu are not sufficient enough to create the filter that you need. Selecting this option also opens the Filter Rows dialog box shown above in Figure 5-4.

The options shown in Figure 5-6 are the **MONTH FILTER OPTIONS** that can be selected.

Figure 5-5 Query Editor date and time functions

Figure 5-6 Month submenu filter options

Using The Search Field To Filter Data

Scrolling through the list of values at the bottom of the filter list can be exhausting.

If you do not want to scroll, type the first few characters of the value that you are looking for in the **SEARCH** field, illustrated in Figure 5-7. This will reduce the number of values in the list.

As shown in the figure, the search returns all entries that have the characters in the order that you typed them in, anywhere in the field. It does not matter whether or not the Select All option is checked.

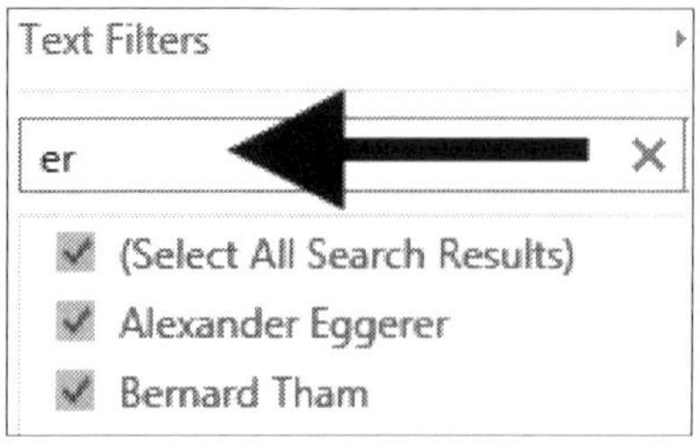

Figure 5-7 Search field filter results

Text Functions

The functions explained in Table 5-1 are used to create filter criteria for text data.

Function	Selects Records That . . .
Equals	Match the text entered.
Does Not Equal	Do not match the text entered.
Begins With	Have the text entered at the beginning of the field.
Does Not Begin With	Do not have the text entered at the beginning of the field.
Ends With	Have the text entered at the end of the field.
Does Not End With	Do not have the text entered at the end of the field.
Contains	Have the text any place in the field.
Does Not Contain	Do not have the text any place in the field.

Table 5-1 Text functions explained

Numeric Functions

The functions explained in Table 5-2 are used to create filter criteria for numeric data.

Function	Selects Records That . . .
Equals	Match the value entered.
Does Not Equal	Do not match the value entered.
Greater Than	Have a value larger than the value entered.
Greater Than Or Equal To	Have the same value entered or a value larger than the value entered.
Less Than	Have a value smaller than the value entered.
Less Than Or Equal To	Have the same value entered or a value smaller than the value entered.
Between	Have a value that is in the range selected.

Table 5-2 Numeric functions explained

Date And Time Functions

The functions explained in Table 5-3 are used to create filter criteria for date and time data.

Function	Selects Records That . . .
Equals	Have the date entered.
Before	Have a date earlier than the date entered.
After	Have a date later than the date entered.
Between	Have a date in the range selected.
In the Next	Have a date in the future range selected. (1)
In the Previous	Have a date in the past range selected. (1)
Is Earliest	Have the oldest date in the column. (2)
Is Latest	Have the most recent date in the column. (2)
Is Not Earliest	Do not have the oldest dates in the column.
Is Not Latest	Do not have the most current dates in the column.
Next Year	Have a date in the next year. (3)
This Year	Have a date in the current year. (3)
Last Year	Have a date in the previous year. (3)

Table 5-3 Date and Time functions explained

Function	Selects Records That . . .
Year To Date	Have a date from January 1 of the current year through today. (3)
Next Quarter	Have a date in the next calendar quarter. (4)
This Quarter	Have a date in the current calendar quarter. (4)
Last Quarter	Have a date in the previous calendar quarter. (4)
Specific Quarter	Have a date in the quarter selected, based on the option selected in Figure 5-9. (4)
Next Month	Have a date in the next calendar month. (5)
This Month	Have a date in the current calendar month. (5)
Last Month	Have a date in the previous calendar month. (5)
Specific Month	Have a date in the month selected on the list shown earlier in Figure 5-6. The year does not matter. (5)
Next Week	Have a date in the next calendar week. (6)
This Week	Have a date in the current calendar week. (6)
Last Week	Have a date in the previous calendar week. (6)
Tomorrow	Have the next days date. (7)
Today	Have the current date. (7)
Yesterday	Have the previous days date. (7)
Next Hour	Have a time within the next hour. (8)
This Hour	Have a time within the current hour. (8)
Last Hour	Have a time within the previous hour. (8)
Next Minute	Have a time within the next minute. (9)
This Minute	Have a time within the current minute. (9)
Last Minute	Have a time within the previous minute. (9)
Next Second	Have a time within the next second. (10)
This Second	Have a time within the current second. (10)
Last Second	Have a time within the previous second. (10)
Custom Filter	Have a date that meets the criteria that you create on the Filter Rows dialog box.

Table 5-3 Date and Time functions explained (Continued)

(1) The **IN THE NEXT** and **IN THE PREVIOUS** functions are used to filter dates in seconds, minutes, hours, days, weeks, months, quarters or years. Both functions have the filter options shown in Figure 5-8.
(2) This function is dynamic, which means that different rows can be retrieved each time the data is refreshed.
(3) This function is on the **YEAR** sub menu, shown earlier in Figure 5-5, and is used as a date range.
(4) This function is on the **QUARTER** sub menu, shown in Figure 5-9 and is used as a date range.
(5) This function is on the **MONTH** sub menu, shown earlier in Figure 5-6, and is used as a date range.
(6) This function is on the **WEEK** sub menu, shown earlier in Figure 5-5, and is used as a date range.
(7) This function is on the **DAY** sub menu, shown earlier in Figure 5-5, and is used as a date range.
(8) This function is on the **HOUR** submenu, shown earlier in Figure 5-5.
(9) This function is on the **MINUTE** submenu, shown earlier in Figure 5-5.
(10) This function is on the **SECOND** submenu, shown earlier in Figure 5-5.

Figure 5-8 In the Next and In the Previous options

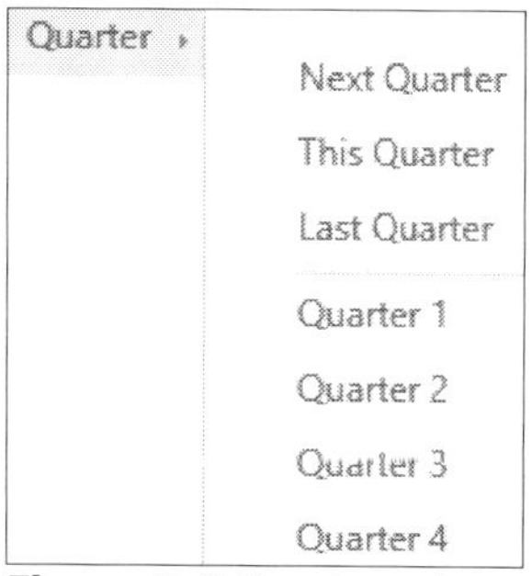

Figure 5-9 Quarter submenu options

Shaping The Data

Depending on the amount and condition of the data, it could take some time to get the data ready to be analyzed or used to create reports. To accomplish this task, in addition to figuring out which fields have data that needs to be cleaned, you need a game plan (a process) to get everything done. As you will see, these tasks need to be done in a somewhat specific order. Yes, there is some wiggle room to change the order, without putting the data in more disarray, then it is already in.

While cleaning the data, make note of items that fall into the categories of consistent missing data and incorrect data entry. The first steps that I take to clean data are listed below. These steps are often referred to as **SHAPING THE DATA**.

① Filter out the columns and rows that are not needed. Filtering data is a popular option for reducing the number of rows.
② Bring in any other data that is needed by using the merge and append options. On my own, I skip the merge portion of this task because I prefer to use the **RELATIONSHIPS VIEW** to join tables.
③ Create calculated columns as needed (only if the data is not going to be loaded into the data model). On my own, I create all formulas in DAX, on the Data view.
④ Give the list of missing and/or incorrect data issues to the appropriate departments, so that they can fix the recurring data problems.

Exercise 5.1: Use The Filter Options In The Query Editor

In this exercise you will learn how to filter data by filtering the Stores table to only display stores in the United States that have less than 30 employees, that are still open.

1. Save the E2.4 file as `E5.1 Filter data`.

2. Duplicate the Stores query ⇒ Rename the query to `1 Filter Stores`.

3. Display the filter list for the Region Country Name column ⇒

   Clear the (Select All) option ⇒

   Scroll down the list and check the United States option, as shown in Figure 5-10 ⇒

   Click OK. The number of rows displayed, has been reduced.

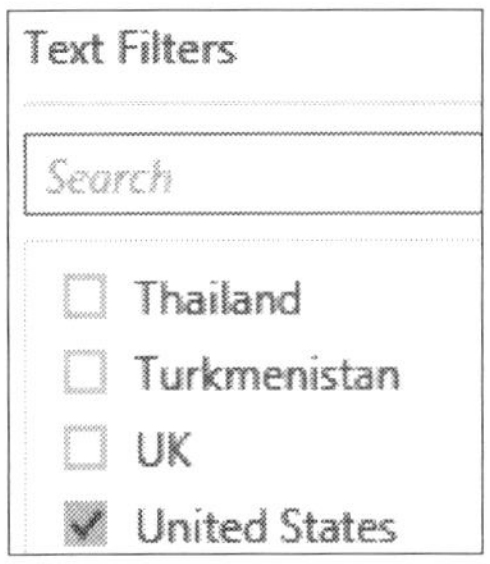

Figure 5-10 Region Country Name column filter options

4. Open the filter for the Employee Count column ⇒ Select the Number Filters option ⇒ Select Less Than.

5. Type `30` in the field, as shown in Figure 5-11 ⇒ Click OK.

   Notice that the table now displays 147 rows of data.

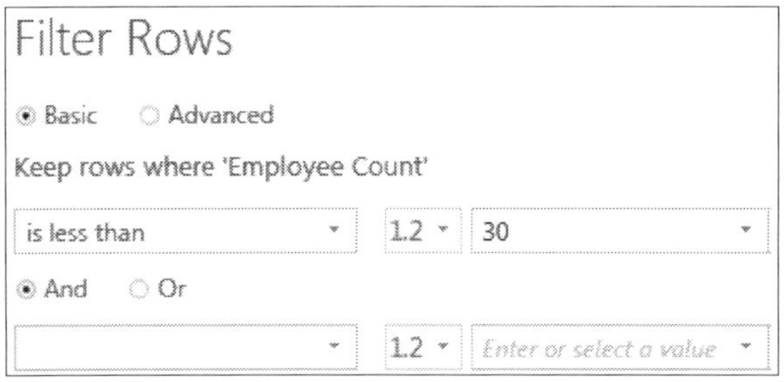

Figure 5-11 Employee Count column custom filter options

6. Open the filter for the Close Date column ⇒ Clear the (Select All) option ⇒ Check the **(NULL)** option. In this exercise, a null value means that the store is still open. ⇒ Click OK.

Based on all of the filters that you created in this query, out of the 306 stores in the table, there are 137 stores in the United States that are open and have less than 30 employees.

Create Date And Text Filters

In this part of the exercise, you will learn how to create a filter that selects dates that fall within a range and a text filter that selects multiple values.

1. Display the Orders query ⇒ Order Date field filter ⇒ Date/Time Filters ⇒ Between.

2. On the first row type `03/01/2006`.

   On the second row type `12/31/2006`, as shown in Figure 5-12.

   All of the rows displayed in the query, will have an order date in the range shown in the figure.

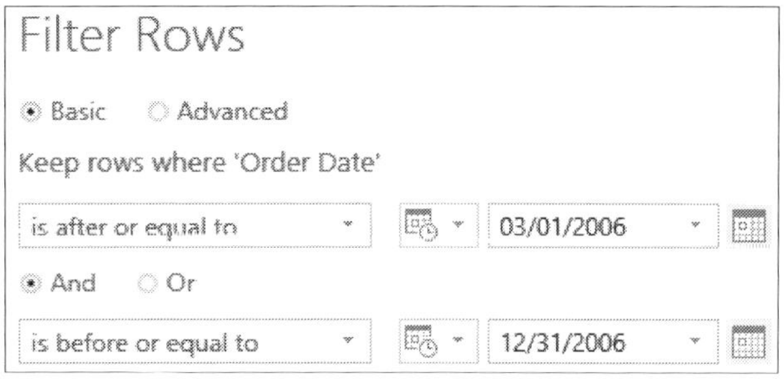

Figure 5-12 Filter options for a date field

Create Filters For More Than One Column

In this part of the exercise, you will create filters for two columns in the same query.

1. Display the Stores query ⇒ Create a filter for the Open Date field, that the date has to be before 12/31/2005.
2. Create a filter for the State Province Name field. The value has to be Florida, Texas or Virginia. There should be 54 rows in the query.
3. Apply and save the changes to the file.

Exercise 5.2: Create A Custom Filter

This exercise will show you how to create custom filters to only display records with a Unit Cost between $1 and $100 and a Discount Quantity between 3 and 4 percent.

1. Save the E2.3 file as `E5.2 Custom filters`.
2. Delete all of the queries except the Fact Sales Txt query ⇒ Display the Fact Sales Txt query.
3. Open the Unit Cost filter drop-down list ⇒ Select the **BETWEEN** function.
4. Type `1` in the field across from the Is greater than or equal to function.

   Type `100` in the field across from the Is less than or equal to function. You should have the options shown in Figure 5-13.

   The values that you just typed in do not have to be in the table, because this criteria is creating a range of values that are acceptable.

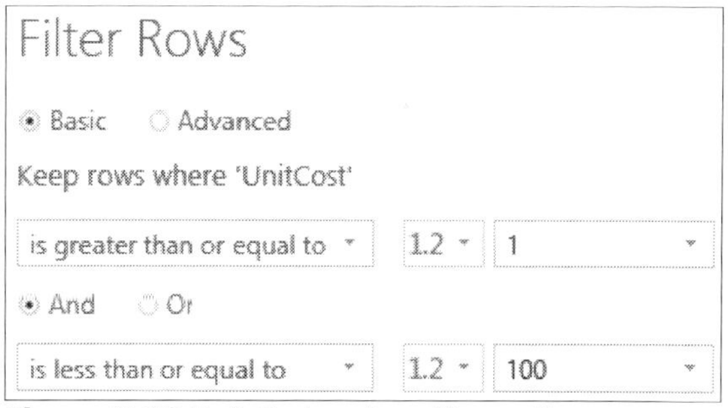

Figure 5-13 Unit Cost custom filter options

   Even though you can't see the exact number of how many rows are in the table, in the Query Editor, the number of rows has been reduced to 1.2 million from over 2.2 million.

Create Another Custom Filter

In this part of the exercise, you will create a filter to only display records that have a Discount Quantity between 3 and 4 percent.

1. Open the Discount Quantity filter drop-down list ⇒ Select the Between function.
2. On the first row type `3` ⇒ On the second row type `4`.
3. Apply the changes.

> **Text Filters Can Be Case Sensitive**
> By default, when you create a filter for a text field that has had the data type changed to Text, the field is case sensitive, meaning typing "Beverages" vs "beverages" will return different results. For example, if the Category column had the data type changed to text and all of the entries started with a capital letter and you typed beverages, all lower case, no records would be retrieved. If the data type for the column has not been changed, you can type either.
>
> There is no option (at least that I could find), to force the search to be **CASE INSENSITIVE**. The only solution that I know is to modify the M formula to force the filter formula to be case insensitive. Figure 5-14 shows the formula with the filter criteria in all lower case letters. Figure 5-15 shows the revised formula, with the **COMPARER.ORDINALIGNORECASE** argument needed to make the filter, case insensitive.

```
= Table.SelectRows(_Products, each Text.StartsWith([Category], "beverages"))
```

Figure 5-14 Case sensitive filter formula

```
= Table.SelectRows(_Products, each Text.StartsWith([Category], "beverages", Comparer.OrdinalIgnoreCase))
```

Figure 5-15 Case insensitive filter formula

Advanced Filter Criteria

If the basic filter options shown earlier in Figure 5-13, do not let you create the filter criteria that you need, select the **ADVANCED OPTION** at the top of the Filter Rows dialog box. This will display the options shown in Figure 5-16.

The options are used to create more than two sets of criteria for the same field or criteria for multiple fields.

Dates can be selected by clicking the Calendar button. When clicked, the current month and year are displayed.

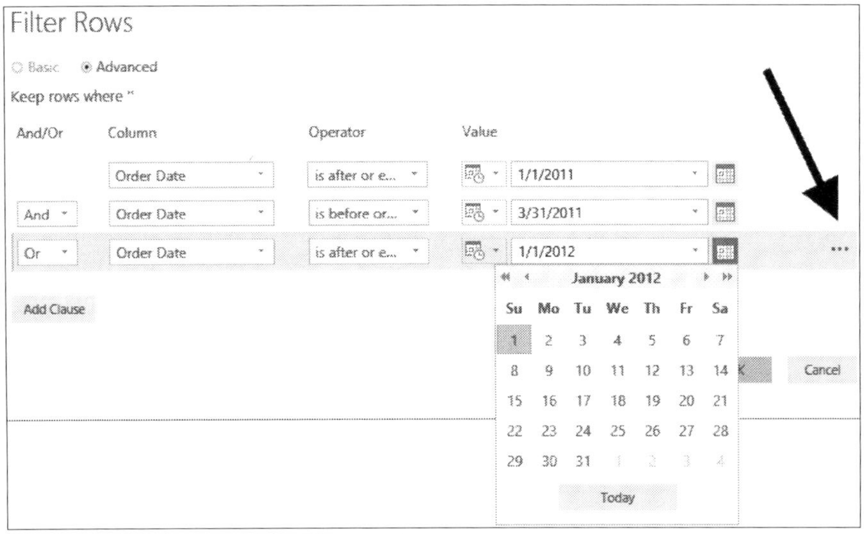

Figure 5-16 Advanced Filter Rows options

Click the arrow to the left of the month to select a date in the past. Click the arrow to the right of the year to select a date in the future.

The **ELLIPSIS BUTTON**, illustrated above in Figure 5-16, is used to move or delete the selected filter criteria.

The **ADD CLAUSE BUTTON** adds another row, so that more filter criteria can be created.

The criteria shown in the figure will select records that have an order date between 1/1/2011 and 3/31/2011 **OR** an order date greater than or equal to 1/1/2012.

Exercise 5.3: Create Advanced Filter Criteria

In this exercise you will learn how to use the Advanced filter options.

Create Advanced Date Filters

In this part of the exercise, you will create multiple date filters. The filters that you will create will select records that fall into one of two date ranges.

1. Save the E2.6 file as `E5.3 Advanced filter options`.

2. Select the Orders table ⇒ Display the filter options for the Order Date column ⇒ Select the Between option.

3. Next to the Is after or equal to option, type `1/1/2011` ⇒ In the next field, type `3/31/2011`. Don't click OK. This criteria will select records with an Order date in the first quarter of 2011.

4. Select the Advanced option ⇒ Click the **ADD CLAUSE BUTTON**.

5. Open the Operator drop-down list for the last Order Date field ⇒ Select **IS AFTER OR EQUAL TO** ⇒ Type `1/1/2012` in the Value field.

6. Because the goal of the filter is to select records that fall into either criteria range, the second And/Or operator needs to be changed. Change the last And operator to **OR**. You should have the options shown earlier in Figure 5-16 ⇒ Click OK.

7. Sort the Order Date column in ascending order ⇒ If you scroll through the records, you will see that all of the order dates are within one of the ranges that you created.

Create Advanced Text And Numeric Filters

In this part of the exercise, you will learn how to create a filter that selects customers in the USA that have a last years sales amount greater than $20,000 or less than $5,000.

1. Display the filter options for the Country column in the Customer table ⇒ Select the Equals filter option ⇒ Select USA in the second drop-down list on the first row.

2. Select the Advanced option ⇒ Click the Add Clause button.

3. Open the second Column drop-down list ⇒ Select the Last Years Sales field ⇒ Change the Operator to **IS GREATER THAN OR EQUAL TO** ⇒ In the Value field type `20000`.

4. On the last row, change the And/Or operator to **OR** ⇒ Select the Last Years Sales field ⇒ Change the operator to **IS LESS THAN OR EQUAL TO** ⇒ In the Value field type `5000`.

   You should have the options shown in Figure 5-17.

   128 records should be displayed in the Customer query.

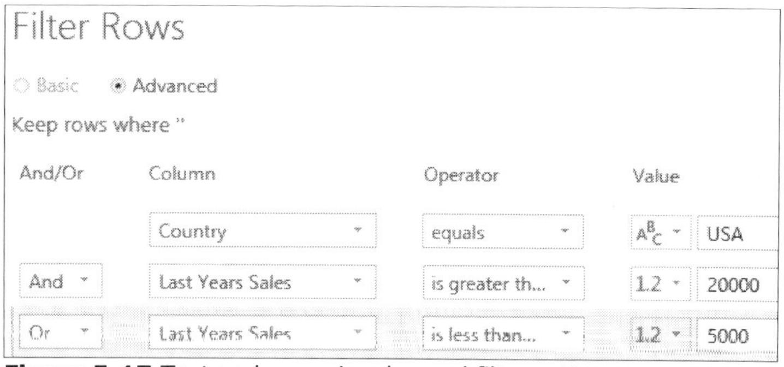

Figure 5-17 Text and numeric advanced filter options

Custom Columns

Custom columns are used to add more data to a table. A custom column in the Query Editor is similar to a **(DAX) CALCULATED COLUMN** in the Data view. It is not a requirement to create custom columns in the Query Editor. I personally prefer to create all calculations in the Data view, instead of some in the Query Editor and some in the Data view, if for no other reason then I only have to look in one place to view and edit all of the formulas. Custom columns are used to:

① Extract part of the data in an existing column
② Create new data
③ Join or combine data from existing columns

Formulas created in the Query Editor look similar to formulas created in Excel. The biggest difference is that in Power BI Desktop and the Query Editor, column names are used in the formulas, instead of cell references. The column names must be enclosed in brackets. Other differences between Excel formulas and Custom columns include the following:

① The data type is a factor in creating a custom column. If there is a data type mismatch, you have to use what is known as a **CONVERSION FUNCTION**, like **NUMBER.TOTEXT** to create the formula.
② A formula created in the Query Editor is case sensitive.
③ There are no tool tips or auto complete options to help you create a formula, using the Custom Column dialog box.

Custom Column Options

This dialog box is used to create expressions (a custom column). These expressions can be based on constant values and values from other data in the same row. The fields in the **AVAILABLE COLUMNS** list are from the query displayed on the Query Editor. To add a field to the formula, select it in the list, then click the Insert button or double-click on the field in the list. The new column is automatically added to the end of the query in the Query Editor.

> A feature that I think is really cool is that if you add a column to a table (using the Merge feature) that is only needed to create a calculation, after the calculation is created, the column that was only added to the query to be used in the calculation can be deleted. Once deleted, the calculation still works because the calculation is saved as a step. And the deleted column action is in a step below the calculation step. This type of calculation and processing cannot be done in Excel.

Exercise 5.4: Add Columns To A Table

In this exercise, you will learn how to create different types of expressions to create data that is usually not stored in a table.

Create A Total Calculated Column

In this part of the exercise, you will create a custom column to calculate the line item total for each row in the Order Details query.

1. Save the E2.4 file as `E5.4 Add columns and use the IF function`.
2. Display the Order Details query.
3. Add Column tab ⇒ Custom Column button ⇒ In the New column name field, type `LineTotal`.
4. In the Available columns list, double-click on the Quantity field ⇒ Type a * after the Quantity field in the formula.

> **Custom Column Error Messages**
> While you are creating the formula for a custom column, you will often see one of the error messages shown in Figure 5-18. You can ignore the error messages until you have finished creating the formula, and the OK button is enabled, on the Custom Column dialog box. If you have finished creating the formula and there is an error message, there is a problem with the formula that you need to fix.

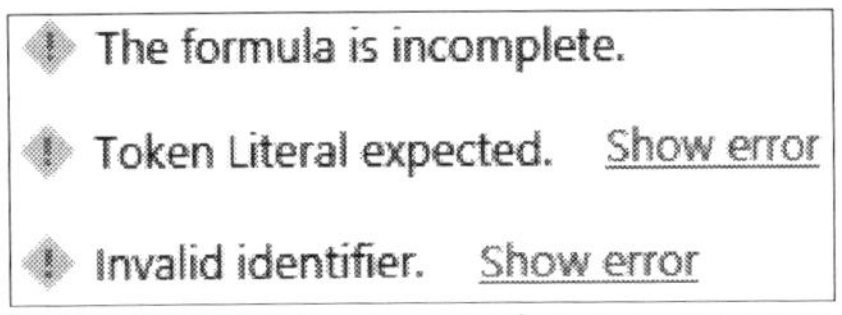

Figure 5-18 Custom Column error messages

5. Double-click on the Unit Price field, in the Available columns list. You should have the formula shown in Figure 5-19 ⇒ Click OK.

   The **LEARN ABOUT POWER BI DESKTOP FORMULAS LINK**, opens a web page that has links for the formula categories, functions and syntax. These documents are helpful if you want to learn about the **M LANGUAGE FUNCTIONS**.

6. Scroll to the far right of the Order Details query. You should see the Line Total column, shown in Figure 5-20. Click in the column. The M formula that you created is in the formula bar. Leave the file open to complete the rest of the exercise.

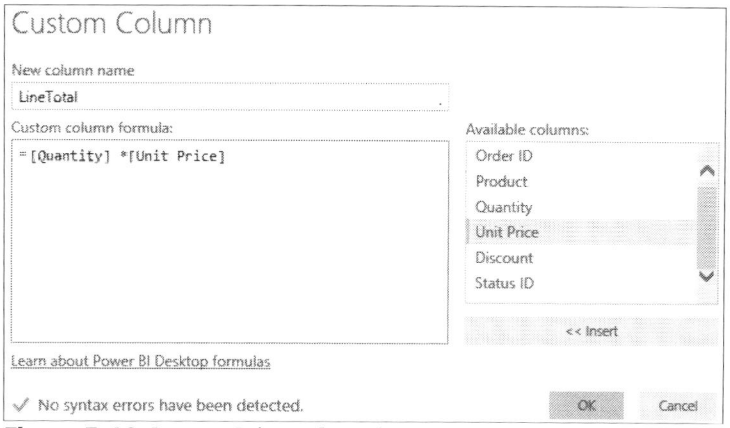

Figure 5-19 Custom Column formula

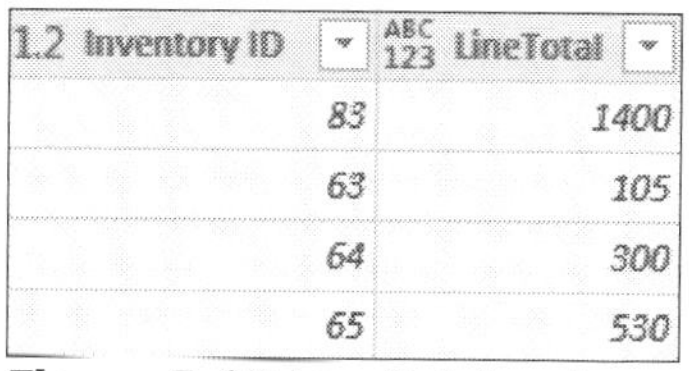

Figure 5-20 Line Total custom column

Congratulations! You just created new data for the query and your first **M FORMULA**. As you see, you can create basic M formulas without knowing a lot about the M language.

Combine Columns Of Data

There may be times when you need to display data from two or more fields together, as one field. A common use of this type of formula is to combine the first and last name fields into one, so that the full name can be displayed together. That is the formula that you will create in this part of the exercise.

1. Display the Customers query.

2. Open the Custom Column dialog box ⇒ In the New column name field, type `FullName`.

3. Click after the equal sign in the formula field and type `[First Name] & " " & [Last Name]`, as shown in Figure 5-21.

   Make sure that there is a space between the quotes. The space between the quotes will place a space between the first and last name fields when they are combined into one field.

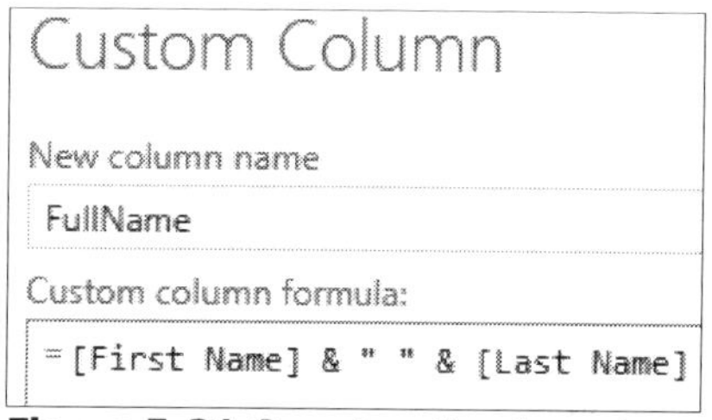

Figure 5-21 Concatenation formula

Figure 5-22 shows the data from the combined fields in one column in the table.

While part of the exercise showed you how to create a formula to combine the data in two columns to create a new column, the Add Column tab ⇒ Merge Columns option can create the same new field.

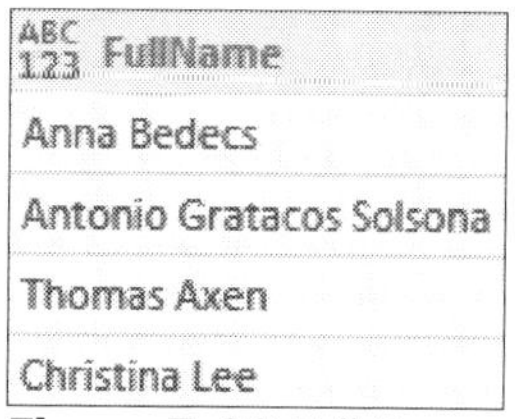

Figure 5-22 Full Name custom column

What Is A Function?

Functions are prewritten, built-in formulas or procedures. The functions that Power BI Desktop supports have been thoroughly tested and from what I can tell, they are error free. However, this does not mean that if there is bad data in a table, that you won't have a problem with the function. If you do not follow the syntax rules or fill in the arguments correctly, when using the function, an error will be generated.

Combine The First Initial And Last Name

The previous part of this exercise showed you how to combine data from two columns. This part of the exercise, will show you how to select the first character from the First Name field and combine it with the Last Name field.

The **TEXT.START FUNCTION** starts at the beginning of the data in the field and extracts a specific number of characters.

1. Display the Customers query.

2. Open the Custom Column dialog box ⇒ Create the formula shown in Figure 5-23. The new column should look like the one shown in Figure 5-24.

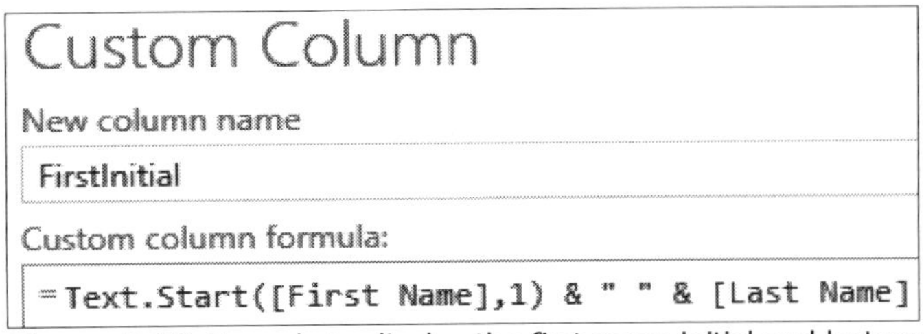

Figure 5-23 Formula to display the first name initial and last name

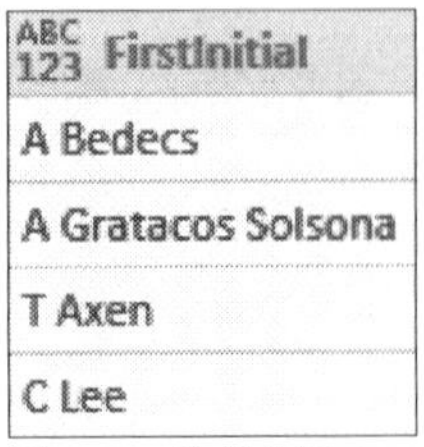

Figure 5-24 Data combined from two columns

Use The IF Function To Create A Formula With Conditional Logic

The **IF FUNCTION** is used to create a conditional formula. It tests to see if the condition that you specify is true or not. Based on the result of the test, different actions are taken.

This function checks the value in a field to see if it meets the criteria in the formula. If the value meets the criteria, the first argument after the criteria, in the formula, is performed. If the value does not meet the criteria, the second argument after the criteria is performed. If you have used the **IF . . . THEN . . . ELSE STATEMENT** in other software, you will see that the IF function in Power BI Desktop works the same way.

The formula that you will create in this part of the exercise will check to see if the shipped date is greater than the order date plus two days. If it is, display "Shipped Late" in the cell, otherwise, display "On Time" in the cell.

1. Display the Orders query.

2. On the Custom Column dialog box, type `Order Shipped On Time`, as the column name.

3. Type the formula shown in Figure 5-25. You can add the fields in brackets, by double-clicking on them in the Available columns list. The column should look like the one shown in Figure 5-26.

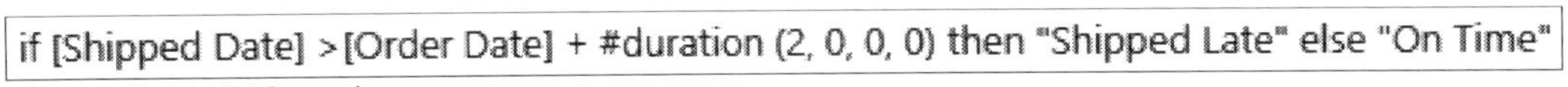

Figure 5-25 IF formula

The cells in the column that have the word "Error", represent rows where one of the fields used in the formula has no value or a null value.

In reality, a formula should be created to verify that both of the fields used in the formula that you just created have data. If either is null, the calculated column should display something like "missing data", so that the person analyzing the data will be alerted to the fact that there is a problem with the data.

Hopefully, when someone sees a message like that, on a report, they will fix the data.

Figure 5-26 Order shipped on time calculated column

The #duration(2, code in the formula, adds two days to the Order Date. You can use any duration number. 2 days, is just what I selected to demonstrate the concept with.

The formula (in Figure 5-25) translates to: If the Order Date is 9/6/14 and if the Shipped Date is 9/19/14, "Shipped Late" will be added to the cell for the row because the Order Date +2 returns a date of 9/8/14, which is the expected ship date. Any date that is greater than 9/8/14 in this example, is considered to be shipped late.

When you apply the changes, you will see the warning shown in Figure 5-27. In the Queries panel, you will see a new group named "Query Errors" and a query named "Error in Orders".

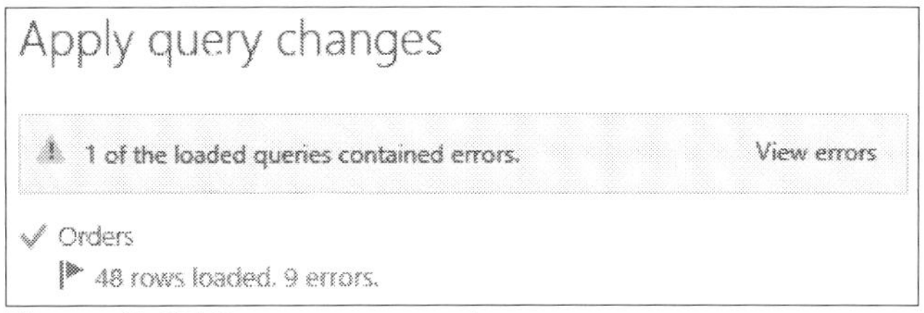

Figure 5-27 Query error warning

Because the formula field on the Add Custom Column dialog box ignores spaces, you can type a formula on multiple lines, as shown in Figure 5-28, instead of typing the formula on one line.

I find formulas that are on multiple lines are easier to read. Doing this is optional.

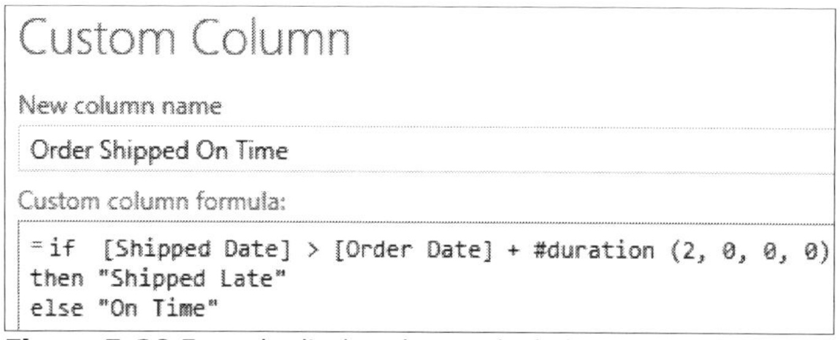

Figure 5-28 Formula displayed on multiple lines

Cell Level Errors

It is very possible that while you are transforming data, you will get a cell level error, as shown earlier in Figure 5-27. This can happen for a variety of reasons, including the following:

☑ Changing the data type from text to a number.

☑ All of the values in the column cannot be converted to the new data type that you select.

Unless fixed, cells that have an error will be loaded into the data model, as a null value. Doing this allows the rest of the data in the column to be updated. The warning message shown earlier in Figure 5-27, displays a count of errors for each query that is being loaded.

Clicking on the **VIEW ERRORS LINK**, shown earlier in Figure 5-27, displays the errors in Orders query, as shown in Figure 5-29. As shown, an index column is added to the query (the Row Number column in Figure 5-29), that displays the row number that has an error.

If you click on the Error link, shown in Figure 5-29, you will see an error message, similar to the one shown in Figure 5 30. This should lead you in the right direction to either fix a step in the query or change the data in the data source.

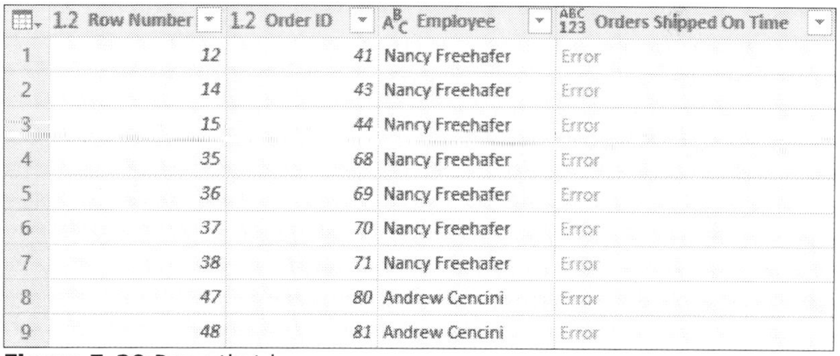

	1.2 Row Number	1.2 Order ID	ABC Employee	ABC 123 Orders Shipped On Time
1	12	41	Nancy Freehafer	Error
2	14	43	Nancy Freehafer	Error
3	15	44	Nancy Freehafer	Error
4	35	68	Nancy Freehafer	Error
5	36	69	Nancy Freehafer	Error
6	37	70	Nancy Freehafer	Error
7	38	71	Nancy Freehafer	Error
8	47	80	Andrew Cencini	Error
9	48	81	Andrew Cencini	Error

Figure 5-29 Rows that have errors

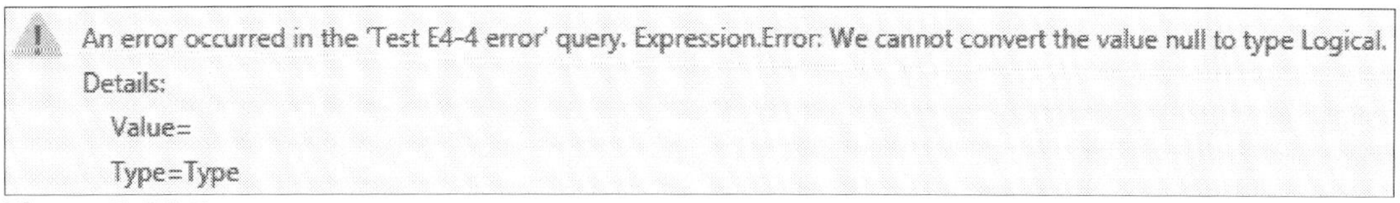

Figure 5-30 Error message

On your own, you could modify the formula to trap for the error or have someone fix the data. You can still save the changes to the file, with this error.

Index Column Options

The first two options shown in Figure 5-31 are used to create a column in the table named "Index", that starts with a zero or 1. These options create an incremental counter that would be useful for tables that need a field with a unique value, because it numbers each row sequentially.

The **CUSTOM** option displays the dialog box shown in Figure 5-32. The options are used to create an index that does not use sequential values or the index needs to start with a specific number other then zero or one. Like the From 0 and From 1 options, custom indexes must also use numeric values.

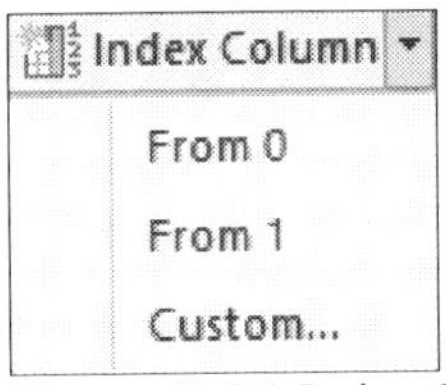

Figure 5-31 Index Column button options

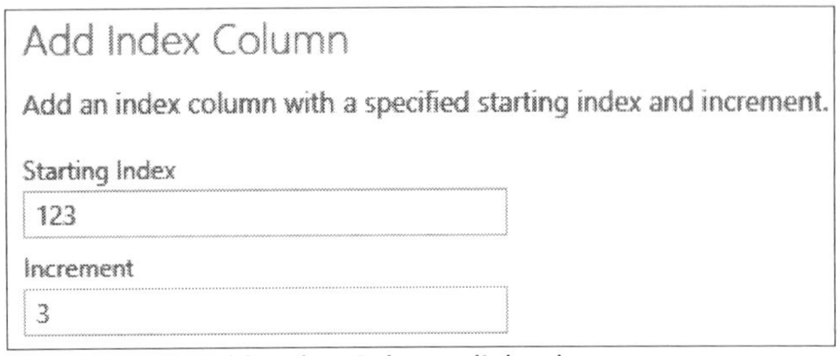

Figure 5-32 Add Index Column dialog box

Viewing A Row Of Data

As you saw earlier when you add a column to a table, you have to scroll to the right to see the new column of data. You can make the grid shorter and display all of the columns for one record. Doing this is similar to clicking on the Table link to display the data in a table, as covered in Chapter 4. Follow the steps below to view one record.

1. Display the query that you want to view ⇒ Click on the row number that you want to view.

2. Resize the grid as needed, as illustrated in Figure 5-33, then drag the grid up.

   As shown at the bottom of Figure 5-33, you can see the data for one record.

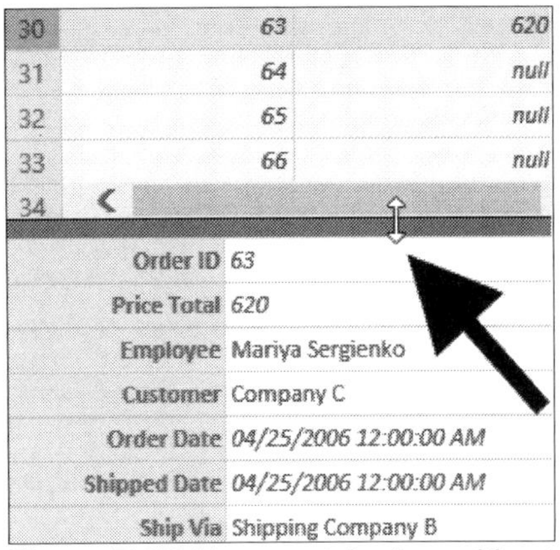

Figure 5-33 Mouse pointer in position to make the grid shorter

Summary

The text, numeric, date and time filter functions were covered in this chapter. The exercises showed you how to create each of these filter types. If you have created filters in Excel, you probably recognized and are familiar with the filter options in the Query Editor.

When you think of transforming data, you also usually think about ways to reduce the number of rows or columns. There are times when columns have to be created because some data that is needed does not exist, in the data source. An example of data that fits into this category is a sales tax field because it is the calculation of at least two other fields. The options used to add new columns are Split Column, Custom Column, Index Column and Duplicate Column.

Creating basic formulas was also covered. This topic introduced you to "writing code", the M language and combining data from different columns. While the exercises only demonstrated combining data from two columns, data can be combined from as many columns as needed. Hopefully, the exercises in this chapter have you wanting to see what else you can do in the Query Editor.

USE THE TRANSFORM TAB OPTIONS TO TRANSFORM DATA

In this chapter you will learn about more transformations in the Query Editor, including the following:

- ☑ How the "Any" data type works
- ☑ Extracting data from a column
- ☑ Splitting data in a column
- ☑ Grouping data
- ☑ Replacing values and errors
- ☑ View tab options
- ☑ Query dependencies

CHAPTER 6

Transforming Data

Chapter 2 covered how to discover and "get" data. Chapter 5 covered how to filter the data and add new columns of data to a query. By this point in the process, you should have all or almost all of the data needed for the analysis process.

This chapter and the next one, will demonstrate techniques on how to clean the data. This is probably what you will spend the most time doing, especially if the data was not imported from a database. If you are not a programmer, completing the exercises in this chapter and the rest of the book will give you a pretty good idea of why we (programmers) do not like working with data that is not stored in a database. No disrespect, but data that is not stored in a database, can be all over the place. It's messy and not always formatted consistently. All of these tasks, can take a while to fix, so that the data is in the correct format to be analyzed, as intended.

Fortunately, the transformations will help you plow through your list of data changes. Equally important as cleaning the data, in my opinion, is understanding the data and how it will be analyzed. For example, the Text filter warning that I discussed in the previous chapter, after Exercise 5.2, discussed that some text filters may not return all of the data that you think it should. To find or discover issues like this, one needs to understand the data and leave no stone unturned. Otherwise, the output (the result of cleaning the data) will be flawed. If the data discussed in that warning was in a database, the fix is easy. Change the setting to force the first letter in the field to be a capital letter. In a spreadsheet that is not as easy to do. In a text file, there usually are no options to force anything. Thus, one should pay extra attention to data that is not imported from a database.

Not to put you on the spot, but on your own, would you have actually looked at any of the data, in the Category column (discussed in the warning after Exercise 5.2) **BEFORE** you created the filter? What value would a report have, that is based on that filter, if 12% of the data that should be included on the report, isn't, because no one bothered to look at the underlying data.

The Transform tab has options that are used to clean the data. Not surprisingly, this is known as **TRANSFORMING THE DATA** and is the "T" in ETL, that was covered in Chapter 4. Splitting data in a column, replacing values and grouping data is also covered, because they transform data.

Transform Tab vs Add Column Tab Transformations

As you have probably seen, these tabs have many of the same transformations. For the most part, they work the same. The **BIGGEST DIFFERENCE** is that the options on the Transform tab **REPLACE THE DATA** in the selected column when the option is applied. The options on the Add Column tab create a new column and place the result of the transformation in the new column, leaving the data in the original column(s) unchanged. On your own, you need to decide whether or not you need or want to keep the original data. That will determine which tab you should select an option from.

How Transformations Are Applied
Keep in mind that transformations are applied, based on the data type. This means that you cannot apply a text transformation to a column that has a numeric data type. Also note that many transformations that are available in the Query Editor, can be created in the Data view, by creating DAX formulas.

Transform Tab

The options shown in Figure 6-1 are used to change the appearance of the data in the selected column. The options are explained in Table 6-1.

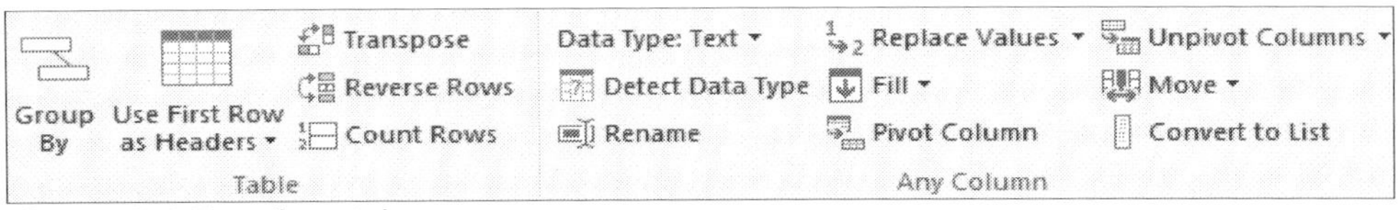

Figure 6-1 Transform tab

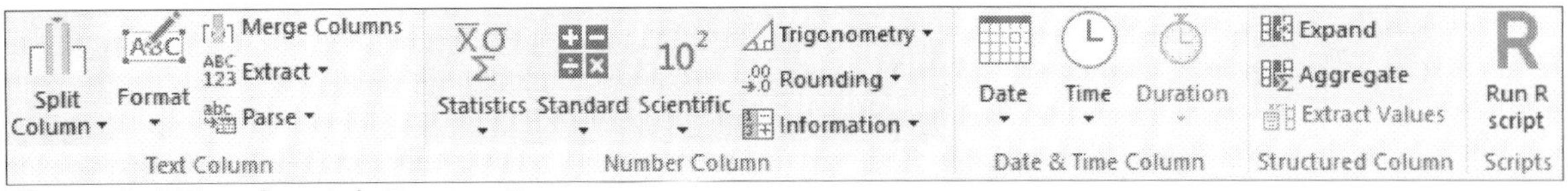

Figure 6-1 Transform tab (Continued)

Option	Description
Group By	[See Chapter 4, Group By Transformation Options] (1)
Use First Row As Headers	[See Chapter 4, Use First Row As Headers Transformation]
Transpose	Switch the rows to columns and the columns to rows.
Reverse Rows	Displays the last rows in the query first.
Count Rows	Displays a count of the number of rows in the table, on the **NUMBER TOOLS TRANSFORM TAB**, as illustrated in Figure 6-2.
Data Type	[See Data Type Options]
Detect Data Type	[See Detect Data Type]
Rename	Rename the selected column.
Replace Values	[See Chapter 4, Replace Values] and Replace Errors, which is covered later in this chapter.
Fill	[See Using The Fill Option]
Pivot Column	[See Chapter 10, Pivot Column Options] (1)
Unpivot Columns	[See Chapter 10, Unpivoting Data] (1)
Move	[See Move Button Options]
Convert to List	Converts the selected column to a list. Lists are usually created to use in a parameter. Once the list is created, it can be modified by using the options on the **LIST TOOLS TRANSFORM TAB**. [See Chapter 4, Figure 4-20]
Split Column	[See Chapter 4, Split Column Options]
Format	The functions shown in Figure 6-3 are used to change the case of characters, as well as, remove spaces from the beginning and end of a cell. The **CLEAN FUNCTION** removes non-printable characters. The **ADD PREFIX** and **ADD SUFFIX FUNCTIONS** are used to add text to the beginning or end of the data in the column.
Merge Columns	This option is only enabled when two or more columns are selected. It combines the data from the selected columns into one new column. The original columns are removed from the table after this process is completed. If you want to keep the original columns, use the Merge Columns option on the Add Column tab.
Extract	[See Extract Button Options]
Parse	Coverts the selected column(s) or cells to **XML** or **JSON** format. This option is only enabled for columns with a Text data type.
Statistics	Applies the statistical functions shown in Figure 6-4, to the values in the selected column and displays the result.
Standard	The functions shown in Figure 6-5 are used to create basic calculations. (2)
Scientific	The functions shown in Figure 6-6 are used to create scientific calculations. (2)
Trigonometry	These functions are used to create formulas that use trigonometry functions. (2)
Rounding	The functions are used to round the values up, down or to a specific number of decimal places. (2)
Information	The functions in this category are used to determine if each value in the column is even, odd, positive or negative. The column on the left of Figure 6-7 shows numeric data. The column on the right, shows the same column of data, after the **IS EVEN FUNCTION** is applied. True means the number is even. False means that the number is not even. (2) (4)
Date	The functions shown in Figure 6-8 are used to extract or return part of the date. The **EARLIEST FUNCTION** retrieves the oldest date in the selected column. The data in the query is replaced with the oldest date. (3)
Time	The functions shown in Figure 6-9 are used to extract or return part of the time. (3)
Duration	The majority of functions shown in Figure 6-11 are used to calculate the duration (the length of time) and display the value in the format that the function represents. The functions in this category are only available for columns that have the **DURATION DATA TYPE**.
Expand	[See Chapter 8, Expand Button Options] (5)
Aggregate	[See Chapter 8, Aggregate Button Options] (5)
Extract Values	Pulls out (extracts) values from each list in the selected column and combines the values into a new Text column, with a delimiter between the values. This option is also available on the column header drop-down list of a column that contains a nested list.
Run R Script	Is used to run an R script that will transform the data.

Table 6-1 Transform tab options explained

(1) This option changes the data structure of the query.
(2) The functions in this category are only available for columns with a numeric data type.
(3) The functions in this category are only available for columns that have any of the Date or Time data types. The functions are used to replace the date or time in the selected column. For example, if the Date button ⇒ Month ⇒ Start of month function is selected, all of the dates in the column will be changed, from the dates shown in the column on the left of Figure 6-10, to the dates in the column on the right of the figure. What you will see is that all of the dates have been changed to the first of the month, which is based on the month of the original date. (4)
(4) I used the option on the Add Column tab for Figures 6-7 and 6-10.
(5) If the Query Editor window is not wide enough, this option will collapse and the Structured Column button shown in Figure 6-12, will be displayed instead.

Number Tools Transform Tab

The options on this tab provide support for scalar queries. The options on this tab are Text, Number and Date/Time transformations.

A **SCALAR EXPRESSION** is one that when evaluated, returns a single value or a column reference, in the evaluation context.

To redisplay the rows of data, delete the **COUNTED ROWS** applied step, or click on the step above the Counted Rows step.

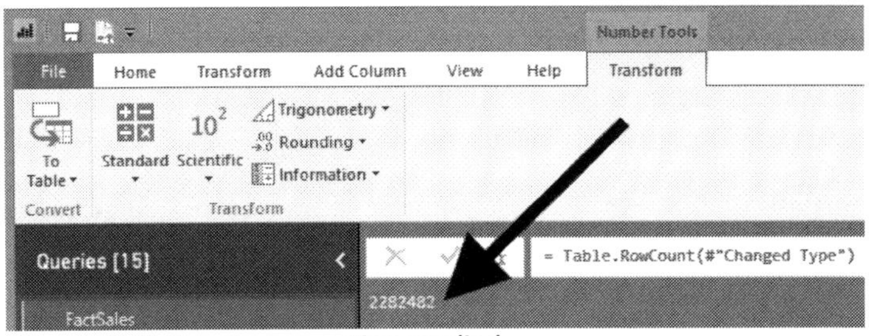

Figure 6-2 Count rows option applied

Transform Tab Options

Figures 6-3 to 6-12 are options on the Transform tab and examples of some of the functions.

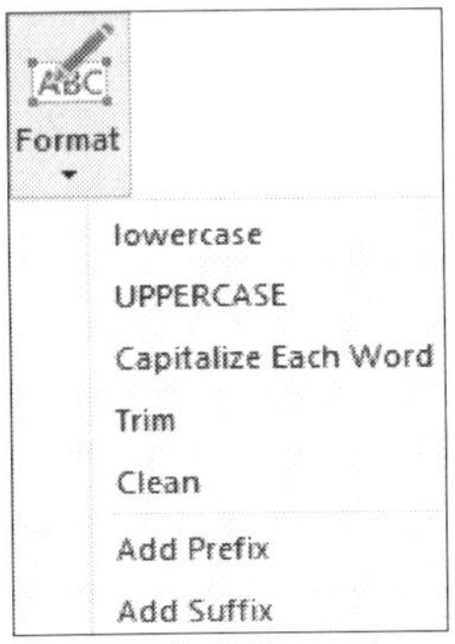

Figure 6-3 Format functions

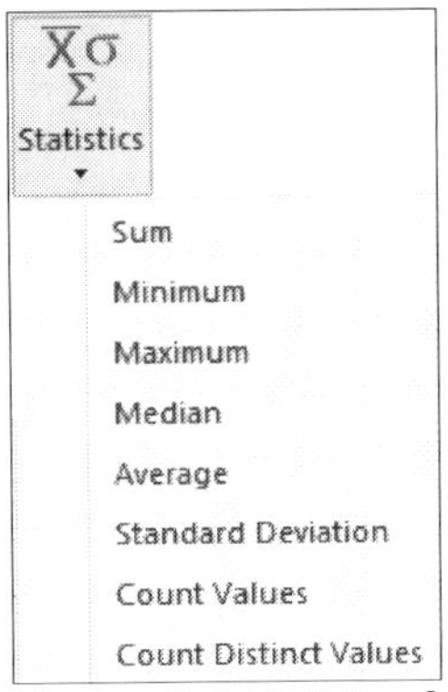

Figure 6-4 Statistics functions

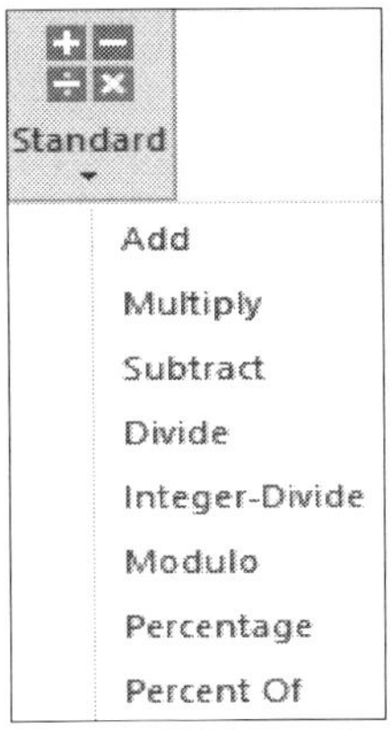

Figure 6-5 Standard functions

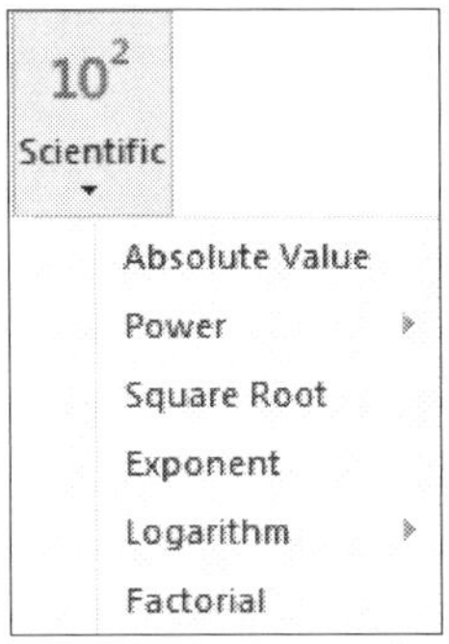

Figure 6-6 Scientific functions

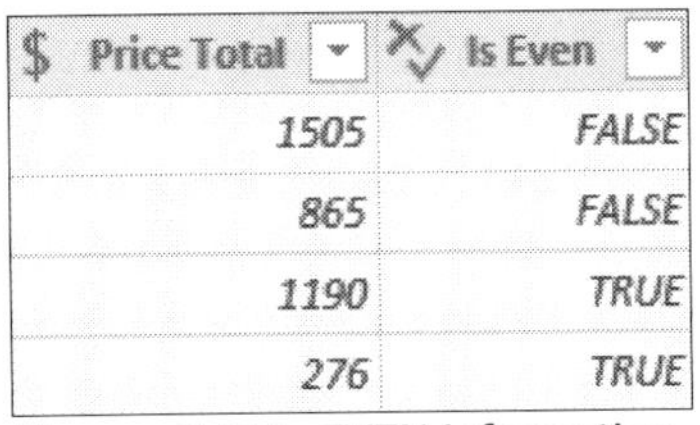

Price Total	Is Even
1505	FALSE
865	FALSE
1190	TRUE
276	TRUE

Figure 6-7 Is EVEN information function applied

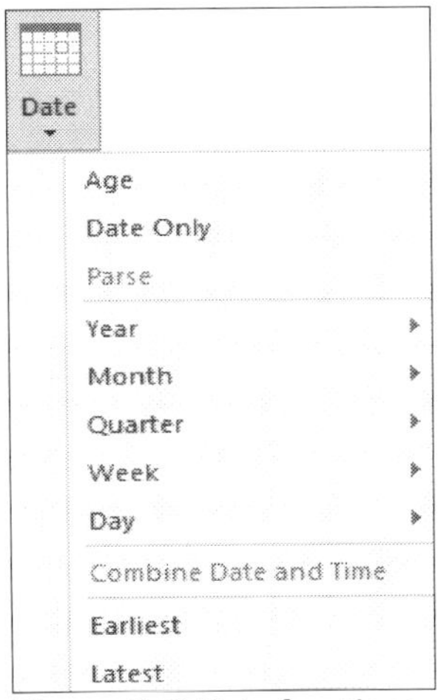

Figure 6-8 Date functions

Figure 6-9 Time functions

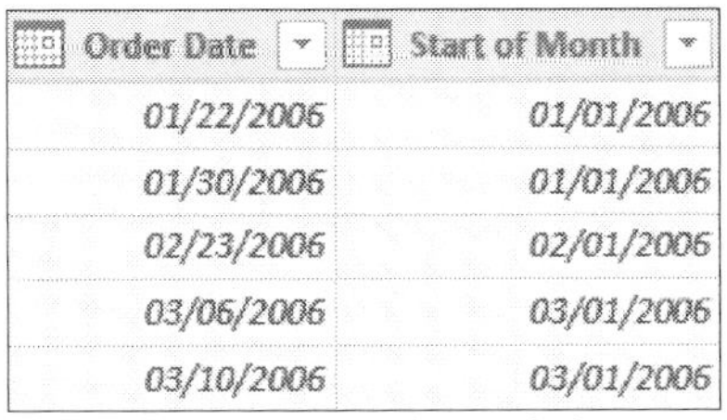

Figure 6-10 Start of month function applied to a date column

Figure 6-11 Duration functions

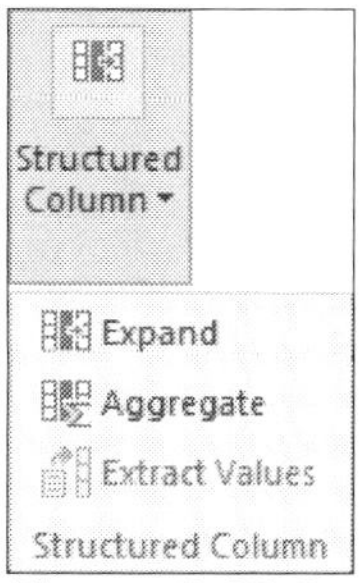

Figure 6-12 Structured Column functions

Data Type Options

The options shown in Figure 6-13 are used to change the data type of the selected column. The options are explained in Table 6-2.

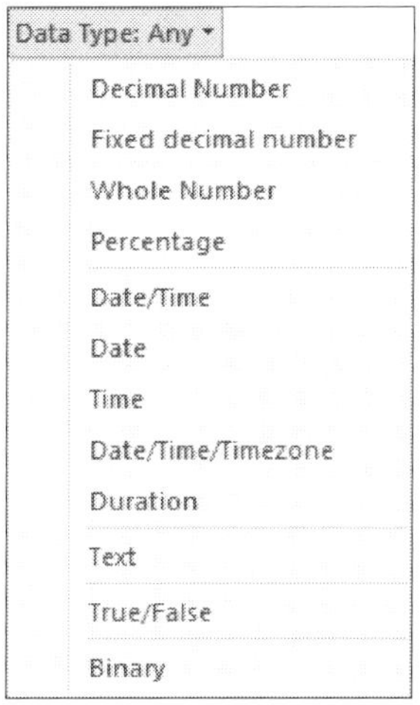

Figure 6-13 Data Type options

Data Type	Select This Data Type When The Data . . .
Decimal Number	Is numeric and needs to display cents or a decimal point.
Fixed Decimal Number	Is numeric and needs to display cents, like currency formatting.
Whole Number	Is numeric and does not need to display a decimal point.
Percentage	[See Percentage Data Type]
Date/Time	Needs to be displayed in a date and time format. (6)
Date	Needs to be displayed in date format.
Time	Needs to be displayed in time format. (6)
Date/Time/Timezone	Should be displayed in date, time and time zone format. The time zone comes from the system settings on your computer. (6)
Duration	[See Table 6-1, Duration]
Text	Should be displayed as alpha numeric. Zip code fields are usually assigned the Text data type, as they are not used in calculations that require numeric data types. At best, they are used with Count and Count (Distinct) functions, which do not require numeric values.
True/False	Should be displayed in Boolean format (on/off).
Binary	Is an object, like a file. This is the data type used when the Query Editor imports files. The binary data type can also be used to store the location of image files.

Table 6-2 Data Type options explained

(6) If the date does not have a time, this option adds the default time of 12:00:00 AM (midnight), to the column.

Percentage Data Type

Select this data type when the data needs to be converted to percent format. The value (like 25%) will automatically be recognized as a percentage value and will be converted to a two digit decimal number (like 0.25), so that it can be used in a calculation.

For data imported from a source without a schema (like a text or csv file), you can select the percentage option for the column, from the Data Type drop-down list, shown above in Figure 6-13 or from the **CHANGE TYPE OPTION** on the columns shortcut menu.

What Is The Any Data Type?

The "Any" data type option, shown above at the top of Figure 6-13, is the data type that the Query Editor gives a column when it cannot figure out what type of data is in the column. This data type can store any value. The easiest way to know if the **ANY DATA TYPE** was applied during the import, is to look at the code for the **CHANGED TYPE STEP**, as shown in Figure 6-14.

```
= Table.TransformColumnTypes(#"Prom    d Headers",{{"Order ID", Int64.Type}, {"Employee ID",
Int64.Type}, {"Cust                    {"Order Date", type any}, {"Shipped Date", type date},
{"Shipper ID", Int64.Type}, {"Ship    me", type text}, {"Ship Address", type text}, {"Ship City",
```

Figure 6-14 Changed Type step code

On the second line of code, you will see that the Order Date column has been assigned the Any Data type and the Shipped Date column has been assigned the Date data type. If you looked at the data, both columns have dates in this format MM/DD/YYYY. I notice inconsistencies like this more, when the data source is not a database.

It is important to ensure that columns that will be used in a calculation have the correct data type. It is best to fix the data types at the end of performing a lot of other steps. This is especially true of columns that have the Any data type. One place where I noticed that changing the data types early in the transformation process does not help is when the **APPEND QUERIES** option is used. The data type will be changed to **ANY**, for matching columns (in the queries that will be appended) that do not have the same data type before the queries are appended.

If you see that there are rows or columns that are missing data, see if the people that created the data can clean up the data. They should know the data the best. If they can't or will not fill in the blanks <pun intended>, you need to figure out what to do with the incomplete data. I personally, do not modify empty fields because if something goes wrong with the analysis, it is not my fault. And because I notified the user group of the empty fields, the ball is in their court.

Structured Data Types

In addition to the data types shown earlier in Figure 6-13, there are three more data types: **TABLE**, **RECORD** and **LIST**. Columns with these data types cannot be changed. These data types are objects that have a lot of values that are bound together. They are explained below. If you want to see these data types, up close and in person, you can use the E2.3 file or make a copy of it to follow along with the next few sections. This file contains the examples that I use to cover these data types.

Table Data Type

The formula bar for the Source step shows the Table data type, as shown at the top of Figure 6-15. As its name suggests, this data type contains a table. The Months table (query), shown in Figure 6-15, was created from an XML file. When clicked, the button (illustrated in Figure 6-16) to the right of the Table column heading, displays a list of the columns in the table, as shown in Figure 6-16.

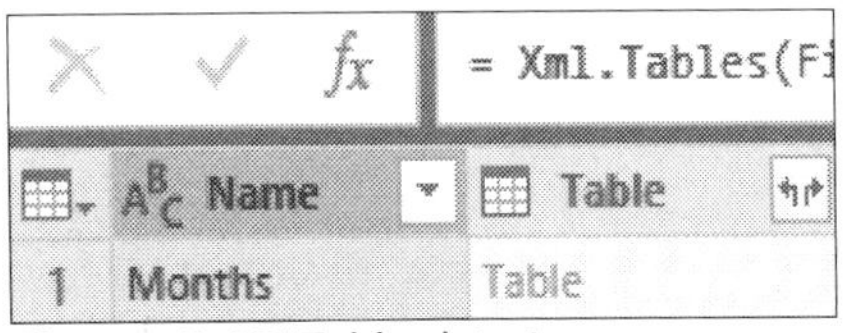

Figure 6-15 Table data type

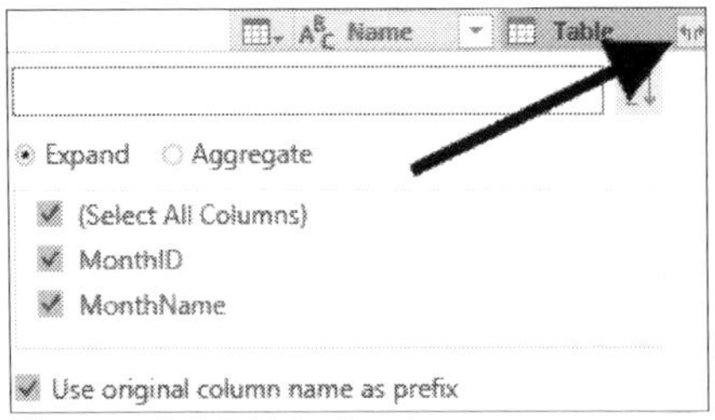

Figure 6-16 List of columns

What may not be obvious is that each row in the query contains a pointer to a different table. Clicking on the **TABLE LINK**, in the Table column, adds a step and displays the data in the table, as shown in Figure 6-17.

In Chapter 8, after completing Exercise 8.1, you will have the option of taking the Table data type for a test drive, if you want.

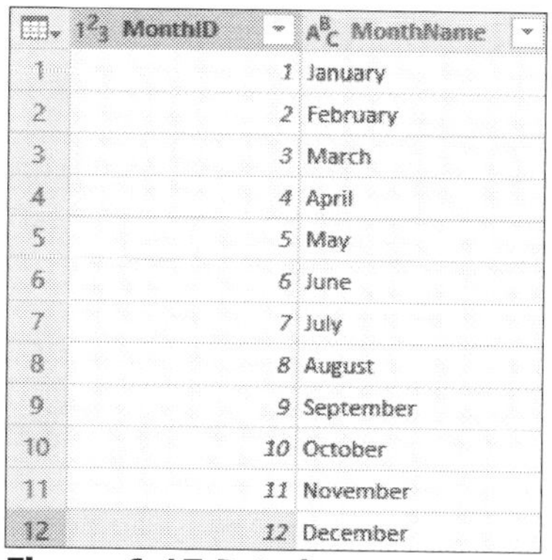

	MonthID	MonthName
1	1	January
2	2	February
3	3	March
4	4	April
5	5	May
6	6	June
7	7	July
8	8	August
9	9	September
10	10	October
11	11	November
12	12	December

Figure 6-17 Data from an XML file

Record Data Type

This data type indicates that the column has more than one field. Figure 6-18 shows the Record and List data types.

To view this figure, click on the JSON Customer Form query ⇒ Click on the Source step.

As you read the discussion below, it may be helpful to refer back to Chapter 2, Figure 2-29, to see where the data is coming from in Figures 6-18 and 6-19.

Clicking on the links explained below will add steps to the query that are not needed and cannot be deleted without modifying the code for the query.

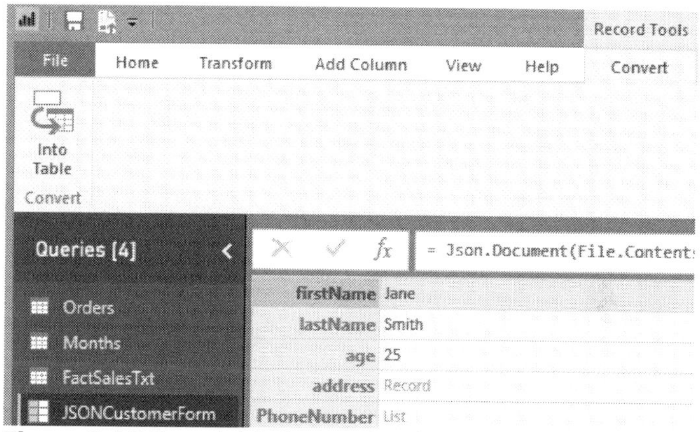

Figure 6-18 Record data type and tools

If you do click on any of these links now, the steps in the next section will prompt you to insert a step. It is ok, because you can close Power BI Desktop and not apply or save the changes.

The **RECORD DATA TYPE** (in the Address field, shown above in Figure 6-18) means that there are multiple fields for the address. Clicking on this link displays all of the address fields, shown in Figure 6-19. Notice that a Navigation step was added to the Applied Steps list.

In Chapter 8, Exercise 8.6, you will create a query that generates the Record Data type.

StreetAddress	21 3rd Avenue
City	New York
State	NY
ZipCode	10021

Figure 6-19 Address fields

List Data Type

This data type means that the element has more than one entry (row of data). The **LIST DATA TYPE** (in the Phone Number field, shown earlier in Figure 6-18) means that there are multiple phone numbers (detail records) for the customer. Clicking on this link displays the table shown in Figure 6-20. (To return to the layout shown earlier in Figure 6-18, click on the Source step.) The table lets you know that there are two phone numbers for the record. This would be the "many" table, in a one-to-many relationship.

Each **RECORD LINK**, shown in Figure 6-20, will display one of the phone numbers for the customer, as shown in Figure 6-21.

	List
1	Record
2	Record

Figure 6-20 Phone number table

type	fax
number	646 555-2345

Figure 6-21 Phone number record

Record Tools Convert Tab

This tab was shown earlier in Figure 6-18. The **INTO TABLE BUTTON** converts the record (data type) into a table.

1. In the Query Settings panel, click on the **SOURCE STEP**.

2. Click the Into Table button, on the toolbar.

   You should see the table shown in Figure 6-22.

	Name	Value
1	firstName	Jane
2	lastName	Smith
3	age	25
4	address	Record
5	PhoneNumber	List

Figure 6-22 Record converted to a table

3. Transform tab ⇒ Transpose button ⇒ Home tab ⇒ Use First Row As Headers button. You will see a table with one row/record of data, as shown in Figure 6-23.

	firstName	lastName	age	address	PhoneNumber
1	Jane	Smith	25	Record	List

Figure 6-23 Table converted to a row

If you are shaking your head and asking "Why?", don't worry. Unless you will be working with a lot of data that is in **XML** or **JSON** format, you probably will not see the Record and List data types. You will see the Table data type in some databases that you may use. And yes, there are exercises in this book, that show you how to work with the Table data type.

Detect Data Type

Click this button to let the Query Editor select the data type for the selected column(s). If you want the data type to be detected for the entire table at one time, you have to select all of the columns in the table before clicking this button. Keep in mind that this function does not always select the correct data type. Therefore, it is a good idea to review the code created for the **CHANGED TYPE STEP**. You can view the code by clicking on the Changed Type step, then looking at the code, in the formula bar, as shown earlier in Figure 6-14.

For example, Figure 6-24 shows the code for the Changed Type step and some of the data in the query. Notice that the Revenue column was changed to the text data type, even though the column has numeric data.

```
= Table.TransformColumnTypes(#"Removed Duplicates",{{"Revenue", type text}})
```

	Product	Region	Revenue
1	Prod A	North America	14.22
2	Prod B	North America	20.12
3	Prod C	North America	12.18

Figure 6-24 Result of using the Detect Data Type option

Using The Fill Option

This option copies the data from the selected cell to the empty cells, (in the same column), above or below the selected cell. Usually, this feature is best suited for data that is grouped on the column that you want to apply the Fill option to. The Fill option will be useful if you have to import a spreadsheet that looks like the one shown in Figure 6-25. To fill in the Store column, you would follow the steps below.

1. Click on the column heading of the column that you want to fill. In this example, you would click on the Store column.

2. Transform tab ⇒ Fill ⇒ Down. The query will look like the one shown in Figure 6-26.

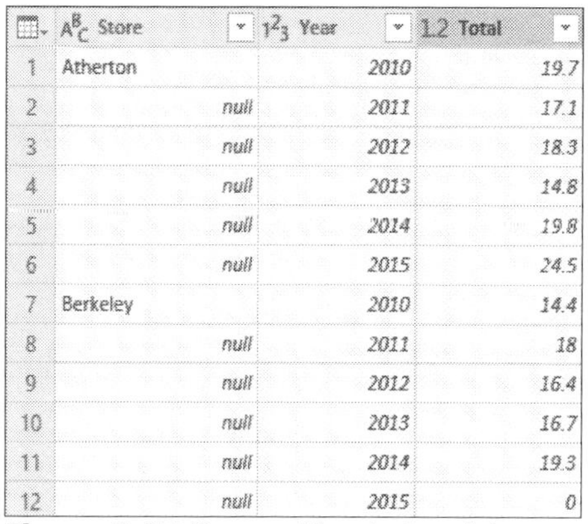

	Store	Year	Total
1	Atherton	2010	19.7
2	null	2011	17.1
3	null	2012	18.3
4	null	2013	14.8
5	null	2014	19.8
6	null	2015	24.5
7	Berkeley	2010	14.4
8	null	2011	18
9	null	2012	16.4
10	null	2013	16.7
11	null	2014	19.3
12	null	2015	0

Figure 6-25 Query with missing data

	Store	Year	Total
1	Atherton	2010	19.7
2	Atherton	2011	17.1
3	Atherton	2012	18.3
4	Atherton	2013	14.8
5	Atherton	2014	19.8
6	Atherton	2015	24.5
7	Berkeley	2010	14.4
8	Berkeley	2011	18
9	Berkeley	2012	16.4
10	Berkeley	2013	16.7
11	Berkeley	2014	19.3
12	Berkeley	2015	0

Figure 6-26 Query data filled in

Move Button Options

The options shown in Figure 6-27, are used to move the selected column(s) left, right, or to the beginning or end of the table.

By default, the columns are loaded in the same order that they are in the data source, which you can view on the Navigator dialog box. When I know which columns I will use the most, I tend to move them (using drop and drag) to the beginning of the query, so that I do not have to keep scrolling to the right to find what I need. Keep in mind that columns cannot be moved in the Data view.

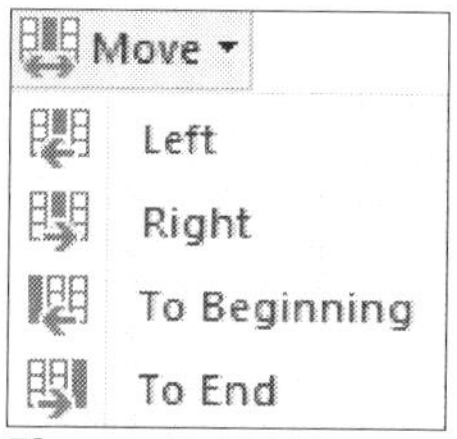

Figure 6-27 Move options

Extract Button Options

The options shown in Figure 6-28 are used to select how many characters to extract (pull out) from the column. The options are explained in Table 6-3.

The Extract option on the Transform tab replaces the values in the column currently selected, with values already in the cell.

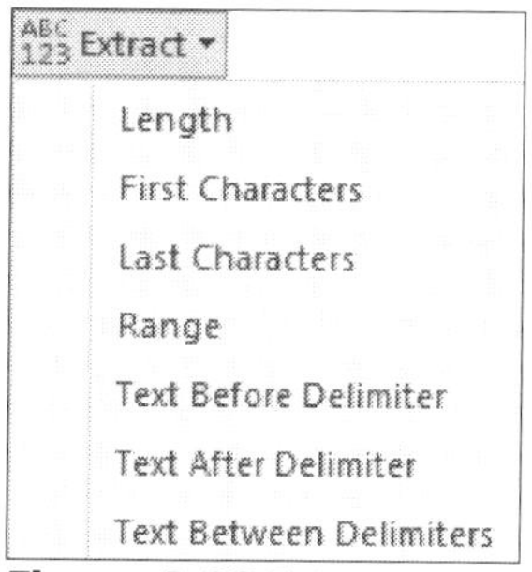

Figure 6-28 Extract options

Option	Description
Length	Replaces the data in each cell with a count of the length of the data in the cell. Doing this changes the columns data type to Decimal Number.
First Characters	Is used to select a specific number of characters from the beginning of the field to keep, as shown in Figure 6-29.
Last Characters	Is used to select a specific number of characters from the end of the field to keep.
Range	Displays the options shown in Figure 6-30. The options are used to select the first position in the field to keep and the number of characters in total to keep. The entries shown in the figure will start at the second character in the field and select three characters to keep. This means that a total of three characters will be kept in the field and the other characters in the field will be removed.
Text Before Delimiter	Extracts the text up to the delimiter that you select. (7)
Text After Delimiter	Extracts the text after the delimiter that you select. In the data shown in Figure 6-31, the first name or last name could be extracted, because the field has a comma, by selecting the appropriate options on the dialog box, shown in Figure 6-32. (7)
Text Between Delimiters	Extracts the text that is between the delimiters that you select. The web sites shown in the column, in Figure 6-33, could be extracted by using the options shown in Figure 6-34. (7)

Table 6-3 Extract options explained

(7) The benefit that this option has is that it can extract an unlimited number of characters, where the first four options in this table extracts a specific number of characters.

Figure 6-29 Extract First Characters option

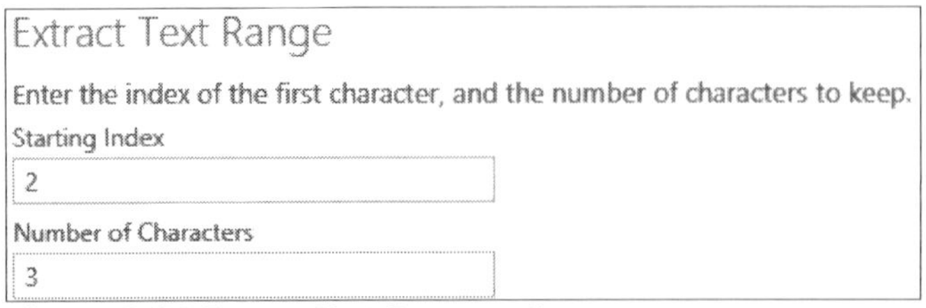

Figure 6-30 Extract Text Range options

Figure 6-31 Text that could be extracted

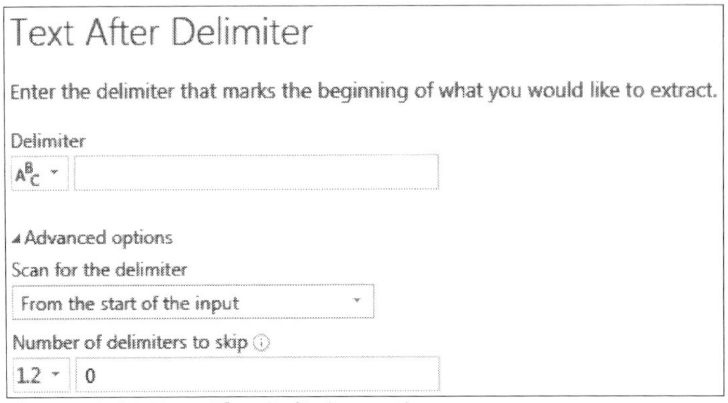

Figure 6-32 Text After Delimiter options

Figure 6-33 Web site data that could be extracted

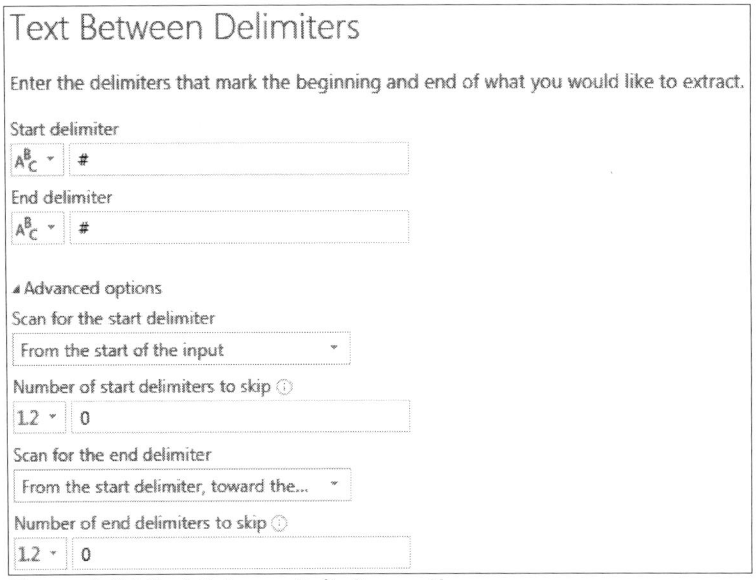

Figure 6-34 Text Between Delimiters options

Exercise Tips

① To make it easier for you to know which queries you modified, the queries will be duplicated and renamed to indicate what was done. The duplicated queries will start with a number to make it easier to recognize the modified queries.

② This is a good time to reread the warning in Chapter 1, below Figure 1-27.

Exercise 6.1: Use The Transform Tab Options

The transformations covered in this exercise are used to change the appearance of data. Keep in mind that options on the Transform tab, overwrite or delete the existing column(s) that you use.

Use The Split Column By Delimiter Transformation

In this part of the exercise, you will use the Split Column option to place the first and last name, which are currently in one column (the Contact Name column), in separate columns.

1. Save the E2.4 file as `E6.1 Transform tab options`.

2. Duplicate the Customers Extended query ⇒ Rename it to `1 Split Contact Name column`.

3. Click on the Contact Name column ⇒ Transform tab ⇒ **SPLIT COLUMN BUTTON** ⇒ By Delimiter ⇒ Open the Delimiter drop-down list and select Space.

If you display the Advanced options, you will see that the suggested number of columns to split the data into, is three. That is because the **EACH OCCURRENCE** split option is selected. Some of the contact names have two spaces, indicating that the name has three words. In this scenario, you do not know if records with three words are middle names or a last name followed by a suffix, like Jr.

4. Select the **LEFT MOST DELIMITER** option ⇒ Click OK. You will see two columns labeled Contact Name.1 and Contact Name.2, in place of the original Contact Name field, as shown in Figure 6-35.

```
= Table.TransformColumnTypes(#"Split Column by Delimiter",{{"Contact Name.1", type text}, {"Contact Name.2", type text}})
```

	Contact Name.1	Contact Name.2
1	Elizabeth	Andersen
2	Catherine	Autier Miconi
3	Thomas	Axen

Figure 6-35 Result of the By Delimiter split column option

The dot notation at the end of a column name indicates that the data in the column came from another column.

The **M FORMULA** to create this data split is shown in the formula bar, at the top of the figure.

Use The Split Column By Number Of Characters Transformation

One way that I find this option useful, is to get the first letter of a first name.

1. Duplicate the 1 Split Contact Name column query ⇒ Rename it to `2 Number of characters`.

2. Click on the First Name column ⇒ Transform tab ⇒ Split Column button ⇒ By Number of Characters ⇒ Type `1` in the **NUMBER OF CHARACTERS** field.

3. Select the Once, as far left as possible option. The table should have the two columns, shown in Figure 6-36.

   More than likely, the First Name.2 column would be deleted, because it is not needed.

First Name.1	First Name.2
E	lizabeth
C	atherine
T	homas

Figure 6-36 Result of the Number of characters split column option

Use The Group By Transformation

In this part of the exercise, you will use the Group By transformation to group the data in the Order Details table, by the Order ID field.

1. Duplicate the Order Details query ⇒ Rename it to `3 Group by Order ID`.

2. Click on the Order ID column ⇒ Transform tab ⇒ Group By button.

3. Change the New column name field to `Item count per order`. The options shown in Figure 6-37 will display a count of items per order. Figure 6-38 shows the top of the Group By query.

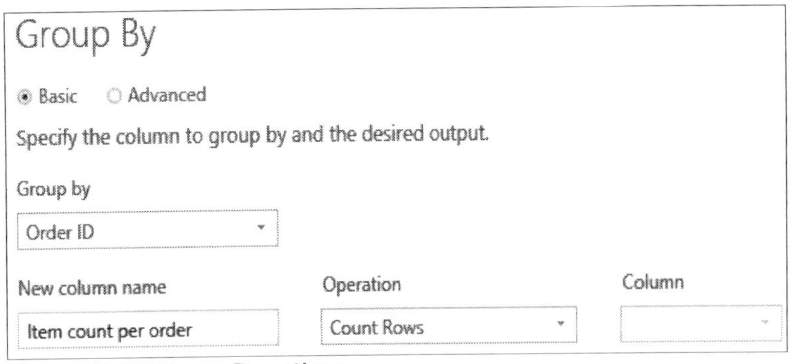

Figure 6-37 Group By options

	1.2 Order ID	1.2 Item count per order
1	30	2
2	31	3
3	32	2
4	33	1

Figure 6-38 Result of the Group By query

On its own, the Item count per order column is not very useful. It would be more useful if it was merged into the Orders table, because that table contains the majority of information for each order.

Use The Replace Values Transformation

If a field does not have data, it has a **NULL VALUE**. When displayed in a visual format, it can be difficult to tell that there are null or missing values. There are times when you need to bring this to someone's attention. One way to do this is to display content in the cell, instead of leaving it blank.

Chapter 4 introduced the Replace Values transformation, because this option is also on the Home tab. In this part of the exercise, you will replace null values with text.

1. Duplicate the Products query ⇒ Rename it to `4 Replace missing description values.` Notice that there are no values in the Description column.

2. Click on the Description column ⇒ Transform tab ⇒ Replace Values button ⇒ Replace Values.

3. Leave the Value To Find field blank.

   In the Replace With field, type `*missing data*`, as shown in Figure 6-39.

   If you wanted to replace cells that have the word "null" in the cell, type `null` in the Value To Find field.

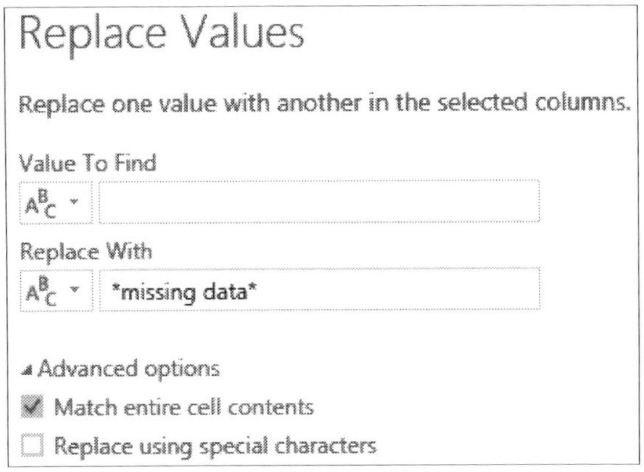

Figure 6-39 Replace Values options

4. Check the **MATCH ENTIRE CELL CONTENTS** option. The Description column in the table should look like the one shown in Figure 6-40.

Product Name	Description
Northwind Traders Chai	*missing data*
Northwind Traders Syrup	*missing data*

Figure 6-40 Description column value replaced, based on a condition

Replace Errors

The previous part of Exercise 6.1 showed you have to replace value in a field. If you have a field that has errors, as shown in Figure 6-41, you may want to replace the word "Error", with a null value. Changing the data type from text to numeric, will cause an error in rows that have text in the field.

If this happens in a transformation that you create, you can follow the steps below to replace the errors.

Order Shipped On Time
On Time
On Time
Error
Shipped Late
Error
Error
On Time

Figure 6-41 Column that has errors

1. Select the column that has errors.

2. Transform tab ⇒ Replace Values button ⇒ Replace Errors option.

3. On the dialog box shown in Figure 6-42, type in the value that you want to replace the word Error with.

If the column is text, you can type in just about anything. If the column is numeric, typing a zero or the word "Null", are usually used. It depends on the calculations that will be created using the column. Null is often the safer choice to indicate that there is no value in the field. If creating a table style report that displays detail rows of data, it is difficult to know if the zero value is the actual value or if it is the result of a formula.

Based on the data type of the column and what you type in the field on this dialog box, you may see a yellow exclamation mark, at the end of the field. This indicates that the value or at least some part of it is not valid for the data type that the column has.

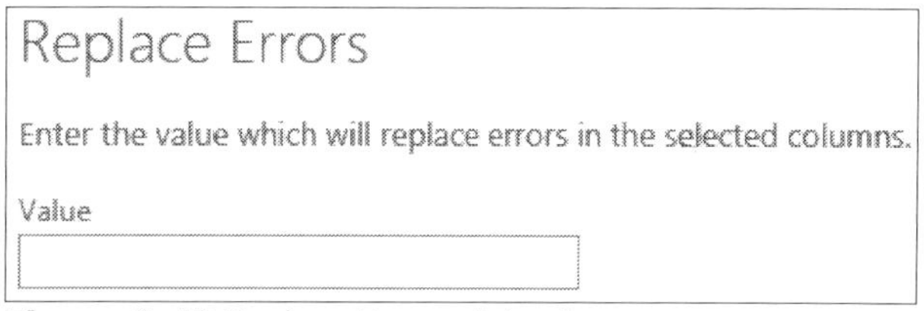

Figure 6-42 Replace Errors dialog box

Working With Dates

There are several date formats that can be used, as shown in Figure 6-43. Data that is not stored in a database, can be entered in any format.

If you have ever created a formula in Excel that used a date, and the formula returned a number like 41,654, you were probably mystified.

Excel stores dates as sequential serial numbers. 41,654 is the number of days since January 1, 1900. The date formula could also return the error #VALUE! This error is generated when Excel does not recognize the date in the cell.

	DifferentDateFormats
1	01/01/2018
2	01/02/2018
3	January 3, 2018
4	February 15, 2018
5	3/22/18 12:00 AM
6	3/26/18 12:00 AM
7	4/5/18
8	4/7/18

Figure 6-43 Date format options

When dates are imported into Power Query, there are some options that can be set to help import dates in a format that Power Query can use. Use one of the options below, then refresh the data.

- ☑ Before you import data, change the **LOCALE FOR IMPORT OPTION** on the Options dialog box ⇒ Current File section ⇒ Regional Settings screen ⇒ Set the option to English (United States) or select the country and language where you are.
- ☑ After the data has been imported, right-click in the date column that you need to change ⇒ Change Type ⇒ Using Locale.

View Tab

The options shown in Figure 6-44 are used to display or hide parts of the Query Editor. They are explained in Table 6-4.

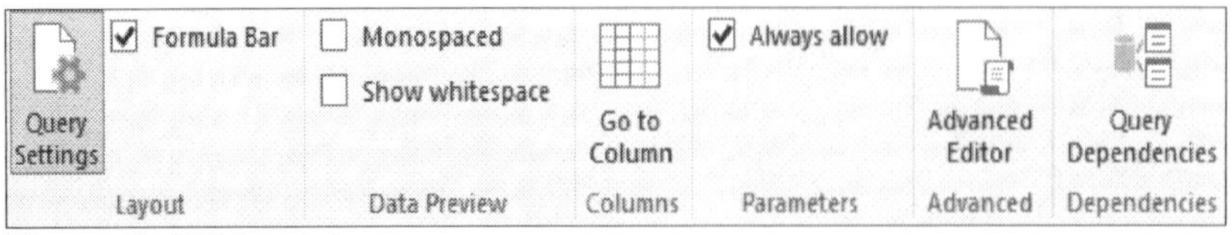

Figure 6-44 View tab

Many of the options on this tab, can be set as a default for all report files, on the Options dialog box. [See Chapter 1, Figure 1-18]

Option	Description
Query Settings	Displays or hides the Query Settings panel.
Formula Bar	Displays or hides the formula bar.
Monospaced	Displays the data in the query with a monspaced font. The font used resembles the `Courier font.`
Show white space	Displays or hides white space characters like line feeds (pressing the Enter key), in the data displayed in the query.
Go To Column	Clicking this button opens the dialog box shown in Figure 6-45. It is used to select or type in the column in the query that you want to see. This option is helpful if the query has a lot of columns and you do not want to scroll to find it. The dialog box only shows fields in the query that is displayed.
Always allow	If checked, many dialog boxes will have the parameter options enabled, as shown in Figure 6-46.
Advanced Editor	[See Advanced Editor]
Query Dependencies	[See Query Dependencies]

Table 6-4 View tab options explained

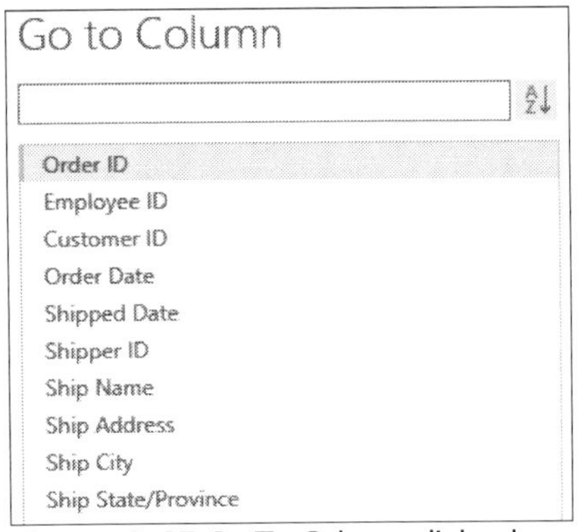

Figure 6-45 Go To Column dialog box

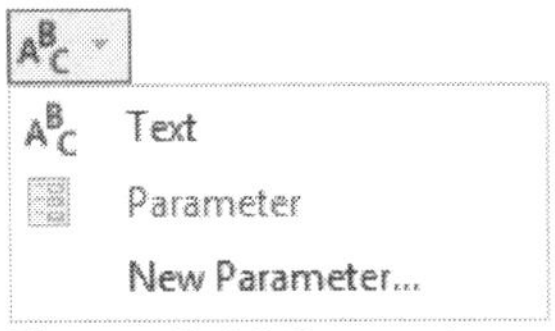

Figure 6-46 Parameter options on a transformation dialog box

Advanced Editor

The dialog box shown in Figure 6-47 displays the M code for a query. Each step in the Query Editor creates its own line of code. The lines of code that start with #, do not wrap on this dialog box. This dialog box is also used to write code from scratch. You can also modify the code on this dialog box, if necessary.

The **LET EXPRESSION** is the first line of an M formula. This expression is used to create/write formulas that are combined into a single value. The **IN KEYWORD** is used to identify that last step of the formula. The last step contains the single value that the formula creates. The step after the in keyword, at a minimum, contains the value of the last step before the in keyword. It can also contain additional text.

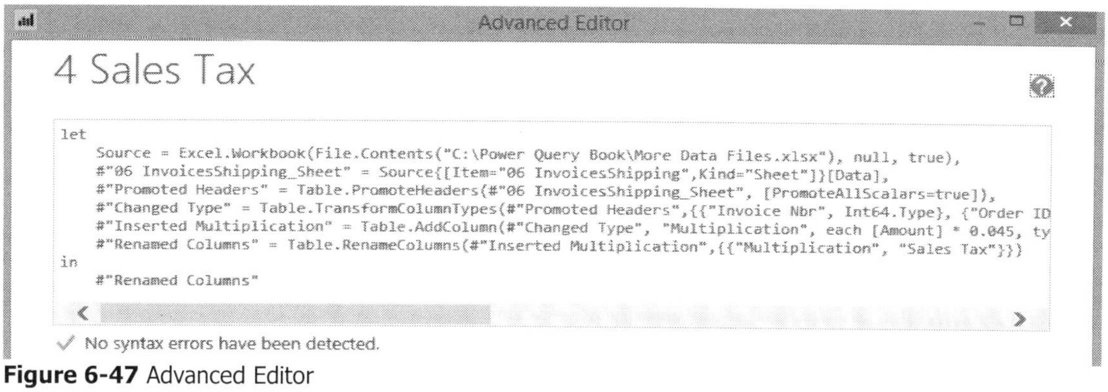

Figure 6-47 Advanced Editor

Query Dependencies

The tool is used to view all of the queries data sources and dependencies (on other queries) in the data model. You can also see the relationships between queries and the load status of each query. In the layout shown in Figure 6-48, there are two data sources and each has several tables.

This option is helpful when the data model has a lot of tables, especially for files that have data from multiple sources. It will let you see which queries (tables) are from the same data source. The top level is the data source. The second level displays the tables in the data source. The remaining levels are the dependencies.

The figure shows the following: That the data model has two data sources (indicated by the different background colors at the top of each square) and the tables for each data source. Notice that there are no reference queries, because the layout only has two levels.

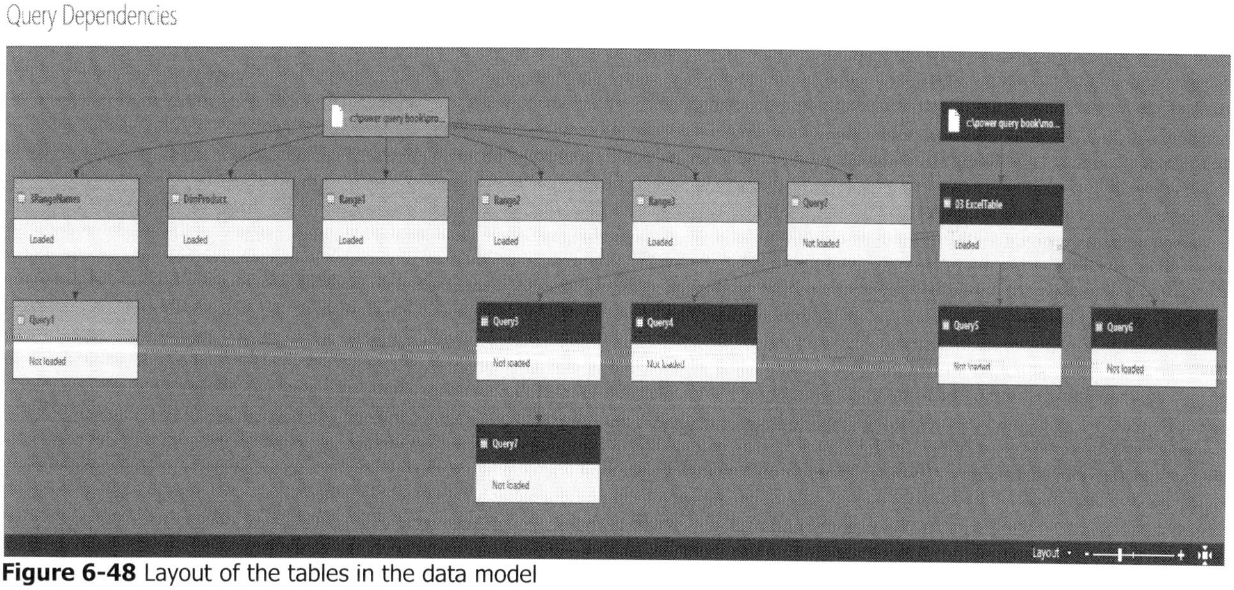

Figure 6-48 Layout of the tables in the data model

> If there is a problem with a query, the icon in the upper left corner of the square, will change to a yellow exclamation mark.

Chapter 4 introduced the concept of **REFERENCES** and how they are used to create query dependencies. The Query Dependencies dialog box is how you can view these dependencies. While the dependency example shown in Figure 6-49 is basic, more complex dependency layouts can be created.

This dialog box displays a diagram of the queries in the file whether or not they are loaded in the data model. While the Queries panel, in the Query Editor, displays all of the queries in the file, it does not indicate whether or not there are any dependent queries. Over time, it is very possible that more queries will be created, in the file. Having this tool, visually lets you know how the queries are related. This dependency "relationship" between queries is different functionality then the relationships that are created between tables and the two cannot be used interchangeably. Relationships between tables are a requirement, dependencies between tables are not.

The reason to create reference queries is because you can create transformations in a query that has dependents, like the International Customers query, shown in Figure 6-49, and those transformations will flow down (be applied to) the Online and Retail Customers queries, thus filtering the data in those queries. This keeps you from having to create some transformations, more than once.

When one query is created using the **REFERENCE OPTION**, a dependency between the queries is automatically created. Each tables dependencies are known as **REFERENCE QUERIES** or **DEPENDENT QUERIES**. When a query has dependents, you cannot delete the query, until the dependent queries are deleted. The layout shows that the Orders table has been loaded into the data model, but its dependencies (the Orders Shipped To USA and Orders Shipped to Canada queries) have not been loaded.

If you try to delete any query shown in the figure that has a dependency, you will get the message shown in Figure 6-50. This message explains why you cannot delete the query. In this case, its because the query has two dependent queries. You would have to delete the dependent queries first.

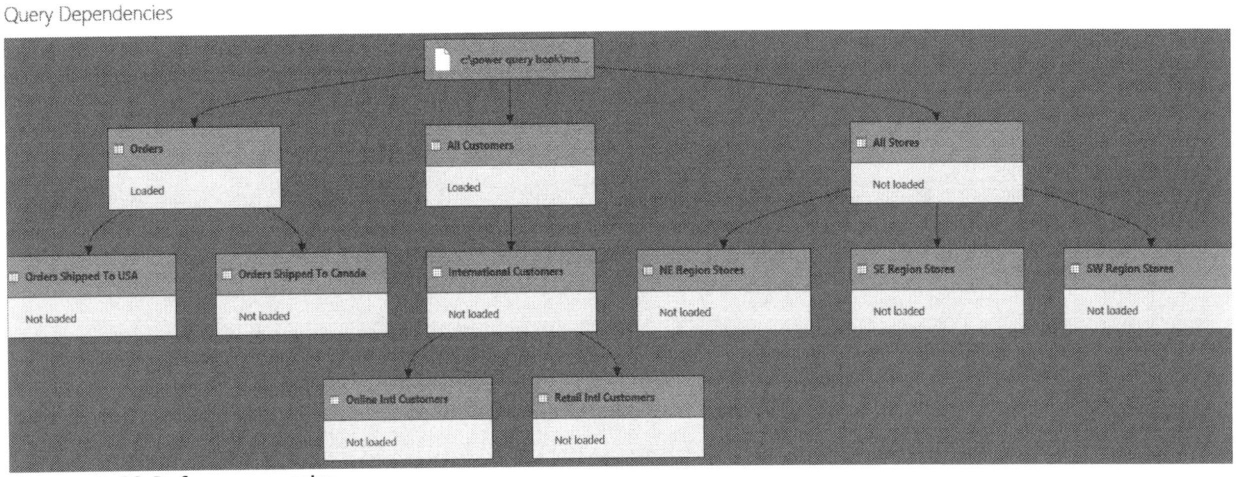

Figure 6-49 Reference queries

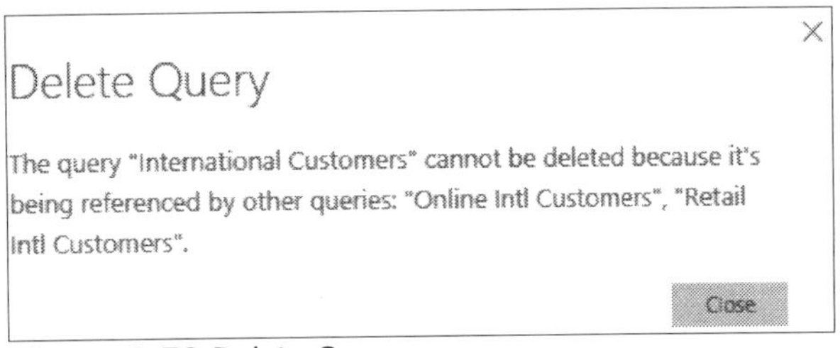

Figure 6-50 Delete Query message

Summary

This chapter covered options on the Transform tab. It is important to understand the **ANY DATA TYPE**, especially when the data source is not a database. While you may not use the structured data types (table, record and list) often, it is good to know that they exist. You also learned another way to extract data from a column.

I don't know for sure, but you may be more comfortable using the options on the Add Column tab, when they are available. This may be helpful when you are doing this on your own, until you get more comfortable with the transformations.

USE THE ADD COLUMN TAB OPTIONS TO TRANSFORM DATA

In this chapter you will learn about more transformations in the Query Editor, including the following:

☑ Merging data
☑ Date functions
☑ Splitting data in a column
☑ Creating conditional columns of data
☑ Use the Column From Examples option to create new columns of data

CHAPTER 7

Overview

The previous chapter introduced you the transformation options on the Transform tab. This chapter picks up where that chapter left off and will introduce you to the transformation options on the Add Column tab. As you learned, some of the options are the same on both tabs and the options on the Transform tab replace data in an existing column and the options on the Add Column tab, place the result of the transformation in a new column in the query.

Add Column Tab

The options shown in Figure 7-1 are used to create new columns in the query. The options are explained in Table 7-1.

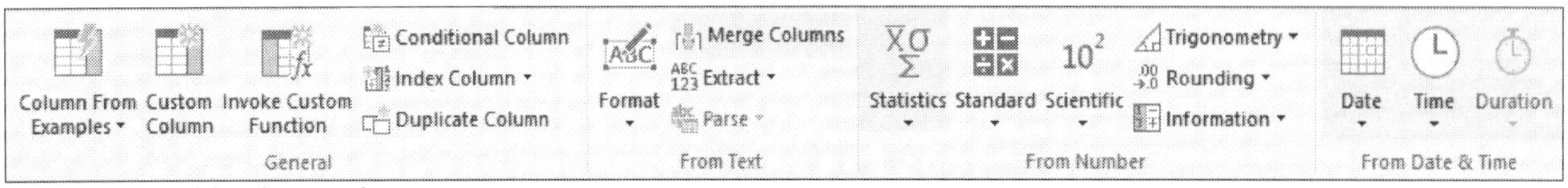

Figure 7-1 Add Column tab

Option	Description
Column From Examples	[See Column From Examples Transformation]
Custom Column	Is used to create a new column in the query, based on a formula. [See Chapter 5, Custom Columns]
Invoke Custom Function	[See Chapter 4, Table 4-1]
Conditional Column	[See Conditional Columns]
Index Column	[See Chapter 5, Index Column Options]
Duplicate Column	[See Chapter 4, Table 4-5]
Format	[See Chapter 6, Table 6-1]
Merge Columns	[See Chapter 6, Table 6-1]
Extract	[See Chapter 6, Table 6-3]
Parse	[See Chapter 6, Table 6-1]
Statistics	[See Chapter 6, Table 6-1]
Standard	[See Chapter 6, Table 6-1]
Scientific	[See Chapter 6, Table 6-1]
Trigonometry	[See Chapter 6, Table 6-1]
Rounding	[See Chapter 6, Table 6-1]
Information	[See Chapter 6, Table 6-1]
Date	[See Date Functions]
Time	[See Time Functions]
Duration	[See Chapter 6, Table 6-1]

Table 7-1 Add Column tab options explained

Merge Columns Options

There are two Merge Columns options. One on the Transform tab and one on the Add Column tab. While the Merge Columns options have the same name, they worked differently.

> When creating a merge column using either option, the order that you click on the columns, is the order that the columns will be merged in.

In both scenarios below, the order that the columns are clicked on is the First Name, then Last Name. Both Merge Columns buttons, display the dialog box shown in Figure 7-2.

The **SEPARATOR** drop-down list has a **CUSTOM** option, which is free form. It is used to type in what character(s) you want displayed between the columns that will be merged into one column.

An example would be combining the city and state fields. The custom option would be used to display a comma and space between the fields, as shown in Figure 7-3.

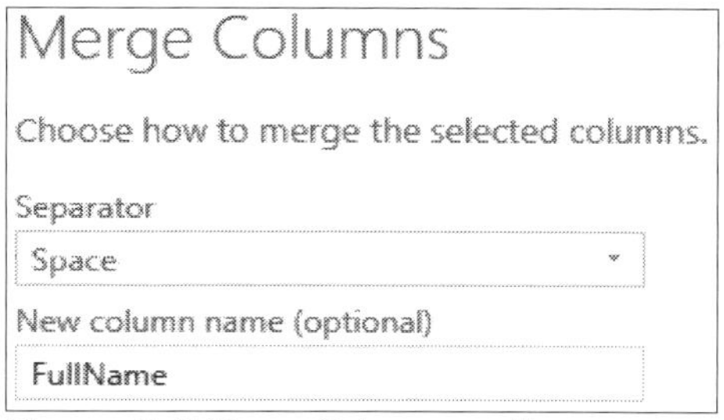

Figure 7-2 Merge Columns options

City State Merge
Seattle,WA
Boston,MA
Los Angeles,CA

Figure 7-3 Custom separator option used

Transform Tab Merge Columns Option

Clicking on the name columns, then clicking the **MERGE COLUMNS** button, replaces both name columns with the Full Name column shown in Figure 7-4.

FullName
Chris Christianson
Ron Cunningham
Pavel Ropoleski

Figure 7-4 Result of the Transform tab merge option

Add Column Merge Columns Option

When this merge columns option is used, a new field is created and the two original fields stay intact.

Exercise 7.1: Create Calculations Using Options On The Add Column Tab

This exercise will show you how to use the Merge Columns option and how to create calculated columns using columns in the query. In previous chapters you learned how to create calculated columns by writing code. There are options on the Add Column tab that can be used to produce the same result.

1. In a new file ⇒ Import the 06 Invoices Shipping table in the More Data Files workbook.

2. Save the file as `E7.1 Add Column Calculations`.

Merge Columns

Chapter 5, Exercise 5.4, covered how to create a formula that combined the data in the first and last name columns and placed the result in a new column. This part of the exercise will show you another way to combine columns of data and place the result in a new column.

1. Duplicate the Invoices Shipping query ⇒ Rename it to `1 Merge First & Last Name columns`.

2. Select the First Name and Last Name columns ⇒ Add Column tab ⇒ Merge Columns button.

3. Select the options shown earlier in Figure 7-2. The new column (at the end of the table) should have the first and last name, as shown earlier in Figure 7-4. The original name columns are still there.

Calculate A Total Using Two Columns Of Data

In this part of the exercise, you will use a function to calculate the invoice total.

1. Duplicate the Invoices Shipping query ⇒ Rename it to `2 Create the invoice total`.

2. Select the Amount and Shipping columns ⇒ Add Column tab ⇒ Standard button ⇒ Add.

3. Rename the **ADDITION** column to `Invoice Total`, as shown in Figure 7-5.

Amount	Shipping	Invoice Total
45	1.8	46.8
479.85	19.19	499.04
107.8	4.31	112.11

Figure 7-5 Invoice total calculation

Calculate The Line Item Total

Chapter 5, Exercise 5.4, covered how to create a formula to calculate the line total of each item ordered. The formula multiplied the values in two columns. In this part of the exercise, you will recreate the Line Total formula, using the **MULTIPLY FUNCTION WITH 2 COLUMNS**.

1. Home tab ⇒ **RECENT SOURCES BUTTON** ⇒ More Data Files workbook ⇒ Import the 06 Invoices Detail table.
2. Duplicate the Invoices Detail query ⇒ Rename it to `3 Create Line Total`.
3. Select the Quantity and Unit Price columns ⇒ Add Column tab ⇒ Standard button ⇒ Multiply.
4. Rename the **MULTIPLICATION** column to `New Line Total`. You should see that the values are the same as the result of the formula that you created in Chapter 5. [See Figure 5-20]

Calculate The Sales Tax Amount

In the previous part of this exercise you used the Multiply function with two columns to create a calculated column. If the **MULTIPLY FUNCTION** is used with one column, you can enter a number that each value in the column will be multiplied by. One way to use this function with one column is to calculate the sales tax.

1. Duplicate the Invoices Shipping query ⇒ Rename it to `4 Calculate sales tax`.
2. Click on the Amount column ⇒ Add Column tab ⇒ Standard button ⇒ Multiply.
3. On the dialog box shown in Figure 7-6, type `.045` in the field next to the Value field.

   This is the sales tax rate of 4.5%.

   Click OK.

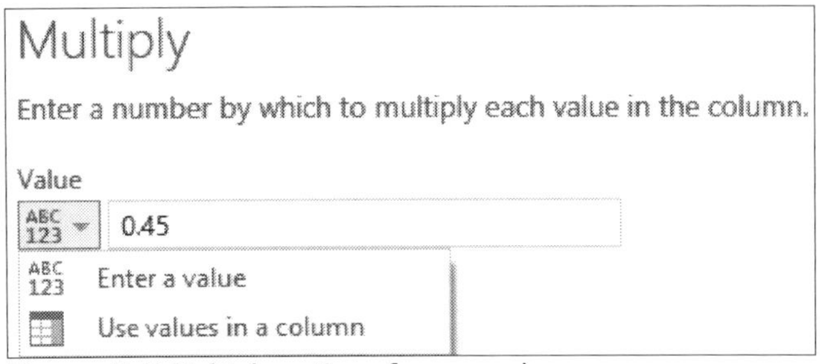

Figure 7-6 Multiply options for one column

The options in the Value field drop-down list, are explained below.

Select the **ENTER A VALUE OPTION** if you want to type in a value, like you did in step 3.

Select the **USE VALUES IN A COLUMN OPTION** to select the column that has the data that you want to use, as shown in Figure 7-7.

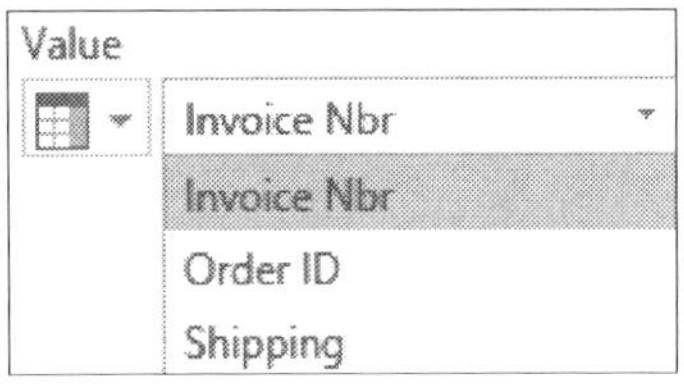

Figure 7-7 Multiply values in column option

4. Rename the **MULTIPLICATION** column to `Sales Tax`.

> **Rename Column Tip**
> Double-clicking on the column heading allows it to be renamed.

Use More Than Two Columns To Create A Calculated Column

More than two columns can be used to create a calculated column. To create an Invoice total, the Amount, Shipping and Sales Tax columns are needed to create the calculation. This part of the exercise will show you how to use multiple columns in a calculation.

1. Duplicate the Sales tax query ⇒ Rename it to `5 Use three columns in the calculation`.
2. Select the Amount, Shipping and Sales Tax columns ⇒ Add Column tab ⇒ Statistics button ⇒ Sum.
3. Rename the Addition column to `Invoice Total`.

Date Functions

Figure 7-8 shows the date functions on the **ADD COLUMN TAB.**

The **AGE FUNCTION** creates a new column that calculates the difference between the local current time (on your computer) and the time in the selected column. This function returns the difference in days and hours.

Figure 7-9 shows the Age function applied to the Date column in the Invoices shipping query. I applied the **DURATION ⇒ DAYS FUNCTION** to the Age From Date column, to display the age in days, as shown in the last column in the figure. You will see different values in the last two columns because the values increment daily.

Figure 7-8 Date functions

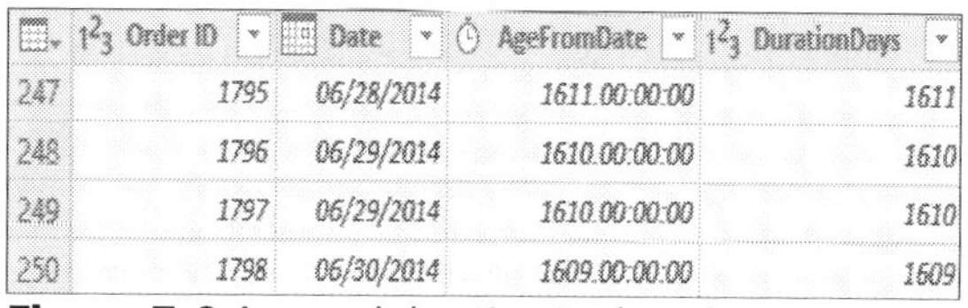

	Order ID	Date	AgeFromDate	DurationDays
247	1795	06/28/2014	1611.00:00:00	1611
248	1796	06/29/2014	1610.00:00:00	1610
249	1797	06/29/2014	1610.00:00:00	1610
250	1798	06/30/2014	1609.00:00:00	1609

Figure 7-9 Age and duration in days functions

The **DATE ONLY FUNCTION** converts the data to a date.

The **PARSE FUNCTION** returns the date portion of the data in the cell. This option is only enabled for Text data type columns.

The **SUBTRACT DAYS FUNCTION** is only enabled when two date columns, with the same date type, are selected. This function creates a new column and calculates the difference between the two dates. Select the columns in the order that you want the function to use them in. For example, if the Order Date and Ship Date are the columns that you will use, select the Ship Date column first.

The **COMBINE DATE AND TIME FUNCTION** is only enabled when a date data type column and a time data type column are both selected. The data in both columns will be combined (merged) into one new column. This option is also on the Time button.

The **EARLIEST FUNCTION** is used to create a new column that contains the earliest date from the columns selected for each row. (1)

The **LATEST FUNCTION** is used to create a new column that contains the most recent date from the columns selected for each row. (1)

(1) This function is only enabled when two or more date columns are selected.

Popular Date Functions

Some of the most popular date fields include the year portion of a date, the quarter that the date is in, the month name of the date spelled out and the month number.

If these are fields that you need, you are in luck, as there are functions for them. As you will probably want to add these columns to a table, so that you can keep the date field intact, select the options listed in Table 7-2, from the Date button on the Add Column tab.

Figure 7-10 illustrates the two month options that I just mentioned. Just select the one(s) you need and a new column will be created and populated with the values.

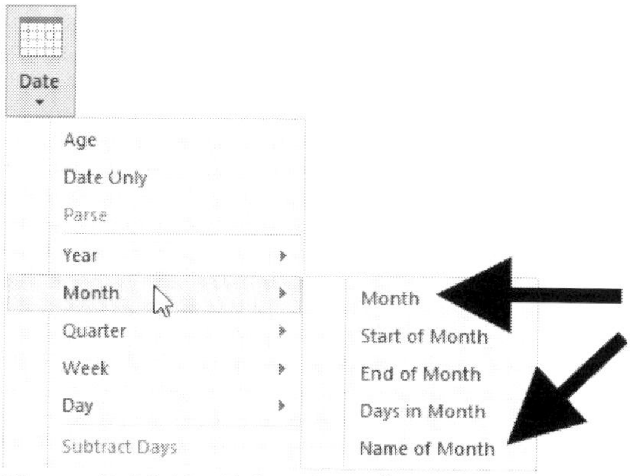

Figure 7-10 Month functions illustrated

The only downside to using these functions, in my opinion, is that they increase the size of each table that they are added to. If you need to add these fields to more than one table, it is better to create a date table, because the date table does not increase the size of each table that is linked to it.

This Function . . .	Displays This Portion Of The Date Field
Year ⇒ Year	The four digit year.
Quarter ⇒ Quarter of Year	The quarter of the year that the date is in (1-4).
Month ⇒ Month	The month number (1-12).
Month ⇒ Name of Month	The month name spelled out (January, February)

Table 7-2 Date functions explained

Time Functions

Figure 7-11 shows the time functions on the Add Column tab.

The **LOCAL TIME FUNCTION** is only enabled for columns that have the **DATE/TIME/TIME ZONE** data type. It converts the time zone of the date to the local time zone.

The **PARSE FUNCTION** returns the time portion of the data in the cell. This option is only enabled for Text data type columns.

The **SUBTRACT FUNCTION** works the same as the Subtract Days function, that was explained earlier.

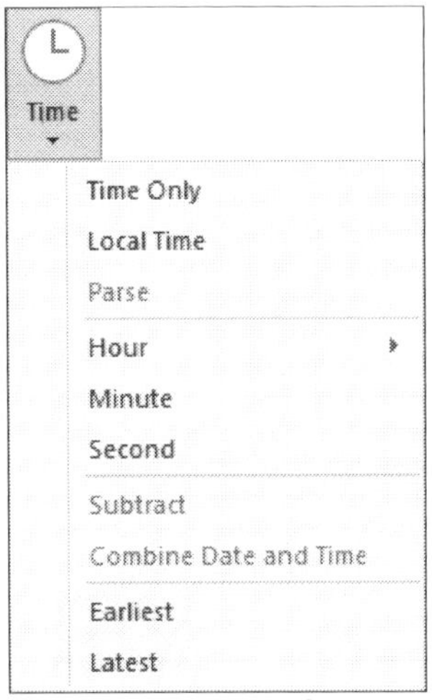

Figure 7-11 Time functions

Duration Functions

Figure 7-12 shows the Duration functions on the Add Column tab. These options are only available for columns that have the Duration data type.

The **TOTAL YEARS FUNCTION** divides the total number of days by 365. This function is demonstrated and shown below, in the second column in Figure 7-14.

The **SUBTRACT FUNCTION** is only enabled when two columns with the Duration data type are selected. This function calculates the difference between the two columns.

Figure 7-12 Duration functions

How To Calculate Age In Years

If you have the need to calculate peoples age or calculate something like the number of years someone has been a customer, the steps below show you how, as long as you have a date field. The number of years calculated, is the difference between the date in the query and today's date.

1. Open the query that has the date field that you want to convert to years ⇒ Click on the date column to use in the calculation.

2. Add Column tab ⇒ Date button ⇒ Age function ⇒ Click on the new column (the Age From Date column, shown below in Figure 7-14) ⇒ Add Column tab ⇒ Duration button ⇒ **TOTAL YEARS FUNCTION**. The number before the decimal point is the age.

3. Click on the Total Years column ⇒ Home tab ⇒ Split Column button ⇒ By Delimiter ⇒ Select the options shown in Figure 7-13.

   The field below the Custom option, shown in the figure, should have a period in it.

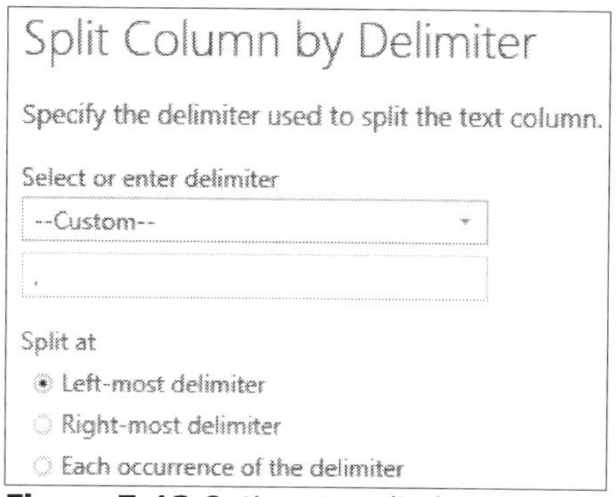

Figure 7-13 Options to split the Total Years column

4. Delete the Total Years.2 column ⇒ Rename the last column in the figure, as needed.

   Figure 7-14 shows the original date (the Birth Date column) and each column that was created in the steps above. The last column in this figure is the age.

BirthDate	AgeFromDate	Age
12/08/1972	16800.00:00:00	46
02/19/1969	18188.00:00:00	49
08/30/1971	17266.00:00:00	47
09/19/1973	16515.00:00:00	45
03/04/1975	15984.00:00:00	43

Figure 7-14 Calculated age in years columns

Keep in mind if you use these steps to calculate a persons age, that the Age function does not take into account the month and day of the persons birthday. This means that if you run a report in June, peoples birthdays that are after the day you run the report on, are pre-maturely incremented. In other words, the **AGE FUNCTION** calculates the age as if today is January 1st, regardless of when during the year that you run the report. I create a DAX formula instead of using the Age function, when I need an age that is based on today's date.

How The Trim And Clean Functions Work

Have you had or seen data in a text file that looked like the file shown in Figure 7-15, that you needed to import and clean?

If so, you know that the data probably has spaces in places where they are not needed.

It is also possible that the data has non-printable characters. This is often the case with **NON-DELIMITED FILES**.

```
Page 1                                                       January 2016

                                                          Invoices

Invoice Nbr    Order ID       Date      Amount   Customer
181     1121   01/01/2016     $851.77            City Cyclists
182     1122   01/01/2016     $1,025.40          Pathfinders
183     1123   01/02/2016     $5,219.55          Bike - A - Holics Anonymous
184     1124   01/02/2016     $59.70  Psycho - Cycle
185     1125   01/02/2016     $75.42  Sporting Wheels Inc.
186     1126   01/02/2016     $3,842.55          Rockshocks for Jocks
187     1127   01/02/2016     $520.35            Poser  &  Cycles
```

Figure 7-15 Non-delimited data

Based on my experiences, when this type of file is imported into the Query Editor, often, all of the data shown above in Figure 7-15 is imported into one column. The functions explained below can help you get non-delimited data ready to be analyzed, after it has been imported into Power BI Desktop.

The **TRIM FUNCTION** removes leading and trailing spaces in cells. This option does not replace duplicate spaces in the middle of the data, like the Trim function does in Excel.

The **CLEAN FUNCTION** removes invisible characters, like non printable characters and carriage returns.

If you import a text file and it looks like the one shown in Figure 7-16, the next few sections demonstrate how to get the data into separate columns.

This figure shows the imported data from the text file shown above in Figure 7-15.

As you can see, all of the data is in one column.

As shown in the Applied Steps section on the Query Settings panel, notice that none of the data was converted.

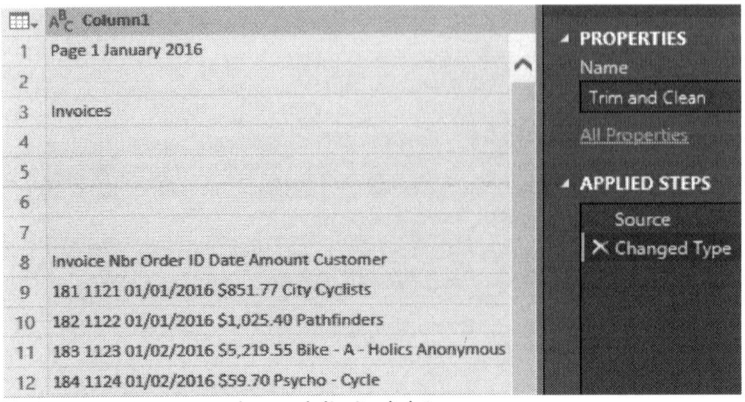

Figure 7-16 Imported non-delimited data

Clean The Data

The first task that needs to be completed is to remove rows of data that are not needed and remove the empty rows at the top of the column. As shown above in Figure 7-16, the first seven rows need to be removed.

In this example, if you kept the column headings row, it would be impossible to create columns of data because the length of some of the column headings is longer then the length of the data in the column. Plus, you can add the column headings back, once the single column of data has been split into several columns. If you need to remove the row of column headings on your own, either write them down, take a screen shot of them or something that will let you see what they were, so that you can recreate them later.

Yes, you could keep switching to the step before the step that deleted the row of column headings, but that may get on your nerves. <smile> The steps below and in the next section, demonstrate how to use the Trim and Clean functions.

1. Home tab ⇒ Remove Rows button ⇒ Remove Top Rows ⇒ Enter the number of rows that need to be deleted.

2. Add Column tab ⇒ Format button ⇒ Trim. Notice the new columns name.

3. Add Column tab ⇒ Format button ⇒ Clean.

   Notice that all of the spaces between the columns have been removed.

   You should have steps similar to those shown in Figure 7-17.

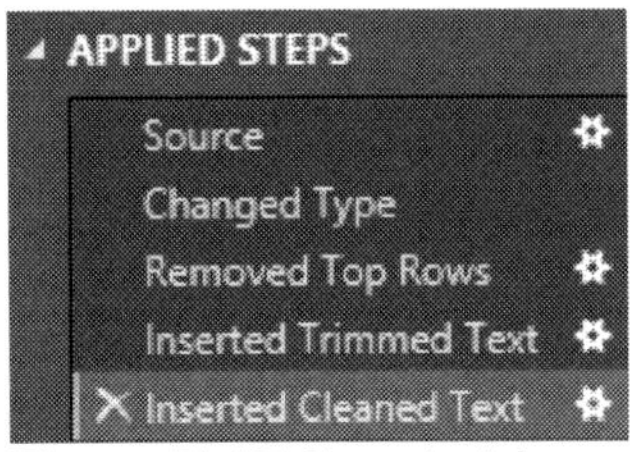

Figure 7-17 Steps to trim and clean the data

Create The Columns

Even though the data is clean, it is still in one column. This section will show you how to separate the data to create the columns. Because the data does not have delimiter characters, most of the columns have to be split by a number of characters, which can take several steps to accomplish.

1. Home tab ⇒ Split Column button ⇒ By Number of Characters ⇒ Type 3 in the field. That is the length of the Invoice number field.

   Select **ONCE, AS FAR LEFT AS POSSIBLE**, as shown in Figure 7-18.

   I prefer to create one column at a time, so that I do not have to split a column that I already split, to put two columns together.

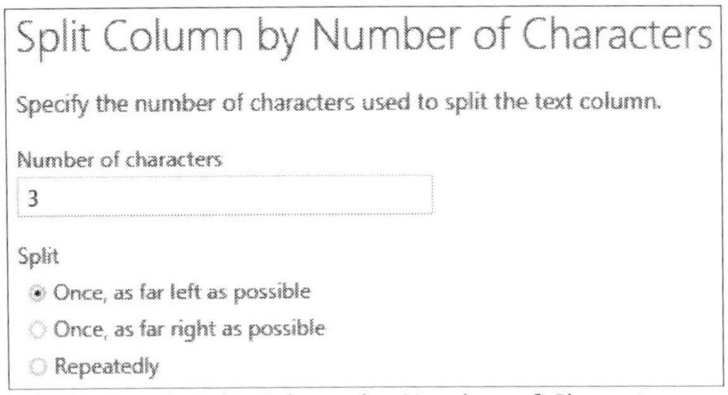

Figure 7-18 Split Column by Number of Characters options

2. Rename the Clean.1 column.

3. Repeat this process for each column that needs to be created.

   It is possible that you may also have to use the Split Column by Delimiter options. When finished, Figure 7-19 shows what the query would look like.

	InvNbr	OrderID	InvDate	InvAmount	Customer
1	181	1121	01/01/2016	$851.77	City Cyclists
2	182	1122	01/01/2016	$1,025.40	Pathfinders
3	183	1123	01/02/2016	$5,219.55	Bike - A - Holics Anonymous
4	184	1124	01/02/2016	$59.70	Psycho - Cycle
5	185	1125	01/02/2016	$75.42	Sporting Wheels Inc.

Figure 7-19 Data after the original column is split into multiple columns

Exercise 7.2: Use Functions On The Transform And Add Column Tabs

This exercise will show you how to use more functions that are available on the Query Editor.

Use The Count Distinct Values Function

If you have the need to display a count of values, text or numeric, the Count Distinct Values function is the solution. This part of the exercise will show you how to display a distinct count of states that have customers.

1. Save the E2.4 file as `E7.2 Using functions`.

2. Duplicate the Customers query ⇒ Rename it to `1 Count distinct states`.

3. Select the State column ⇒ Transform tab ⇒ Statistics button ⇒ **COUNT DISTINCT VALUES.** You should see the value shown on the left side of Figure 7-20.

   I displayed the query name next to it in the figure, so that if you look at this figure again, a month from now, you will know what the number represents.

15	1 Count distinct states

Figure 7-20 Distinct count value

Use The Round Up Function

The Round functions are used to make numbers, especially long numbers, easier to read, while keeping the rounded value close to the original value. The **ROUND UP FUNCTION** removes the decimal point and digits after it and adds "1" to the value. The value after the decimal point is ignored. This may be different then the round up function that you may be use to, that only rounds up when the number after the decimal point is .50 or larger.

This part of the exercise will show you how to round values up to the next whole number.

1. Duplicate the Monthly Sales Pivot Table query ⇒ Rename it to `2 Round Up function`.

2. Click on the 2012 column ⇒ Add Column tab ⇒ Rounding button ⇒ Round Up.

3. Rename the new column to `2012 Rounded Up` ⇒ Drag this column next to the 2012 column, as shown in Figure 7-21.

   Moving the column just makes it easier to see how the Round Up function works.

1.2 2012	123 2012 Rounded Up
2233575.113	2233576
3705635.498	3705636
2611621.26	2611622
3041865.441	3041866

Figure 7-21 Round Up function applied

Use The Quarter Of Year Function

Many reports need to display or group the data by the quarter of the year (which is based on a date field). This part of this exercise will show you how to add a column that displays the quarter for the order date.

1. Duplicate the Orders query ⇒ Rename it to `3 Quarter of Year function`.

2. Select the Order Date column ⇒ Change the Data Type to Date ⇒ Add Column tab ⇒ Date button ⇒ Quarter ⇒ Quarter of Year.

3. Rename the Quarter column to `Order Date Quarter` ⇒

   Move the column left, next to the Order Date column, as shown in Figure 7-22.

	Order Date	Order Date Quarter
14	03/24/2006	1
15	03/24/2006	1
16	04/07/2006	2
17	04/05/2006	2
18	04/08/2006	2

Figure 7-22 Order Date Quarter column

Use The Subtract Days Function

This part of the exercise will show you how to calculate the number of days between two dates.

1. Duplicate the Orders query ⇒ Rename it to `4 Subtract Days function`.
2. Change the Data Type of the Order Date and Shipped Date columns to Date.
3. Select the Shipped Date column ⇒ Hold down the CTRL key ⇒ Select the Order Date column.
4. Add Column tab ⇒ Date button ⇒ Subtract Days ⇒ Rename the column to `Date Difference` ⇒ Move the Date Difference column to the left, after the Shipped Date column.

You should see the values shown in Figure 7-23. In this exercise, the Date Difference column displays how many days are between the date the order was placed and the date the order was shipped.

Null values in the new column means that at least one of the cells in the columns used to create the column, does not have a date.

Order Date	Shipped Date	DateDifference
01/15/2006	01/22/2006	7
01/20/2006	01/22/2006	2
01/22/2006	01/22/2006	0
01/30/2006	01/31/2006	1

Figure 7-23 Subtract Days calculation

A zero in the Date Difference column means that the order was shipped in less than 24 hours after it was placed. This is true, even if the order and shipped dates are a date apart. That is because the Subtract Days function actually uses the time portion of a date field, whether or not the date has a time value. In order for the Subtract Days function to really be accurate, the date fields used, need to also have the time portion of the date field being used.

Creating Percents

The Standard button on the Transform and Add Column tabs have the following **PERCENT FUNCTIONS**.

① **PERCENTAGE** Use this function to calculate a percent of the values in the selected column. For example, you need to know what 25% of the monthly sales is, for a specific year. On the dialog box shown in Figure 7-24, you would type in 25. A column would be created that displayed what 25% of each months sales is.

② **PERCENT OF** Use this function to display the values in the column as a percent of a value that you select.

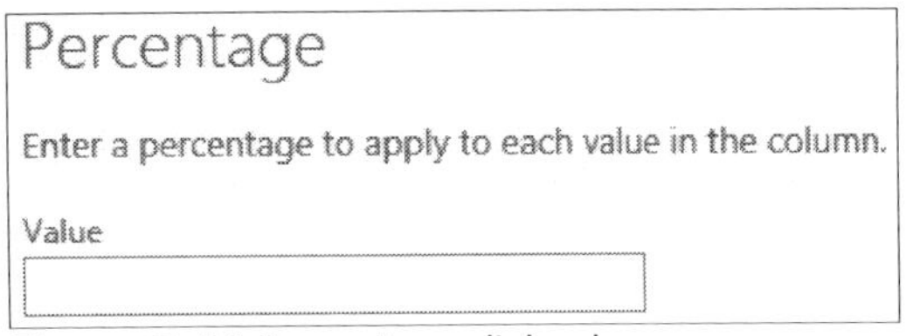

Figure 7-24 Percentage dialog box

Conditional Columns

The Add Conditional Column dialog box is used to create criteria that selects the value to be added to the new column that is created. This dialog box is used to create an IF Then Else statement without writing code. In Chapter 5, Exercise 5.4, you typed in code to create an IF statement [See Chapter 5, Figure 5-25]. Instead of typing in all of the code, you can use this dialog box to create it, as you will see in the next exercise.

The Add Conditional Column dialog box is used to create new columns of data in a query, using values from other columns in the same query. It can also be used to create "buckets" to categorize data.

The options shown in Figure 7-25 are used to select a **VALUE** (the data used for the comparison), the **OUTPUT** (what you want to happen if the value meets the criteria rule) and **OTHERWISE** (what to do if the data does not meet any of the rules created for the column. Using the Otherwise condition is optional. If it is not used, rows that do not meet any of the rules will not have any data in the conditional column.

Select the **ENTER A VALUE OPTION** to type in a value.

The **SELECT A COLUMN OPTION** is used to select a column from the query that has the data to use for the value.

The **PARAMETER OPTION** is used to select an existing parameter, to get the data to use for the value.

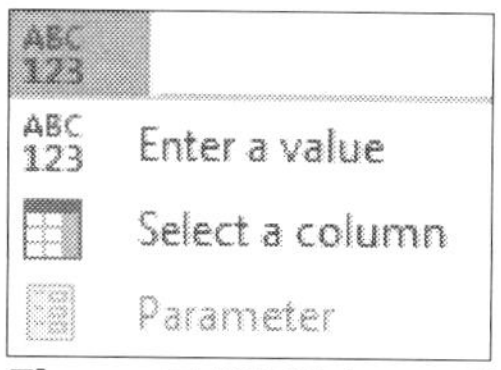

Figure 7-25 Value options

Exercise 7.3: Create A Conditional Column

In this exercise, you will duplicate the IF Then Else statement that you created in Exercise 5.4. The Add Conditional Column dialog box does not support the "duration" part of the formula, so you will create a custom column for that portion of the formula and use it in place of the Order Date field.

Create The Duration Custom Column

In this part of the exercise, you will create a column that replaces the duration portion of the formula in Chapter 5, Figure 5-25.

1. Save the E2.4 file as `E7.3 Conditional column`.
2. Duplicate the Orders query ⇒ Rename it to `1 Conditional column`.
3. Create the custom column shown in Figure 7-26 ⇒ Apply and save the changes.

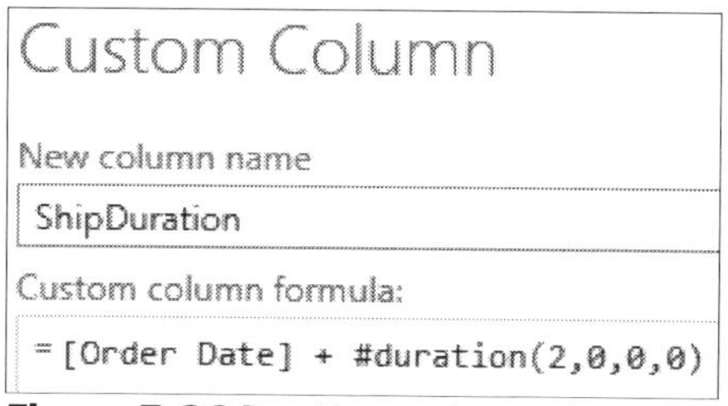

Figure 7-26 Duration custom column formula

Create The Shipped On Time Conditional Column

1. In the 1 Conditional column query ⇒ Add Column tab ⇒ **CONDITIONAL COLUMN BUTTON**.
2. In the New column name field type `Shipped On Time`.
3. In the Column Name field drop-down list, select the Shipped Date field ⇒ Select the **IS AFTER OR EQUAL TO** operator.
4. In the Value field drop-down list, select the **SELECT A COLUMN** option (See Figure 7-25) ⇒ Select the Ship Duration field in the next drop-down list.
5. In the Output field drop-down list, select Enter a Value ⇒ Type `Shipped Late` in the next field.

Create The Else If Portion Of The Condition

1. Click the **ADD RULE BUTTON**.
2. In the Column Name field, select the Shipped Date field ⇒ Select the **IS BEFORE** operator.
3. In the Value field drop-down list, select the **SELECT A COLUMN** option ⇒ Select the Ship Duration field in the next drop-down list.

4. In the Output field drop-down list, select Enter a Value ⇒ Type `On Time` in the next field.

Create The Otherwise Portion Of The Condition

1. Open the Otherwise drop-down list and select Enter a Value.

2. Type `Problem with Order or Shipped Date field`. You should have the options shown in Figure 7-27 ⇒ Click OK.

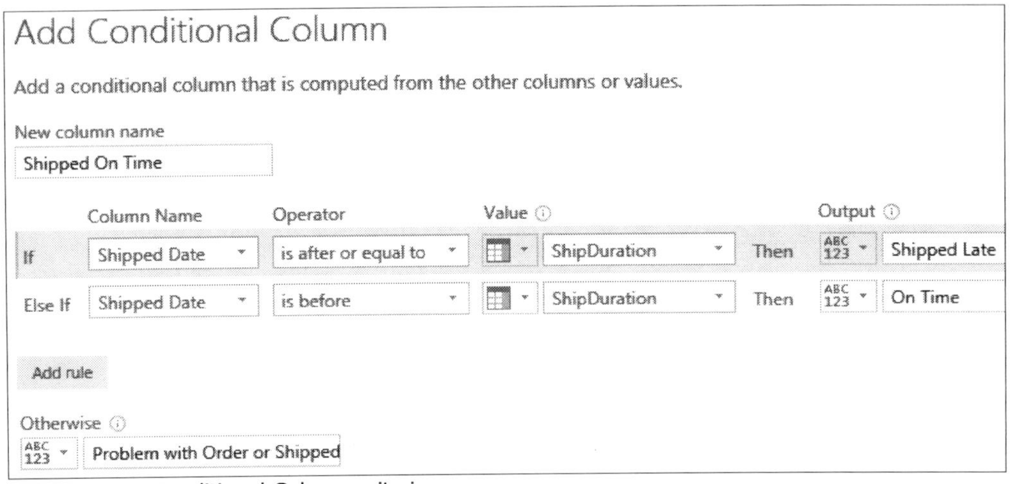

Figure 7-27 Conditional Column criteria

If you scroll down the Shipped On Time column, you will see some cells have the word **ERROR**, as shown in Figure 7-28. That is because the Shipped Date field does not have a date for some rows of data. I was expecting to see the text entered in the "Otherwise" field, shown above in Figure 7-27.

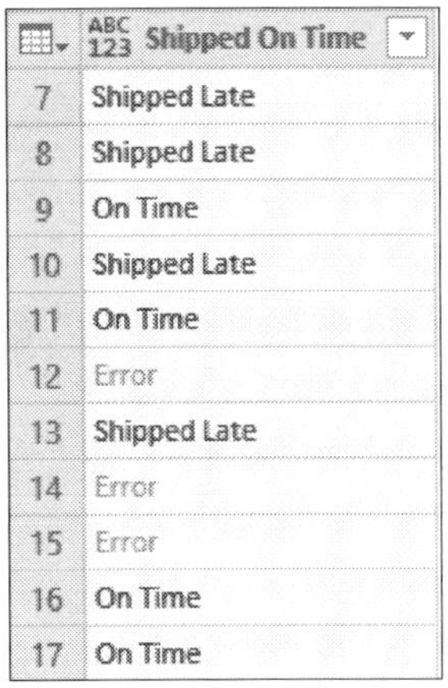

Figure 7-28 Result of conditional column criteria

I then created the criteria shown in Figure 7-29. I left the "Otherwise" field blank. Initially, the condition to check for a null value was the last condition, but that did not work. As shown in Figure 7-30, the check for null values works. Compare this to Figure 7-28. No, I do not understand why! <smile>

Figure 7-31 shows the conditions to check for a null value. Notice in Figure 7-32, that the "Otherwise" condition works. Hopefully, these inconsistencies will eventually be fixed.

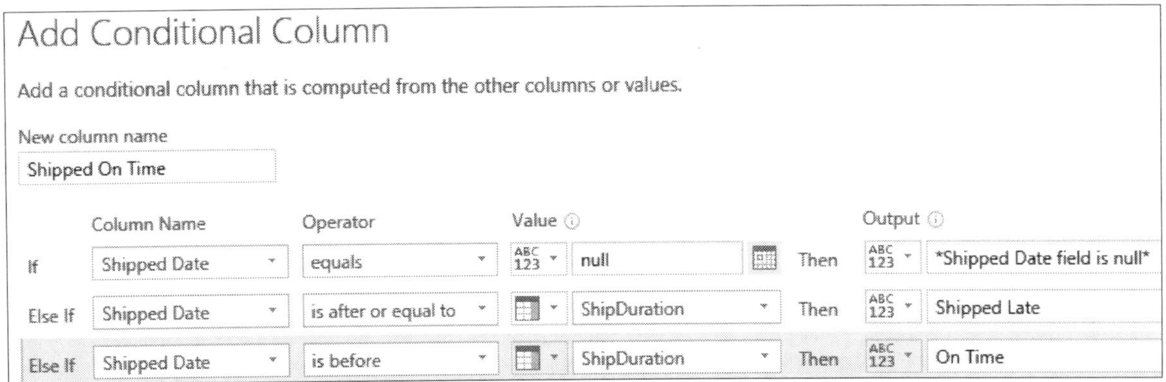

Figure 7-29 Criteria to check for null values with other criteria

	Shipped On Time
7	Shipped Late
8	Shipped Late
9	On Time
10	Shipped Late
11	On Time
12	*Shipped Date field is null*
13	Shipped Late
14	*Shipped Date field is null*
15	*Shipped Date field is null*
16	On Time
17	On Time

Figure 7-30 Result of the null value condition in Figure 7-29

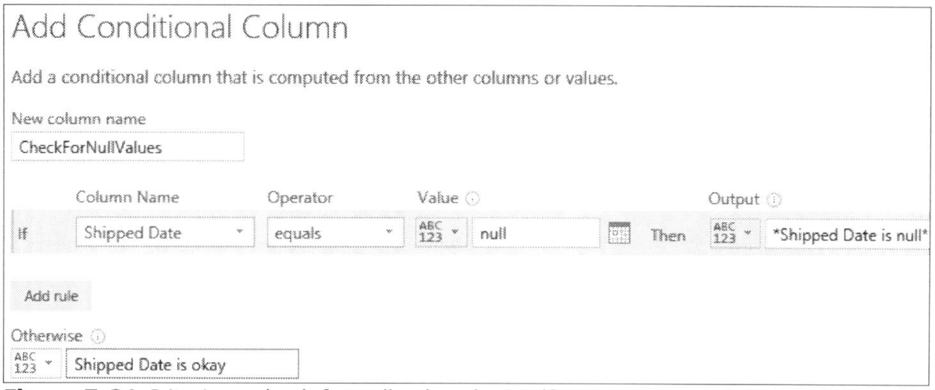

Figure 7-31 Criteria to check for null values by itself

	CheckForNullValues
13	Shipped Date is okay
14	*Shipped Date is null*
15	*Shipped Date is null*
16	Shipped Date is okay
17	Shipped Date is okay

Figure 7-32 Result of the null value conditional checking by itself, in Figure 7-31

Add Conditional Column Dialog Box Issues

Even though multiple requests were submitted to have the following issues resolved, at the time this book went to print, the bugs had not been fixed.

① **ISSUE #1** The criteria created for the **OTHERWISE OPTION** on this dialog box does not work, if there is more than one condition created at the top of the dialog box. I was expecting the text that I entered to be displayed for records that do not meet the criteria that I created at the top of the dialog box, but that doesn't happen. Instead, cells that do not meet the criteria, have the word "Error" in them.

② **ISSUE #2** When checking for null values, the criteria only works if the null value criteria is first on the Conditional Column dialog box. If it isn't, the word Error is displayed, instead of the value in the Output field.

Column From Examples Transformation

The Column From Examples transformation is used to create a new column of data, that is based on the sample data that you type in, from existing columns. This tool is good for people that are not familiar with the transformation options or do not know where the option is, in the Query Editor, that they need, but know the type of data that they need to create a report. The benefit that many will find using the Column From Examples transformation, is that they can create new columns of data without having to know which transformation(s) to use.

This transformation can also be used to replace null values and to create buckets, to place data in. Since it's release, this transformation has been updated on a regular basis to include more functionality.

What is also helpful is that after creating a column using this transformation, you can see the formula on the dialog box. And when you close the dialog box, you can also see the formula, in the formula bar. This will help you learn more about the transformations that you use and should make it easier over time, for you to be able to select the transformation that you need, from a toolbar, in the Query Editor.

Based on the values that you type in, the Query Editor tries to create the appropriate transformation. More than one column can be created using the Column From Examples transformation, in the same query.

There are two ways to use this feature, as shown in Figure 7-33. The options are explained below.

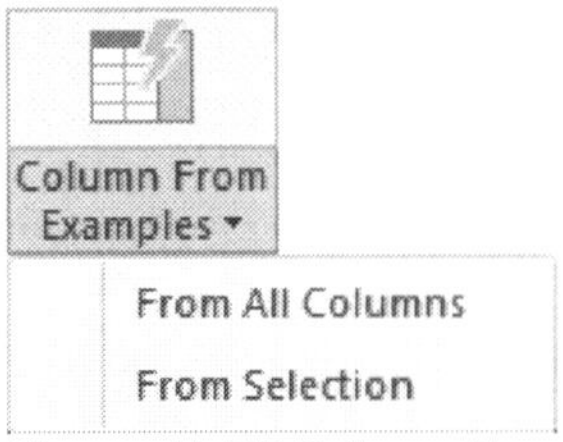

Figure 7-33 Column From Examples options

Select the **FROM ALL COLUMNS OPTION** when you are not sure which columns have the data that you will create the example data from. This option will check all of the columns in the table, on the Add Column From Examples dialog box, shown in Figure 7-34. This is the default option when you click the top half of the Column From Examples button.

Select the **FROM SELECTION OPTION** if you know the column(s) that have the data that you will create the example data from. If you select the columns on the Query Editor before selecting this option, the selected columns will be the only columns checked, on the Add Column From Examples dialog box, shown in Figure 7-34. Doing this lets Power Query know to only use the selected columns to base the transformation on. If you do not select the columns before you open the dialog box, you can clear the check mark for the columns that you do not want to search, after the dialog box is open. Doing this is optional, but it can help Power Query narrow down the example data that you are creating and create the transformation that you are looking for.

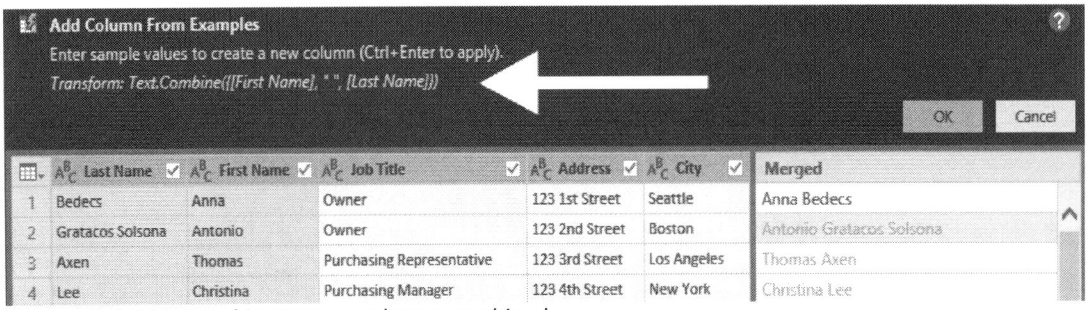

Figure 7-34 First and Last name columns combined

The **ADD COLUMN FROM EXAMPLES DIALOG BOX**, shown above in Figure 7-34, has the options to transform the data. The section on the left, with the columns, is the **DATA PREVIEW AREA**. It displays the data from the query.

The section on the right is the **NEW COLUMN PREVIEW AREA**. This is where you type examples of the data that you want in the output column. As you create new columns of data using the Column 1 field (renamed to Merged in the figure), they are added to this section.

The Column From Examples dialog box is used to create new columns of data without having to know which button, on which tab in the Query Editor, should be used. This is accomplished by typing in one or more examples of what you want the data in the new column to look like. As you will see, a benefit of using this option is that you do not have to know function names or how to create formulas. Behind the scenes, the correct transformation function is selected, which creates the formula.

When you click in a row in the Column 1 field, the corresponding row in the data preview area is selected. Type in the transformation that you want to create. For example, you want to change a date/time field to a date field. In the data preview area, click on the date column that you want to change, then type in the date, without the time in the Column 1 field. When you press Enter, the column will display the dates without a time. At the top of the window, you will see the transformation formula, as illustrated above, in Figure 7-34.

As you are typing in the Column 1 field, Intellisense will display a list of options, that it thinks match what you are typing, as shown in Figure 7-35.

If you see what you need in the drop-down list, double-click on it, to select it.

The options in the drop-down list is data that Power Query thinks could be used to create the transformation.

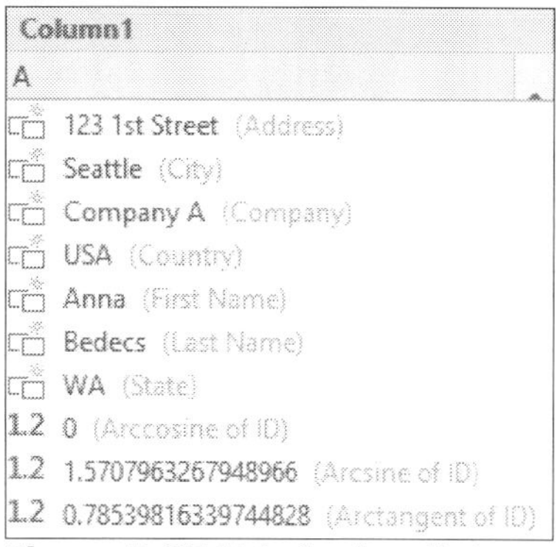

Figure 7-35 List of values that you can select from

Query Editor Tip Reminder
Behind the scenes, the Query Editor captures your transformation steps and creates the formula. It will remind you of creating a macro in Excel. Each entry in the Applied Steps section, has it's own formula.

Add Column From Examples Transformation Limitations
While the Column From Examples feature supports a lot of transformations, not all of them are supported. Clicking the question mark icon, on the Column From Examples dialog box, opens the web page listed below, which covers the Add Column From Examples transformation. This web page lists the transformations that are supported. https://docs.microsoft.com/en-us/power-bi/desktop-add-column-from-example

Exercise 7.4: Create Columns Of Data From Examples

In this exercise, you will learn how to use the Column From Examples options to create columns of data that you have already created. This will let you see another way to accomplish the same transformation.

Combine Data From Two Columns

In Chapter 5, Exercise 5.4, you learned how to create new columns of data, from data already in the data model. In this part of the exercise, you will learn another way to perform the same transformation of combining the first and last name fields into one column.

1. Save the E2.4 file as `E7.4 Columns of data from examples`.

2. Duplicate the Customers query ⇒ Rename it to `1 Combine name fields`.

3. Add Column tab ⇒ Column From Examples button ⇒ From All Columns.

4. On the first row in the Column 1 field, type the name that is in the First Name and Last Name columns, then press Enter. For me, the name on the first row is Anna Bedecs. The column should have filled in the name for each row, as shown earlier in Figure 7-34.

Notice that the column name was changed to "Merged", because that is the type of transformation that was created.

Notice in the upper left corner, that you see a transform formula. That formula was created because you typed in a name. Pretty cool!

It is not a requirement to type the example criteria on the first row, in the Column 1 field.

5. Double-click on the Merged column heading ⇒ Type `Customer Full Name` ⇒ Click OK. The column will be added to the query.

Extract Data From A Column

In this part of the exercise, you will create an example that will combine the first letter in the First Name column with the Last Name column.

1. Duplicate the Customers query ⇒ Rename it to `2 Combine first letter and last name`.

2. Add Column tab ⇒ Column From Examples button ⇒ From Selection.

> When you are not going to type in the entire contents of a field, you have to select the field(s) that you want to create the example from. There are two options for selecting the columns that you need, as explained below.
>
> ① Select the columns on the query before opening the Add Column From Examples dialog box.
> ② Use the From Selection option, then check the columns on the Add Column From Examples dialog box.

3. On the Add Column From Examples dialog box, check the Last Name and First Name columns ⇒ If any other columns are checked, remove the check mark from them ⇒ If necessary, make sure that the name columns are visible.

4. On a row in the Column 1 field, type the first initial of the first name and last name of the customer that corresponds to the row that you are using ⇒ Press Enter.

As shown in Figure 7-36, you did not get the result that you were expecting, as the first initial is the same for each row. If you look at the formula that was created (in the upper left corner), you can see that it will display the same letter (for me that is the letter "A"), for every row. This means that you need to type in more examples, for this transformation to work with.

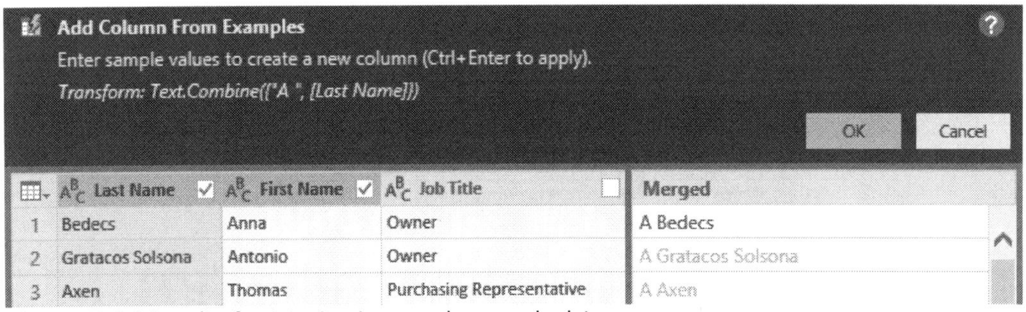

Figure 7-36 Result of not typing in enough example data

5. On another row, type in the first initial and last name. You may see the results that you were expecting, as shown in Figure 7-37. Notice that the letter is not in the formula, as shown above in Figure 7-36, and it has been replaced with the First Name column.

   If you do not see the result that you are expecting, on another row, type in another name. There is no set limit to the number of examples that you will have to provide, to get the results that you are looking for.

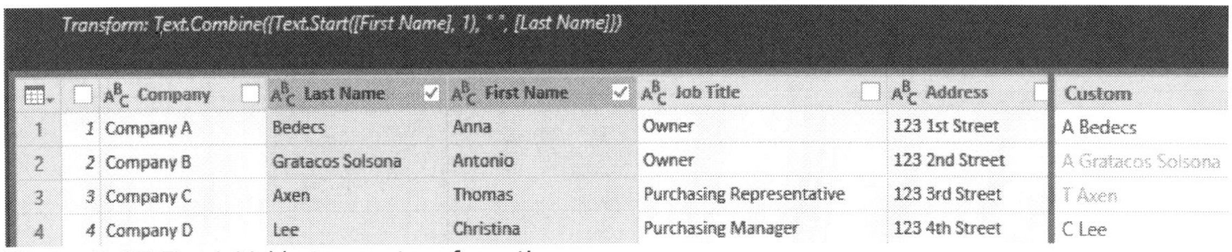

Figure 7-37 First initial last name transformation

If you compare this formula to the one shown in Chapter 5, Figure 5-23, you will see that it is almost identical. The reason that they are not identical is because there is often more than one way to write the same formula.

6. Rename the column to `First Initial Last Name` ⇒ Click OK.

Combine Data From Three Columns

In this part of the exercise, you will learn how to combine three columns and punctuation, to create a new column.

1. Duplicate the Customers query ⇒ Rename it to `3 Combine city state zip`.

2. Add Column tab ⇒ Column From Examples button ⇒ From All Columns.

3. Display the City, State and Zip Code fields on the left.

4. In the Column 1 field, type the city name ⇒ Type a comma ⇒ Press the space bar ⇒ Type the state abbreviation ⇒ Press the space bar ⇒ Type the zip code ⇒ Press Enter ⇒ Rename the column to `CityStateZip`.

You should see all three fields and a comma in the column, as shown in Figure 7-38.

Notice that the example data that you type in, is bold and that the data that is created is gray.

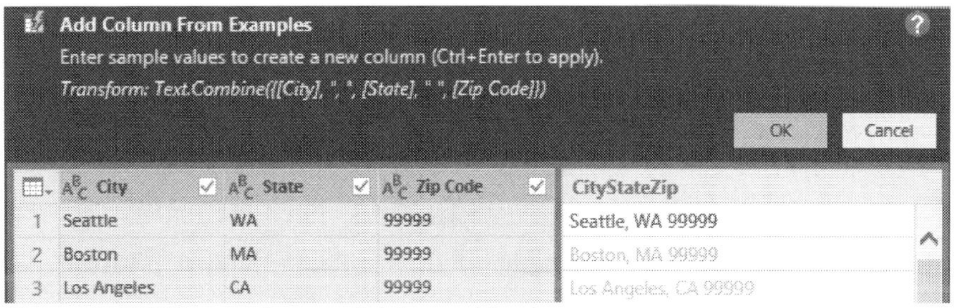

Figure 7-38 Three columns of data combined

If you are really interested in learning about the transformations that are on the tabs, and reading the formula for the step (on the formula bar) isn't helping that much, in the Applied Steps section on the Query Settings panel, click on the icon for the step to display the dialog box for the transformation.

For example, in the transformation that you just created, the Insert Merged Column transformation was created when you used the Add Column From Examples dialog box. The name of the step is the first hint of the type of transformation that was created.

If you click on the cog wheel icon for this transformation (Inserted Merged Column), you will see the dialog box shown in Figure 7-39. This is another view of the formula that was created.

The name of the dialog box is often the same name as the button on one of the tabs in the Query Editor.

Knowing this should help you find the transformation button to use, the next time that you need to combine data from two or more columns.

Figure 7-39 Dialog box used to merge columns of data

Modify The Data Type Of A Date Field

This part of the exercise will show you how to change the data type of a date field. Changing the data type, changes how the dates in the column will be displayed.

1. Duplicate the Orders table ⇒ Rename it to `4 Change Order Date data type`.

2. Select the Order Date column.

3. Add Column tab ⇒ Column From Examples button ⇒ From Selection.

4. In the Column 1 field, type the date portion of the Order Date field ⇒ Press Enter.

5. Rename the Date column to `Removed Time`.

   You should have the options shown in Figure 7-40.

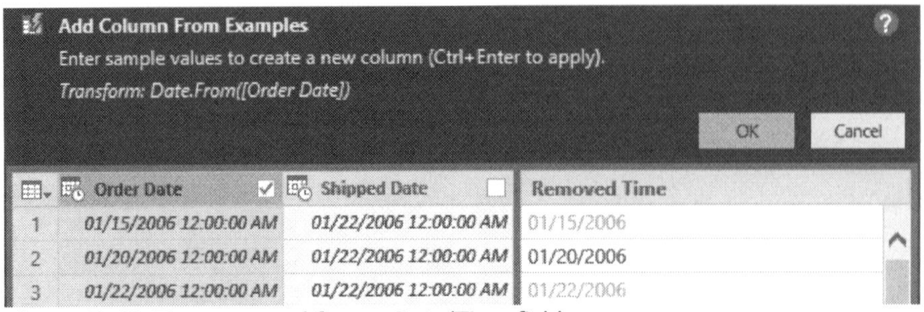

Figure 7-40 Time removed from a Date/Time field

Extract The Month Name From A Date Field

In this part of the exercise, you will learn how to get the month name from a date field.

1. Duplicate the Orders table ⇒ Rename it to `5 Get month name`.
2. Click on the Order Date column ⇒ Add Column tab ⇒ Column From Examples button ⇒ From Selection.
3. In the Column 1 field, type out the month name for the Order Date in the corresponding row ⇒ Press Enter.
4. Rename the column to `Month Name`, as shown in Figure 7-41.

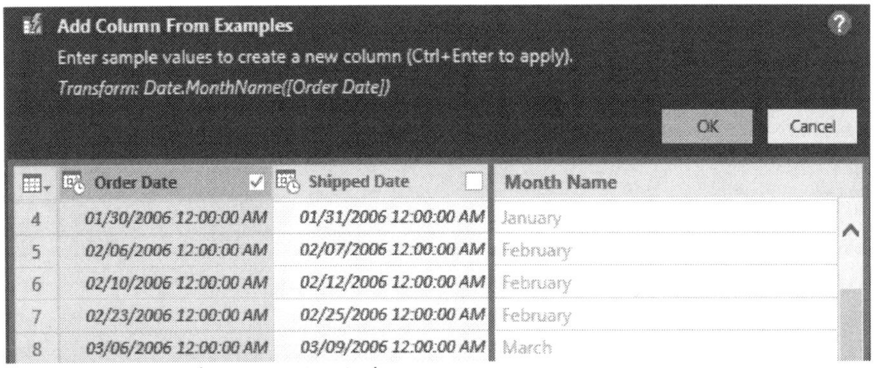

Figure 7-41 Month name extracted

If you typed the month name and year, the formula at the top of Figure 7-42, would be created.

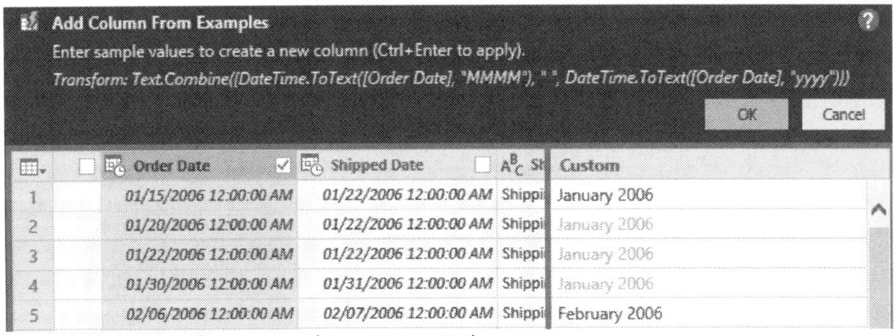

Figure 7-42 Month name and year extracted

Extract The Year From A Date Field

In this part of the exercise, you will learn how to extract the year from a date field.

1. Duplicate the Orders table ⇒ Rename it to `6 Get year`.
2. Click on the Order Date column ⇒ Add Column tab ⇒ Column From Examples button ⇒ From Selection.
3. In the Column 1 field, type the year portion of the Order Date field.

This table only has data for one year, so you will not see different values in the column. The column was renamed appropriately, so there is no need to change it.

Handling Different Date Formats In The Add Column From Examples Dialog Box

If a date field is imported from a source other then a database, there could be different date formats in the same field, as shown in Figure 7-43. The goal is to have all of the dates in the same format. You may be thinking that if you changed the data type for the column to "Date", the problem would be solved. Figure 7-44 shows the result of changing the Data Type to Date. As you can see, the dates with a time, generated an error.

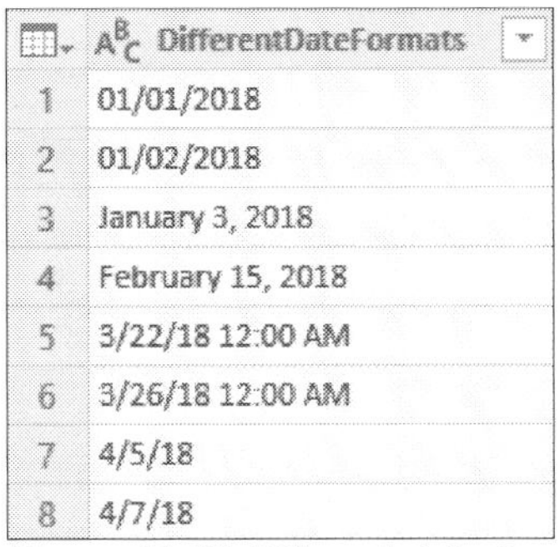

Figure 7-43 Different date formats in a column

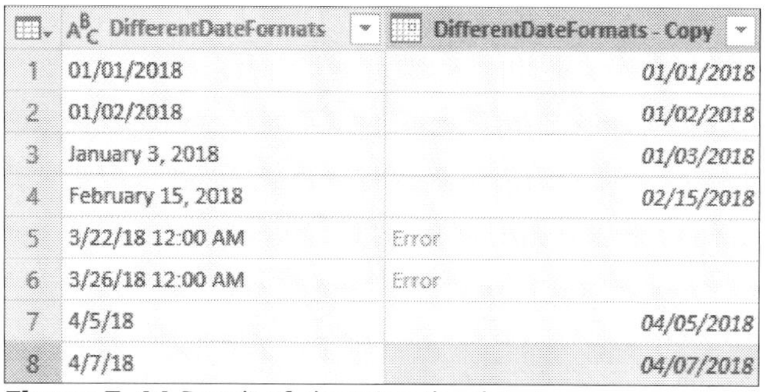

Figure 7-44 Result of changing the data type

If you were new to Power Query, you may not have any idea, which transformation to use, to fix the problem. This is where the **COLUMN FROM EXAMPLES** tool would be very helpful.

As the dates with times generated the error, I would type in the date format example on one of those rows first, as shown in Figure 7-45.

Notice that all of the dates did not convert the day portion of the date to two digits. If you wanted a two digit day, you would have to type in at least one more example. I would use a date with a day that was not already two digits.

Did you see how long the formula is, for this transformation?

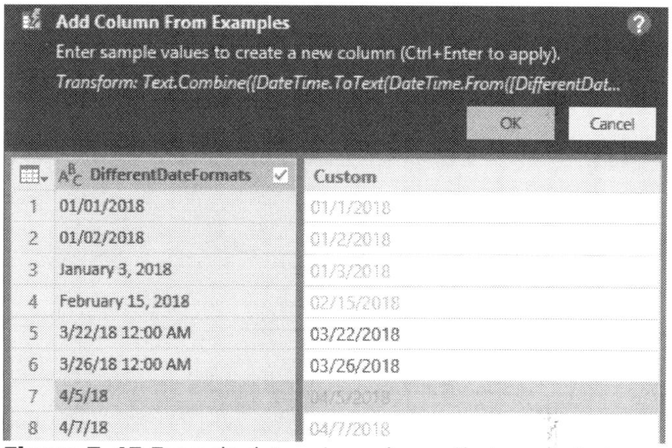

Figure 7-45 Example data using columns that generated an error

Figure 7-46 shows that starting with dates in the format that you want for the new column, does not convert any of the other dates. This means that you would have to type in more example data.

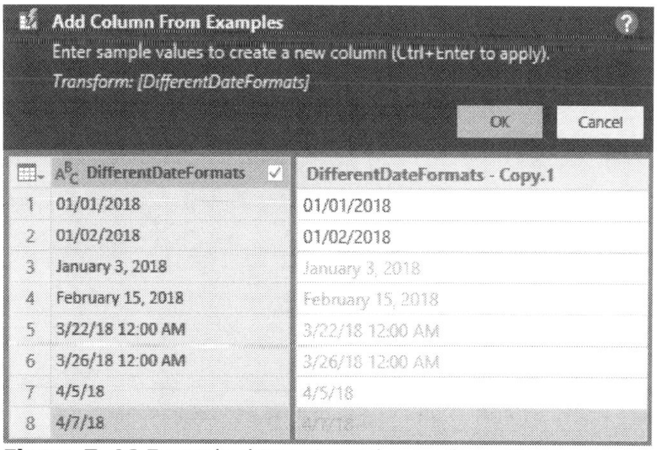

Figure 7-46 Example data using columns that did not generate an error

Creating Categories, Buckets Or Bins To Group Data

There may be times when you need a way to group data based on a range of values in a field. While the Group By transformation is available, it groups by specific values in a field. If you need one group that has more than one value, or a range of values to be included in the same group or category, the Group By transformation is not the solution, at least not initially. For example, you need order totals in three categories or groups, like 0-100, 100.01 - 250 and 250.01 - 500. To accomplish this, category, **BUCKETS** or **BINS** need to be created and applied to each row. These three terms refer to the same concept and can be interchangeably.

Another example would be creating categories for products. Once these categories or bins are created, you could use this new column of data to group the products on, to get a total amount of sales per product category.

Exercise 7.5: Create Product Categories

In this exercise, you will create the following categories for the Products table: Gloves and Helmets.

1. In a new file, import the 09 Products table in the More Data Files workbook.
2. Save the file as `E7.5 Create product categories by example`.
3. Select the Product Name column ⇒ Use the From Selection option to open the Add Column From Examples dialog box.
4. Rename Column 1 to `Product Category`.
5. Create the example criteria in Table 7-3.

In Rows . . .	Type This . . .
1 and 6	Gloves
12 and 14	Helmets

Table 7-3 Criteria to create the categories

Notice how the Locks and Saddles categories were automatically created, as shown in Figure 7-47.

	ProductID	ProductName	Product Category
37	*4106*	InFlux Lycra Glove (l)	Gloves
38	*5201*	Xtreme Adult Helmet (m white)	Helmets
39	*5202*	Xtreme Adult Helmet (m green)	Helmets
40	*5203*	Xtreme Adult Helmet (m red)	Helmets
41	*5204*	Xtreme Adult Helmet (l white)	Helmets
42	*5205*	Xtreme Adult Helmet (l green)	Helmets
43	*5206*	Xtreme Adult Helmet (l red)	Helmets
44	*5301*	Xtreme Mtn Lock	Locks
45	*5302*	Xtreme Rhino Lock	Locks
46	*5303*	Xtreme Titan Lock	Locks
47	*5207*	Xtreme Youth Helmet (black)	Helmets
48	*5208*	Xtreme Youth Helmet (red)	Helmets
49	*5401*	Xtreme Anatomic Mens Saddle	Saddles

Figure 7-47 Product categories created

Summary

This chapter took transforming data up a notch or two. One way this was accomplished was learning another way to merge columns in one query into another query.

The options on the Add Conditional Column dialog box were covered, in this chapter. The options are used to add a column to a table. For example, it can be used to display whether or not each row of data meets the criteria. Exercise 7.3 demonstrated using this tool to determine if the data in a field is valid. A report could be created using this data checking feature to let users know which records they need to fix.

As I have said, usually queries are created for reporting purposes. When working with large datasets, it is a good idea, to only keep the columns needed to create the report, in the query. While many people use the same query to create multiple reports, that is okay if several reports all use the same fields. I create a query for each report. Doing that, increases the performance of the query and the report. Plus, when a report needs to be modified, from a data perspective, I know which query to modify and do not have to consider or worry about whether or not the changes will break another report that uses the same query. It also helps to name the query, the same (or a very similar) name, as the report.

USING THE QUERY EDITOR TO MASHUP DATA

After completing this chapter you will be able to perform the following tasks:

- ☑ Merge data
- ☑ Append data
- ☑ Group data

CHAPTER 8

What Does Mashup Mean?

The terms **MASHUP** and **DATA MASHUP** often refer to the process of pivoting and unpivoting data, adding columns and rows to tables and joining tables or datasets. Usually, these are some of the last tasks that are applied to the data before reports are created. Some of these topics were covered in previous chapters, but the two most popular ways to mashup data (merge and append) are covered in this chapter. On your own, you can use the features in the order that works best for the data that you are working with.

Why Would I Need To Combine Data From Different Tables?

While some of the terminology used in this chapter is only used when discussing databases, the concepts also apply to data not stored in a database. The ability to join tables and use the data from multiple tables to create one report, may be the number one reason that many people will use Power BI Desktop.

A relationship is a link between two tables. Relationships are created between a column of data that the two tables have in common. Relationships between tables allow for a higher level of analysis, because columns of data from different tables can be reported on, as if they were one table. Data in one table can be filtered by data in another table, which provides even more flexibility and control over the data that is displayed on a visualization. Relationships were covered in detail in Chapter 3.

Merge Data vs Append Data, Which One Should I Use?

These are the two ways to combine data from different tables. Use the **MERGE QUERIES OPTION** when you want to add columns of data in one table to another table. While this may sound good, it is really just duplicating data unnecessarily. Use the **APPEND QUERIES OPTION** when you want to add all of the rows of data in one table to another table. Both options are covered in more detail in this chapter.

Merging Data

Merging data in Power BI Desktop is the process of adding columns from one table to another table. This is also known as **COMBINING DATA** or **MERGING DATA FROM LOOKUP TABLES**. The reason data is merged is because there is a need to create a report or perform analysis that needs to display data from two or more tables. If you have used the **VLOOKUP FUNCTION** in Excel to combine data from different tables, those days are over. Some, or all of the columns in the second table can be added to the first table. Having said that, even though the best choice is to create relationships between tables then to merge data from one table to another, the merge functionality is covered.

Merge Queries Option

Home tab ⇒ **MERGE QUERIES**, displays the dialog box shown in Figure 8-1. You select the columns that will be added after the queries are merged. The columns that you select to join on, must have similar data types.

Display the table that you want the columns to be added to, before opening this dialog box.

While Power BI Desktop has the ability to link tables (create relationships), queries only support one table. That is why you have to add columns from one table to another, while using the Merge Queries option.

The icons illustrated in the figure are used to refresh the data.

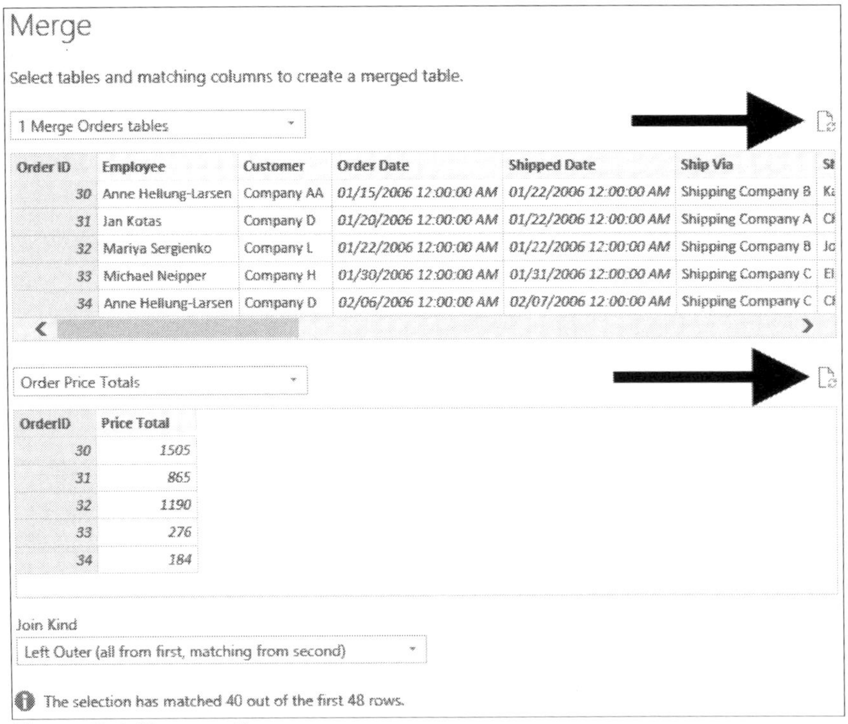

Figure 8-1 Merge options

The first drop-down list contains all of the queries in the file.

If you do not want to alter either table, use the **MERGE QUERIES AS NEW OPTION**, to create a new table.

Selecting Columns To Match On
What may not be obvious is that more than one column in each query, on the Merge dialog box, can be selected to create the matching criteria. The order that multiple columns are selected in, in each query matters.

Join Kind Options

The Join Kind drop-down list, at the bottom of the Merge dialog box, contains options for selecting how the tables will be joined. The options also decide what happens to records in a table that do not have matching records in the other table, in the join. If you have used joins in a programming language like SQL, the options explained in Table 8-1 will be familiar.

Option	This Join Kind Option Selects . . .
Left Outer	All records in the first query and the matching records in the second query. This is the default join option. This option will retrieve/display all records in the first table. This option is useful if you are trying to ensure that each record, in the first table, has at least one matching record in the second table. This provides another way to clean the data. This option is often used to merge data from a lookup table, into another table.
Right Outer	All records in the second query and the matching records in the first query.
Full Outer	All records from both queries, without using any matching criteria.
Inner	Records from both queries that have an exact match on the column that is selected for the join. Unlike the Left Outer join option, which selects all records in the first table, regardless of whether or not there is a matching record in the second table, the Inner join option only retrieves records when there is a match.
Left Anti	Records in the first query that do not have a matching record in the second query.
Right Anti	Records in the second query that do not have a matching record in the first query.

Table 8-1 Join Kind options explained

Exercise 8.1: Merge Columns Of Data

Figure 8-2 shows part of the Order Details table. This table contains one row for each item ordered by all of the customers. The Product ID column contains the item number of the product that was ordered.

	A	B	C	D	E
1	OrderID	ProductID	UnitPrice	Quantity	StatusID
2	1	1101	$14.50	1	2
3	1	1102	$14.50	2	2
4	1	7038	$479.85	2	2
5	2	1103	$14.50	3	2

Figure 8-2 Order Details table

People that will use this table probably do not know what the Product ID column name means, even if it was renamed to item number. They will however, know what the data is, in a product name column. As shown, the Order Details table does not store the product name. That value is stored in the Products table, which is the correct table to store it in.

Figure 8-3 shows part of the Orders table. As shown, you do not know the name of the customer that placed the order or the sales rep that took the order. The customer and sales rep names are stored in other tables. This is the same dilemma that that table in Figure 8-2 has.

	A	B	C	D	E
1	Order ID	Order Amount	Customer ID	Sales Rep ID	Order Date
2	1001	41.90	1	13	12/02/2013
3	1002	5,060.28	41	14	12/02/2013
4	1003	186.87	77	4	12/02/2013
5	1004	823.05	18	4	12/02/2013

Figure 8-3 Orders table

If the goal is to display the product, customer or sales rep name on a report, there are two options, as explained below.

① **CREATE RELATIONSHIPS** between the tables. This is the easiest option and does not make any of the tables (queries) larger in size. Relationships are created on the Relationships tab, that was covered in Chapter 3.

② **MERGE THE COLUMNS IN ONE TABLE INTO ANOTHER TABLE.** This option copies a column of data in one table into another table. For example, in the table shown earlier in Figure 8-2, the Product Name column, in the Products table would be copied to the Order Details table. This is the option that Power Query supports. However, this is the least efficient way to be able to display data from two tables on the same report. On the other hand, this option is apparently easier for non technical people to understand. Honestly, the only reason to use the Merge transformation to combine data from two or more tables, is if you do not create relationships between the tables.

This exercise will show you how to merge data from the tables discussed above and more.

1. In a new file, open the Options dialog box ⇒ On the Data Load screen, in the Current File section, clear the check mark for the following options:

   ☑ Automatically detect column types . . .
   ☑ Auto detect new relationships . . .
   ☑ Auto Date/Time . . .

2. Import the following tables from the More Data Files workbook.

   ☑ 07 Orders
   ☑ 07 Sales Reps
   ☑ 08 Customers
   ☑ 08 Order Details
   ☑ 08 Products
   ☑ 08 Regions

3. Promote the headers on all of the tables that you just imported.

4. Save the file as `E8.1 Merge columns of data.`

Merge The Product Name Column Into The Order Details Table

Earlier in this chapter, the available join types were covered for merging and you learned that the Left Outer join type is often used for merging data from a lookup table. In the Product Name column merge discussed earlier, the Products table is the lookup table. This means that it needs to be the second table on the Merge dialog box. This section and the next one, are the equivalent of using **VLOOKUP** in Excel.

1. Display the Order Details table.

2. Home tab ⇒ Merge Queries button ⇒ Merge Queries.

3. Open the drop-down list and select the Products table. This is the table that has the Product Name column that will be added to the Order Details table.

4. In both tables, click on the Product ID column.

This is how you create a virtual join. If you were creating a relationship between these tables, as covered in Chapter 3, this would be the only step that you would need to do.

Notice the message at the bottom of the dialog box. It displays how many matching rows between the tables were found. The numbers let you know that a match was found in the Products table, for every row in the Order Details table. In this example, there should be a match for every row in the Order Details table. If not, there is a problem with the data in at least one of the tables on the Merge dialog box. You should have the options shown in Figure 8-4.

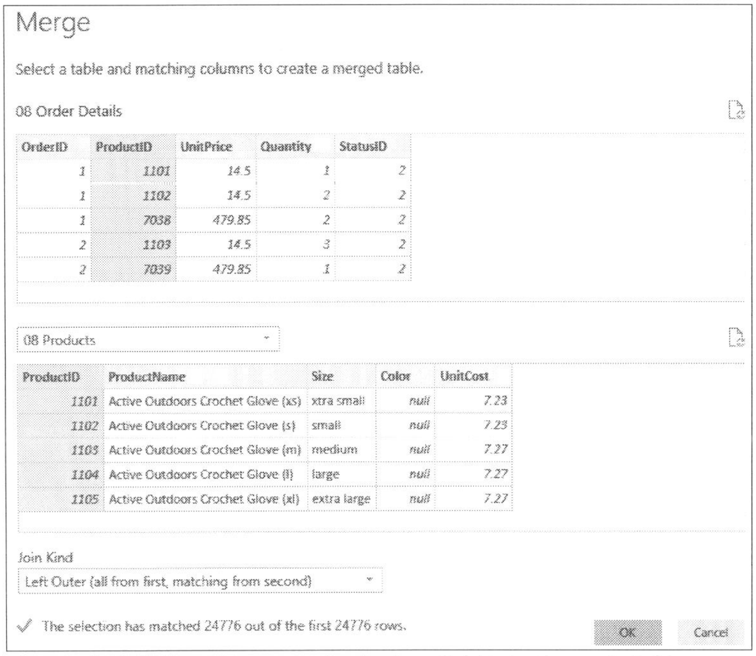

Figure 8-4 Options to merge the lookup field into the main table

5. Click OK.

Add The Lookup Columns

The Products column, is the link between the tables. The next task is to select the column(s) from that table that you want to add to the Order Details table.

1. Click the Expand button at the end of the Products column.

   The options shown in Figure 8-5 are the columns in the Products table. They are the same columns shown at the bottom of the Merge dialog box, shown above in Figure 8-4.

   The field(s) selected on this list, will be added to the query.

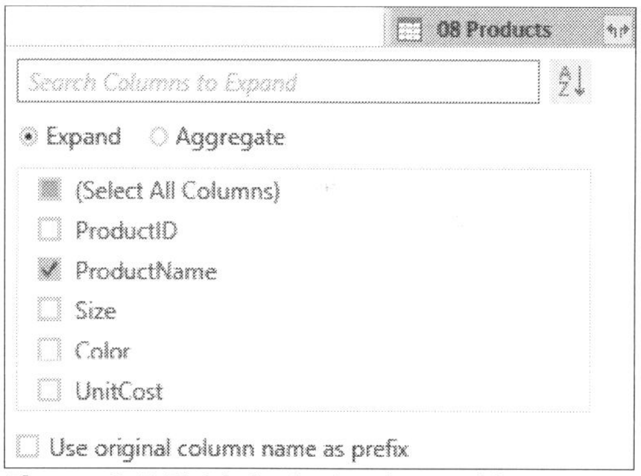

Figure 8-5 Fields in the Products table

> Another way to display the Expand options shown above in Figure 8-5, is to click on the Products column ⇒ Transform tab ⇒ Expand button.

> For all of the Merge and Append exercises in this chapter, clear the check mark for the **USE ORIGINAL COLUMN NAME AS PREFIX OPTION**, shown above in Figure 8-5. Clearing the check mark for this option keeps the original column name (which is really the name of the table) from being added to the beginning of the column name.

2. Clear the (Select All Columns) option ⇒ Clear the Use original column name as prefix option ⇒ Check the Product Name column.

3. Click OK ⇒ Move the Product Name column left, after the Product ID column. The Order Details table should look like the one shown in Figure 8-6.

	OrderID	ProductID	ProductName	UnitPrice	Quantity	StatusID
1	1	1101	Active Outdoors Crochet Glove (xs)	14.5	1	2
2	1	1102	Active Outdoors Crochet Glove (s)	14.5	2	2
3	1	7038	Rapel (ladies black)	479.85	2	2
4	13	7038	Rapel (ladies black)	479.85	2	2

Figure 8-6 Product Name lookup field added to the Order Details table

Add Columns From Different Lookup Tables

In this part of the exercise, you will add columns from two different lookup tables to the Orders table, shown earlier in Figure 8-3. You will add the Customer Name field (First and Last Name) from the Customers table and the Sales Rep name field from the Sales Reps table to the Orders table.

1. Display the Orders table.
2. Home tab ⇒ Merge Queries button ⇒ Merge Queries option.
3. Select the Customers table in the drop-down list ⇒
   Click on the Customer ID column in both tables.

   Notice that one row in the Orders table does not have a match in the Customers table, as illustrated in Figure 8-7.

   This could be a problem, as all orders should have a customer.

   The Left Outer join type should be selected.

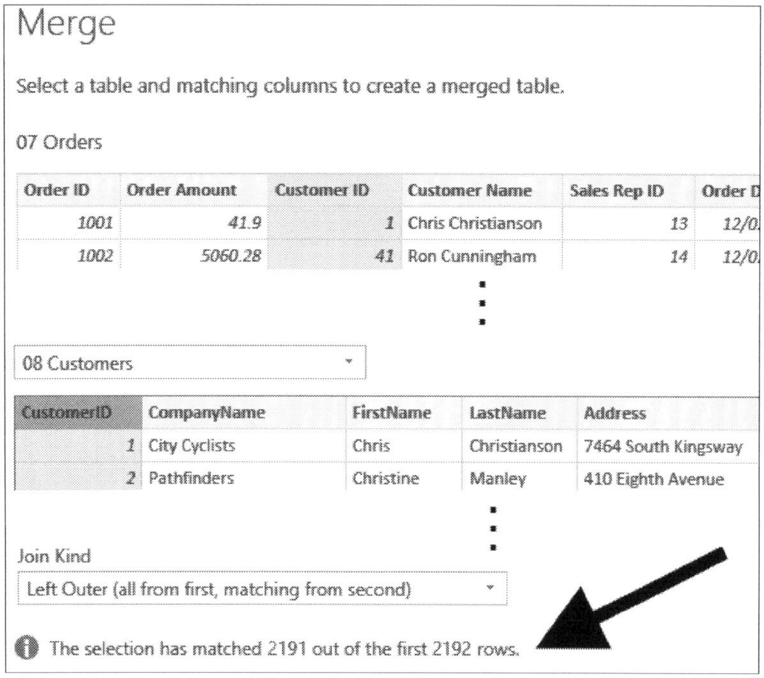

Figure 8-7 Warning message illustrated

4. Click OK.
5. Click the Expand button at the end of the Customers column ⇒ Check the First Name and Last Name columns.

> Now that the columns that you need have been merged into the table, the Customer ID column (in the Orders table) can be deleted, even though it is the column used to create the link between the tables. While deleting it is optional, I keep columns that can be used to link to another table, as I do not know whether or not I will need it in the future.

Merge And Rename The First And Last Name Columns

1. Select the First Name and Last Name columns ⇒ Right-click on one of the selected column headings ⇒ Merge Columns.
2. In the Separator drop-down list, select **SPACE**.
3. Type `Customer Name` in the New column name field on the Merge Columns dialog box, as shown in Figure 8-8.

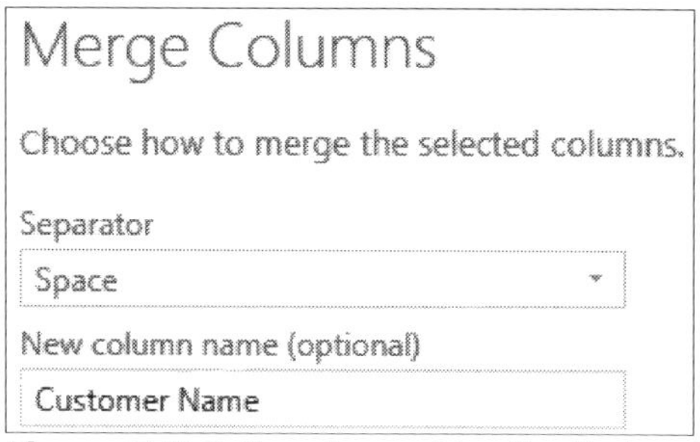

Figure 8-8 Options to combine the first and last name into one column

> Selecting the **SPACE SEPARATOR** on the Merge Columns dialog box will add a space between the columns being merged into one column.

4. Move the Customer Name column left, and place it after the Customer ID column.

5. Sort the Order ID column in ascending order.

   The beginning of the table should look like the one shown in Figure 8-9.

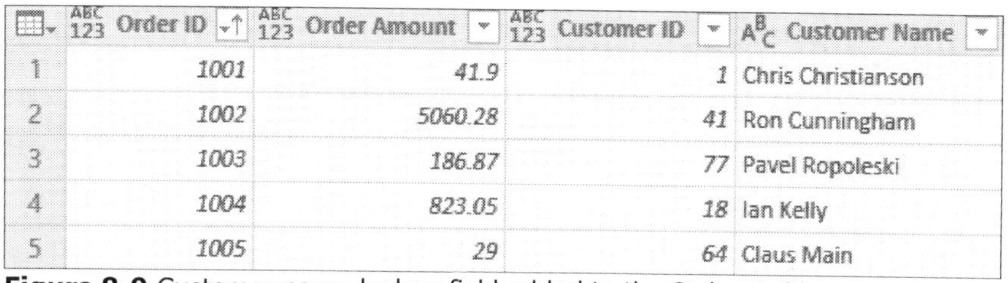

	Order ID	Order Amount	Customer ID	Customer Name
1	1001	41.9	1	Chris Christianson
2	1002	5060.28	41	Ron Cunningham
3	1003	186.87	77	Pavel Ropoleski
4	1004	823.05	18	Ian Kelly
5	1005	29	64	Claus Main

Figure 8-9 Customer name lookup field added to the Orders table

If you recall, the message at the bottom of the Merge dialog box indicated that one row in the Orders table, did not have a customer name. This is a good time to look into that warning. If you scroll through the list of names on the Filters drop-down list, there isn't any value (name) that does not look right. You should see the **LOAD MORE LINK**. Click on it to display more names.

As shown in Figure 8-10, there is a record in the Customers table (the table that the data in this column is from) that does not have a name.

If you display the record without a customer name, you will see that the Customer ID for that blank row is 200.

At this point, you should look in the Customers table for Customer ID 200. What you will find is that there is no record that has that Customer ID.

Either a record needs to be created in the Customers table for that Customer ID, or the Customer ID number in the Order Details table is wrong. You would have to decide which of these options are appropriate.

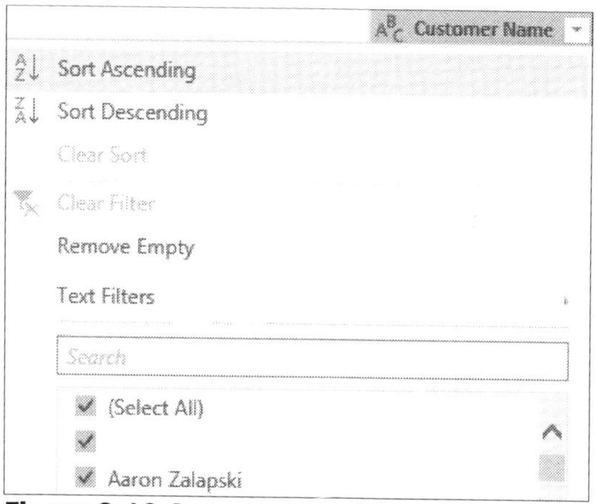

Figure 8-10 Customer Name filter options

Merge Another Lookup Field Into The Orders Table

In this part of the exercise, you will merge the Sales Rep name into the Orders table.

1. Display the Orders table ⇒ Home tab ⇒ Merge Queries button ⇒ Merge Queries.

2. Select the Sales Reps table, in the drop-down list below the Orders table.

3. Select the Sales Rep ID column in both tables ⇒ Click OK.

> It is not a requirement that the column names are the same, when selecting the column to link on.
> The columns just need to have compatible data types, which sadly, are not displayed on the Merge dialog box.

4. Click the Expand button at the end of the Sales Reps column heading ⇒ Select the options shown in Figure 8-11.

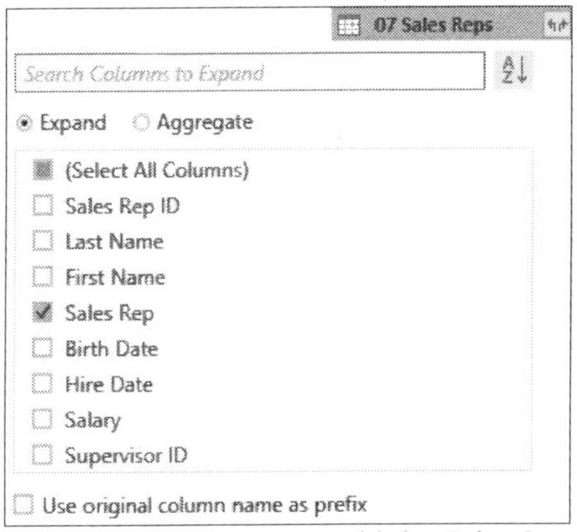

Figure 8-11 Options to add the Sales Rep column to the Orders table

5. Move the Sales Rep column left, before the Sales Rep ID column, as shown in Figure 8-12.

	Order ID	Order Amount	Customer ID	Customer Name	Sales Rep	Sales Rep ID
1	1001	41.9	1	Chris Christianson	Justin Brid	13
2	1002	5060.28	41	Ron Cunningham	Xavier Martin	14
3	1003	186.87	77	Pavel Ropoleski	Margaret Peacock	4
4	1004	823.05	18	Ian Kelly	Margaret Peacock	4
5	1005	29	64	Claus Main	Margaret Peacock	4

Figure 8-12 Sales Rep column added

Merge The Lookup Data Into A New Table

So far, the merge queries that you have created in this chapter, merge data into an existing query. There may be times when it is best to merge the data into a new query. In this part of the exercise, you will learn how to merge the data in one query to a new query and add a column from the lookup table into the new query, as well.

1. Display the Customers table.

2. Home tab ⇒ Merge Queries button ⇒ **MERGE QUERIES AS NEW.**

3. On the Merge dialog box, select the Regions table ⇒ Select the Region ID column in both tables.

   As shown at the bottom of Figure 8-13, only 377 rows in the Customers table have a match in the Regions table.

   Yes, you could create the merge using the State and State Abbr columns and possibly get the same results, but it is not the best option.

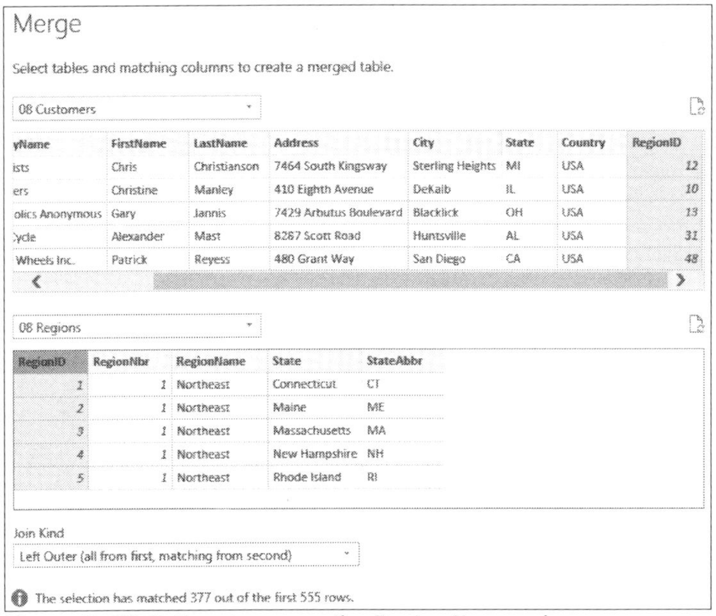

Figure 8-13 Options to merge the Region Name column

4. Rename the Merge 1 query to `Merged Region Name`.

5. Click the Expand button at the end of the Regions column heading ⇒ Only select the Region Name field.
6. Scroll down the table and display row 60.

As shown in Figure 8-14, the Region ID field is null in some rows. That is because the Regions table only has regions for the USA.

This is why all of the rows in the Customer table did not have a matching record in the Regions table on the Merge dialog box. However, on your own, you should verify that the rows that have a null value in the Region Name column, have a country other then USA. If any records have USA, but no region, that is a data problem that needs to be fixed.

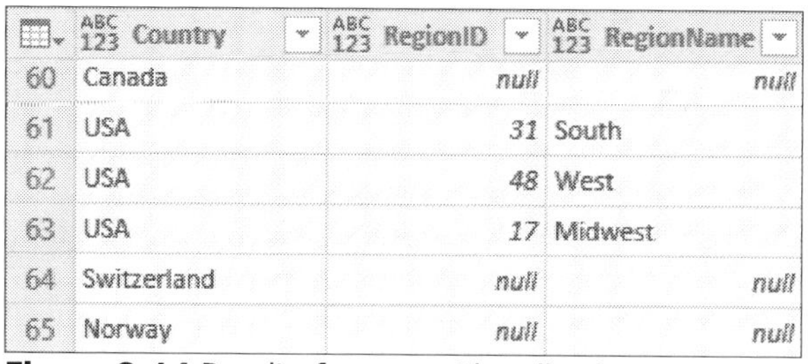

Figure 8-14 Result of merge with null values

Seeing What The Table Data Type Can Do

The **TABLE DATA TYPE** was covered in Chapter 6. Now that you have created a transformation that has a Table data type, you can test it out for yourself. If you want to follow along, make a copy of the Orders query and rename it to `test the table data type`.

As you have seen, the Table data type displays as a link. That means when you click on it something will happen. The options are explained below. What you will see is that using the **LIST** and **RECORD DATA TYPES** that were discussed in Chapter 6, pretty much work the same way as the Table data type.

☑ Clicking in any cell that has the Table data type object, displays the corresponding row (below the query) in the table that has the data that will be merged. For example, clicking in the Table cell, on row 2, displays the customer data shown at the bottom of Figure 8-15. This is the customer that placed order #1002.

☑ Clicking on the Table link produces the same outcome as clicking in the cell (discussed above). The difference is the clicking on the link, inserts a step.

☑ A new query can be created by right-clicking on the Table link and selecting Add as new query, as shown in Figure 8-16. The new query that is created, has all of the steps that the original query has.

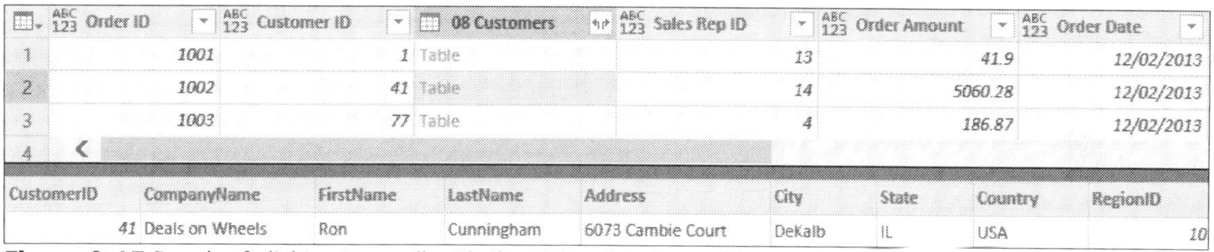

Figure 8-15 Result of clicking in a cell with the Table data type object

Figure 8-16 Table data type link shortcut menu

Appending Data

Appending data is the process of combining the data in two or more queries. The data in one query is added after the end of the data in another query. The Query Editor provides several ways to append data, as explained below.

① Append data in one query to another query. This option adds data to the first query that is selected. To create this type of query, use the **APPEND QUERIES OPTION** on the Append Queries button. This option adds the data from one query to the query selected before the Append Queries option is selected. This query option does not keep the original query intact.

② Append data from two queries to create a new query. This option keeps both of the original queries intact. To create this type of query, use the **APPEND QUERIES AS NEW OPTION** on the Append Queries button.

③ Append data from three or more queries at the same time.

> **Append Queries As New Option**
> While you can use the Append Queries option with a **REFERENCE QUERY** to accomplish the same result as using the Append Queries as New option, if you plan to modify M formulas on a regular basis, the Append Queries as New option creates fewer lines of code.
>
> In addition to that, the reason that I like creating new queries is that you can leave the original queries intact. If you append one query to another, its hard to tell where the data really came from. Most of the time queries that will be used to create a report, I rename the query to match the report name, thus removing any clue of the original query (table) that was used. If the query for the report used three queries, they could all be unloaded. I do not know if there is an official list of reasons of when not to load data, but intermediate queries that are used to append data do not have to be loaded.

While you may think that appending the data in Power Query is tedious, keep reading because this process is more painful to do in Excel, and it is very easy to make a mistake and not even know it.

The primary reason that you would not cut and paste the data in one spreadsheet and paste it at the end of another spreadsheet is because you would have to do this over and over, every time another spreadsheet needed to be appended. You would also have to constantly check all of the spreadsheets that were copied and pasted, to see if any had new rows of data or if rows of data were deleted. Basically, every time you needed to run a report that used this copied and pasted data, you would have to copy and paste all of the data again. No thank you. That would be a hot mess. <smile>

How Appending Data Works

The new query is created by adding the data from existing queries to it. Columns that have the same name in both queries are usually appended. All columns in the first query selected, are added to the new query, as is. Columns in the second query that do not have a matching column name in the first query, create new columns in the first or new query. When this happens, rows from the first query are filled in with null values for these new columns. If you need to append more than one query, select the Append Queries as New option.

If the column names are identical in the queries and you want to rename a column or if you want to change something else, it is best to make this type of change after all of the queries have been appended, so that you only have to make the change (like rename a column) once, instead of multiple times before the append.

As long as the structure (the columns have the same name, are in the same order and have the same number of columns) is the same, the tables can be from different source types (for example, one table could be imported from a text file and another table from a database) can be appended.

Append Queries Option

Home tab ⇒ **APPEND QUERIES BUTTON** ⇒ Append Queries, displays the dialog box shown in Figure 8-17. The options are used to select one or more queries (tables) that have data that you want to add to the table, currently displayed in the Query Editor.

Figure 8-17 Append options

What I found interesting about the Append Queries option is that the data being appended does not have to have the same structure as the table that it is being appended to.

By that I mean, if the structures and/or data types are not the same for each column, no error is generated and the data is not appended. Null values are appended instead.

Structured Column Options

The options in this section are on the Transform tab. The first two options are used to add columns of data from one query to another query. These two options are only enabled when a column, like the one shown on the left of Figure 8-18, is selected that contains a link to a related table.

An example is a field in one table that is merged from a different table, like you will see in Exercise 8.2. You should see the word "Table" in each cell in the column, as shown in Figure 8-18.

The first two options in the Structured Column section, are explained below.

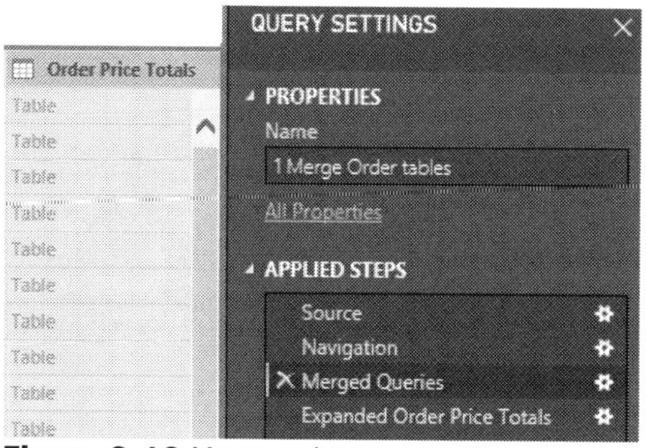

Figure 8-18 Merge column created

The **EXPAND DIALOG BOX** (Figure 8-19) and the **AGGREGATE DIALOG BOX** (Figure 8-20) will display a Load more link, when a table has more than 1,000 rows of nested data. Clicking on this link, forces Power BI Desktop to look at more rows to try and find more nested fields to display on these dialog boxes.

Expand Button Options

Clicking this button displays the dialog box shown in Figure 8-19. The options are used to add fields from the linked table to the current table.

The **DEFAULT COLUMN NAME PREFIX** option is used to enter what you want added to the beginning of column names for the columns that are selected to be added to the current table. The prefix default is the column name.

One option is to use the table name or an abbreviated table name that the merge columns are from. Doing this will visually let you know what table the column is from. Using this field is optional. If you delete the default prefix and leave the field empty, no prefix will be added to the column headings.

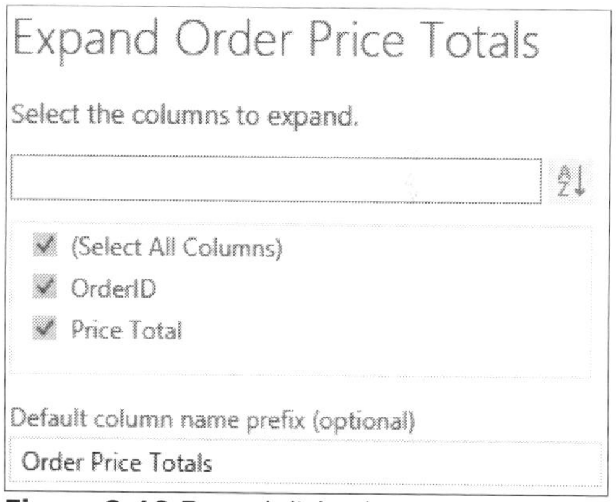

Figure 8-19 Expand dialog box

The options on the Expand dialog box add a step to the query. The step starts with the word "Expanded", as shown earlier, at the bottom of Figure 8-18.

Aggregate Button Options

Clicking this button displays the dialog box shown in Figure 8-20. If you hold the mouse pointer over a field on the dialog box, you will see a button at the end of the field.

Clicking the button will display the aggregate options, shown in the figure. Check the option(s) for how you want the column to be summarized (aggregated).

The default aggregate type is **SUM**. You can change the aggregation type.

If checked, the **USE ORIGINAL COLUMN NAME AS PREFIX** option adds the name of the aggregate type that you selected, to the beginning of the column header name, as shown in Figure 8-21.

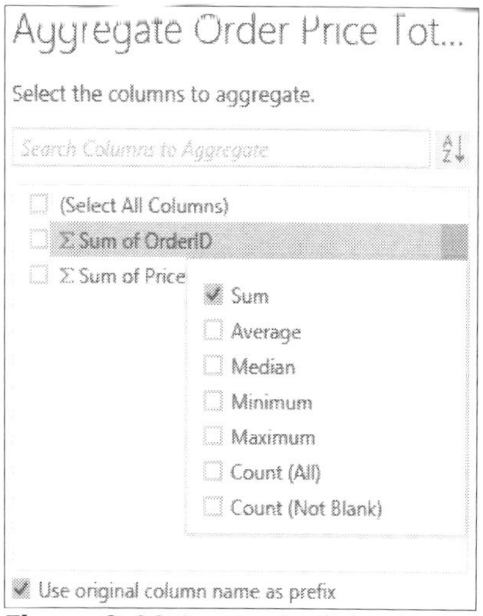

Figure 8-20 Aggregate dialog box

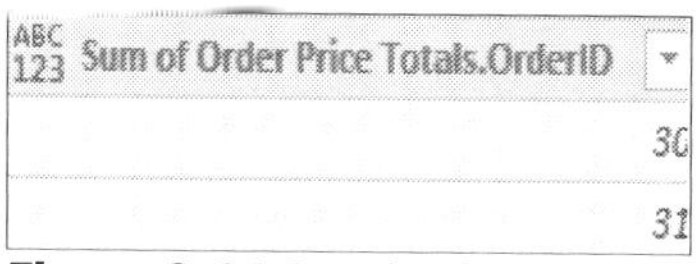

Figure 8-21 Result of selecting the Use original column name as prefix option

The product of a numeric column in another query can also be calculated. [See Table 4-5, Product option]

The options on the Aggregate dialog box add a step to the query. The step starts with the word "Aggregated". The functions on the Aggregate dialog box are the same as the **PIVOT COLUMN AGGREGATE** value functions that are covered later in Chapter 10, Table 10-1.

Exercise 8.2: Use The Merge And Append Options

This exercise will show you how to merge columns of data and how to create aggregate columns of data.

Use The Merge Queries Option

This part of the exercise will show you how to add columns from one table to another table.

1. Save the E2.4 file as `E8.2 Add Columns options`.
2. Duplicate the Orders query ⇒ Rename it to `1 Merge Order tables`.
3. Home tab ⇒ **MERGE QUERIES** button ⇒ Merge Queries option.
4. Open the drop-down list below the table and select the Order Price Totals table.
5. Click on the Order ID column in both tables. Your dialog box should look like the one shown earlier in Figure 8-1 ⇒ Click OK.
6. Scroll to the end of the table (on the right). You should see a column named Order Price Totals ⇒

   Click the Expand button to the right of the column heading. You should see the options shown in Figure 8-22.

   The options are used to select which field(s) from the second table (Order Price Totals) will be copied (merged) into the first table (the Orders table).

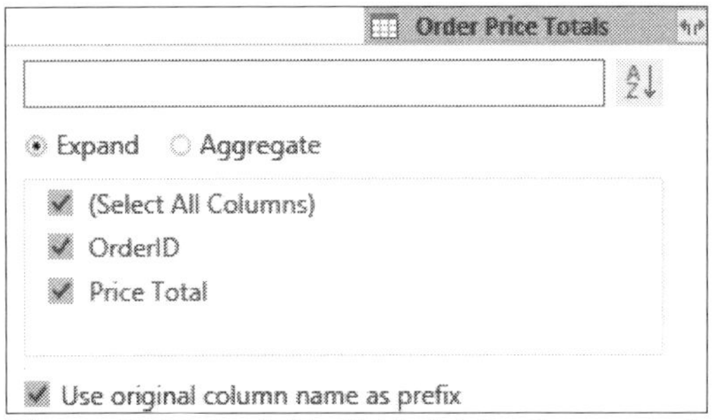

Figure 8-22 Available fields list for the merged query

7. Clear the check mark for the (Select All Columns) option ⇒ Check the Price Total field. There is no reason to add the Order ID field because it is already in the first table ⇒ Click OK.
8. Rename the Price Total column to `Order Sub Total`.
9. Right-click on the Order Sub Total column heading ⇒ Move ⇒ To Beginning ⇒
   Move the column to the right, so that it is after the Order ID column, as shown in Figure 8-23.

	1.2 Order ID	$ Price Total
1	30	1505
2	31	865
3	32	1190

Figure 8-23 Merged column from another query (table)

Aggregate The Data, Then Merge It

Aggregating data means to create a total, for a column of data. Figure 8-20 shown earlier, displays the list of aggregate functions that are available, when merging data. In this part of the exercise, you will learn how to change the default aggregate function and add aggregated columns of data to a table.

1. Duplicate the Orders query ⇒ Rename it to `2 Aggregate data`.
2. Merge Queries button ⇒ Merge Queries ⇒ Open the first drop-down list on the Merge dialog box and select the Order Details table.
3. Select the Order ID column in both tables ⇒ Click OK.

4. Click the button at the end of the Order Details column ⇒ Select the **AGGREGATE** option. You will see the options shown in Figure 8-24.

   If you want to create or change the calculation, click the button illustrated at the end of the field. You will see the aggregate options, shown earlier in Figure 8-20. Select the option that you want to use.

   Check the Sum of Unit Price option ⇒
   Check the Sum of Quantity option ⇒
   Click the button at the end of the Sum of Quantity column ⇒
   Check the **COUNT (NOT BLANK)** aggregate option on the drop-down list.

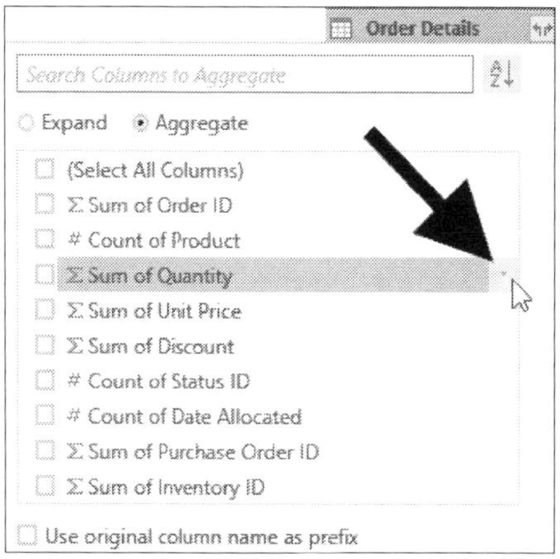

Figure 8-24 Aggregate options

Keep in mind that more than one aggregate value can be added at the same time for the same column, to create additional columns.

5. You should have the options checked, that are illustrated in Figure 8-25 ⇒ Click OK. At the end of the table, you will see the three new columns shown in Figure 8-26.

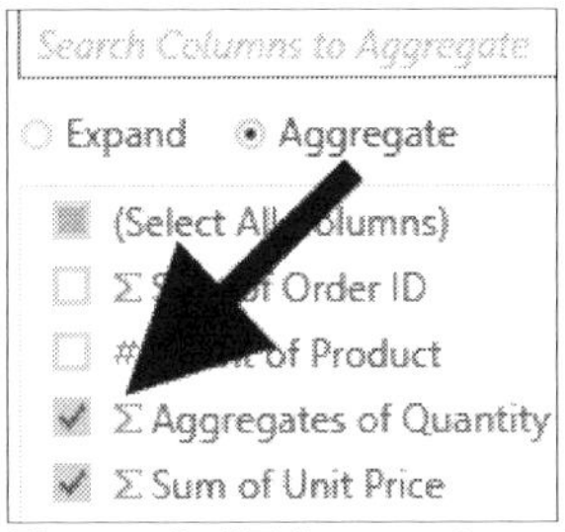

Figure 8-25 Aggregate options selected

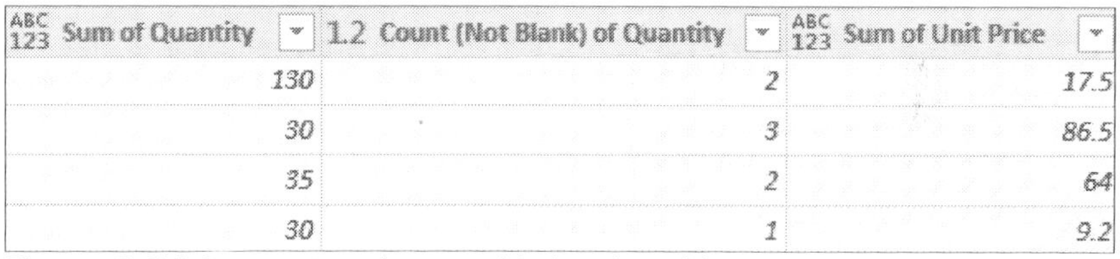

Sum of Quantity	Count (Not Blank) of Quantity	Sum of Unit Price
130	2	17.5
30	3	86.5
35	2	64
30	1	9.2

Figure 8-26 Aggregate columns added to the table

Use The Append Queries Option

In this part of the exercise, you will learn how to append data in one query to another query.

1. Duplicate the New Products query. Rename it to `3 Append queries`. Notice that there are 20 records in the query.

2. Home tab ⇒ Append Queries button ⇒ Append Queries ⇒ Open the drop-down list and select the Append_Products table. The records in the Append_Products table will be added to the bottom of the 3 Append queries table ⇒ Click OK. The table should now have 27 rows of data.

The (Current) Option
As shown in Figure 8-27, the 3 Append queries query has the word (**CURRENT**) next to it. This indicates the query that data will be appended to.

There is nothing stopping you from selecting the current query, as the one to append. If the current query is selected as the table to append, the data in it will be appended to itself. Doing so will cause the current query to have duplicate records. The probably is not what you want to happen. Merging queries has the same (Current) option.

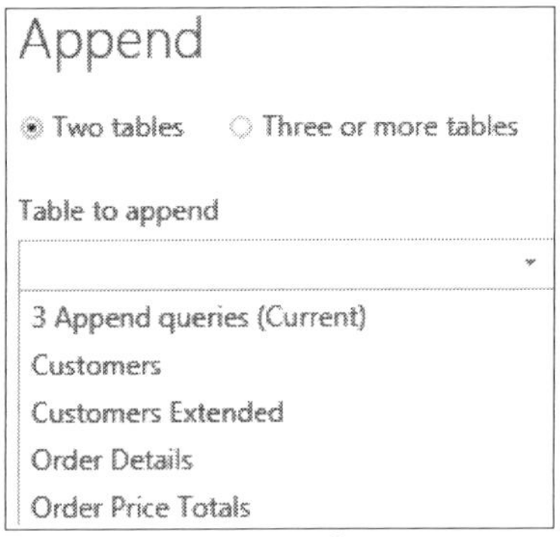

Figure 8-27 Append options

Grouping Data

Grouping data is a way to sort data. Grouping forces the data to be displayed in a particular order, based on the fields selected to create the group(s). Grouping is used when you need to create a total or subtotal another or aggregate value for all of the rows that have the same value in a column.

For example, you need to create an order total amount for each sales rep. You would create a group using the sales rep field and a calculated field (a total) to sum the order totals for each order that the sales rep has. These totals are known as **SUMMARIZED** data. Each time the value in the field being grouped on changes, a subtotal is created.

Exercises in this chapter take grouping up a notch, from what was covered in previous chapters, by creating what is known as **NESTED GROUPS**. (A group within a group. It is a way to create subtotals.)

Exercise 8.3: Merging Data To Group By

This exercise will show you how to combine the merge and group by features, plus a few others, to prepare data to be used to create reports. Not to scare you, but this exercise is long. Keep in mind that on your own, all of the merging parts of the exercise can be handled by creating a few relationships between the tables and that it is far less steps to create relationships. <smile>

Transform The Data

This part of the exercise will show you how to create new columns, bring in columns from another table and create calculations. These tasks are needed to be able to group data in different ways.

1. In a new file ⇒ Import all of the 07 tables in the More Data Files workbook.

2. Save the file as `E8.3 Transform and group data`.

Add A Year Field To The Orders Table

There is often a need to display data by a portion of a date field, like by year, quarter or month. Normally, these fields are not stored in non date tables. The Query Editor has some functionality to help. Creating a date table is beyond the scope of this book. Creating a year column will let the data be grouped by year.

3. Display the Orders query ⇒ Duplicate the Order Date column ⇒ Rename the duplicate column to `Order Year`.

Insert A Step Between Existing Steps

This part of the exercise will show you how to add a step between steps in the Applied Steps section of the Query Settings panel. To do this, click on the step right above where you want to add a step.

1. In the Applied Steps list, click on the Changed Type step ⇒ Delete (Remove) the Required Date column, from the query. You should see the Insert Step message ⇒ Click the **INSERT** button. The column will be deleted.

2. Click on the Renamed Columns step ⇒ Right-click on the Order Year column ⇒ Transform ⇒ Year ⇒ Year ⇒ Move the Order Year column next to the Order Date column.

Merge The Sales Rep Name Column

The Orders table contains the Sales Rep ID column. Displaying that column on a report will not be helpful unless the person viewing the report has memorized all of the sales reps ID numbers. <smile> A better solution is to display the sales reps name. This part of the exercise will add the Sales Rep name field (in the Sales Reps table) to the Orders query.

1. Select the Orders query ⇒ Click on the last step in the Applied Steps list ⇒ Home tab ⇒ Merge Queries button ⇒ Merge Queries.

2. Open the first drop-down list and select the Sales Reps table ⇒ Select the Sales Rep ID column in both tables.

   Notice at the bottom of the dialog box, that all of the rows in the Orders table have a matching value (in this exercise, a sales rep) in the Sales Reps table.

   This is known as a **ONE-TO-ONE RELATIONSHIP**.

   There does not have to be a 100 percent match for the merge to be valid.

   Figure 8-28 shows the options that should be selected ⇒ Click OK.

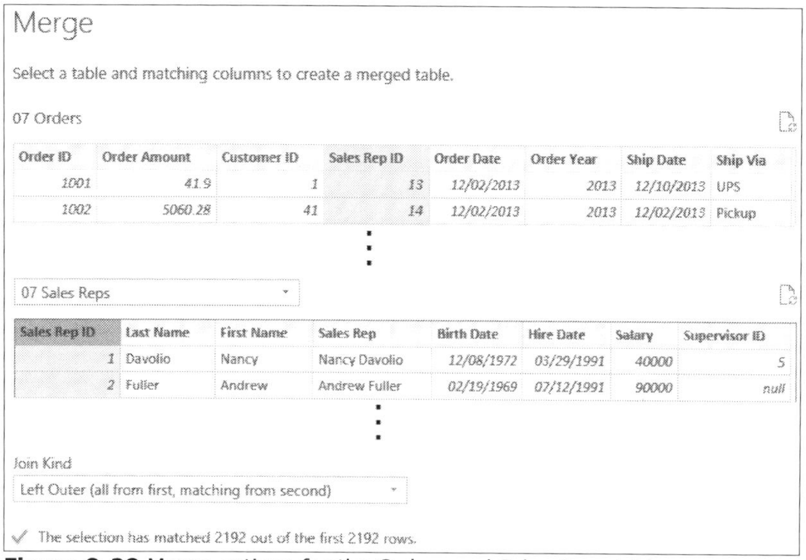

Figure 8-28 Merge options for the Orders and Sales Reps tables

3. Click the button at the end of the 07 Sales Reps heading ⇒ Clear the **(SELECT ALL COLUMNS)** option ⇒ Check the Sales Rep field ⇒ Click OK. Now, each order displays the sales reps name.

4. Rename the Merged Queries step to `Merge Sales Reps table`.

Merge The Customer Name Column

Just like the Orders table needs the Sales Reps name, having the Customer Name in the Orders table would also be helpful. In this part of the exercise, you will add the Customer Name column (that you will create) to the Orders table. The goal is to **COMBINE** (merge) the first and last name columns into one new column. If you view the Customers table, you will see that the name is in two fields, which is the norm.

1. Display the Customers query ⇒ Select the First Name and Last Name columns.

2. Add Column tab ⇒ Merge Columns button.

3. Open the Separator drop-down list and select Space.

4. In the New column name field, type `Customer Name`. You should see the first and last name in a new column, at the end of the table

5. Display the Orders query ⇒ Home tab ⇒ Merge Queries button ⇒ Merge Queries ⇒ Select the Customers table ⇒ Use the Customer ID column to join the tables.

6. Using the new 07 Customers column, add the Customer Name column that you just created to the Orders table ⇒ Also add the State and Country columns to the Orders table.

Merge Columns From A Date Table

Earlier in this chapter, you used the Year transform function. The Transform shortcut menu has a month option. If you select that option, the date will be converted to the number value for the month of the date field.

I exported a portion of a custom date table that I created, to use in this book. Part of the My Date Table is shown in Figure 8-29. This table can be created in Power BI Desktop by creating DAX formulas or using transform functions. In this part of the exercise, you will add columns in the date table to another table.

	DateKey	Year	MonthFull	MonthAbbr	QuarterAbbr	WeekDay	WeekDayAbbr
1	01/01/2012	2012	January	Jan	Q1	Sunday	Sun
2	01/02/2012	2012	January	Jan	Q1	Monday	Mon
3	01/03/2012	2012	January	Jan	Q1	Tuesday	Tue
4	01/04/2012	2012	January	Jan	Q1	Wednesday	Wed
5	01/05/2012	2012	January	Jan	Q1	Thursday	Thu

Figure 8-29 A portion of the My Date Table

1. Add the Month Abbr and Quarter Abbr columns in the My Date Table to the Orders table ⇒ Use the Date Key column in the My Date Table to link to the Order Date column in the Orders table.

2. Rename the Quarter Abbr column to `QTR`. You have just merged data from three tables into another table!

Modify The Merge Query Formula

Oops! You just realized that you would rather use the Month Full Name column instead of the Month Abbr column, to display the month name. You could delete the column that you do not want and merge the column that you need. Another option is to modify the formula for the column that you want to replace.

1. Display the Orders query ⇒ Click on the last **EXPANDED** step, in the Applied Steps list.

2. Look at the formula. You should see "Month Abbr" in the formula, twice ⇒ Change the first occurrence to `MonthFull`. This is the column name.

3. The second occurrence of Month Abbr, is the column heading name that will be displayed ⇒ Change Month Abbr to `Month`, as illustrated in Figure 8-30 ⇒ Press Enter. Yes, you just modified the M formula.

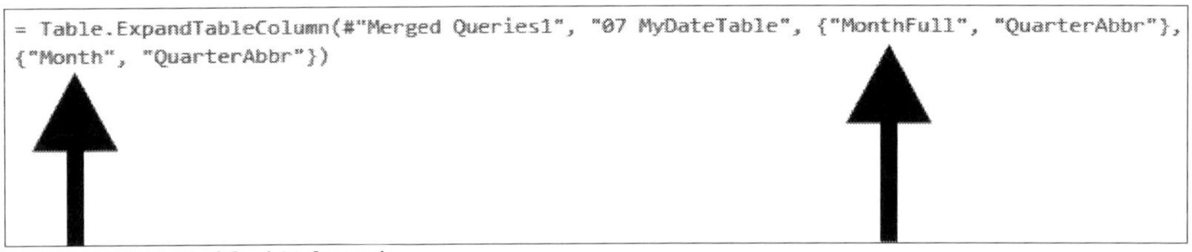

Figure 8-30 Modified M formula

Group The Order Records By Year

This part of the exercise will show you how to display orders by year and display a count of orders per year and quarter.

1. Duplicate the Orders query ⇒ Rename it to `1 Orders Grouped By Year` ⇒ In the Description field, on the Query Properties dialog box, type `Based on the Orders table`, as shown in Figure 8-31.

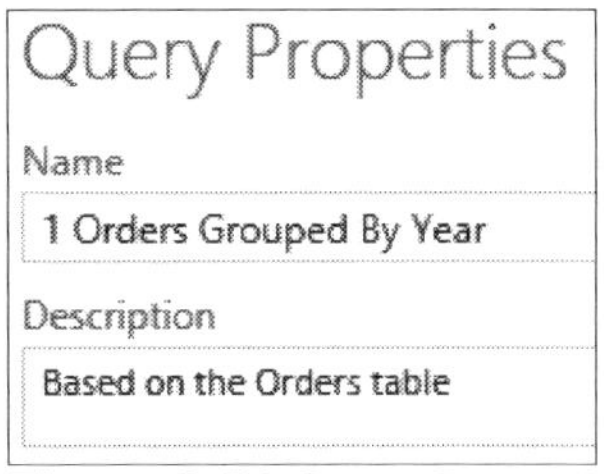

Figure 8-31 Query Properties dialog box

2. Home tab ⇒ Group By button ⇒ On the Advanced screen, create these three groups: Order Year, QTR, Sales Rep.

3. Change the New column name to `# Of Orders`.

4. Add another row to create an aggregation ⇒

   In the New column name field, type `Total Order $` ⇒

   Select the Sum operation ⇒

   Select the Order Amount field.

   You should have the options shown in Figure 8-32.

   Click OK.

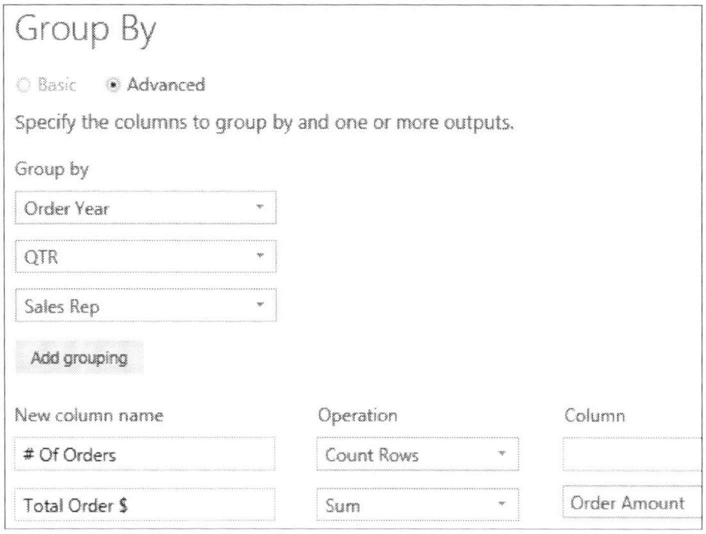

Figure 8-32 Group By options

5. Sort the data in ascending order, on the Order Year column, then sort the QTR column in ascending order.

   The groups should look like the ones shown in Figure 8-33. Each row displays the sales reps order totals for each year and quarter.

	Order Year	QTR	Sales Rep	# Of Orders	Total Order $
1	2013	Q1	Robert King	2	2687.05
2	2013	Q1	Anne Dodsworth	3	6988.4
3	2013	Q1	Laurent Pereira	1	70.5
4	2013	Q1	Albert Hellstern	2	1707.9
5	2013	Q1	Laura Callahan	1	2447.34
6	2013	Q1	Caroline Patterson	5	19478.16

Figure 8-33 Order amount grouped by year, quarter and sales rep

Modified Sort Order

If the sales rep column, shown above in Figure 8-33, was moved to the beginning of the table, the data would be displayed, as shown in Figure 8-34.

The sort order was changed to sort on the Sales Rep, Order Year and QTR columns.

	Sales Rep	Order Year	QTR	# Of Orders	Total Order $
3	Albert Hellstern	2014	Q1	14	9318.61
4	Albert Hellstern	2014	Q2	13	30119.23
5	Albert Hellstern	2014	Q3	2	7596.21
6	Albert Hellstern	2014	Q4	25	42425.83
7	Albert Hellstern	2015	Q1	10	14542.35
8	Albert Hellstern	2015	Q2	3	3203.25
9	Andrew Fuller	2013	Q1	4	1833.83
10	Andrew Fuller	2013	Q4	5	9246.33

Figure 8-34 Modified sort order

Group The Order Records By Sales Rep

This part of the exercise will show you how to create a group that will display one row for each sales rep. In addition to the sales reps name, each row will include the total number of orders and total order amount.

1. Duplicate the Orders grouped by year query ⇒ Rename it to `2 Orders grouped by sales rep`.

2. Delete the Sorted Rows step.

3. Open the Group By dialog box by clicking the button at the end of the Grouped Rows step ⇒
Delete the Order Year and QTR group by options, by clicking the ellipsis button next to them.

The query should look like the one shown in Figure 8-35. This query would be considered a top level query because there are no sub groups.

On a chart, users may want to drill-down on a sales rep to see the order detail records.

	Sales Rep	# Of Orders	Total Order $
1	Justin Brid	90	132842.14
2	Xavier Martin	122	284616.8
3	Margaret Peacock	174	415165.89
4	Albert Hellstern	82	149025.61
5	Steven Buchanan	110	168408.76
6	Anne Dodsworth	218	422262.77
7	Caroline Patterson	99	131020.36

Figure 8-35 Orders grouped by sales rep

Display The Orders Grouped By Customer

If you wanted to display the orders grouped by customer, instead of by sales rep, change the Group By option to Customer Name, as shown in Figure 8-36.

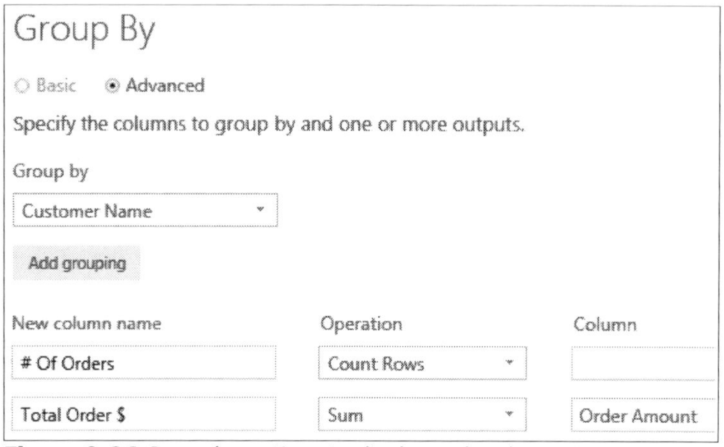

Figure 8-36 Group by options to display orders by customer

Change The Sort Options

The data is grouped by sales rep, but there is a problem with the Sort step. That happened because some of the columns that were sorted on, are no longer displayed in the query. In this part of the exercise, you will add the Last Name column from the Sales Rep query, so that the data can be sorted by the sales reps last name. If you sorted the data by the Sales Rep column, it would not be sorted by the last name, because the Sales Rep column starts with the first name.

1. Duplicate the Orders grouped by sales rep query ⇒ Rename it to `3 Grouped & sorted by sales rep`.

2. Add the Last Name column from the 07 Sales Reps query. Use the Sales Rep column to join the tables, in the merge.

3. Sort the Last Name column in ascending order.

The table should look like the one shown in Figure 8-37.

	Sales Rep	# Of Orders	Total Order $	Last Name
1	Justin Brid	90	132842.14	Brid
2	Steven Buchanan	110	168408.76	Buchanan
3	Laura Callahan	98	149768.8	Callahan
4	Nancy Davolio	224	423904.36	Davolio

Figure 8-37 Data sorted by the last name

It may be better if the Last Name column could be hidden, but there is no option to hide a column. However, the order that the steps are currently in, allows for the following solution. Each time the data is refreshed, the Last Name column would be added to the query. The data will be sorted on the Last Name column, then the Last Name column could be deleted. As long as these steps, in particular, the step to delete a column are done as the last or one of the last steps, you should not run into any problems.

On the other hand, the data is being transformed for reporting purposes. So, other then the person creating the report, users will not use or view the queries.

Group The Order Records By State

The group options needed to display orders by state are similar to the options used to display orders by sales rep.

1. Duplicate the Orders grouped by sales rep query ⇒ Rename it to `4 Orders grouped by state`.

2. Click on the icon for the Grouped Rows step ⇒ Change the Group By field to State.

3. Change the # of Orders column name to `# of Sales` ⇒

   Change the Total Order $ column name to `Total Sales Amount`.

   The table should look like the one shown in Figure 8-38.

	State	# Of Sales	Total Sales Amount
1	MI	81	124970.6
2	IL	199	389455.97
3	Warsaw	35	41055.83
4	MN	98	207211.94

Figure 8-38 Orders grouped by state

Modify The Data Displayed In The Group

As you can see, there are some international customers in the data displayed above in Figure 8-38. In this part of the exercise, the goal is to only display orders shipped to a USA address. Because the country is not used as a group, the filter has to be created before the group is created.

1. Click on the step above the **GROUPED ROWS** step. You should see all of the columns in the table.

2. Open the Country column filter ⇒ Clear all options ⇒ Select USA.

3. Click on the Grouped Rows step. You should only see rows for the states in the USA.

4. Sort the Total Sales Amount column in descending order.

   The table should look like the one shown in Figure 8-39.

	State	# Of Sales	Total Sales Amount
1	IL	199	389455.97
2	CA	148	275657.93
3	PA	102	232311.69
4	AL	83	223506.47
5	MN	98	207211.94

Figure 8-39 Orders grouped by state

Add Currency Formatting To Numeric Data

If the Fixed Decimal Number (currency) data type was applied to the Total Sales Amount column shown above in Figure 8-39, the values would not be displayed with currency formatting that you are probably expecting to see.

The formula that I use to display a dollar sign and commas, to emulate currency formatting, is shown in Figure 8-40.

It displays the values shown in the last column in Figure 8-41.

Custom Column

New column name

TotalSalesAmountFormatted

Custom column formula:

```
= "$" & Number.ToText([Total Sales Amount], "N", "")
```

Figure 8-40 Formula to display data in currency format

	State	# Of Sales	Total Sales Amount	TotalSalesAmountFormatted
1	IL	199	389455.97	$389,455.97
2	CA	148	275657.93	$275,657.93
3	PA	102	232311.69	$232,311.69

Figure 8-41 Result of currency formatting

Keep in mind that the new column is created using the **NUMBER.TOTEXT FUNCTION**, which converts numeric values to text.

This means that the new column, that displays currency formatting, cannot be used in a calculation.

A better solution is to apply the currency formatting in the Data view, because the data type is not changed, as illustrated in Figure 8-42.

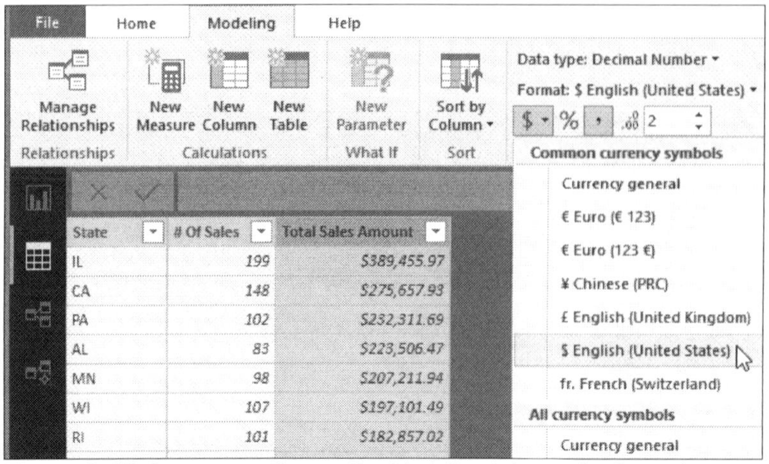

Figure 8-42 Currency option on the Modeling tab, on the Data view

Conversion Functions

Table 8-2 lists some other M conversion functions that you may find useful.

Function	This Function Converts . . .
Date.From	Numeric dates to a date format.
Date.FromText	A text field date to a date format.
Date.ToText	A date to text.
Number.FromText	Text to a number.
Time.ToText	Time data to text.

Table 8-2 Conversion functions explained

Use The Merged Queries Step To View The Matching Rows Of Data

Clicking on this step will display the matching record(s) from the second table. To follow the steps below, use Exercise 8.3.

1. Display the Orders query.
2. Click on the first Merged Queries step. You should see the 07 Sales Reps column at the end of the query.
3. Click to the right of the word "Table" in a cell, in the column. At the bottom of the window, you will see the matching row(s) of data from the second table, as illustrated in Figure 8-43.

Figure 8-43 Matching row of data illustrated for row 2 in the query

Clicking on the word "Table" will add a step to the query. This step will replace the source data, with the linked data. More than likely, when creating a merge, this is not what you want to have happen.

Create An Aggregated Column To Merge

In the previous parts of this exercise, one-to-one relationships were used to add columns to the Orders table. One way to tell what type of relationship you are creating is if the number of matching records between the tables is the same on the Merge dialog box.

The Order Details table can have multiple rows of data for each order. It is very common to have the need to get an aggregation of a column in the "many" table (the Order Details table, in this exercise) and add the aggregation to the "one" table (the Orders table).

The next few sections of this exercise will show you how to:

☑ Create a formula in the Order Details table to calculate the line total for each row in the table.
☑ Add the Line Total column to the Orders table to get a sub total for each order. It is a subtotal versus a grand total because shipping and taxes are calculated at run time.
☑ Create a count of items per order, that will also be added as a column in the Orders table.

Create A Calculated Column

In this part of the exercise, you will create a formula that calculates the total for each item that was ordered. Keep in mind that each order can have more than one item. If you looked at the data in the Order Details table, you will see multiple rows with the same Order ID number. All of the rows with the same Order ID number belong to one record (in this case, one order) in the Orders table.

Aggregate data must have a numeric data type to be used in a calculation.

1. Display the Order Details table ⇒

   Add Column tab ⇒ Custom Column button ⇒ Create the formula shown in Figure 8-44.

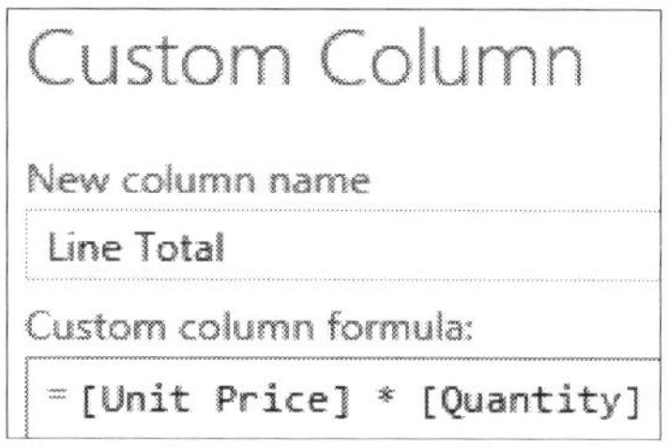

Figure 8-44 Line Total formula

2. Change the data type of the Line Total column to Fixed Decimal Number.

Create And Merge Aggregated Columns

In this part of the exercise, you will merge the Line Total column into the Orders table and create a column that displays a count of items for each order.

Before creating this type of calculation, it is a good idea to make all other changes to the table first, as calculations that use data in another table can take longer to run.

1. Duplicate the Orders query ⇒ Rename it to `5 Orders with detail sub total`.

2. Filter the table to only display orders in the USA.

3. Home tab ⇒ Merge Queries button ⇒ Merge Queries ⇒ Select the Order Details table ⇒ Select the Order ID column in both tables.

4. With the new column selected ⇒ Transform tab ⇒ Aggregate button ⇒ Check the Sum of Order ID field ⇒ Change the aggregation type to Count (All) ⇒ Clear the Sum option.

5. Check the Sum of Line Total field ⇒ Clear the Use original column name as prefix option ⇒ Click OK.

   You may see circles moving above the formula bar. This indicates that the data is being generated to display the new columns of data that you just created.

6. Rename the Count of Order ID column to `Count of items on order` ⇒
   Rename the Sum of Line Total column to `Order Subtotal Amount`.

7. Move both columns to the beginning of the table, right after the Order ID column, so that your table looks like the one shown in Figure 8-45.

	Order ID	Count of items on order	Order Subtotal Amount
1	1001	1	41.9
2	1002	2	260.28
3	1004	1	823.05
4	1033	3	146.32

Figure 8-45 Calculated columns from data in different tables

If you look in the Order Details table, you will see two rows of data that have Order ID 1002. If you add up the Line Total column values for these two rows, it will equal $260.28, which is what is displayed as the Order Subtotal Amount in the Orders table, shown above in Figure 8-45. The reason that you see Order ID's in the Order Details table that are not in the Orders table, is because the Orders table has a filter to only display Orders in the USA. Filtered records are not displayed.

The Basic Group By Options

If the Group By options covered in the previous exercise are more than you need to group data, the basic group by options are what you are looking for. The difference between the basic and advanced options, is that the basic group by options only group on one field and only create one new column.

The good thing is that if you start with the basic options and then decide that you need to group on more than one field or need to create more than one new column, you can, by selecting the Advanced option and not loose what you created on the basic window.

Exercise 8.4: Use The Basic Group By Options

In this exercise, you will learn how to group data by only using one field and there are no merge queries steps in this exercise. <smile>

1. In a new file, load the 07 Customers and 07 Orders tables in the More Data Files workbook.
2. Save the file as `E8.4 Basic Group By Options`.

Group And Count The Number Of Customers By State

In this part of the exercise, you will group the customers by state and create a count of the number of customers in each state.

1. Duplicate the Customers query ⇒ Rename it to `1 Customer count by state`.
2. Filter the Country column to only display customers in the USA.
3. Transform tab ⇒ Group By button. The Basic group by options should be displayed.
4. Select the State column in the Group By drop-down list.
5. In the New column name field, type `Nbr Of Customers`.

   You should have the options shown in Figure 8-46 ⇒ Click OK.

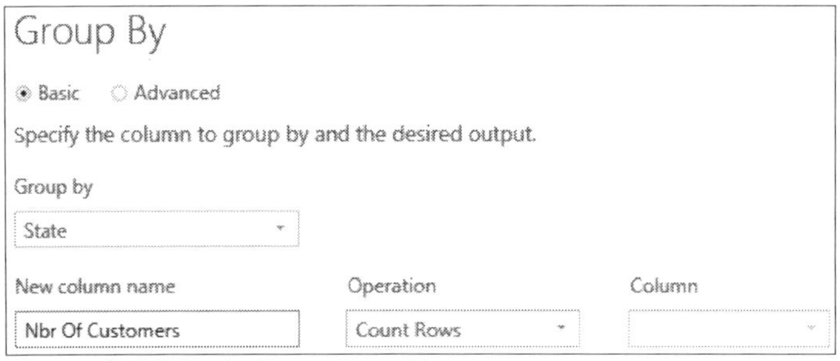

Figure 8-46 Basic Group By options

6. Sort the Nbr Of Customers column in descending order. The table should look like the one shown in Figure 8-47.

	State	Nbr Of Customers
1	IL	7
2	CA	6
3	PA	5
4	RI	4
5	MN	4

Figure 8-47 Customers grouped by state

Group The Orders By Year

In this part of the exercise, you will group the orders by year and create a total order amount for each year. To get the order year from the Order Date field, you will use the **EXTRACT FUNCTION**.

1. Duplicate the Orders table ⇒ Rename it to `2 Total Order Amount by year`.

2. Select the Order Date column ⇒ Add Column tab ⇒ Extract ⇒ Last Characters ⇒
   Type `4` in the Count field, as shown in Figure 8-48.
   Four is the number of characters for the year ⇒ Click OK.

Figure 8-48 Insert Last Characters options

3. Rename the Last Characters column to `Order Year`.

4. Home tab ⇒ Group By button.

5. Select the Order Year column in the Group By drop-down list.

6. In the New column name field, type `Total Order Amount`.

7. Change the Operation to Sum.

8. Select the Order Amount field in the Column drop-down list. You should have the options shown in Figure 8-49. The table should look like the one shown in Figure 8-50.

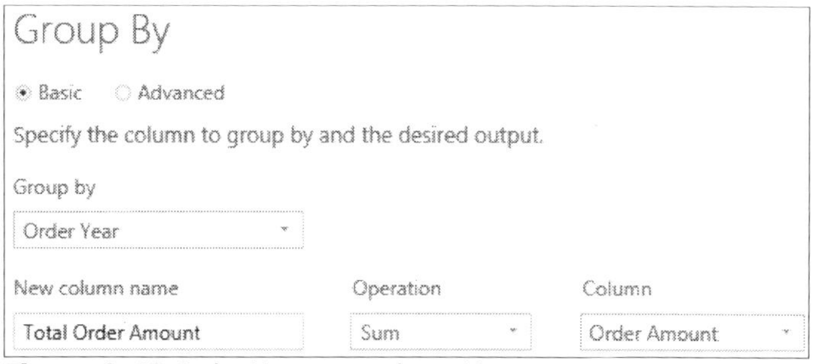

Figure 8-49 Order Year group by options

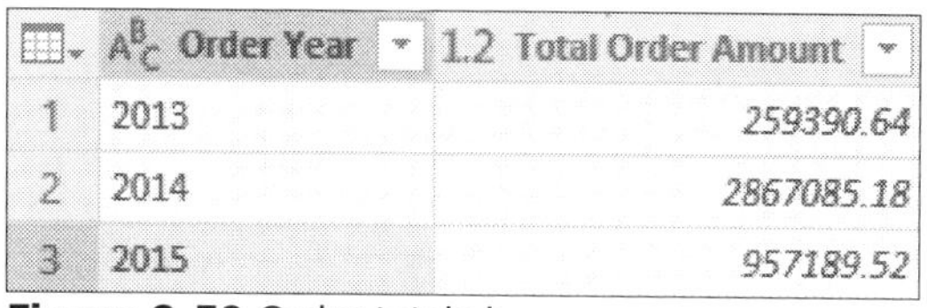

	Order Year	Total Order Amount
1	2013	259390.64
2	2014	2867085.18
3	2015	957189.52

Figure 8-50 Order totals by year

Merge Queries To Create A New Table

This chapter has covered merging columns from one table into another table. There is one more merge option. This option is used to create a new table by selecting columns from two queries. This leaves both of the original queries intact.

Exercise 8.5: Create A New Table By Merging Queries

This exercise will show you how to create a new table by merging columns from two queries. The **MERGE QUERIES AS NEW OPTION** on the Merge Queries button is used to start from scratch, to create a query with just the columns that you need. As you will see, the options are similar to the **MERGE QUERIES** options. The difference is that you select both tables. This option works the same as duplicating an existing query and then using it as the first table on the Merge dialog box.

This option could be used to create a table that will be used as the basis for a lot of reports. It is a great tool to use when you have tables like Products, Products Category and Product Subcategory and need a few fields from each of these tables. It will allow you to create a table that only has the fields that you need, then either unload tables from the data model or delete the tables from the report file.

1. In a new file, load the 07 Customers and 07 Orders tables in the More Data Files workbook.

2. Save the file as `E8.5 My New Table`.

3. Merge Queries button ⇒ Merge Queries as New ⇒ In the first drop-down list, select the Orders table ⇒ In the second drop-down list, select the Customers table.

4. Select the Customer ID column in both tables.

   You should have the options shown in Figure 8-51.

   Click OK.

   From here, the process is the same as using the Merge Queries option.

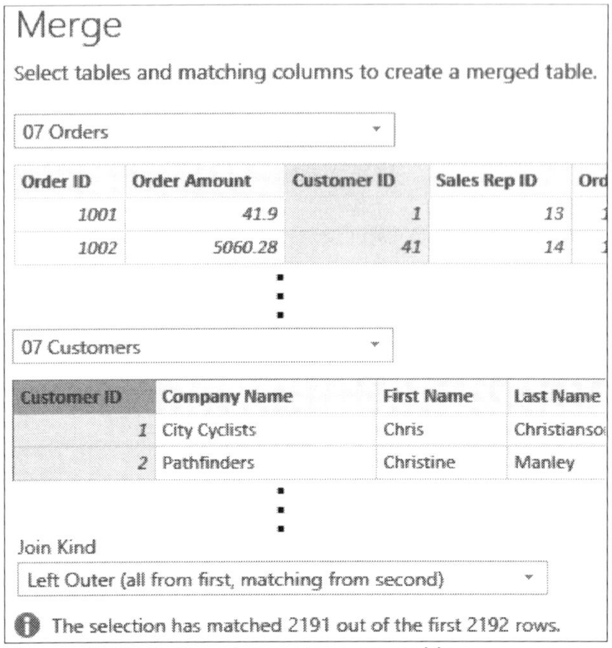

Figure 8-51 Options to create a new table

5. Rename the query to `1 My Custom Orders`.

At this point, you would display the options on the new column at the end of the query and select the columns from the Customers table that you want to add to the new query, just like you have done in previous exercises. After that, you would delete the columns in the Orders table that are not needed.

Many-To-Many Merge Criteria

So far, all of the merge exercises have used the one-to-many relationship criteria. There are times when you need to create a many-to-many merge. Sometimes, it is possible to create a many-to-many merge and not even know it. When you do, additional rows will be added to the query. A one-to-one merge has the same or fewer rows (then the first table selected for the merge) that have a match. Many-to-many merges produce more rows than the first table has.

For example, Figure 8-52 shows two tables that can be used to create a merge. Notice that the table on the left has more rows of data than the table on the right side of the figure. Figure 8-53 shows the result of a one-to-many merge. In the lower left corner of the figure, you can see the number of rows after the merge.

3	Order ID	Product ID	Unit Price	Quantity	Vendor
4	1001	1001	$18.88	1	Roadster
5	1002	1101	$14.50	4	Active Outdoors
6	1002	1102	$14.50	2	Active Outdoors
7	1003	2161	$9.85	3	Wheeler
8	1003	1150	$4.85	3	SlickRock
9	1004	1151	$39.85	3	Descent
10	1005	2002	$24.35	2	Changing Gears
11	1006	2151	$19.29	1	Mozzie
12	1006	2161	$9.85	1	Wheeler
		⋮			
25	1012	1151	$39.85	3	Descent
26	1013	2002	$24.35	2	Changing Gears
27	1013	2151	$19.29	3	Mozzie
28	1014	2161	$9.85	2	Wheeler

Product ID	Vendor	Show Room	Color	Price (SRP
1001	Roadster	Online	blue	$18.88
1101	Active Outdoors	Retail Location	red	$14.50
1102	Active Outdoors	Online	green	$14.50
1150	SlickRock	Kiosk	champagne	$4.85
1151	Descent	Retail Location	steel satin	$39.85
2002	Changing Gears	Expo	purple	$24.35
2151	Mozzie	Expo	green	$19.29
2161	Wheeler	Expo	purple	$9.85
2162	Rapel	Online	silver	$9.85
2206	Triumph Pro Helmet	Online	white	$11.90

Figure 8-52 Tables for a merge

	Order ID	Product ID	Unit Price	Quantity	Vendor	Products
1	1001	1001	18.88	1	Roadster	Table
2	1002	1101	14.5	4	Active Outdoors	Table
3	1002	1102	14.5	2	Active Outdoors	Table
4	1003	2161	9.85	3	Wheeler	Table

6 COLUMNS, 25 ROWS

Figure 8-53 One-to-many merge result

Exercise 8.6: Use Some Of The Advanced Merge And Append Options

This exercise will show you other ways to use the merge and append options.

1. In a new file ⇒ Import the following tables from the Store Sales workbook: June_invoices, Nov_invoices, Order Details, Products, Sept_invoices and Sales.

2. Save the file as `E8.6 Merge And Append New Table Options`.

3. Import the two CSV files in the 2016 invoices folder.

Create A Many-To-Many Merge

In this part of the exercise, you will learn how to create a many-to-many merge.

1. Duplicate the Order Details query ⇒ Rename the query to `1 Merged On Vendor`.

2. Home tab ⇒ Merge Queries button ⇒ Merge Queries ⇒ Select the Products table in the drop-down list.

3. Select the Vendor column in both tables. Notice that the message at the bottom of the dialog box says that 25 of 25 rows were matched ⇒ Click OK.

4. As shown at the top of Figure 8-54, the two rows with the Order ID 1002 have different Product ID's, which is what is expected ⇒ Click next to the word "Table", in the new column, in row 2. You will see that there are two matching records in the Products table.

This is probably not what you were expecting. The reason that two matches were found for row 2 is because the Vendor column was used to link the tables for the merge. Both products are from the same vendor, which is fine. Row 3 will also display two rows. This means that two rows will be created in the query that are not needed (one for the current row 2 and one for the current row 3).

	Order ID	Product ID	Unit Price	Quantity	Vendor	Products
1	1001	1001	18.88	1	Roadster	Table
2	1002	1101	14.5	4	Active Outdoors	Table
3	1002	1102	14.5	2	Active Outdoors	Table
4	1003	2161	9.85	3	Wheeler	Table

Product ID	Vendor	Show Room	Color	Price (SRP)
1101	Active Outdoors	Retail Location	red	14.5
1102	Active Outdoors	Online	green	14.5

Figure 8-54 Result of a many-to-many merge

5. Use the button (on the Products column), to add the Show Room column from the Products table.

Notice that there are now 27 rows in the query. Figure 8-55 illustrates the duplicate rows. Most of the time, this is not the result that you want.

	Order ID	Product ID	Unit Price	Quantity	Vendor	Show Room
1	1001	1001	18.88	1	Roadster	Online
2	1002	1101	14.5	4	Active Outdoors	Retail Location
3	1002	1101	[illegible]	4	Active Outdoors	Online
4	1002	1102	14.5	2	Active Outdoors	Retail Location
5	1002	1102	[illegible]	2	Active Outdoors	Online
6	1003	2161	9.85	3	Wheeler	Expo
7	1006	2161	9.85	1	Wheeler	Expo

Figure 8-55 Duplicate rows of data illustrated

This is also an example of why many IT people cringe when end users want to link tables on a text field. This is why tables in a database use automatic sequential numeric values, as the Primary key field to link on.

If you have data that is part of a many-to-many relationship and want to use it in Power BI Desktop, unpivoting it will be helpful. An example of this type of data is orders that have different bill to and ship to addresses. Another example would be a customer that has multiple ship to addresses.

> **Adding More Data To A New Table**
> If you wanted to merge (or append) more data to the new merge table after initially creating it, use the Merge Queries option with the new table. Using the Merge (or Append) Queries as New option will create another new table, which would not hurt anything, but it is probably not what you want.

Append Queries To Create A New Table

Earlier in Exercise 8.2, the Append Queries option was used to append data in one table to an existing table.
In Exercise 8.5, the Merge Queries as New option on the Merge Queries button was used to create a new table.
The Append Queries as New option on the Append Queries button is also used to create a new table.

Create A New Table From Appended Queries

This part of the exercise will show you another way to create a new table and how to append data with different column names.

1. Append Queries button ⇒ Append Queries as New ⇒

   In the first drop-down list, select the June Invoices table ⇒

   Select the Sept Invoices table, in the last drop-down list, as shown in Figure 8-56.

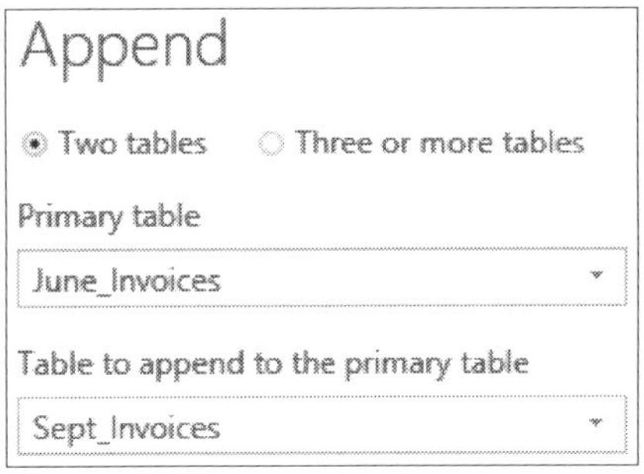

Figure 8-56 Append options

2. Click OK ⇒ The new query will be created. Rename the query to `2 Append invoices`.
   The query should have 368 rows.

Appending Queries With Different Column Names

The append exercise that you just completed, went off without a problem. That is because during the append process, the column headings from the first table were loaded into memory and the data in the query was added to the new table. When the second table was scanned, the column headings were compared to the ones from the first table, so that the columns can be appended to the new table. As hard as you try to get people to follow naming conventions, at some point, you will get data that does not follow the rules.

> **Column Order For Appending Queries**
> As long as the column heading names are the same, the data will be appended, even if the columns are not in the same order, as the table that the data will be appended to. The column names will be matched and appended to the correct column.

This part of the exercise will show you what happens when the column names are not the same.

1. Duplicate the Append Invoices query ⇒ Rename it to `3 Append with different headings`.

2. Append Queries button ⇒ Append Queries ⇒ Select the Nov Invoices query ⇒ Click OK.

As illustrated in Figure 8-57, there is a new column named Order Nbr. The existing records in the table have "null" in this column because the table that they are from, does not have a column with this name.

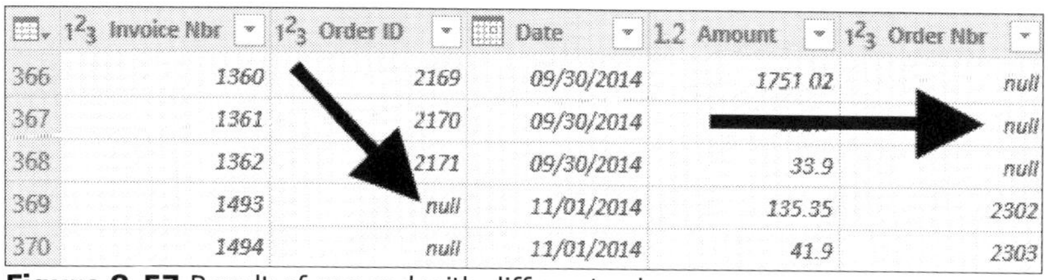

	Invoice Nbr	Order ID	Date	Amount	Order Nbr
366	1360	2169	09/30/2014	1751.02	null
367	1361	2170	09/30/2014	[illegible]	null
368	1362	2171	09/30/2014	33.9	null
369	1493	null	11/01/2014	135.35	2302
370	1494	null	11/01/2014	41.9	2303

Figure 8-57 Result of append with different column names

If you scroll down the table and view the data for November, you will see values in the Order Nbr column.

Also notice that there are null values in the Order ID column for the Nov Invoice rows. That is because the Nov Invoices table does not have this column.

If the Nov Invoices table had three columns of data that the current table did not have, three new columns would be added to the new query. When Power BI Desktop cannot find a match for the column heading, a new column is created. This is easy to fix. The Order Nbr column heading needs to be renamed to Order ID.

3. Click on the Nov Invoices query ⇒ Rename the Order Nbr column to `Order ID`.

4. Display the Append with different headings query. You will not see the last column shown above in Figure 8-57, that was created when the Nov Invoices query was initially appended, because the column names are the same.

Append Three Or More Tables At One Time

The previous part of this exercise demonstrated appending two queries. As shown below in Figure 8-38, there is an option to append three or more tables, which is what this part of the exercise covers.

1. Duplicate the Append with different headings query ⇒ Rename it to `4 Append five tables`.

2. Home tab ⇒ Append Queries button ⇒ Append Queries ⇒ Select the **THREE OR MORE TABLES** option.

3. Add the following tables to the Tables to append column: Jan 2016, Feb 2016, June Invoices, Sept Invoices and 2 Append Invoices, as shown in Figure 8-58 ⇒ Click OK.

   The new query will be created.

   The append order of the queries can be changed before the query is created, by selecting the query that you want to move, then clicking the Up and Down buttons.

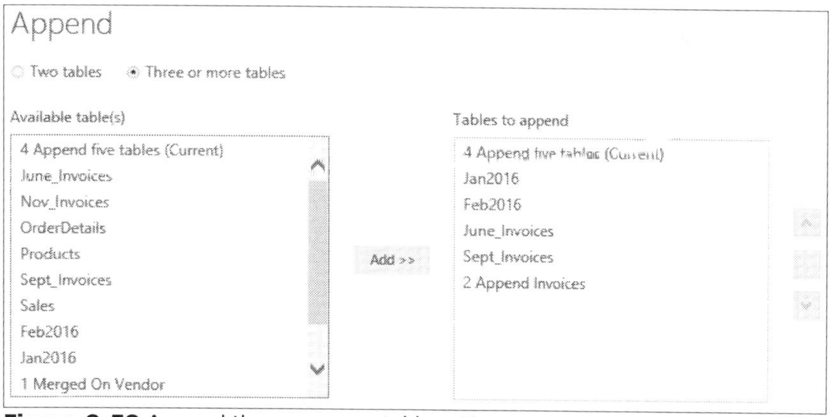

Figure 8-58 Append three or more table options

> If, in the future you need to append more tables to this query, import the table that you want to append ⇒ Double-click on the icon across from the **SOURCE STEP** (of the query that you want to append data to), to open the dialog box shown above in Figure 8-58.

Instead of using the Append dialog box, you can modify the formula, for the Source step, as shown in Figure 8-59. Type in the query name that you want to add, between the curly brackets. The order that the queries are listed in, is the order that they are appended in. This means that just like on the Append dialog box, you can change the order of the queries. For example, if you need to add a table that has July invoices, you would add it between the tables shown in Figure 8-59, as shown in Figure 8-60.

```
= Table.Combine({June_Invoices, Sept_Invoices})
```

Figure 8-59 Source step formula to modify

```
= Table.Combine({June_Invoices, July_Invoices, Sept_Invoices})
```

Figure 8-60 Modified Source step formula

Discover The Top Selling Product By Year

There seems to always be a need to find the top this or top that. At the time this book went to print, Power Query does not have what is known as Top 10 functionality built in. There is a TOPN function in DAX that you can use in the Data view, to create Top N formulas.

This part of the exercise will show you how to find each sales reps top selling product per year, based on the largest line total amount.

Create The Group

The group that you will create in this part of the exercise, will display the orders by order year and sales rep.

1. Duplicate the Sales query ⇒ Rename it to `5 Sales reps orders`.
2. Home tab ⇒ Group By button ⇒ Create the groups shown in Figure 8-61.

   The **ALL ROWS OPERATION** creates a new column of tables. The table contains the detail rows that are used to create the calculation for the row above it on the Group By dialog box.

   In this exercise, the Sales Detail table will display the rows needed to create the values in the Total Sales column.

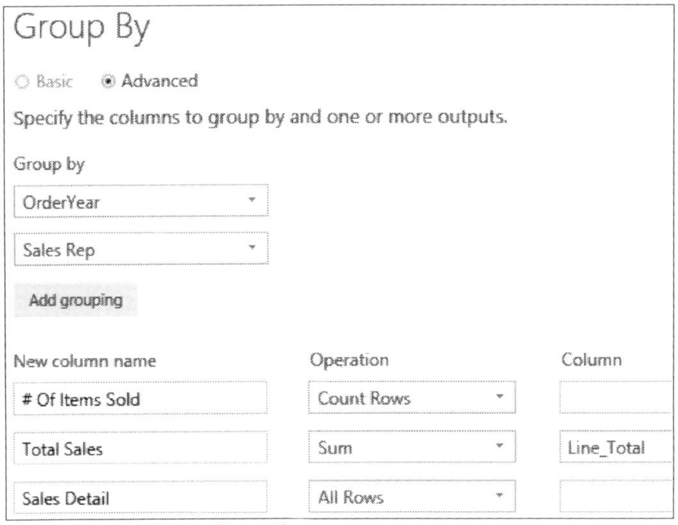

Figure 8-61 Group By options

The top of Figure 8-62 shows some of the grouped data. Clicking next to the word "Table", displays the rows (shown at the bottom of the figure) that are used to create the Total Sales calculation for the selected row in the table at the top of the figure. Remember that when the data is grouped, columns that are not used to create the groups, are not displayed, once the Group By options are applied.

	OrderYear	Sales Rep	# Of Items Sold	Total Sales	Sales Detail
1	2013	Justin Brid	23	7163.08	Table
2	2013	Xavier Martin	16	7647.46	Table
3	2013	Margaret Peacock	30	11938.05	Table

Order ID	Order Date	OrderYear	QTR	Sales Rep	Customer Name	Product ID
1002	12/02/2013	2013	Q4	Xavier Martin	Ron Cunningham	2181
1002	12/02/2013	2013	Q4	Xavier Martin	Ron Cunningham	5205
1072	12/16/2013	2013	Q4	Xavier Martin	Zach Fabro	7402
1075	12/16/2013	2013	Q4	Xavier Martin	Christopher Carmine	2204
1096	12/27/2013	2013	Q4	Xavier Martin	Gary Jannis	4105

Figure 8-62 Result of the group by options shown above in Figure 8-61

3. Change the data type of the # Of Items Sold column to Whole Number.

Discover The Top Selling Products By Dollar Amount

This part of the exercise will show you how to create a formula to find each sales reps highest selling product for each year, based on the Line Total value. This value will be displayed in the query.

1. Click on the last Changed Type step.

2. Add Column tab ⇒ Custom Column button ⇒ Create the column using the formula shown in Figure 8-63.

   In this formula, the **TABLE.MAX FUNCTION** looks in the Sales Detail records for each row (shown above, at the bottom of Figure 8-62) and pulls out the row that has the largest value in the Line Total column, for each sales rep.

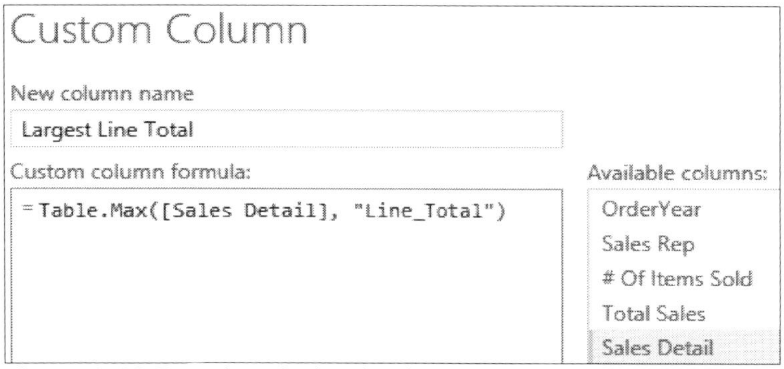

Figure 8-63 Formula to find each sales reps largest selling product

You should see a column with the word "Record", as shown in the upper right corner of Figure 8-64.

This is an example of the **RECORD DATA TYPE**, that was discussed in Chapter 6.

Clicking next to the word "Record", displays the row (from the rows retrieved in the table, in the Sales Detail column) with the largest Line Total value, as shown at the bottom of the figure.

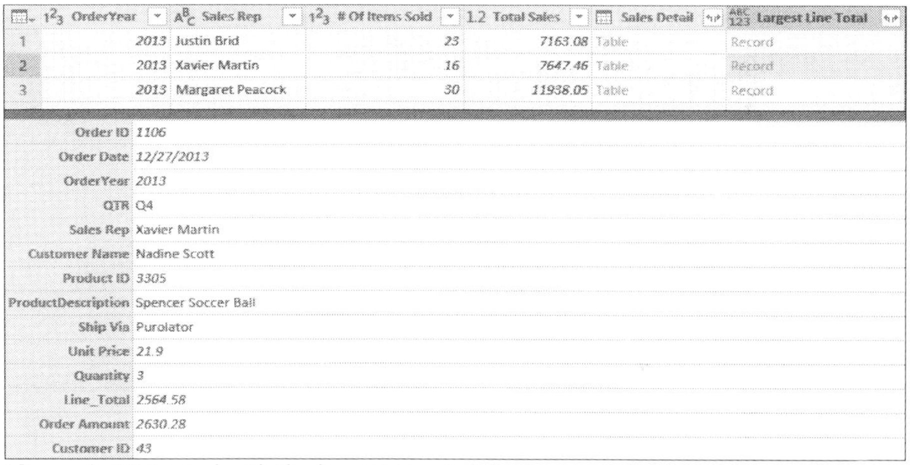

Figure 8-64 Record with the largest Line Total amount for the selected sales rep

The next step is to add columns from the record with the largest value.

3. Click the button to the right of the Largest Line Total column heading ⇒

   Check the fields shown in Figure 8-65.

   When selecting columns, if you are not 100% sure, if you need to display a column, it is best to select it now. If you find that you do not need it, you can always delete it later. This is a step that I would rename, in case I needed to change the columns.

   If you need to add more columns later, repeat this step. You will see an error message. Delete the old Expanded step.

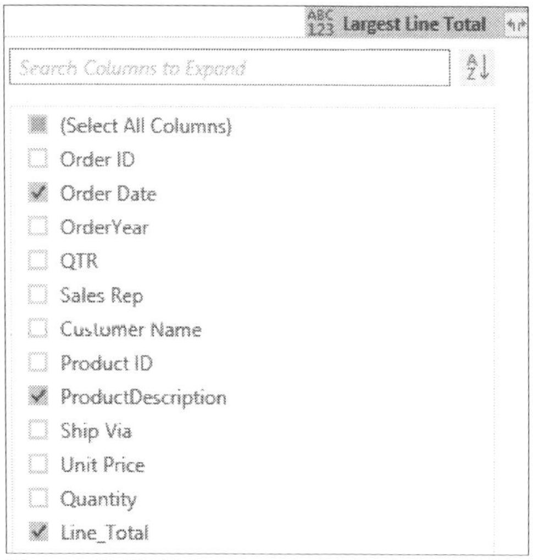

Figure 8-65 Columns selected to be added to the table

Clean Up The Table

1. Rename the Product Description column to `Best Seller`.
2. Rename the Line_Total column to `$Best Seller` ⇒ Change the $Best Seller column data type to Fixed Decimal Number.
3. Delete the Sales Detail column.
4. Change the Order Date column data type to Date.

Calculate The Best Seller Percent

The steps below show you how to create a formula that will display what percent of the yearly total, each best selling product represents. Keep in mind that the percent may not be displayed as you expect in the Query Editor, but in the Data view, you can format the column to display as a percent. You can also create a formula in the Query Editor, to display the values with a percent symbol.

1. Add Column tab ⇒ Custom Column button ⇒ Create the formula shown in Figure 8-66.

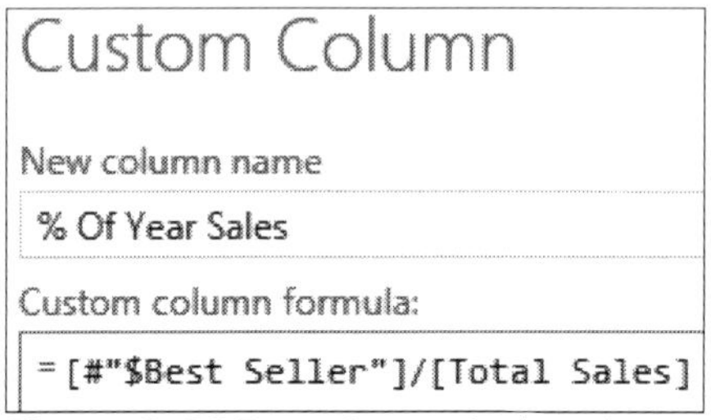

Figure 8-66 Formula to calculate the percent

2. Click on the % Of Year Sales column ⇒ Transform tab ⇒ Rounding button ⇒ Round ⇒ Type 2 in the Decimal Places field. The query should look like the one shown in Figure 8-67. The % Of Year Sales values are actually whole numbers.

	OrderYear	Sales Rep	# Of Items Sold	Total Sales	Order Date	Best Seller	$Best Seller	% Of Year Sales
1	2013	Justin Brid	23	7163.08	12/19/2013	ProTech Bike Helmet	1079.7	0.15
2	2013	Xavier Martin	16	7647.46	12/27/2013	Spencer Soccer Ball	2564.58	0.34
3	2013	Margaret Peacock	30	11938.05	02/27/2013	Gold Coast Volleyball Set	2497.05	0.21
4	2013	Anne Dodsworth	32	8778.38	12/17/2013	Johnson Bowling Ball	2372.19	0.27
5	2013	Albert Hellstern	25	8473.76	12/13/2013	Flexall Dual Stack Gym M...	2497.05	0.29

Figure 8-67 Query showing each sales reps best selling item for each year

Add Percent Formatting To Numeric Data

Earlier in this chapter you saw how to use the **NUMBER.TOTEXT FUNCTION** to display values with currency formatting. The same function can also be used to display values with percent formatting. Figure 8-68 shows the formula used to display the % Of Year Sales values with percent formatting, as shown in Figure 8-69. The "P" in the formula is what displays the percent sign.

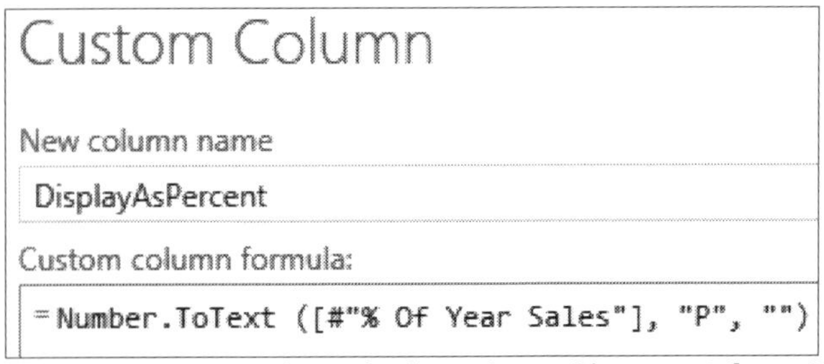

Figure 8-68 Formula to display values with percent formatting

% Of Year Sales	DisplayAsPercent
0.15073125	15.07 %
0.335350561	33.54 %
0.209167326	20.92 %

Figure 8-69 Result of percent formatting

Summary

This chapter covered using the merge and append options, to help get the data ready to be analyzed. The Group By dialog box was used to create calculations that are often needed for analysis purposes.

One reason some exercises contained multiple queries is to emulate what would be needed for different analysis and reporting requests for the same dataset. In this chapter, I tried to include more real life scenarios of the types of transformations that you may need to create.

This chapter covered appending three or more tables. Using the Append dialog box made it easy. But if you know that you will need to add another table or two, on a regular basis, that process probably isn't very appealing. If that is the case and the files that you will need to append, can be saved in the same folder, there is a folder import option that accomplishes the same append process. Once you set it up, you only need to refresh the data for the folder and any new tables in the folder are automatically appended to the existing query. This functionality is covered in the next chapter.

ADVANCED IMPORTING AND CREATING PARAMETERS

After completing this chapter you will be able to perform the following tasks:

- ☑ Import all files (with the same file type) in a folder, at one time
- ☑ Create parameters to use with queries and drop-down lists in Power Query

CHAPTER 9

Overview

So far, this book has covered importing tables of data from different file types. Most of the time, this will handle your needs. Chapter 8 covered using the Append dialog box, to append two or more tables. As good as that functionality is, if you need to append tables to the same query over time, that is not the best solution. There is another way to import data, which can save you from having to create a separate append transformation after the tables are imported. That is because the import option has the append functionality built in. This chapter covers different ways of importing an unlimited number of files from a folder and appending the data in that files that are imported. The **FOLDER CONNECTOR** is used to import and append the data from files in a folder.

You will also learn how to create parameters, which will make the queries interactive and have more functionality.

A benefit that the Folder import (and append) option has over the Append transformation is that you do not need to know the name of the files that will be imported.

What Is Metadata?

Metadata is data about other data. In the context of Power BI Desktop, this would be data that describes files in a folder.

For example, Windows Explorer can display any of the data shown in Figure 9-1 about files on the hard drive. Each field shown in the Details list, is a piece of metadata.

Metadata is often used with the Folder import option on the Get Data dialog box.

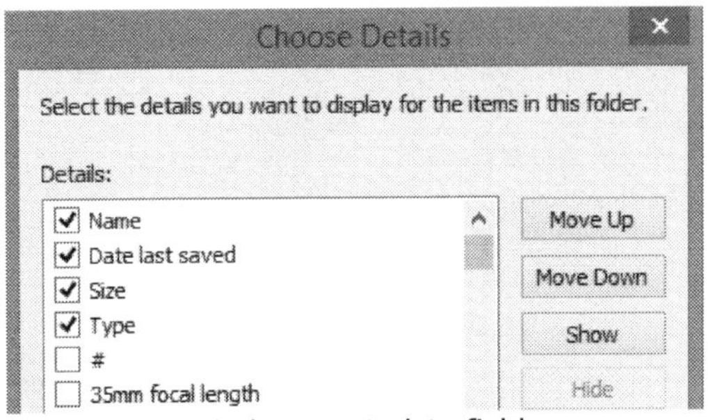

Figure 9-1 Windows metadata fields

Exercise 9.1: Import And Append Multiple CSV Files From A Folder At One Time

If you have several files with the same file type and data structure, in a folder or folder/subfolder structure, Power BI Desktop can import and refresh all of them at the same time.

If you are of a particular age <smile>, you may have used the DOS command prompt to combine the contents of files that are in the same folder, by typing something like "copy * .csv Newfilename.csv". The Folder import option is a similar concept.

This exercise will show you how to complete the same task of appending data from several CSV files into one file. You may find this exercise helpful if you have data that is sent to you on a regular basis, like daily sales or monthly invoice data. Instead of manually appending them one by one, using the Append Queries as New option, never mind formatting each files columns, you can set up a query to import each file, filter out file types in the folder that you do not want to import, and more.

Once the initial query is set up and works the way that you need it to, with the click of a button, new files can be imported, transformed and appended to the main table. As you will see, the end result of importing several files from a folder is another way to append data. There are four main steps to setting up a query that will import CSV files from a folder or subfolder, to create one large table.

This exercise uses CSV files. The same steps can be used with other types of files. While this exercise uses CSV files that are on your hard drive, you can use CSV files that are on the web or a server, as long as they are in the same folder.

Step 1: Select The Folder With The Data

The goal of this step is to select the folder that will be used by the query to get the files from. This folder should already be in the location that you need and have the name that you want. If the folder name or location needs to be changed later, the query will have to be modified. If you need to import files from different folders, you could create a parameter that has a list of folders that has files that you need to import.

1. In a new file ⇒ Get Data button ⇒ More ⇒ Select the Folder option.

2. Click the Browse button ⇒
   Select the invoice import files folder, in your folder.

   You should have the options shown in Figure 9-2 ⇒
   Click OK. You will see the dialog box shown in Figure 9-3.

Figure 9-2 Folder that has the files to import

All of the buttons, in the lower right corner of Figure 9-3, will append the files shown at the top of the dialog box.

The **LOAD BUTTON** will load all of the files in the folder, into the data model and display them in the Query Editor.
The **EDIT BUTTON** displays all of the files in the folder, in the Query Editor.

The difference between these buttons and the options on the Combine button, is that the buttons bypass the Combine Files dialog box, shown in Figure 9-4.

Both options on the **COMBINE BUTTON** open the dialog box shown in Figure 9-4. It displays all of the files in the folder that you selected. Notice the Extension column. It contains the type for each file in the folder. At this point in the process, it is okay that the files in the folder are different file types. As you will see later in the import process, you can (and should) select the file type that you want to import.

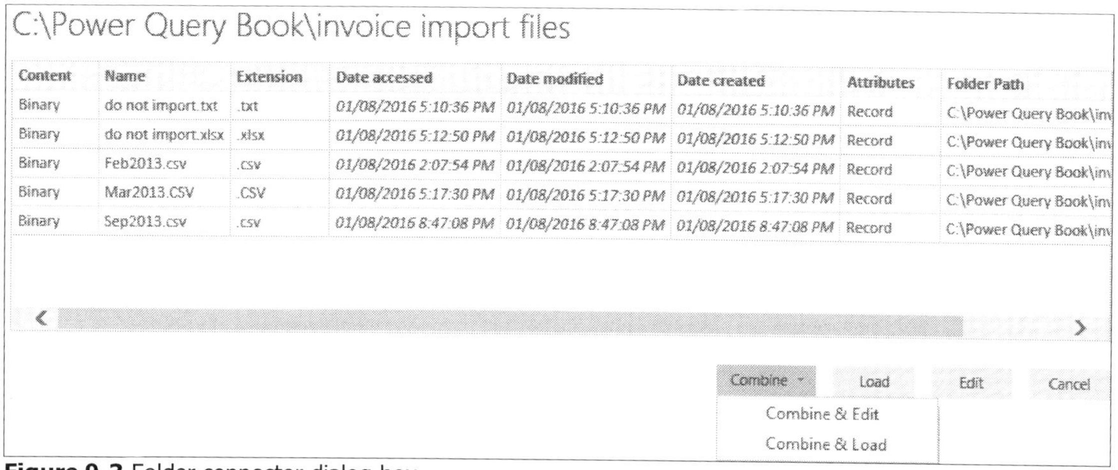

Figure 9-3 Folder connector dialog box

Combine Files Dialog Box

The options on the **COMBINE FILES DIALOG BOX** are used to select the settings for each file in the **EXAMPLE FILE** drop-down list, if necessary. The files in this list are the files shown above in Figure 9-3. If you do not need to change any settings, use the Load and Edit buttons, discussed above, instead of the Combine button options.

The **EXAMPLE FILE FIELD** is used to select which file in the folder should be used as the sample file to use to select any transformation, when needed. The default value selected is **FIRST FILE**.

This option forces the first file in the folder to be used as the example file, regardless of the file name. You can select a specific file in the folder to use as an example file.

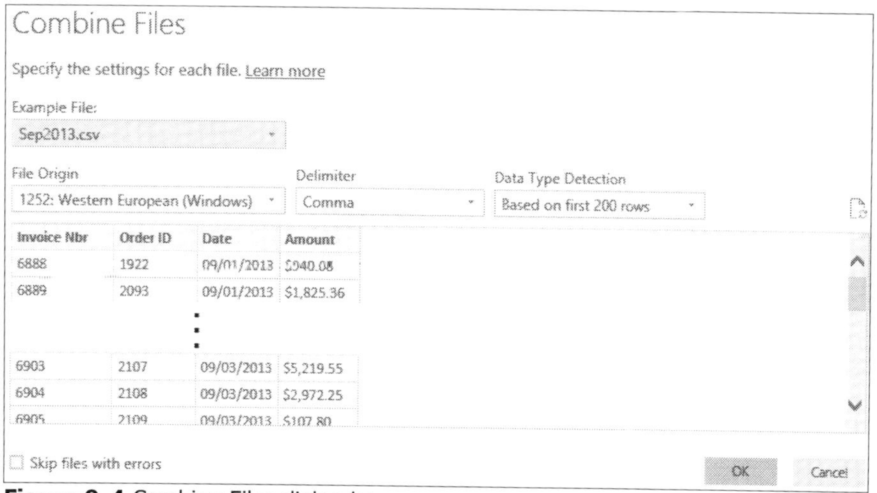

Figure 9-4 Combine Files dialog box

If you select a specific files in the Example File drop-down list and that file gets deleted or renamed, you will get an error when you refresh the data.

The Combine Files dialog box is the equivalent of the Navigator dialog box. One difference that I noticed is that you can select a table on a worksheet or a worksheet to combine. Once you make the selection, all tables or worksheets in each workbook in the folder will be combined. For example, the workbook shown in Figure 9-5 has a worksheet (a tab) named 3 Range Names, with four tables defined (created using the Range Name Manager) on the same sheet. Notice that the worksheet has a different icon, then the four tables.

If you had multiple workbooks that had a table named "Range 2" for example, that you wanted to import, you would select that and each workbook in the folder that has a table named Range 2, would be imported.

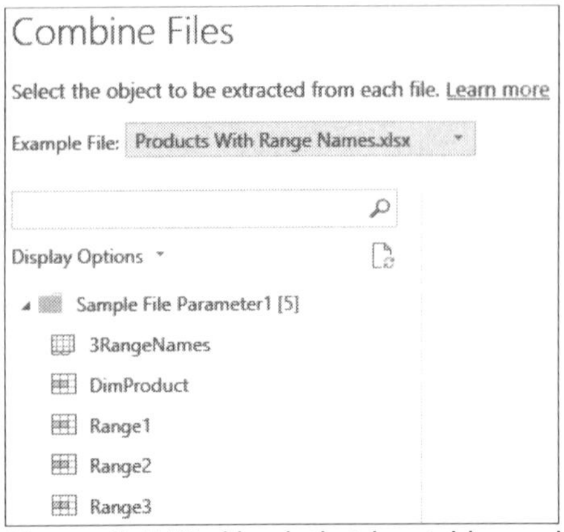

Figure 9-5 Workbook that has tables and a worksheet

In this exercise, you only want to import CSV files. As shown earlier in Figure 9-3, there are other file types in the folder. They should not be imported.

3. Click the Edit button.

4. Save the file as `E9.1 Import csv files from a folder.`

Understanding The Folder Connector Query Results

You should see the files shown in Figure 9-6. They are the same files shown earlier in Figure 9-3. As you can see, there are files in the folder that are not CSV files. That is okay, because the other file types can be filtered out. I purposely added non CSV files to the folder, to demonstrate how to filter out other file types.

As hard as you try, if other people are suppose to place files in the import folder, at some point, someone will place a file in the folder that has a different file type. That would cause the query to fail, if you do not set up a filter to exclude other file types.

Each row shown in Figure 9-6 represents a table. The **CONTENT COLUMN** stores a link to the data for the file in the Name column. In the Content column, clicking on the word **BINARY**, will import the data in the associated table into the query.

The button next to the Content column heading is called the **COMBINE BUTTON** (illustrated in Figure 9-6). When this button is clicked, the Query Editor will try to combine all of the data in all of the binary files displayed in this query, into one table. This is done by importing and appending the data, hopefully, error free. <smile>

For this to work, the files must be the same type and the fields should be in the same order. If the fields are not in the same order, the data can still be combined, but it can be difficult to clean up the data.

The **COMBINE FILES BUTTON** on the Home tab in the Query Editor, works the same as the Combine button on the Content column, shown in Figure 9-6. This transform option analyzes the files (.xlsx, JSON, csv) and selects the correct format to use, then creates the following queries, that are shown later in Figure 9-9, in the Queries panel.

① A sample query that performs all of the extraction steps in a single file.
② A **FUNCTION QUERY** (as shown later in Figure 9-26) that creates parameters for the files that will be imported.
③ A **FUNCTION QUERY** that points back to the original query (like a folder import query), which expands the data.

These queries make it easier to combine all of the files in a folder, as long as they have the same structure and data type.

The **EXTENSION COLUMN** displays the extension for the file.

The **DATE MODIFIED** column will be helpful if you need to know when the file (in the Name column) was last saved.

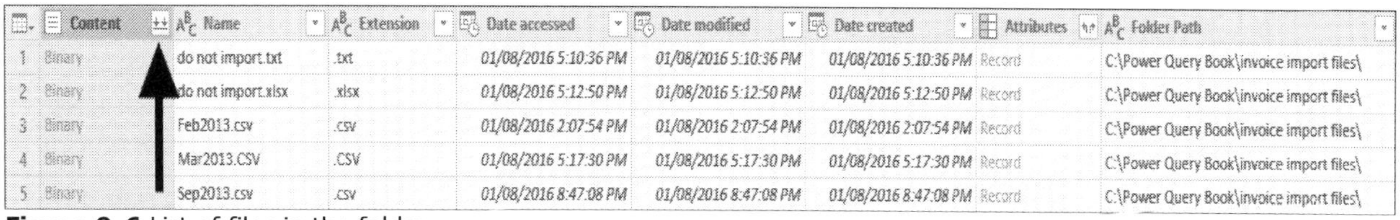

	Content	Name	Extension	Date accessed	Date modified	Date created	Attributes	Folder Path
1	Binary	do not import.txt	.txt	01/08/2016 5:10:36 PM	01/08/2016 5:10:36 PM	01/08/2016 5:10:36 PM	Record	C:\Power Query Book\invoice import files\
2	Binary	do not import.xlsx	.xlsx	01/08/2016 5:12:50 PM	01/08/2016 5:12:50 PM	01/08/2016 5:12:50 PM	Record	C:\Power Query Book\invoice import files\
3	Binary	Feb2013.csv	.csv	01/08/2016 2:07:54 PM	01/08/2016 2:07:54 PM	01/08/2016 2:07:54 PM	Record	C:\Power Query Book\invoice import files\
4	Binary	Mar2013.CSV	.CSV	01/08/2016 5:17:30 PM	01/08/2016 5:17:30 PM	01/08/2016 5:17:30 PM	Record	C:\Power Query Book\invoice import files\
5	Binary	Sep2013.csv	.csv	01/08/2016 8:47:08 PM	01/08/2016 8:47:08 PM	01/08/2016 8:47:08 PM	Record	C:\Power Query Book\invoice import files\

Figure 9-6 List of files in the folder

Step 2: Prepare The Files To Be Combined

This step will show you have to create a filter that selects a specific file type.

The query name cannot be the same as any table name or folder name used in the query.

1. Display the Extension column filter options ⇒ Check both .csv extensions, as shown in Figure 9-7.

   As shown above in Figure 9-6, one file has the csv extension in all capital letters, which really is not correct.

   I would force all extensions to be lower case, but I am trying not to bog you down with too many steps. <smile>

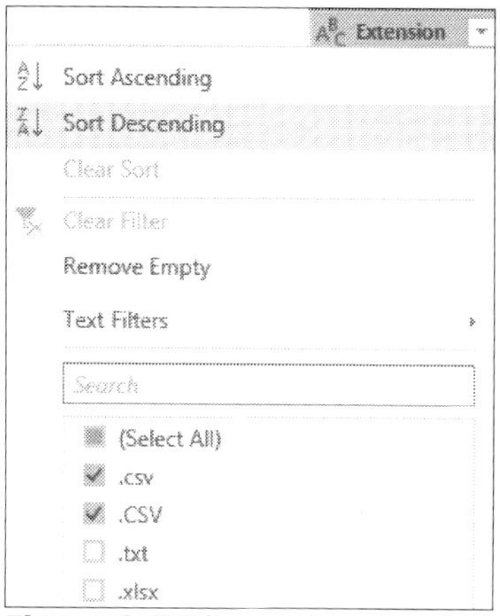

Figure 9-7 Filter options to select the file type

2. Rename the query to `Import Invoices`.

If your folder initially only had files with the file type that you wanted to import, using the Extension column filter option would not work. The reason is because when the filter only has one item to filter on, the **(SELECT ALL)** option stays enabled by default. With the (Select All) option being selected, all file types would be acceptable and would appear in the list of tables, just like what was shown above in Figure 9-7. On your own, if this is the case, follow the steps below to force the filter to only select the file type that you want. You would do this after completing step one above.

1. Right-click on the Extension column header ⇒ Transform ⇒ Lowercase. This step is optional, if it does not apply to your data files. It changes the extension to be lowercase. Remember, **TEXT FILTERS ARE CASE SENSITIVE**.
2. Open the Extension column filter ⇒ Text Filters ⇒ Equals ⇒ On the dialog box shown in Figure 9-8, type the extension, including the period before the letters in the field, as illustrated ⇒ Click OK.

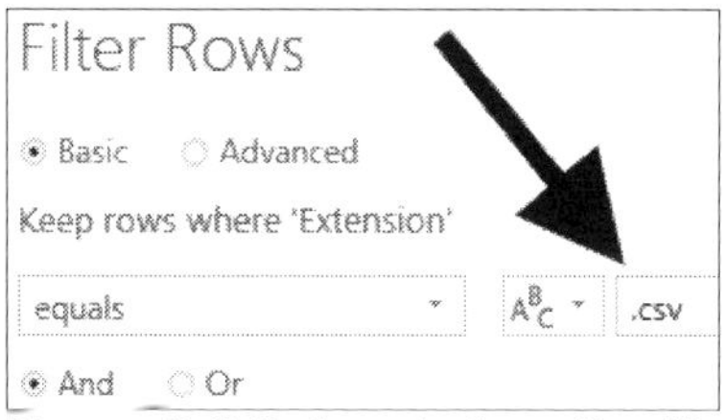

Figure 9-8 Options to force the filter to use a specific file extension

Step 3: Import The Data

The transformations that are applied, depend on the data. Sometimes you will need to rename columns, change the data or add columns.

1. Click the Content column **COMBINE FILES BUTTON** (illustrated earlier in Figure 9-6) ⇒ On the dialog box shown earlier in Figure 9-4, click OK. 353 rows of data will be imported.

The first few rows are shown in Figure 9-9. This is the data in the three CSV files, in the folder.

The **SOURCE.NAME COLUMN** is the file name that the row of data was imported from. This column is automatically created and is helpful if you have data that you need someone else to fix, because you can tell them which file that data is in.

In the Queries panel, notice all of the transformations and parameters that were created during the import.

You should have the steps shown in Figure 9-10. Pretty good for not writing code, huh!

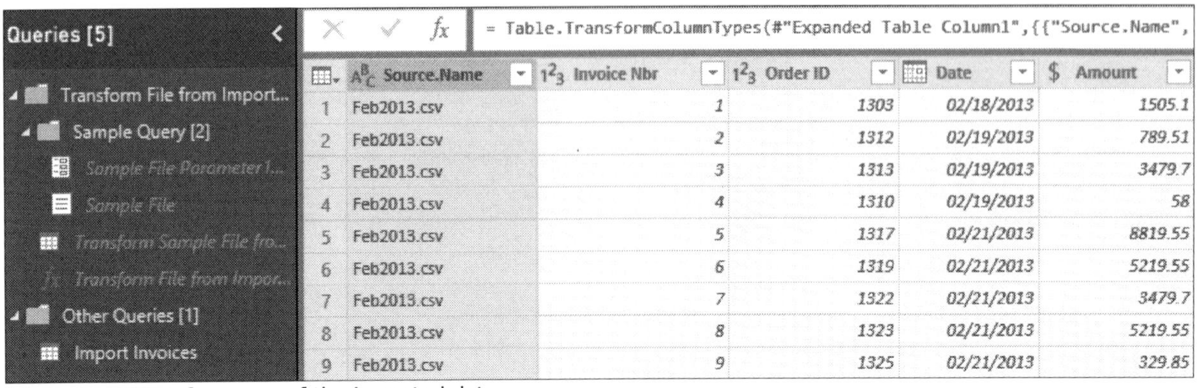

Figure 9-9 First few rows of the imported data

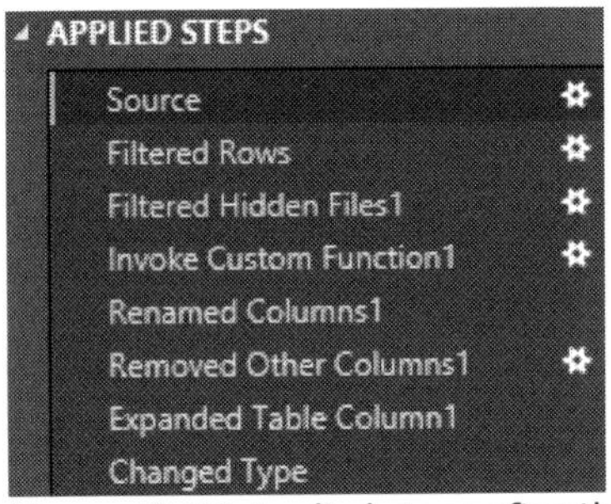

Figure 9-10 Applied steps after the import

Step 4: Transform The Data

Notice the formula for the Changed Type step. It contains what Power BI Desktop thinks the data type is for each column of data that was imported. I prefer to select the data types manually, as the actual data on future imports is based on this criteria and may also need to be converted. I have noticed that when the first row of data is not used as the column headings, that at least some of the data types that were selected are not correct.

Before you boo me for adding more steps, remember that the data type only has to be changed now. Going forward, the same data types that are applied now, override what Power BI Desktop thinks the data type is, when more data is imported and appended to this file.

1. Delete the Changed Type step.

2. Home tab ⇒ Remove Rows button ⇒ Remove Blank Rows.

   Unless you plan to view all of the rows each time you append new files to the one that you just created, this is a good transformation to apply. If there are no blank rows, this step will not hurt anything.

3. Rename the Date column to `Inv Date` ⇒ Rename the Amount column to `Inv Amount`.

4. Right-click on the Invoice Nbr column ⇒ Change Type ⇒ Whole Number.

5. Change the data types for the columns in Table 9-1.

Column	Change The Data Type To . . .
Order ID	Whole Number
Inv Date	[See Figure 9-11]

Table 9-1 Columns to change the data type of

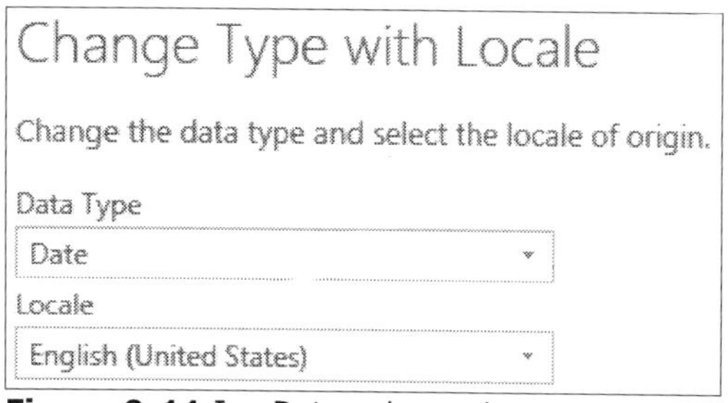

Figure 9-11 Inv Date column change type options

If you scroll down and view row 49, you will see that three of the data columns have the word "null", as shown in Figure 9-12. This is a blank row in the Mar2013.csv file. This row, and any other rows like it, should not be saved in the data model. One way to fix this is to create a filter for one of the columns that has the null value.

On your own, you should check the data files before making a decision about what to do with the data. The reason that I know what to do is because I created the data files.

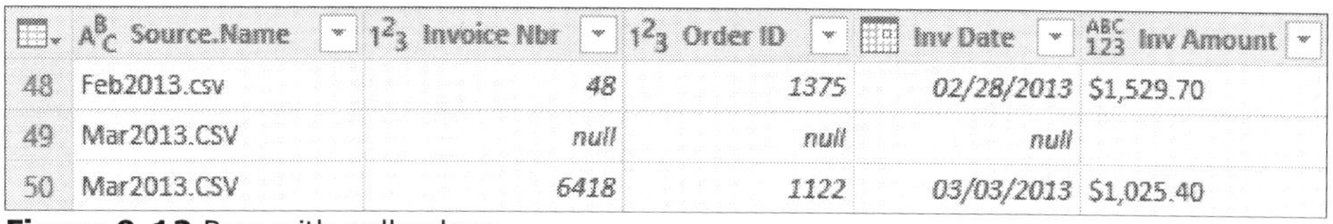

	Source.Name	Invoice Nbr	Order ID	Inv Date	Inv Amount
48	Feb2013.csv	48	1375	02/28/2013	$1,529.70
49	Mar2013.CSV	null	null	null	
50	Mar2013.CSV	6418	1122	03/03/2013	$1,025.40

Figure 9-12 Row with null values

6. Display the filter options for the Order ID column ⇒ Clear the check mark for the (null) option ⇒ Click OK. If you view the data, you will not see the rows that have a null value, in the Order ID column.

You can use any of the three columns that have a null value and the result would be the same. On your own, if your data source has more than 999 rows, you can open the filter options for each column to see if there is a null option. If all of the columns have a null option, clear the check mark, as that indicates the row does not have any data.

7. Save and apply the pending changes.

Any time that you import data using the Get Folder option, you should at least look at the data displayed in the Query Editor, to make sure that you have the data in the format that you need. Depending on the data source type, column headings can be imported, that are not needed, as shown earlier in Figure 9-12. This happens mostly when the data source is not a database.

Keep in mind that if more files are added to the folder and the Refresh button is clicked, the files that were added to the folder will automatically be imported also. This is why creating a filter for the file type to be imported is important. If someone adds files that have a different file type, like .pdf for example, to the folder, the import would fail.

Exercise 9.2: Import Data From Other Folders

Hopefully, you found the previous exercise helpful. I think the Folder connector will save a lot of people a lot of time. Keep in mind that like all other connectors, the Folder connector can be used more than once in the same query. That means that if you used it a second time in Exercise 9.1 to import Excel files, after they are imported and appended by the connector, you could create an append transformation and append the Excel data to the csv data.

Set Up The Folders

The files that were imported in the previous exercise were in the Invoice import files folder. I am sure by now, that you have seen the four folders that have a year in their name, in your folder for this book. If you moved those folders under the Invoice import files folder, guess what? The query that you created in the previous exercise would import the CSV files in those folders also, the next time the query is refreshed.

Yes, if you were doing this on your own, those four folders may have been moved into the Invoice import files folder before you started creating the query. I left them out on purpose so that you could see how the **FOLDER CONNECTOR** import option works. It is also possible that you may have the need to set up sub folders also, and this part of the exercise would serve as the template, if you will, of what to do.

1. In Windows Explorer, display your folder ⇒ Drag/move the four yearly Invoices folders into the invoice import files folder, as shown in Figure 9-13.

Figure 9-13 Structure to have files in multiple folders imported at the same time

2. Save the E9.1 file as `E9.2 Import and append data from other folders.`

3. On the Query Editor ⇒ Refresh the Import Invoices query. The lower left corner of the window should display that there are more than 999 rows. To be exact, there are 1,734 rows. The reason that I know the exact number of rows is because I created all of the files that were imported. <smile>

Group The Data

It would be great to be able to see totals for all of the tables, that were imported in the previous part of this exercise. In this part of the exercise, you will group the data to calculate the total number of invoices and total dollar amount for each year of data in the table.

1. Duplicate the Import Invoices query ⇒ Rename the duplicated query to `1 Invoices grouped by year.`

2. Duplicate the Inv Date column ⇒ Rename it to `Inv Year` ⇒ Right-click on the column ⇒ Transform ⇒ Year ⇒ Year.

3. Change the Inv Amount column data type, to Fixed decimal number.

4. Home tab ⇒ Group By button ⇒ Change the Group By field to Inv Year.

5. Rename the Count column name to `Nbr of Invoices.`

6. Add an aggregate column named `Total $ For Year` ⇒ Select the Sum operation ⇒ Select the Inv Amount column.

   The table should look like the one shown in Figure 9-14.

	Inv Year	Number of Invoices	Total $ For Year
1	2013	484	748402.13
2	2014	712	1295045.44
3	2015	228	385715.57
4	2016	310	483600.83

Figure 9-14 Invoices grouped by year

Exercise 9.3: Import And Append Multiple Sheets From A Workbook

So far in this chapter, you have learned how to append data that was stored in different files. You may come across a file that has data on several sheets in a workbook that needs to be appended and saved in the query.

In Chapter 2, Exercise 2.1, you learned how to import multiple sheets in a workbook. Doing that created a query for each sheet, which is the right thing to do when each sheet has different data. The difference between that exercise and this one, is that the data on each sheet in the workbook for this exercise has the same type of data. By that I mean, the workbook could have three sheets of invoice data. Each sheet has the same data, just for three different years, as shown in Figure 9-15.

If this data was created in a database, instead of Excel, all three sheets of invoice data would be in the same table, regardless of the year of the data.

In this exercise, the Folder import option, creates one query and adds the data from the three sheets to one table. That is the correct way that the data on the three sheets should be set up.

In this exercise, you will learn how to import multiple sheets in one workbook and append the data in them. Figure 9-15 shows some of the data from some of the sheets that will be appended in this exercise.

Invoice Nbr	Order ID	Date	Amount
6107	1121	01/01/2016	$851.77
6108	1122	01/01/2016	$1,025.40
6109	1123	01/02/2016	$5,219.55
6110	1124	01/02/2016	$59.70

2016Jan 2016Feb 2015Apr

Invoice Nbr	Order ID	Date	Amount
6240	1	02/02/2016	$41.90
6241	1002	02/02/2016	$5,060.28
6242	1003	02/02/2016	$186.87
6243	1004	02/02/2016	$823.05

2016Jan 2016Feb 2015Apr

Invoice Nbr	Order ID	Date	Amount
1245	2054	09/01/2014	$4,078.95
1246	2055	09/01/2014	$1,457.61
1247	2056	09/01/2014	$83.80
1248	2057	09/01/2014	$125.70

2016Jan 2016Feb 2015Apr 2015May 2014Sept

Figure 9-15 Data on sheets that will be appended

While you can select (check) all of the individual sheets in the workbook shown in Figure 9-16 and then append them, as covered in Chapter 8, that will not give you the automation that you are looking for. When new sheets are added to the workbook, they will not be imported and appended automatically. **Hint**: The keyword is "automatically". <smile>

Import The Data

1. In a new file ⇒ Home tab ⇒ Get Data button ⇒ Excel ⇒ Select the Import Multiple Sheets workbook.

2. On the Navigator dialog box, notice that there are five sheets (tables). Right-click on the workbook file name and select Edit, as shown in Figure 9-16.

   The options on this shortcut menu are applied to all of the tables in the data source. The Load and Edit buttons, on the Navigator dialog box, are for individual tables that you check.

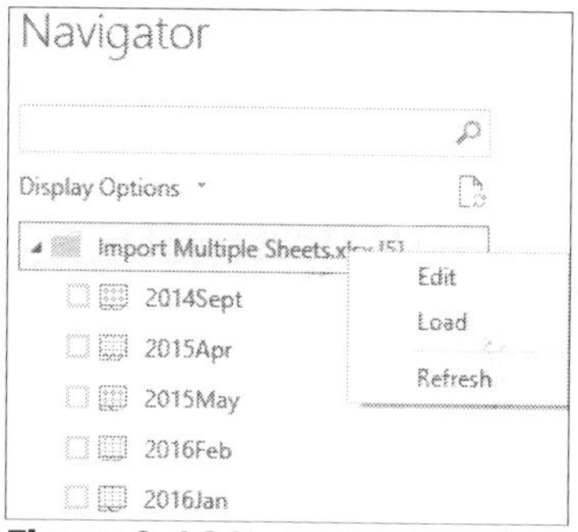

Figure 9-16 Navigator dialog box options

Figure 9-17 shows the result of the import. Notice that there are five rows, one for each sheet in the workbook. The data for each worksheet is currently stored in the **DATA COLUMN**. The **NAME COLUMN** is the sheet name in the workbook.

As you will see, when the table is expanded, each row will have the table name.

	Name	Data	Item	Kind	Hidden
1	2016Jan	Table	2016Jan	Sheet	FALSE
2	2016Feb	Table	2016Feb	Sheet	FALSE
3	2015Apr	Table	2015Apr	Sheet	FALSE
4	2015May	Table	2015May	Sheet	FALSE
5	2014Sept	Table	2014Sept	Sheet	FALSE

Figure 9-17 List of sheets (tables) in the workbook

3. The **ITEM**, **KIND** and **HIDDEN COLUMNS** are not needed. Delete them.

4. Save the file as `E9.3 Append multiple sheets from an Excel file.`

On your own, if the workbook has sheets that you do not need (you will see them in the list of sheets in Figure 9-17), filter them out before you append the data. If the workbook has a hidden sheet, the row will have TRUE in the **HIDDEN COLUMN**.

Transform The Data

In previous exercises, you used the **EXPAND BUTTON** when adding (appending) columns from one table to another. The Expand button on the Data column, appends the data on all of the sheets shown above in Figure 9-17.

Usually, there are three transformations that you have to do. They are explained below.

- ☑ Promote the first row to headers [See Figure 9-18].
- ☑ Filter out the heading row from each table that was appended [See Figure 9-19].
- ☑ Rename a column [See Figures 9-20 and 9-21].

1. Click the **EXPAND BUTTON** to the right of the Data column heading, shown above in Figure 9-17 ⇒ Clear the check box for the Use original column name as prefix option ⇒ Click OK.

The tables will now be appended/combined. As shown in Figure 9-18, the first row needs to be promoted to become the column headings.

	Name	Data.Column1	Data.Column2	Data.Column3	Data.Column4
1	2016Jan	Invoice Nbr	Order ID	Date	Amount
2	2016Jan	6107	1121	01/01/2016	851.77
3	2016Jan	6108	1122	01/01/2016	1025.4
4	2016Jan	6109	1123	01/02/2016	5219.55

Figure 9-18 Appended/combined data

2. On the Home tab, click the Use First Row As Headers button.

If you scroll down and view rows 30, 55, 75 and 89, you will see the column headings for each sheet, as shown in Figure 9-19. In Exercise 9.1, you saw something similar with the combined table that had null values, in some rows.

	2016Jan	Invoice Nbr	Order ID	Date	Amount
29	2016Jan	6135	1149	01/07/2016	329.85
30	2016Feb	Invoice Nbr	Order ID	Date	Amount
31	2016Feb	6240	1	02/02/2016	41.9

Figure 9-19 Column heading rows

3. Display the Amount column filter options ⇒ Scroll to the bottom of the list and clear the check mark for the Amount option ⇒ Click OK. If you scroll down the table, you should not see the rows with the column headings.

The first column (2016Jan), is the name of the sheet that the row of data came from. This column name is a problem because it does not clarify what the data is, in the column.

4. Rename the first column to `FromSheet`.

What may not be obvious is that the sheets were combined, into one table, in the order that they are in the workbook. If the sheets are rearranged in the workbook or if new sheets are added before the 2016Jan sheet and then the data is refreshed in Power BI Desktop, this query will fail because the **RENAMED COLUMNS STEP** hard codes the original name (2016Jan, in this exercise) of the column that is renamed, in the formula, as shown in Figure 9-20.

```
fx  = Table.RenameColumns(#"Filtered Rows",{{"2016Jan", "FromSheet"}})
```

Figure 9-20 Formula to rename a column

The **TABLE.COLUMNNAMES FUNCTION** returns a list of the column names in the table. In Figure 9-20, the table name is #Filtered Rows. The table name came from the previous step, which filtered the data. The 2016Jan portion of the formula needs to be modified to make the column name reference generic. To accomplish this, the formula has to tell Power Query to use the index number, which is in curly brackets, that you specify in the formula. [See Figure 9-21]

In this exercise, you want to rename the first column name in the list, so zero is used in the formula. The M language uses zero (instead of 1), to represent the first item in the list.

5. Select the Renamed Columns step ⇒ Replace "Jan2016", in the formula (in the formula bar), with `Table.ColumnNames(#"Filtered Rows") {0}`

The revised formula says to rename the first column in the query to FromSheet. The formula should look like the one shown in Figure 9-21.

```
= Table.RenameColumns(#"Filtered Rows",{{Table.ColumnNames(#"Filtered Rows") {0},"FromSheet"}})
```

Figure 9-21 Formula to use a generic name for the column name

When you rename a column (step 4 above), it creates what is known as an **EXPLICIT REFERENCE**. This will cause an error when the data is refreshed, or if a new sheet was added to the beginning of the sheets in the workbook.

Renaming A Column

There are several reasons to rename a column, including making it more user friendly or to better convey the data in the column.

Test The Rename Column Formula

In this part of the exercise, you will test refreshing the data in the Import Multiple Sheets workbook with the formula that you just changed. To test this, you will need to add another sheet to the workbook.

Currently, the second table in the query (see row 30 in the query) is from the 2016 Feb sheet in the Import Multiple Sheets workbook. After completing the steps in this part of the exercise, you will see a new sheet, starting at row 30.

1. Open the Import Multiple Sheets workbook in Excel.

2. Make a copy of the 2015Apr sheet ⇒ Rename it to `2017Sept` ⇒ Move the sheet left and place it after the 2016Jan sheet.

3. Save the changes and close the workbook.

4. In the Query Editor ⇒ Home tab ⇒ Refresh Preview button ⇒ Refresh All.

If you scroll down to row 30, you will see the rows from the new sheet, named 2017Sept. Now, the data from the 2016Feb sheet in the workbook starts at row 49. Data on new sheets are added to the query in the order of the tabs in the workbook that they were imported from. If the 2017Sept sheet was added to the end of the workbook, it would be appended at the end of the data already in the query.

> Any sheets that are deleted from the Excel file, will automatically be deleted from the query, when the query is refreshed. There is no warning that data has been deleted from the query.

> Because you cannot control where in the workbook new sheets will be added, on your own, the Renamed Columns step may need to be moved up or created earlier in the list of steps. Where it is now, the refresh will fail if a new sheet is added as the first tab in the workbook. A quick fix would be to move any new sheets in the Excel file to the end of the sheets, then refresh the data.

> From experience, when you create an auto append query, like the one in Exercise 9.3 and something goes wrong when you refresh the data, it is easier to make the change in the Excel file, like move a sheet tab to a new location in the workbook, then to figure out how or what query step needs to be modified.

As covered in Chapter 4, a **CHANGED TYPE STEP** can automatically be created when data is loaded into Power Query. This change type step can cause problems when the data is refreshed or a column is renamed or deleted. The Promoting the first row as headers step can also cause the refresh to generate an error. If the Automatically detect column types . . . option [See Figure 1-25] on the Options dialog box is unchecked, before the data is loaded, the chances of problem happening is greatly reduced.

Personally, I think this option should be in the global section of the Options dialog box, so that it could be applied to all files. Since it's not, I created my own template and selected options on this dialog box, that I want applied to all non database, data source files that I import. I save this file with a new name and use it as the starting point for importing Excel data, instead of using the "New" option to create a new file.

Another solution is to delete the Change Type step that is automatically created, then create it manually. The columns that have to be changed, are the ones that will be used in a calculation. Ironically, creating a Change Type step should be done as close to the end of all of the steps as possible, for the following reasons:

☑ It reduces the chances of getting errors in cells.
☑ Refreshing data takes less time.
☑ Creating the Change Type step, early in the process may not be forced down to all of the appended data.
☑ It increases the performance of the query. When this step is added after the data has been filtered, there is less data that has to be processed.

Exercise 9.4: Import And Append Excel Files

Exercise 9.1 showed you how to import text (CSV) files that are in the same folder. This exercise will do the same using Excel files. The process is similar to importing and appending text files, that have one sheet per workbook, that needs to be imported.

1. In a new file ⇒ Get Data button ⇒ More ⇒ Folder ⇒ Select the Import_Excel folder ⇒ Click OK twice.

2. Click the Load button.

3. In the Query Editor, Home tab ⇒ Combine Files button.

4. On the dialog box shown in Figure 9-22, click on the Load File table ⇒ Click OK.

   Load File, is the name of the tab that all workbooks have, that will be imported.

   On your own, you can name the tab what you want in Excel, before you import the worksheet.

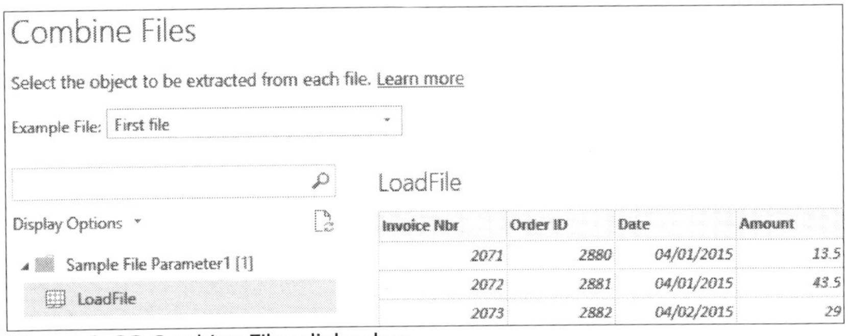

Figure 9-22 Combine Files dialog box

Like the E9.1 CSV exercise, you will see that queries and parameters will be created. On your own, you should change the data types like you did in the CSV exercise and check for values that represent column headings.

Figure 9-23 shows the Removed Other Columns 1 step. It shows the transform step that selects all of the files in the Import_Excel folder that will be imported and appended.

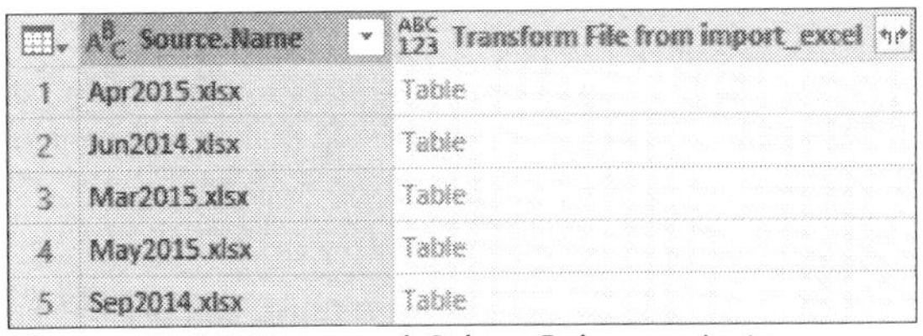

Figure 9-23 Removed Other Columns 1 step

5. Save and apply the changes ⇒ Save the file as `E9.4 Import & Append Excel files in a folder.`

Exercise 9.5: Import An Unlimited Number Of Excel Files From A Folder At One Time

Exercise 9.1 showed you how to import and append CSV files that are in the same folder. This exercise will do the same for Excel files. The difference is that a function will be created. This function will let you select the folder to import files from. This means that you will have the option of importing the same type of file (in this exercise, Excel files) from different folders. The good news is that most of the function can be created by using the macro (M language) functionality that is built into Power Query.

This exercise is also an introduction to creating a parameter. The difference in this exercise, is that you will not use the Parameters dialog box to create the parameter, that is used in the next exercise.

To import multiple Excel files successfully, **THE TAB (WORKSHEET) IN EACH WORKBOOK THAT WILL BE IMPORTED, HAS TO HAVE THE SAME NAME.** If you need to know which workbook each row of data comes from, the Name column, shown later in Figure 9-28, is automatically included when the tables in the figure are expanded. Chapter 11, has an exercise that provides another way to maintain the Excel tab (sheet) name, when appending data.

Load An Excel File

1. In a new file ⇒ Get Data button ⇒ Excel ⇒ Select any Excel file in the Import_Excel folder.

2. On the Navigator dialog box, check the Load File table ⇒ Click the Edit button. (Load File is the name of the tab that all workbooks have, that will be imported.) On your own, you can name the tab what you want in Excel, before you import the worksheet.

On your own, at this point, you should do any or all of the following, as needed:

☑ Rename the query ☑ Create calculations
☑ Transform the data ☑ Any task that you want to be applied to all tables that will be imported

3. Rename the query to `fn_loadfiles`.

> **Function Naming Conventions**
> **fn** is a prefix that is often used to indicate that the query is a function. Using a prefix is optional. (And yes, fn is suppose to be all lower case. <smile>)

Create The Function That Will Select The Files To Load

In this part of the exercise, you will modify the formula to change it to a function.

1. Home or View tab ⇒ Advanced Editor button. You will see the dialog box shown in Figure 9-24. On your own, you will see more lines of code if you performed any of the tasks listed above step 3, in the previous section.

```
fn_loadfiles

let
    Source = Excel.Workbook(File.Contents("C:\Power Query Book\import_excel\Sep2014.xlsx"), null, true),
    LoadFile_Sheet = Source{[Item="LoadFile",Kind="Sheet"]}[Data],
    #"Promoted Headers" = Table.PromoteHeaders(LoadFile_Sheet, [PromoteAllScalars=true]),
    #"Changed Type" = Table.TransformColumnTypes(#"Promoted Headers",{{"Invoice Nbr", Int64.Type}, {"Order ID", Int64.Type}, {"Date"
in
    #"Changed Type"
```

Figure 9-24 Formula before the changes

2. Add a blank line at the top of the window ⇒ Type the line of code shown in Figure 9-25.

   The => is a tag that indicates that you are creating a function.

```
let LoadExcelFiles = (FilePath, FileName) =>
         ①                    ②
```

Figure 9-25 First line of the formula to create the function

The illustrated parts of the formula are explained below.

① This is the function name, which can be whatever you want.
② The **FILEPATH ARGUMENT** will pass the folder name that the Excel files are in, that you want to import. The **FILENAME ARGUMENT** is a place holder for the name of the Excel files that have the data that will be imported.

3. On the Source line, replace "C:\Power Query . . . with `FilePath&FileName`, as illustrated below in Figure 9-26.

4. After the last line of code, type `in LoadExcelFiles`.
   This tag (line of code) indicates that this is the end of the function. Figure 9-26 illustrates the changes that you should have made to the formula.

fn_loadfiles

```
let LoadExcelFiles = (FilePath, FileName)=>
let
    Source = Excel.Workbook(File.Contents(FilePath&FileName), null, true),
    LoadFile_Sheet = Source{[Item="LoadFile",Kind="Sheet"]}[Data],
    #"Promoted Headers" = Table.PromoteHeaders(LoadFile_Sheet, [PromoteAllScalars=true]),
    #"Changed Type" = Table.TransformColumnTypes(#"Promoted Headers",{{"Invoice Nbr", Int
in
    #"Changed Type"

in LoadExcelFiles
```

Figure 9-26 Modified formula for the function

5. Click Done.

   You should see the parameters shown in Figure 9-27, for the function that you just created.

   Because the function will pass the data to the parameters, you will not actually see the parameters during the process of importing the files in this exercise. On your own, you could run the function and use the parameters to get the path to the files that you want to import. This will let you import Excel files from any folder that you select.

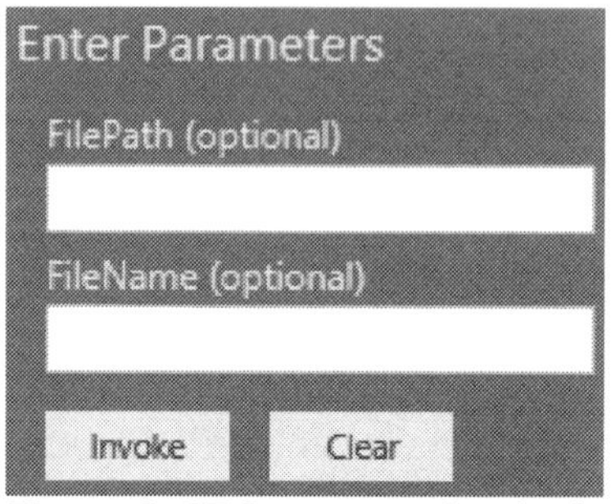

Figure 9-27 Parameters for the function

If you wanted to import a different type of file, you would have create another function or modify this one to allow multiple data sources.

This type of query is known as a **QUERY FUNCTION**. If you have used a programming language like Visual Basic, the concept of one query calling/using another query will be familiar.

6. Save the file as `E9.5 Function to load Excel files`.

Create The Query To Import The Workbook Files

In this part of the exercise, you will create a query that will use the function that you just created. You will create a formula that will pass the folder path and file name fields to the function.

This is the query that you will run to the import the Excel files. If you find that you need to import workbooks that have the same tab as the one used in the function, but are in a different folder (location), duplicate the query in this part of the exercise, open the Advanced Editor and change the path. If you can copy or move the workbooks to the folder used in the current function, you do not have to duplicate the query. The other option is to create a parameter that has a list of folders that have the Excel files to import.

1. Get Data button ⇒ More ⇒ Folder ⇒ On the Folder dialog box, select the Import_Excel folder ⇒ Click OK twice ⇒ On the dialog box that shows all of the files in the Import_Excel folder, click Edit. You will see the query shown in Figure 9-28.

	Content	Name	Extension	Date accessed	Date modified	Date created	Attributes	Folder Path
1	Binary	Apr2015.xlsx	.xlsx	05/11/2016 4:02:32 PM	05/11/2016 4:02:32 PM	05/11/2016 4:02:32 PM	Record	C:\Power Query Book\import_excel\
2	Binary	Jun2014.xlsx	.xlsx	05/11/2016 4:02:18 PM	05/11/2016 4:02:18 PM	05/11/2016 4:02:18 PM	Record	C:\Power Query Book\import_excel\
3	Binary	Mar2015.xlsx	.xlsx	05/11/2016 4:02:02 PM	05/11/2016 4:02:02 PM	05/11/2016 4:02:02 PM	Record	C:\Power Query Book\import_excel\
4	Binary	May2015.xlsx	.xlsx	05/11/2016 4:01:48 PM	05/11/2016 4:01:48 PM	05/11/2016 4:01:48 PM	Record	C:\Power Query Book\import_excel\
5	Binary	Sep2014.xlsx	.xlsx	05/11/2016 4:01:20 PM	05/11/2016 4:01:20 PM	05/11/2016 4:01:20 PM	Record	C:\Power Query Book\import_excel\

Figure 9-28 Query with all of the files in the folder to import

Exercise 9.1 demonstrated how to make sure that the only files imported are ones that have a specific file extension. On your own, you may want to incorporate that functionality into any Folder query that you set up. As Excel supports two file extensions, the filter should include the .xls and .xlsx options, unless you are 100% sure that only one of these file extensions will be used.

2. Add Column tab ⇒ Custom Column button ⇒ Create the formula shown in Figure 9-29 ⇒ Click OK.

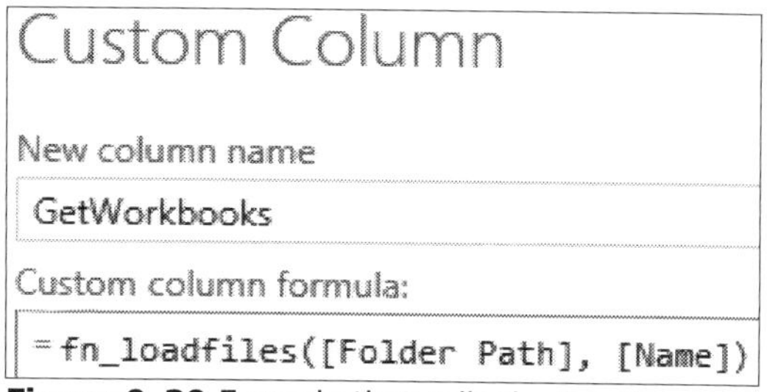

Figure 9-29 Formula that calls the function to get the files in the folder

3. In the import_excel query, click the button at the end of the Get Workbooks column header ⇒ Clear the check mark for the Use original column name as prefix option on the Expand window ⇒ Click OK.

   You will see that the columns of data from the tab in the Excel workbooks have been added (scroll right) to the query. On your own, you do not have to import all of the columns.

4. Perform any tasks that are needed to get the data ready for analysis. Below are some examples.

   ☑ Delete the columns of data that are not needed, like the ones shown earlier in Figure 9-28.
   ☑ Rearrange the remaining columns as needed.
   ☑ Rename the query.

> I don't know about you, but I would like a Folder import option, that imports an unlimited number of files **WITHOUT** having to combine the data into one table.

Parameters

While this topic may seem out of place being in this chapter, I added it here on purpose, because I wanted the parameter exercises to be created after you had learned how to create a variety of queries. That way, adding parameters to queries, makes sense Trust me. There is a method to what appears to be madness. <smile>

Parameters are another way to filter data. They can be used to select a data source to import data from, filter data in the Query Editor, filter data during the import process or filter data on a chart. A parameter can be created or used any place in the Power BI Desktop where you see the last two options shown on the drop-down list, in Figure 9-30.

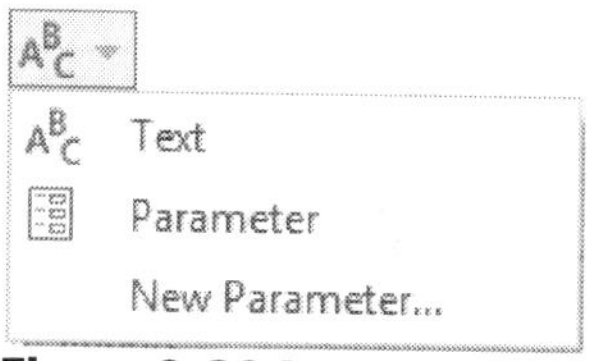

Figure 9-30 Parameter options

Parameters can also be used in DAX formulas and referenced from other queries.

If you have used other software like Crystal Reports™, which has parameter fields, you are already familiar with the concept.

Figure 9-31 shows the dialog box used to create and edit a parameter. The options are explained below.

The column on the left is a list of parameters in the report file.

The **NAME FIELD** is used to give the parameter a descriptive name.

The **DESCRIPTION FIELD** is used to explain how the parameter should be used. The content in this field will be displayed next to the parameter name, when the parameter is displayed. Using this field is optional. It can be used as a tool tip, as shown later in Figure 9-41.

Check the **REQUIRED OPTION** to force a value to be selected for the parameter.

If a parameter is required, you are not prevented from using the other parameter(s) in the file. This means that if you only want to use one parameter of four, for report A and two parameters for report B, you can.

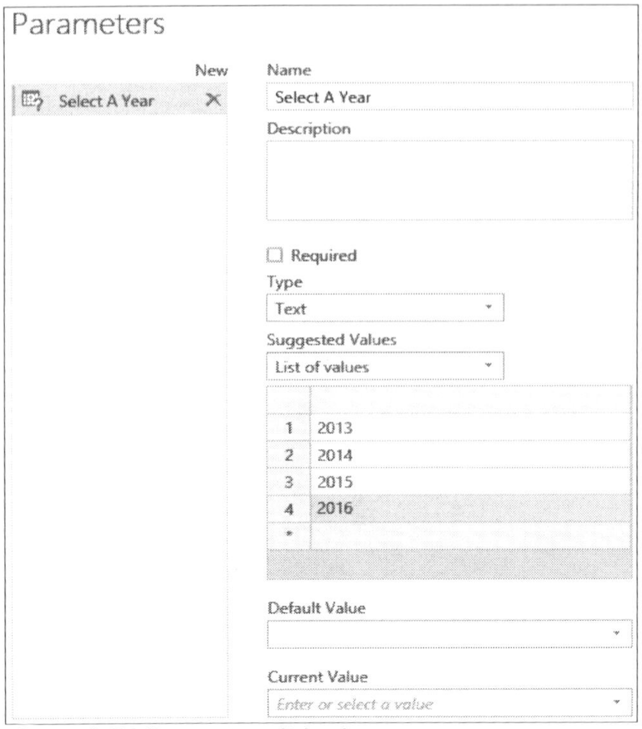

Figure 9-31 Parameters dialog box

The options in the **TYPE FIELD** are the data types that the parameter supports. Select the one that matches the type of data that will be used in the parameter field. Select **ANY** to make the parameter free form.

The **SUGGESTED VALUES OPTION** is used to select where the values for the parameter come from. Figure 9-32 shows the options currently available. The options are explained below.

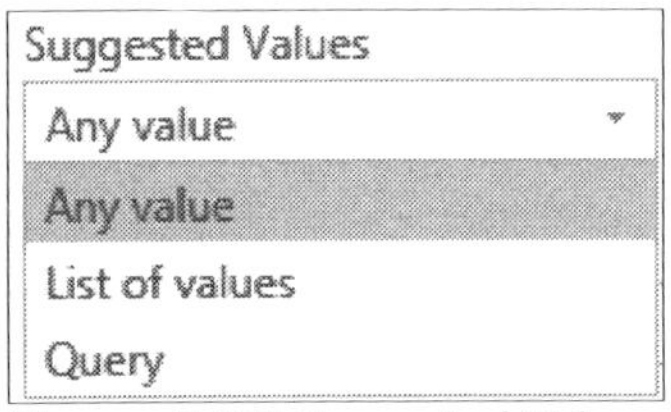

Figure 9-32 Suggested Values options

① Select **ANY VALUE** to allow basically anything to be entered as a value.
② Select **LIST OF VALUES** to provide the values that can be selected. This option requires you to manually type in the list of values and is best suited for a short list of values, unless you like to type a lot. <smile>
③ **QUERY** This option is used to select what is known as a **LIST QUERY**. It contains a list of values that can be selected from. In Exercise 9.6, you will learn how to create a list query.

The **CURRENT VALUE OPTION** is used to enter a value for the parameter. Once the parameter is used, the value selected is added to this field.

The **DEFAULT VALUE OPTION** is currently only available when the List of values option, shown above in Figure 9-32, is selected. This option is used to enter the value that you think will be used the most for the parameter. This value will automatically be selected when the parameter is first displayed. Entering a value in this field is optional.

Exercise 9.6: Create Parameters

In this exercise, you will learn how to create parameters that use a list of values and query.

Create The Year Parameter

Many reports need to filter the data by year. Having a consistent way to perform this task from page to page (on the Report view), makes it easier for users.

1. Save the E8.2 file as `E9.6 Parameters`.

2. Query Editor ⇒ Home Tab ⇒ Manage Parameters button ⇒ New Parameter.

3. In the Name field, type `Select A Year`.

4. Clear the check mark for the Required field.

5. Open the Type drop-down list and select Text.

6. Open the Suggested Values drop-down list and select List of values.

7. Type the following values in the table, one per row. `2013`, `2014`, `2015`, `2016`.
   You should have the options shown earlier in Figure 9-31 ⇒ Click OK.

   You will see that a query was created and the parameter input field is displayed, as shown in Figure 9-33. (I moved the parameter query up, on the Queries panel) By default, no data is displayed because parameters do not store data.

The **CURRENT VALUE FIELD** drop-down list contains the values that you entered for the Value list.

The **MANAGE PARAMETER BUTTON** displays the Parameters dialog box, shown earlier in Figure 9-31.

Parameter queries are like the other queries. They can be loaded to the data model, used in other queries and referenced in DAX formulas.

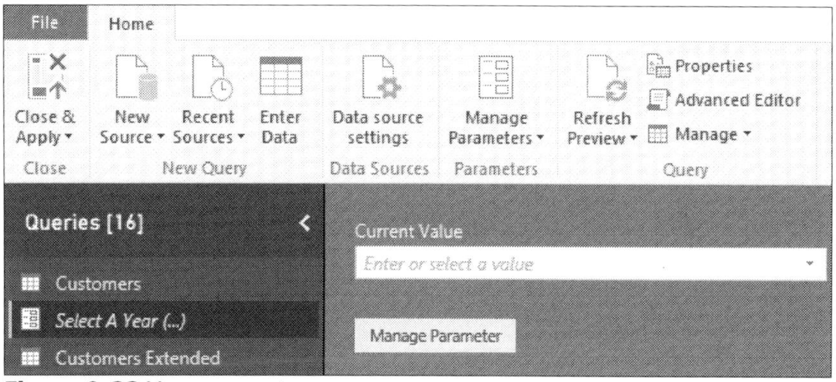

Figure 9-33 Year parameter query

Figure 9-34 shows the formula that was created for the Select A Year parameter.

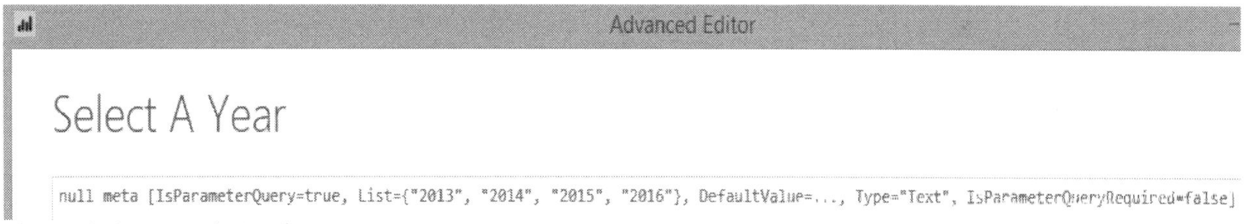

Figure 9-34 Formula for the year parameter

> **Creating More Than One Parameter**
> If you need to create more than one parameter at the same time, click the **NEW LINK**, that is above the list of parameter names on the Parameters dialog box, instead of clicking the OK button.

Load The Parameter Query Into The Data Model

By default, parameter queries are not loaded to the data model.

1. Right-click on the parameter query, on the Queries panel, and select **ENABLE LOAD**.

2. Save and apply the changes.

Create The Country Parameter

1. Create a new parameter using the options shown in Figure 9-35.

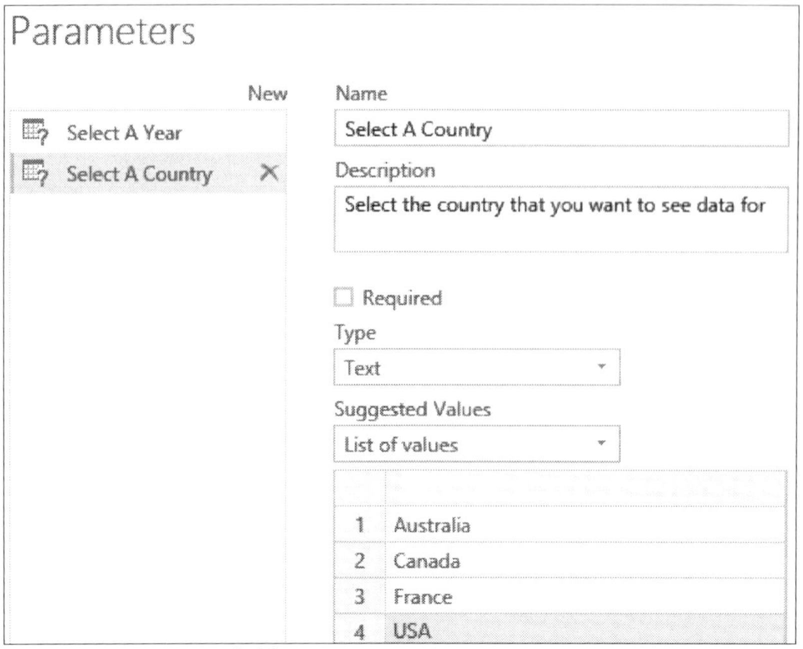

Figure 9-35 Country field parameter options

2. Load the parameter into the data model ⇒
   Apply and save the changes.

   You should see the query options shown in Figure 9-36.

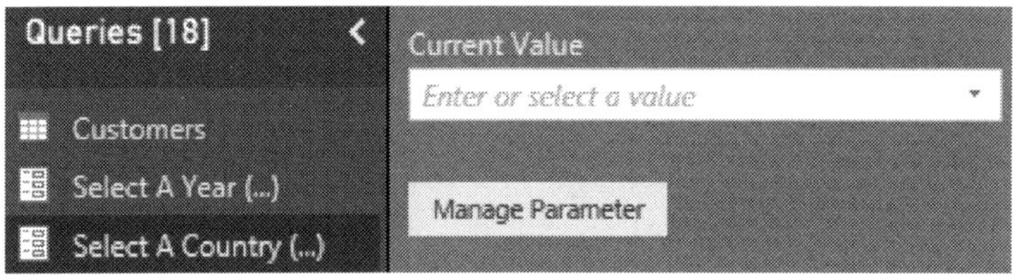

Figure 9-36 Select A Country query

Use The Query Suggested Values Parameter Option

This option uses a list of values from a query to populate the parameter, like the List of Values, Suggested Values option that was covered in the previous section of this exercise. While a list may look like a query in the Queries panel, they are not the same.

Chapter 6 covered the **LIST DATA TYPE**. One way to create a list query is by using the M language, to create a formula. This type of query contains a list of values, which is also known as an **ORDERED LIST**. Don't worry, creating a formula to create the list is painless.

Create The List Query

In this part of the exercise, you will learn how to create a list of query values. This list will be used in a parameter, as the list of values. Chapter 4 covered the **LIST TOOLS TRANSFORM TAB OPTIONS**. The steps below are used to manually create a list of specific values.

1. Query Editor ⇒ Home tab ⇒ New Source ⇒ **BLANK QUERY OPTION** ⇒ Advanced Editor button.

2. Delete all of the code in the Advanced Editor ⇒ Type the expression shown in Figure 9-37.

Figure 9-37 Values for the list query

3. Click Done.

   You should see the list shown in Figure 9-38.

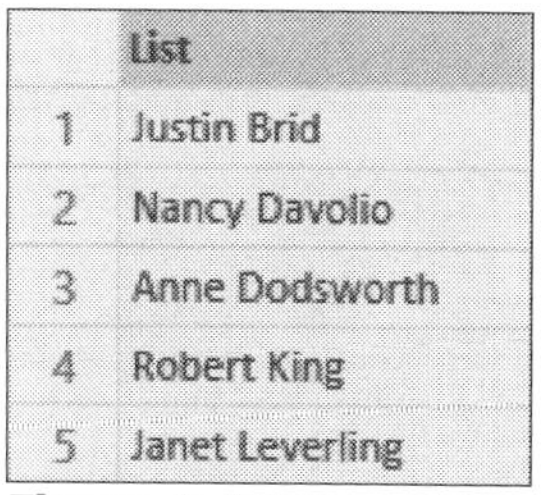

Figure 9-38 List of values for a parameter

4. Rename the query to `Sales Reps List` ⇒ Save the changes.

Create A Parameter That Uses A List Query

In this part of the exercise, you will create the parameter that will use the list query created in the previous part of this exercise.

1. Home tab ⇒ Manage Parameters button ⇒ Manage Parameters option. (Clicking the top half of the Manage Parameters button, will also open the Manage Parameters dialog box, which is the same dialog box as the Parameters dialog box.)

2. On the Parameters dialog box, click the New link.

3. Select the options shown in Figure 9-39 ⇒

   Save the changes.

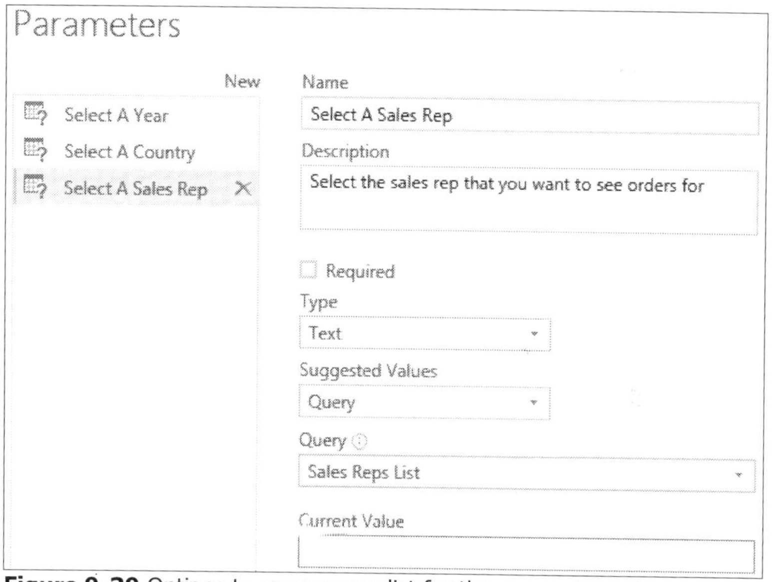

Figure 9-39 Options to use a query list for the parameter values

Manage Parameters

The options on the button shown in Figure 9-40 are explained below.

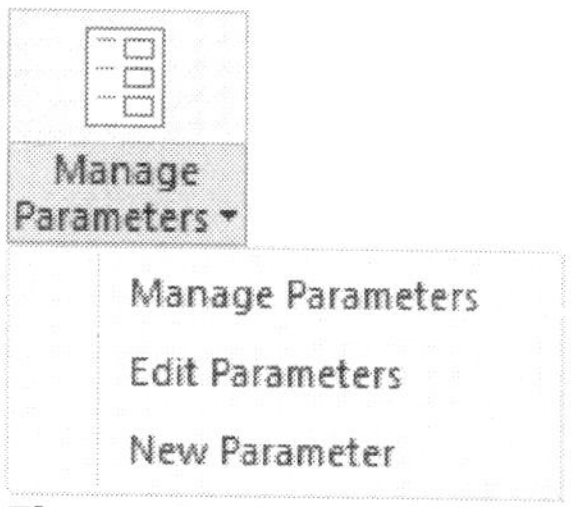

Figure 9-40 Manage Parameters button options

The **MANAGE PARAMETERS** and **NEW PARAMETER OPTIONS** open the Parameters dialog box. New parameters can be created and existing parameters can be edited on the dialog box.

The **EDIT PARAMETERS OPTION** displays the dialog box shown in Figure 9-41. The options are used to select the values for the parameters.

The values that you select on this dialog box, are the ones that will be displayed in the Current Value field, shown earlier, at the bottom of Figure 9-39. They will also be displayed when the query is first run.

Like the Parameters dialog box, all of the parameter fields, for the report file are displayed on the same dialog box.

Notice that the description created for the country parameter is displayed as a tool tip.

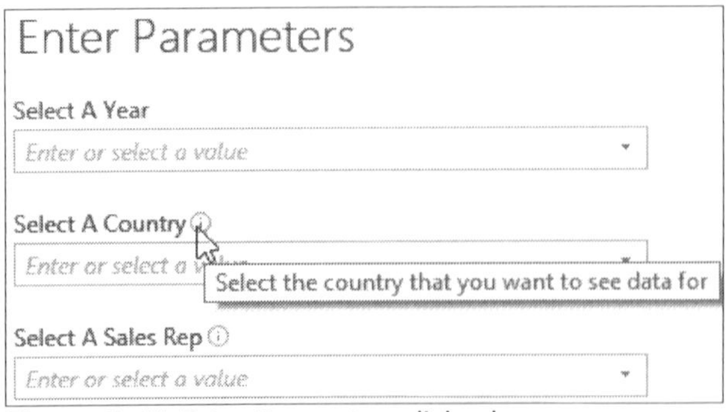

Figure 9-41 Enter Parameters dialog box

Selecting The Parameter Values

> **Using Parameter Values**
> As you will see, parameters may not work the way that you think they will. I suspect that in time, the process of using them will become more intuitive.

Before using the parameters to filter or load data, you have to select the value(s) that you want to filter on. You can select the value on the individual query [See Figure 9-36] or you can use the Enter Parameters dialog box. Use this option when you need to select values for more than one parameter.

Exercise 9.7: Use A Parameter With A Query

In this exercise, you will use a parameter to filter data in a query. You will use the country parameter, to filter records in the Customer query.

1. Save the E9.6 file as `E9.7 Use a parameter with a query.`
2. Import the 07 Customers table from the More Data Files workbook.
3. In the Queries panel, click on the Select A Country query ⇒ Open the Current Value drop-down list and select USA.
4. Display the 07 Customers query ⇒ Display the filter options for the Country column ⇒ Select Text Filters ⇒ Equals.
5. On the Filter Rows dialog box, open the first "ABC" drop-down list and select Parameter, as shown on the right side of Figure 9-42.

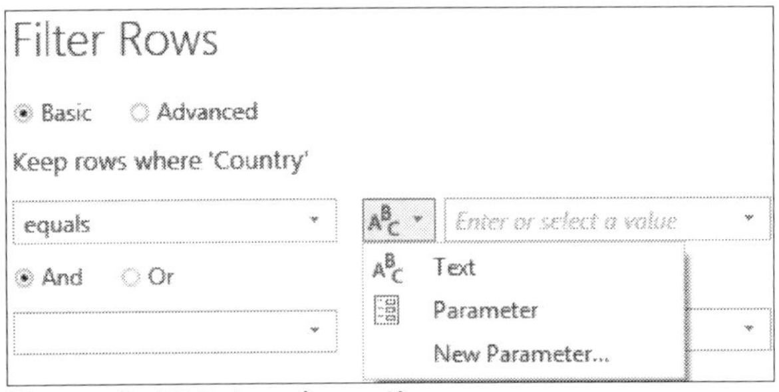

Figure 9-42 Data value options

6. In the next field, select the Select A Country parameter ⇒ Click OK. The 07 Customers query will only display records that have USA in the Country column ⇒ Save the changes.

Parameter Tips
Below are some tips for making parameters useful.

① **WHERE TO CREATE PARAMETERS** If you are creating a template file and know that the dataset would benefit from parameters, create the parameters in the file that will be used as the template file, so that you do not have to create the same parameters over and over in different files.
② When you create a function out of a query (aka query parameter), you can use the function input values to replace the parameter values.
③ Parameters that have the **TABLE DATA TYPE** can be used to invoke a built in or custom function.
④ Keep in mind that the parameters that have a value selected, filter the visualizations that are created in the report file. I clear them in the query, when creating visualizations, to ensure that all of the data that I am expecting to see is displayed.

Summary

This chapter covered how to import and append data automatically. While this process is not appropriate for every situation, when it is appropriate, it can be a life saver. Some of the exercises used the Folder import option. The append options covered in this chapter are different from the Append transformation that was covered in Chapter 8, because you do not have to know the table names or the number of tables that need to be imported and appended.

As a result of learning how to automate the append process, you learned how the Change Type step and renaming a column can causes the refresh process to fail.

I suspect that the parameter functionality will be enhanced in the future. New features that I think would make parameters much more useful are:

① To have the option of selecting more than one value in the parameter.
② To connect two or more parameters together to create a new parameter (think merge two queries to a new table), so that they appear together. The way parameters currently work is that all of the parameters created in the report file are used on every report page. You should be able to select which parameter(s) to use on a particular page or chart or table on a page. You should also have the option to not use parameters on a page.

I hope that you see the benefits that the Folder connector provides. Yes, there are things that can go wrong when the data is refreshed. I tried to explain them without scaring you and provide some solutions and ways to avoid them from happening.

Keep in mind that the append options covered in this chapter, work under the condition that the fields have the same format and the same number of columns. How to handle tables that have columns with different names was covered in Chapter 8. [See Appending Queries With Different Column Names]

USING THE PIVOT AND UNPIVOT TRANSFORMATIONS

After completing this chapter, you will be able to pivot and unpivot columns of data.

CHAPTER 10

Overview

So far, the transformations that have been covered are used to add columns, cleanse the data, join tables, filter data, merge and group data. There will be times when the topics covered so far in this book, still will not let you get the data in a format or layout that can be used to create the reports that you need. Often, this means that the original data structure is not correct. The transformations listed below are available to reshape the data. This process is known as **CHANGING THE DATA STRUCTURE**. This is different then the **STRUCTURED COLUMN OPTIONS** that were covered in Chapter 8.

① **PIVOT DATA** changes the structure of the data by switching the data in columns to rows.
② **UNPIVOT DATA** changes the structure of the data by switching the data in rows to columns.
③ **TRANSPOSE COLUMNS AND ROWS** changes the columns to rows and the rows to columns.

Pivot And Unpivot Options

These options do not cleanse, join, filter or merge data. They are used to change the structure of tables that have a layout that will not work as expected, after the data has been imported. Data that has been imported in multiple columns (like data in a pivot table layout), but really needs to be in one column, is an example of when you would use these options. These transformations are primarily used with data that does not come from a database. Often, these transformations are used with data on a spreadsheet.

Pivoting and unpivoting data when needed, allows the data to be used to create charts or other types of visuals, that give the data meaning.

Learning How To Recognize Tables With A Poor Layout

First, let me say that this section does not apply to tables in a database. Just the opposite. This section applies to any file, (like an Excel file or text file for example), other then tables in a database. When tables are not well designed, it is usually very difficult to create reports. That is because it is hard, if not impossible to get the data out of the table, the way that you need, to display on a chart. While the tables shown later in Figures 10-7, 10-13 and 10-14 are easy to read, the tables are not in a format that works in the Query Editor.

The data in the Year columns in both tables (Figures 10-7 and 10-13) represent the same value, a yearly total. In Figure 10-13, the total row and total column should not be saved in a table. Instead, totals should be created as a DAX measure for the report. In a table in a database, the total row and column in Figure 10-13 are never stored.

The easiest way that I can think of to know if a table is in a layout that will work in Power Query is if each row in the fact table has a unique key field or when the data source is not a database, the table should have two fields, that when combined, make the row unique, like car manufacturer and model name/number. The same concept applies to lookup tables. Each row needs a unique key field.

Examples of layouts that have a good table design, are shown later in Figures 10-9 and 10-21. In Figure 10-9, the Invoice Nbr field has a unique value for each record/row. While the data in Figure 10-21 does not have one field that has a unique value for each row, combining, the data in the first two columns make each row unique.

Pivot Column Options

If you have not guessed already, the Pivot Column transformation creates a pivot table from the data in the query. The options selected in Figure 10-1 take the data shown later in Figure 10-13 and pivots it, so that it is in the layout shown later in Figure 10-21. These options are used to create a table that has an aggregate value for each unique value in the selected column. This is another way to group raw data. An example would be providing a count of customers per state.

The Pivot Column transformation creates a column in the table for each unique value in the column that you select, before opening the Pivot Column dialog box. Figure 10-2 shows part of a Products pivot table. This option is used when the source data has multiple rows for the same entity. The Pivot Column transformation works the opposite of the Unpivot transformation.

The **AGGREGATE VALUE FUNCTION** options shown in Figure 10-1, are used to create a calculated field for the column selected in the **VALUES COLUMN** field. The functions are explained in Table 10-1, based on how they work in Power Query. For example, if the query needed to have quarterly totals for each store, for each year, you would use the Sum function to get a total per store, per year. These functions are also available on the Aggregate dialog box that was covered in Chapter 8. [See Figure 8-20]

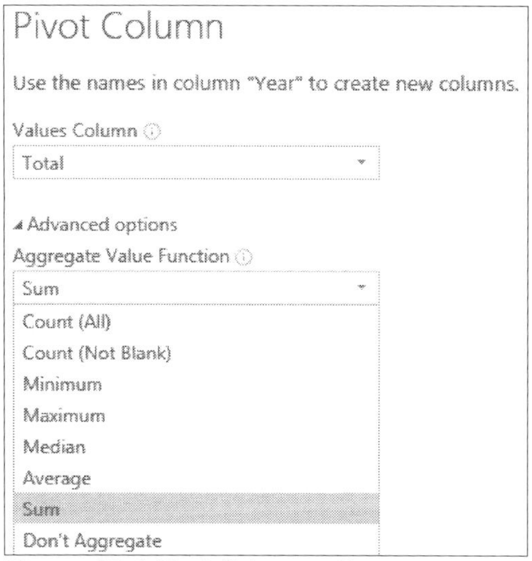

Figure 10-1 Pivot Column options

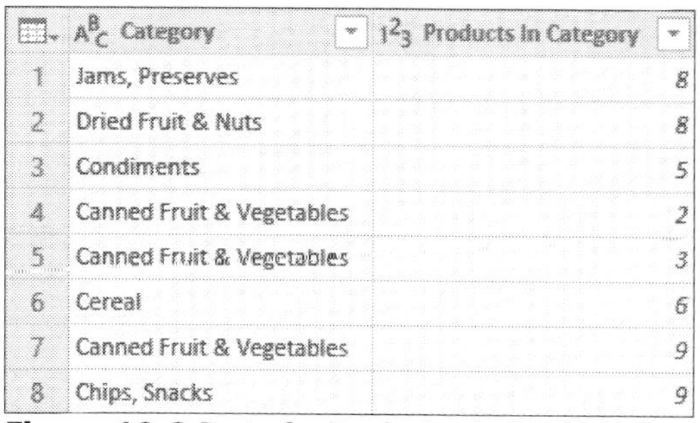

	Category	Products In Category
1	Jams, Preserves	8
2	Dried Fruit & Nuts	8
3	Condiments	5
4	Canned Fruit & Vegetables	2
5	Canned Fruit & Vegetables	3
6	Cereal	6
7	Canned Fruit & Vegetables	9
8	Chips, Snacks	9

Figure 10-2 Part of a Products pivot table

Function	Description
Count (All)	Counts the number of all rows, whether or not there is a value in the column.
Count (Not Blank)	Only counts the number of rows that have a value in the column.
Minimum	Creates columns that display the smallest value in each category.
Maximum	Creates columns that display the largest value in each category.
Median	Creates columns that display the middle value for each category.
Average	Creates columns that display the average value for each category.
Sum	Creates columns for each unique category and adds the values for all rows that have the same category, to calculate the total.
Don't Aggregate	Does not create a calculation for the categories.

Table 10-1 Aggregate functions explained

DISPLAY A COUNT PER CATEGORY The options selected in Figure 10-3 create the columns shown in Figure 10-4.

If the table was sorted by the Category column before selecting the pivot column options, the new columns will be displayed in alphabetical order.

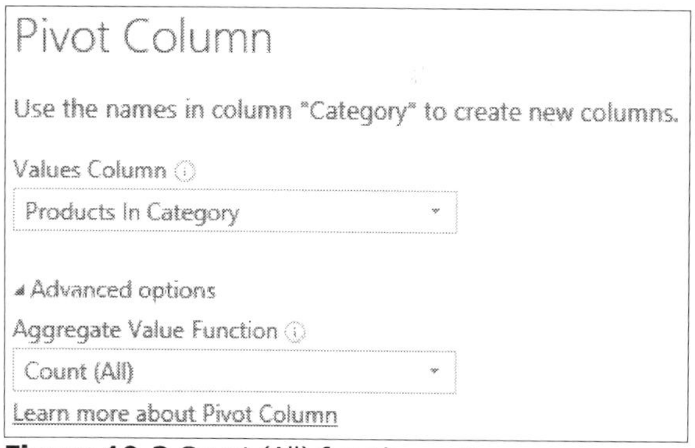

Figure 10-3 Count (All) function options

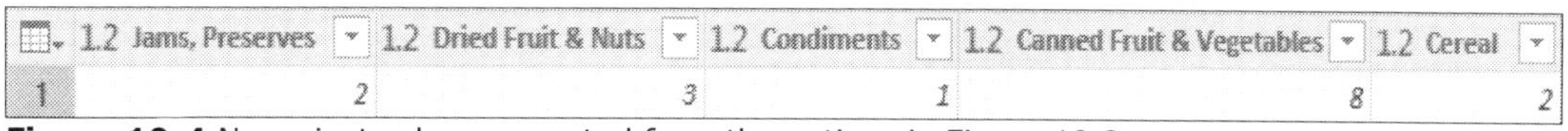

	Jams, Preserves	Dried Fruit & Nuts	Condiments	Canned Fruit & Vegetables	Cereal
1	2	3	1	8	2

Figure 10-4 New pivot columns created from the options in Figure 10-3

COUNT (NOT BLANK) The options selected in Figure 10-5 create the columns shown in Figure 10-6.

Notice that some of the counts are smaller then shown above in Figure 10-4. That is because I removed some values in the Products In Category column.

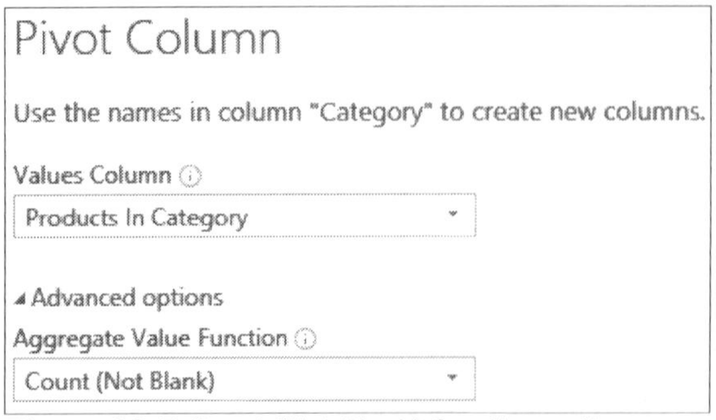

Figure 10-5 Count (Not Blank) function options

	Jams, Preserves	Dried Fruit & Nuts	Condime...	Canned Fruit & Vegetables	Cereal
1	1	0	1	7	2

Figure 10-6 New pivot columns created from the options in Figure 10-5

Exercise 10.1: Use The Pivot Column And Reverse Rows Transformations

This exercise will show you how to use the Pivot Column dialog box and Reverse Rows transformation.

Create A Pivot Table

In this part of the exercise, you will learn how to create a table that displays a yearly total per store, in a column layout, like a pivot table.

1. Import the Yearly Sales table in the More Data Files workbook ⇒ Save the file as `E10.1 Yearly sales data`.
2. Duplicate the Yearly Sales query ⇒ Rename it to `1 Pivot table`.
3. Click on the Year column ⇒ Transform tab ⇒ Pivot Column button.
4. Select Total, from the Values Column drop-down list.

   In this exercise, the values in the Total column have already been aggregated.

   Selecting Sum or Don't Aggregate will produce the same results in this exercise, because each store only has one total per year.

   Click OK. The pivot table should look like the one shown in Figure 10-7.

	Store	2010	2011	2012	2013	2014	2015
1	Atherton	19.7	17.1	18.3	14.8	19.8	24.5
2	Berkeley	14.4	18	16.4	16.7	19.3	0
3	Carmel-by-the-Sea	18.8	13.5	18.7	13.9	15.7	17.2
4	Cupertino	12	16.2	17.5	17.8	13.8	15.55
5	Fresno	19.2	15.6	19.6	15.9	14.4	14.3
6	Laguna Beach	18.9	14.6	16.7	12.1	13.9	16.2
7	Los Angeles	0	12.75	0	0	0	130
8	Mailbu	18.7	17.8	14	18.5	13.7	19.1
9	Palm Springs	0	0	0	0	0	6.55
10	Pasadena	17	19.4	17.1	17.3	17.3	18.88
11	San Francisco	14.4	14	13.9	15.4	18.3	0
12	Santa Barbara	0	0	0	0	8.2	9.19

Figure 10-7 Pivot table

Use The Reverse Rows Transformation

This transformation works similar to sorting in descending order. The difference is that there is no ranking involved. The Reverse Rows transformation moves the physical last row in the query to the first row and vice versa.

1. Duplicate the Pivot table query ⇒ Rename it to `2 Reverse Rows`.
2. Transform tab ⇒ Reverse Rows button. The table should look like the one shown in Figure 10-8.

This transformation does not seem to add any value to a pivoted data layout. What can I say? <smile>

	Store	2010	2011	2012	2013	2014	2015
1	Santa Barbara	0	0	0	0	8.2	9.19
2	San Francisco	14.4	14	13.9	15.4	18.3	0
3	Pasadena	17	19.4	17.1	17.3	17.3	18.88
4	Palm Springs	0	0	0	0	0	6.55

Figure 10-8 Reverse Rows transformation applied to a pivot table

Exercise 10.2: Use The Pivot Column Transformation To Fix A Problem

There may be a time when you use the Unpivot transformation to try and get the data in the correct format and it does not turn out as expected. Often, the unpivot step is done before you have added a lot of transformations to the query. Yes, you have the option of inserting a step or two above the unpivot step, to try and fix the problem. When I have tried that, more times then not, at least one step below the step that I inserted, generates an error.

Once you have created several steps to transform the data and the unpivot does not work, the last thing you want to do is start over. I have used the steps in this exercise to get our of trouble a few times.

While you will not create several steps to clean the data, just pretend that you have. <smile> You will unpivot the data, shown in Figure 10-9, even though the unpivot options have not been covered yet in this chapter.

	Invoice Nbr	Order ID	Date	First Name	Last Name	Subtotal	Shipping	SalesTax	InvoiceTotal
1	740	3065	06/01/2018	Chris	Christianson	45	1.8	2.7	49.5
2	741	3066	06/01/2018	Ron	Cunningham	479.85	19.19	28.791	527.831
3	742	3067	06/01/2018	Pavel	Ropoleski	107.8	4.31	6.468	118.578
4	743	3068	06/01/2018	Ian	Kelly	17.5	0.7	1.05	19.25

Figure 10-9 Data that will be used in this exercise

Unpivot The Data

1. In a new file, import the June Invoices table in the More Data Files workbook ⇒ Save the file as `E10.2 Use the Pivot And Unpivot transformations`.

2. Combine the First Name and Last Name columns into a new column ⇒ Name the new column `Customer` ⇒ Move the Customer column after the Order ID column.

3. Delete the First Name and Last Name columns.

4. Select the last four columns ⇒ Transform tab ⇒ Click the Unpivot Columns button. The table should look like the one shown in Figure 10-10.

	Invoice Nbr	Order ID	Customer	Date	Attribute	Value
1	740	3065	Chris Christianson	06/01/2018	Subtotal	45
2	740	3065	Chris Christianson	06/01/2018	Shipping	1.8
3	740	3065	Chris Christianson	06/01/2018	SalesTax	2.7
4	740	3065	Chris Christianson	06/01/2018	InvoiceTotal	49.5
5	741	3066	Ron Cunningham	06/01/2018	Subtotal	479.85
6	741	3066	Ron Cunningham	06/01/2018	Shipping	19.19

Figure 10-10 Table after the Unpivot Columns option was applied

As shown above in Figure 10-10, the four columns that were unpivoted, are not in the Attribute and Value columns. The first four rows in the table, equal the data that was in one row before the structure of the table was changed. [See Figure 10-9] The current structure is very complicated and would be difficult to use to create a report.

Fix The Data Structure Problem

While this problem was created on purpose to demonstrate how to fix it, it is very possible that a spreadsheet could be created with the structure shown above in Figure 10-10. If that was the case, there would not be an unpivot step that you cold possibly delete. The steps in this part of the exercise will show you how to fix the problem, regardless of how the problem came to be.

1. Select the Attribute column ⇒ Transform tab ⇒ Click the Pivot Column button.

2. The Pivot Column dialog box, should have the phrase "Use the names in column "**ATTRIBUTE**" to create new columns. If you do not see the word Attribute, click Cancel because you did not select the Attribute column. The pivot column options will not work as expected in this scenario, if that column is not selected ⇒ If this is the case, go back to step 1, in this part of the exercise.

3. Open the **VALUES COLUMN** drop-down list and select Value.

4. In the Advanced Options section, open the **AGGREGATE VALUE FUNCTION** drop-down list and select Don't Aggregate.

   You should have the options shown in Figure 10-11.

   The values in the Value column, do not need to be summarized in the pivot table, because they are already summarized. If totals or counts were needed, they would be created when the report is created.

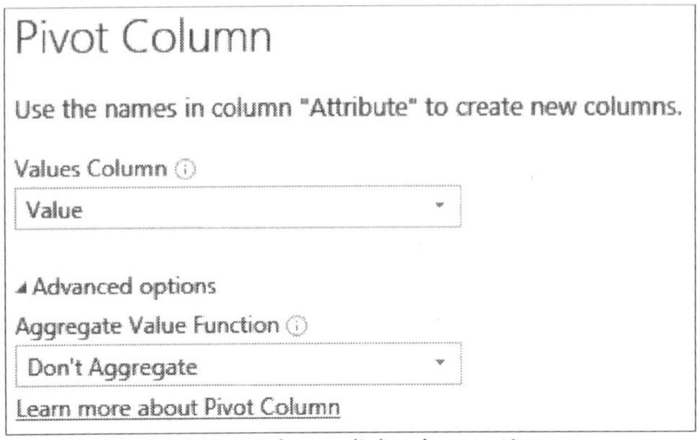

Figure 10-11 Pivot Column dialog box options

5. Click OK. The table should look like the one shown in Figure 10-12. This layout can be used to create a report because it is in a format that the Query Editor supports.

	Invoice Nbr	Order ID	Customer	Date	Subtotal	Shipping	SalesTax	InvoiceTotal
1	740	3065	Chris Christianson	06/01/2018	45	1.8	2.7	49.5
2	741	3066	Ron Cunningham	06/01/2018	479.85	19.19	28.791	527.831
3	742	3067	Pavel Ropoleski	06/01/2018	107.8	4.31	6.468	118.578
4	743	3068	Ian Kelly	06/01/2018	17.5	0.7	1.05	19.25
5	744	3069	Claus Main	06/01/2018	5879.7	235.19	352.782	6467.672

Figure 10-12 Modified pivot table

While the techniques in Exercise 10.2 can be used to reverse data that has been unpivoted incorrectly, you may find it easier to just start over. I just wanted to show you that it could be done.

Unpivoting Data

These options work the opposite of the Pivot Column option, that was covered in the previous exercise.

The Unpivot transformation options are used with data that has been summarized, like the data shown in Figure 10-13 and convert it into a fact table.

The unpivot transformations are used to transform, pivot or summarized tables into fact tables, that were discussed earlier in Chapter 4.

	A	B	C	D	E	F	G
1	(In Millions)						
2							
3	Store	FY 2010	FY 2011	FY 2012	FY 2013	FY 2014	Total
4	Atherton	$19.70	$17.10	$18.30	$14.80	$19.80	$89.70
5	Berkeley	$14.40	$18.00	$16.40	$16.70	$19.30	$84.80
6	Carmel-by-the-Sea	$18.80	$13.50	$18.70	$13.90	$15.70	$80.60
7	Cupertino	$12.00	$16.20	$17.50	$17.80	$13.80	$77.30
8	Fresno	$19.20	$15.60	$19.60	$15.90	$14.40	$84.70
9	Laguna Beach	$18.90	$14.60	$16.70	$12.10	$13.90	$76.20
10	Mailbu	$18.70	$17.80	$14.00	$18.50	$13.70	$82.70
11	Pasadena	$17.00	$19.40	$17.10	$17.30	$17.30	$88.10
12	San Francisco	$14.40	$14.00	$13.90	$15.40	$18.30	$76.00
13	Total	$153.10	$146.20	$152.20	$142.40	$146.20	$740.10

Figure 10-13 Data in a pivot table layout

The Unpivot transformations are also designed to handle tables that have a bad or poorly designed data layout. Changing the data structure of a table is done to improve how the data can be presented in a visualization. The unpivot process takes a cells column name and value from unpivoted columns and creates a row that has the following columns: Anchor, Attribute and Value.

The Unpivot options take data in a pivot table format (also known as a **DENORMALIZED FORMAT**) or data that is in a non tabular format and changes it to a flat file (unpivoted layout), as shown later in Figure 10-18.

In addition to the unpivot options being on the Transform tab, these options are also on some shortcut menu's, when one or more columns are selected, as shown earlier in Chapter 4, Figures 4-12 and 4-13. The unpivot options are explained below.

The **UNPIVOT COLUMNS OPTION** adds the columns (of data) that have not been selected, to the unpivoted table. This option does unpivot new columns of data that are added to the query in the future. Select the columns that you do not want unpivoted.

The **UNPIVOT OTHER COLUMNS OPTION** adds the columns (of data) that are not selected, to the unpivoted table. This option will unpivot new columns that are added to the query in the future, after the transformation is created, without you having to modify the query.

The **UNPIVOT ONLY SELECTED COLUMNS OPTION** works the opposite of the Unpivot Other Columns option. It only unpivots the selected columns. This creates an explicit list of columns. When the data is refreshed, the only columns that are unpivoted are the ones in the list of columns. This is the most limited unpivot option.

Understanding How The Unpivot Options Work

What you will see is that while these options produce the same result initially, if new columns are added to the data source table, the output from these unpivot options will differ.

When an unpivot function is applied to a table, the table is divided into two types of columns, as explained below.

① **ANCHOR COLUMNS** These are the columns from the original table that are not unpivoted. They are the attributes that you want to keep. There can be more than one anchor column in a table. Attributes are explained in the next section.

② **UNPIVOTED COLUMNS** These are the columns that have different values for the same attribute. For example, in Figure 10-13 above, the "FY" columns are the unpivoted columns because they have the same attribute. They contain the yearly total. Each column heading should be in the same unpivoted column. Each years total should be in the same unpivoted column, as shown later in Figure 10-18.

Anchor Columns

Keep the following in mind, when using the **UNPIVOT COLUMNS** and **UNPIVOT OTHER COLUMNS FUNCTIONS.**

① If a new anchor column is added to the data source after the unpivot option has been applied, the new anchor column will be unpivoted, and may generate an error.

② If the column(s) in the data source, that will be used as an anchor column, are renamed in the data source, the query will fail when the data in the query is refreshed.

③ If you think that your data source table could eventually have a new anchor column, use the **UNPIVOT ONLY SELECTED COLUMNS OPTION.**

Attribute And Value Columns

If you have a spreadsheet that looks like the one shown above in Figure 10-13, you will appreciate how the Unpivot Column option can help you import this non table data. This option is used to change the layout into one that Power BI Desktop supports. By support, I mean that the data will be changed to a layout that can be used to create a table or chart visualization. This data layout is often referred to as a **PIVOTED LAYOUT**. It does not lend itself to be used to create reports, because the data is already pivoted (not in **TABULAR FORMAT**).

The unpivot options rearrange the layout of the data. The columns selected before either of these unpivot options are selected, are placed in the left most columns of the new table query (the **ANCHOR COLUMN**). The other data is placed in the columns explained below. The **UNPIVOT COLUMNS** options create the following columns:

① The **ATTRIBUTE COLUMN** contains the data for each original column heading, of the cell in the data source.

② The **VALUE COLUMN** contains the original data value from each cell in the data source. The columns in the data source become rows, once the unpivot option is applied.

Like the table shown earlier in Figure 10-13, the table in Figure 10-14 is readable, but not useable in the Query Editor because of the design/layout.

The data in this table is a subset of the data shown earlier in Figure 10-13. It is just presented in a different layout.

Store	FY2010
Altherton	$19.70
Berkeley	$14.90
Carmel-by-the-sea	$18.80
Store	**FY2011**
Altherton	$17.10
Berkeley	$18.00
Carmel-by-the-sea	$13.50

Figure 10-14 Layout of data that the Query Editor cannot use

Unpivot Columns vs Unpivot Other Columns Options

Both transformations switch data from columns to rows. The difference between these options is that the Unpivot Other Columns option will also unpivot columns that are added to the query after the initial query is created.

The reason that these two unpivot options use the same transformation is because they both work on the premise that the anchor columns do not change and that the unpivoted columns can change over time. The **UNPIVOT OTHER COLUMNS TRANSFORMATION** allows the query to unpivot new columns without having to modify the query. This transformation is well suited when the data source has several columns that have the same **ATTRIBUTE** with different time periods, like years or months.

For example, a spreadsheet currently has columns for January, February and March when you first import it. In the Query Editor, you would apply the Unpivot Other Columns transformation to the non month columns. Then, when the query is refreshed, it has two more month columns, April and May. These new columns will automatically be unpivoted, when the Unpivot Other Columns transformation step is applied.

Exercise 10.3: Use The Unpivot Columns Option

This exercise will show you how to transform the data shown earlier in Figure 10-13, into a layout that the Query Editor supports.

Import The Data

1. In a new file, load the Stores table in the More Data Files workbook.

2. Delete the first row of data.

3. Click the Use First Rows as Headers option.

4. Delete the Total column and Total row. They are not needed for this exercise.

   The table should look like the one shown in Figure 10-15.

   Hold on, you are just a few clicks away from having the data in the correct layout to create visuals.

	Store	FY 2010	FY 2011	FY 2012	FY 2013	FY 2014
1	Atherton	19.7	17.1	18.3	14.8	19.8
2	Berkeley	14.4	18	16.4	16.7	19.3
3	Carmel-by-the-Sea	18.8	13.5	18.7	13.9	15.7
4	Cupertino	12	16.2	17.5	17.8	13.8
5	Fresno	19.2	15.6	19.6	15.9	14.4
6	Laguna Beach	18.9	14.6	16.7	12.1	13.9
7	Mailbu	18.7	17.8	14	18.5	13.7
8	Pasadena	17	19.4	17.1	17.3	17.3
9	San Francisco	14.4	14	13.9	15.4	18.3

Figure 10-15 Data in a pivoted layout

5. Save the file as `E10.3 Unpivot columns.`

Handling Rows And Columns With Totals

In the previous part of this exercise, you were instructed to delete the Total row and columns, that were shown earlier in Figure 10-13, before the Unpivot transformation was applied. Most of the time, rows and columns that have totals are not needed in Power Query, because they are created on the report. More importantly, having totals in the query will make it difficult to create reports. Equally important, is that deleting the total rows and columns before applying the unpivot transformation, means that the unpivot transformation has less data to process, thus reducing the process time of the query, which is always a good thing. <smile>

For example, the data in Figure 10-16 has a total row and column row. If you right-clicked on the Store column and selected Unpivot Other columns, the table would look like the one shown in Figure 10-17. A first glance, this table may not seem to be problematic, until you notice several rows like row 6 and the rows with "Total" in the Store column, at the end of the table.

Yes, you could create a filter or two, to remove these rows, but that is less efficient then deleting the total row and column **BEFORE** the Unpivot transformation is applied. If these rows were included in the calculation, the result of the calculation would be incorrect.

Because the total column in Figure 10-16 has a name, opposed to "Column 7", it is okay to delete it. If the column name was "Column 7" and it was deleted, in this unpivot scenario, it would cause unexpected results if other columns were added to the able in the future. For example, if a FY2015 column was added after the FY2014 column and the headers had not been promoted, "Column 7" would be the FY2015 column, which isn't the column that should be deleted.

For reports that need totals, you would create a DAX measure. The measure will calculate the last value in the Total column (740.1) in Figure 10-16.

When the measure is added to the report, it will also display the individual row and column totals, depending on the chart style.

	Store	FY 2010	FY 2011	FY 2012	FY 2013	FY 2014	Total
1	Atherton	19.7	17.1	18.3	14.8	19.8	89.7
2	Berkeley	14.4	18	16.4	16.7	19.3	84.8
3	Carmel-by-the-Sea	18.8	13.5	18.7	13.9	15.7	80.6
4	Cupertino	12	16.2	17.5	17.8	13.8	77.3
5	Fresno	19.2	15.6	19.6	15.9	14.4	84.7
6	Laguna Beach	18.9	14.6	16.7	12.1	13.9	76.2
7	Malibu	18.7	17.8	14	18.5	13.7	82.7
8	Pasadena	17	19.4	17.1	17.3	17.3	88.1
9	San Francisco	14.4	14	13.9	15.4	18.3	76
10	Total	153.1	146.2	152.2	142.4	146.2	740.1

Figure 10-16 Table with totals

	Store	Attribute	Value
1	Atherton	FY 2010	19.7
2	Atherton	FY 2011	17.1
3	Atherton	FY 2012	18.3
4	Atherton	FY 2013	14.8
5	Atherton	FY 2014	19.8
6	Atherton	Total	89.7
		⋮	
54	San Francisco	Total	76
55	Total	FY 2010	153.1
56	Total	FY 2011	146.2
57	Total	FY 2012	152.2
58	Total	FY 2013	142.4
59	Total	FY 2014	146.2
60	Total	Total	740.1

Figure 10-17 Table with totals after the Unpivot option was applied

Unpivot The Data

In this part of the exercise, you will use the **UNPIVOT COLUMNS OPTION** to unpivot the fiscal year (FY) total columns.

1. Duplicate the Stores query ⇒ Rename the query to `1 Unpivot columns`.

2. Select all of the FY columns ⇒ Transform tab ⇒ Unpivot Columns button ⇒ Unpivot Columns.

   The table should look like the one shown in Figure 10-18. Now you can applaud. <smile>

	Store	Attribute	Value
1	Atherton	FY 2010	19.7
2	Atherton	FY 2011	17.1
3	Atherton	FY 2012	18.3
4	Atherton	FY 2013	14.8
5	Atherton	FY 2014	19.8
6	Berkeley	FY 2010	14.4

Figure 10-18 Result of using the Unpivot Columns option

How To Choose Between The Unpivot Columns And Unpivot Other Columns Transformations

Earlier in this chapter, I discussed the biggest difference between these two transformations. The exercise that you just completed, used the Unpivot Columns transformation. If you look in the formula bar, you will see the formula shown in Figure 10-19. Notice that the Unpivot Columns function actually uses the Unpivot Other Columns function. Also notice that the formula references the anchor column (the Store column), by name. When I saw this formula, I thought that the step name may have changed to Unpivot Other columns, but that didn't happen.

```
= Table.UnpivotOtherColumns(#"Removed Bottom Rows", {"Store"}, "Attribute", "Value")
```

Figure 10-19 Unpivot Columns formula

I am not 100% sure why this happens, but my guess is that both functions work on the premise that the anchor column(s) (the Store column in Figure 10-13) will not change, and the unpivoted columns (the "FY" columns in Figure 10-13) will probably change over time. In the table used in Exercise 10.3, new stores can be added to the table without changing the structure of the table. When new fiscal year data is added to the table, new columns have to be created, thus changing the structure of the table.

One way to look at it, is that since the Unpivot Columns and Unpivot Other Columns functions use the same code, there really is no difference. Use the one that you understand the best. Hopefully, the following will help.

☑ When there are more anchor columns than columns to unpivot, select the columns to unpivot and select the **UNPIVOT COLUMNS OPTION**.

☑ When there are more columns to unpivot than anchor columns, select the anchor columns and select the **UNPIVOT OTHER COLUMNS OPTION**.

Unpivot Columns And Unpivot Other Columns Transformation Tips
Keep the following in mind when using these transformations:

① Both of these transformations reference the **ANCHOR COLUMN(S)** by name. If an anchor column is renamed in the data source, the query will fail, when the data is refreshed.
② If a new anchor column is added to the data source, it will be unpivoted, when using either of these transformations. This will cause unexpected results in the query.

Exercise 10.4: Use The Unpivot Other Columns Option To Transform The Data

In this exercise, you will use the Unpivot other columns transformation. This will give you a foundation to be able to compare the Unpivot Other Columns transformation to the Unpivot Columns transformation.

1. Save the E10.3 file as `E10.4 Unpivot Other Columns`.
2. Duplicate the Stores query ⇒ Rename the query to `1 Yearly Sales`.
3. Right-click on the Store column and select **UNPIVOT OTHER COLUMNS**. You should see the same data, shown earlier in Figure 10-18.
4. Rename the Attribute column to `Year` ⇒ Rename the Value column to `Year Total`.

Remove Part Of The Data In A Column

To make the Year column easier to work with, the letters FY and the space after it, need to be removed.

1. Right-click on the Year column header ⇒ Replace Values.

2. In the Value To Find field, type `FY` ⇒ Press the space bar, as shown in Figure 10-20 ⇒ Click OK.

   While you may have been tempted to rename the column heading in Excel, it would work the first time the data was imported. When the data is refreshed, the changes would not be there, if for no other reason then the person using the worksheet will probably change the heading back to the way it was. The table should look like the one shown in Figure 10-21.

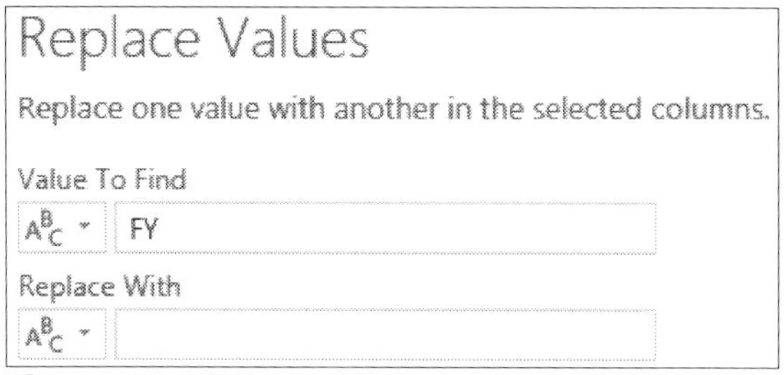

Figure 10-20 Replace Values criteria

	Store	Year	Year Total
1	Atherton	2010	19.7
2	Atherton	2011	17.1
3	Atherton	2012	18.3
4	Atherton	2013	14.8
5	Atherton	2014	19.8
6	Berkeley	2010	14.4

Figure 10-21 Data in the Year column modified

Create Averages In A Pivot Table Layout

Figure 10-15 shown earlier, displays data in a pivot table layout. If you have the need to display an average per row, in this case, an average per store, the steps below will show you how. The **LIST.AVERAGE FUNCTION** is used to calculate the average of the selected values in a row. If you are using your own data, you would start with step 3.

1. Duplicate the Yearly Sales query ⇒ Rename it to `2 Display averages`.

2. Delete the Unpivoted Other Columns step and all steps after it.

3. Add Column tab ⇒ Custom Column button.

4. Create the formula shown in Figure 10-22. Don't forget to add the ({ }) brackets around the first and last column names. Figure 10-23 shows the average sales amount for each store.

   It is not a requirement to use all of the columns in the formula.

   You can pick and choose the columns that you want to create the average for.

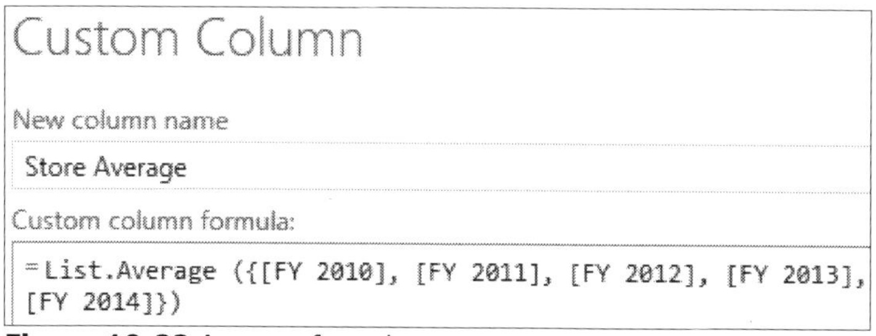

Figure 10-22 Average formula

	Store	FY 2010	FY 2011	FY 2012	FY 2013	FY 2014	Store Average
1	Atherton	19.7	17.1	18.3	14.8	19.8	17.94
2	Berkeley	14.4	18	16.4	16.7	19.3	16.96
3	Carmel-by-the-Sea	18.8	13.5	18.7	13.9	15.7	16.12
4	Cupertino	12	16.2	17.5	17.8	13.8	15.46
5	Fresno	19.2	15.6	19.6	15.9	14.4	16.94
6	Laguna Beach	18.9	14.6	16.7	12.1	13.9	15.24
7	Mailbu	18.7	17.8	14	18.5	13.7	16.54
8	Pasadena	17	19.4	17.1	17.3	17.3	17.62
9	San Francisco	14.4	14	13.9	15.4	18.3	15.2

Figure 10-23 Average yearly sales amount per store

Exercise 10.5: Unpivot Data Using The Unpivot Only Selected Columns Transformation

As discussed earlier, this is the unpivot option to use if you think that the data source table will have new (additional) anchor columns in the future. When anchor columns change, the **UNPIVOT OTHER COLUMNS** transformation will fail. This transformation is like an insurance policy. Right now, you do not have to file a claim, but just in case something happens in the future, you are covered.

1. In a new file, load the Revenue By State sheet in the More Data Files workbook.

2. Select all of the columns except the State column.

3. Transform tab ⇒ Unpivot Columns button ⇒ **UNPIVOT ONLY SELECTED COLUMNS.**

As shown in Figure 10-24, the fiscal years were hard coded in the formula. When another fiscal year of data is added, it will be treated as an anchor column. This means that the new fiscal year column will not be unpivoted. In this scenario, using the Unpivot Other Columns option is the best option to use.

```
= Table.Unpivot(#"Changed Type", {"FY2013", "FY2014", "FY2015", "FY2016", "FY2017"}, "Attribute", "Value")
```

Figure 10-24 Unpivot only selected columns formula

4. Save the file as `E10.5 Unpivot only selected columns.`

Refreshing The Data

Once the raw data has been changed in a table in Excel, the user should not remove the table characteristics, if the data needs to be refreshed in Power BI Desktop. More rows or columns can be added (to the table in Excel), as long as they are adjoining to the current table. If any data is added outside of the table in Excel, that needs to be refreshed, Power BI Desktop will not automatically include that data as part of the refresh process.

What happens if the spreadsheet shown earlier in Figure 10-13, now looks like the one shown in Figure 10-25.

The changes listed below were made to the spreadsheet.

	A	B	C	D	E	F	G	H
3	Store	FY 2010	FY 2011	FY 2012	FY 2013	FY 2014	FY 2015	Total
4	Atherton	$19.70	$17.10	$18.30	$14.80	$19.80	$24.50	$89.70
5	Berkeley	$14.40	$18.00	$16.40	$16.70	$19.30		$84.80
6	Carmel-by-the-Sea	$18.80	$13.50	$18.70	$13.90	$15.70	$17.20	$80.60
7	Cupertino	$12.00	$16.20	$17.50	$17.80	$13.80	$15.55	$77.30
8	Fresno	$19.20	$15.60	$19.60	$15.90	$14.40	$14.30	$84.70
9	Laguna Beach	$18.90	$14.60	$16.70	$12.10	$13.90	$16.20	$76.20
10	Los Angeles		$12.75				$130.00	
11	Mailbu	$18.70	$17.80	$14.00	$18.50	$13.70	$19.10	$82.70
12	Pasadena	$17.00	$19.40	$17.10	$17.30	$17.30	$18.8[illegible]	$88.10
13	Palm Springs						$6[illegible]5	
14	San Francisco	$14.40	$14.00	$13.90	$15.40	$18.30		$76.00
15	Santa Barbara					$8.20	$9.19	
16	Total	$153.10	$158.95	$152.20	$142.40	$146.20		$740.10

Figure 10-25 Modified table in Excel

① Rows for the following cities are new: Los Angeles, Palm Springs and Santa Barbara.
② The column FY 2015 has been added to the worksheet, but it is not part of the table.
③ Some cells do not have a total.

How To Tell What Data Is Not Part Of The Table

The last cell in the table frame is cell F15, as illustrated above in Figure 10-25. Any rows below row 15 or columns after Column F, are not part of the table.

Empty Cell Considerations

When the data is refreshed in Power BI Desktop, rows will not be created for cells that do not have data, when the data is unpivoted. For example, a row would not be created for Los Angeles 2010 or Berkeley 2015.

Figure 10-26 shows the data that was unpivoted for Los Angeles. This could make the reports created based on this data skewed. Also, people reading the reports may not notice that data is missing, which would be a problem. If you need rows to be created for every cell in the table, a zero or null value needs to be added to the cells, that currently do not have data. The Total column and row can remain empty in this scenario because they are not used in the Query Editor.

	Store	Attribute	Value
33	Laguna Beach	FY 2013	12.1
34	Laguna Beach	FY 2014	13.9
35	Laguna Beach	FY 2015	16.2
36	Los Angeles	FY 2011	12.75
37	Los Angeles	FY 2015	130

Figure 10-26 Unpivoted data for Los Angeles

Handling Rows And Columns That Have Subtotals

Earlier in this chapter, you learned how to handle rows and columns that have totals. You have probably seen a spreadsheet that has subtotals. Like totals, subtotals need to be filtered out also. The difference is that often, each subtotal name is slightly different. For example, if the data is grouped by the sales rep, each subtotal will have a slightly different name, like "A Jones Subtotal" and "B Smith Subtotal".

The other difference is that subtotals have to be filtered out **AFTER** the data has been unpivoted. That is because the location (position) of the subtotal columns and rows in the data source can change. Also, there is usually more than one subtotal row and each subtotal row label is slightly different. Figure 10-27 shows part of a weekly sales report with subtotals.

Notice that the subtotal rows (8 and 19) have different labels. In addition to unpivoting data, the next exercise will show you how to handle rows and columns that have subtotals.

	A	B	C	D	E	F	G
1	**Sales Rep**	**Customer**	**Bicycles**			**Bicycle Total**	**Bicycle Locks**
2			Mountain Bicycle	Touring Bicycle	Children's Bicycle		Guardian Chain Lock
3	Nancy Davolio	City Cyclists	$2,645.87			$2,645.87	
4		Pathfinders	$8,908.05	$27.00		$8,935.05	
5		Bike-A-Holics Anonymous		$6,839.10	$39.80	$6,878.90	
6		Psycho-Cycle			$43.80	$43.80	
7		Sporting Wheels Inc.	$65.70			$65.70	
8	**Totals For Nancy Davolio**					**$18,569.32**	
9							
10	Andrew Fuller	Spokes 'N Wheels Ltd.	$9,612.47			$9,612.47	$40.50
11		Trail Blazer's Place			$31.00	$31.00	$4,304.10
12		Rowdy Rims Company			$46.50	$46.50	$1,583.15
13		Clean Air Transportation Co.			$950.97	$950.97	$701.54
14		Hooked on Helmets			$959.70	$959.70	$116.21
15		C-Gate Cycle Shoppe				$0.00	$40.50
16		Alley Cat Cycles				$0.00	
17		The Bike Cellar				$0.00	
18		Hercules Mountain Bikes				$0.00	
19	**Totals For Andrew Fuller**					**$11,600.64**	

Figure 10-27 Weekly sales report with subtotals

Exercise 10.6: Filter Out Subtotals In An Unpivoted Table

In this exercise, you will learn how to create a filter to remove the subtotal rows from the table after the data is unpivoted.

1. In a new file, import the Subtotals sheet in the More Data Files workbook.

2. If the column headers are "Column 1", "Column 2" etc, promote the first row to be the column headers ⇒ What you see, depends on whether or not the Automatically detect column types and headers for unstructured sources, in the Current File ⇒ Data Load section, on the Options dialog box is selected.

3. Use the Fill option on the Transform tab, to fill in the Sales Rep column. This will replace the null values in the column with the sales reps name.

4. Save the file as `E10.6 Filter subtotal rows.`

Unpivot The Data

In this part of the exercise, you will unpivot the product columns. There are two anchor columns in this table, the Sales Rep and Customer columns.

1. Select the Sales Rep and Customer columns.

2. Transform tab ⇒ Unpivot Columns button ⇒ Unpivot Other Columns.

As shown in Figure 10-28, there are several rows that are not needed, at the top of the table. In this exercise, many of the values in the Attribute column need to be changed, because they do not correspond to the product name, which is on the second row in the table that was imported. [See Figure 10-27]

Also notice in rows 12 and 13, that the Attribute column value is not correct. The values in the Value column, at the top of Figure 10-28, are the values that should be in the Attribute column, as they are the products that were sold.

	Sales Rep	Customer	Attribute	Value
1	null	null	Bicycles	Mountain Bicycle
2	null	null	Column4	Touring Bicycle
3	null	null	Column5	Children's Bicycle
4	null	null	Bicycle Locks	Guardian Chain Lock
5	null	null	Column8	Guardian U Lock
6	null	null	Column9	Xtreme Mtn Lock
7	null	null	Column10	Xtreme Titan Lock
8	null	null	Gloves	Active Outdoors Crochet Glove
9	null	null	Column13	Active Outdoors Lycra Glove
10	Nancy Davolio	City Cyclists	Bicycles	2645.87
11	Nancy Davolio	City Cyclists	Bicycle Total	2645.87
12	Nancy Davolio	City Cyclists	Column8	296.87
13	Nancy Davolio	City Cyclists	Column10	659.7

Figure 10-28 Result of using the Unpivot Other Columns option

The easiest way to fix this (in my opinion) is to delete the Unpivoted Column step, promote the values on row 1 (click on the Filled Down step, to see the values that should be the column headers), then rename the five columns that are not currently correct, but will get changed when the row is imported (the columns in row 1 on the Filled Down step). Yes, you could insert a step below the Unpivoted step, instead of deleting it. I prefer to delete it and then recreate it. On your own, you can try inserting a step.

If you scroll down and view rows 48-50, you will see the sales reps totals for each of the categories that they sold products in.

3. Delete the Unpivot Other Columns step.

4. Promote the first row to be the column headers.

5. Rename the columns in Table 10-2.

Column	Rename The Column To . . .
Column 1	Sales Rep
Column 2	Customer
Column 6	Bicycle Total
Column 11	Bicycle Locks Total
Column 14	Gloves Total

Table 10-2 Columns to rename

6. Select the Sales Rep and Customer columns.

7. Transform tab ⇒ Unpivot Columns button ⇒ Unpivot Other Columns.

8. Rename the Attribute column to `Product` ⇒ Rename the Value column to `Sales Amount`.

Your table should look like the one shown in Figure 10-29.

Now you can see the products each sales rep sold to customers.

	Sales Rep	Customer	Product	Sales Amount
1	Nancy Davolio	City Cyclists	Mountain Bicycle	2645.87
2	Nancy Davolio	City Cyclists	Bicycle Total	2645.87
3	Nancy Davolio	City Cyclists	Guardian U Lock	296.87
4	Nancy Davolio	City Cyclists	Xtreme Titan Lock	659.7
5	Nancy Davolio	City Cyclists	Bicycle Locks Total	956.57
6	Nancy Davolio	City Cyclists	Active Outdoors Crochet Glove	23.8
7	Nancy Davolio	City Cyclists	Gloves Total	23.8
8	Nancy Davolio	Pathfinders	Mountain Bicycle	8908.05

Figure 10-29 Revised result of using the Unpivot Other Columns option

Filter Out The Total Rows

Clearing the check mark for the Subtotal and Grand Total options on the columns Filter drop-down list, for the Sales Rep column, illustrated in Figure 10-30, will work initially. If the label name changes or new subtotal rows are added, the options on this drop-down list, will not capture these types of changes. You would have to manually keep selecting the subtotal and grand total rows. Additionally, when applicable, any rows with a null value are not needed.

In the next part of this exercise, you will create criteria to filter out the total rows illustrated above in Figure 10-30. As shown above in Figure 10-29, rows 2, 5 and 7 are total rows, based on the values in the Product column. They need to be filtered out also.

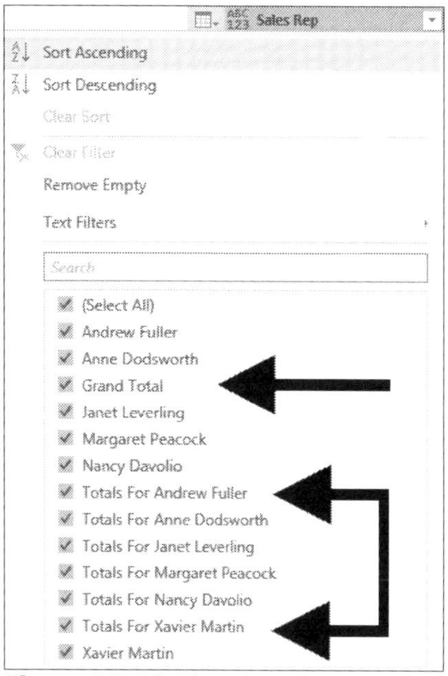

Figure 10-30 Filter drop-down list values to filter subtotal and grand total rows illustrated

Filter The Sales Rep Column

In this part of the exercise, you will create a filter for the total rows. To kill two birds with one stone, the filter criteria created, will also remove the Grand Total rows that are at the end of the table. On your own, you will have to decide if combining the filter criteria is appropriate.

1. Open the Filter drop-down list for the Sales Rep column ⇒ Text Filters ⇒ **DOES NOT CONTAIN**.

2. In the field across from the Does not contain option, type `Total`, as shown in Figure 10-31. This will work for both types of rows that need to be filtered on the Sales Rep column.

   The reason that I selected this filter criteria is because the sales rep total rows use the word "Totals", at the end of the name and the grand total rows, use the word "Total".

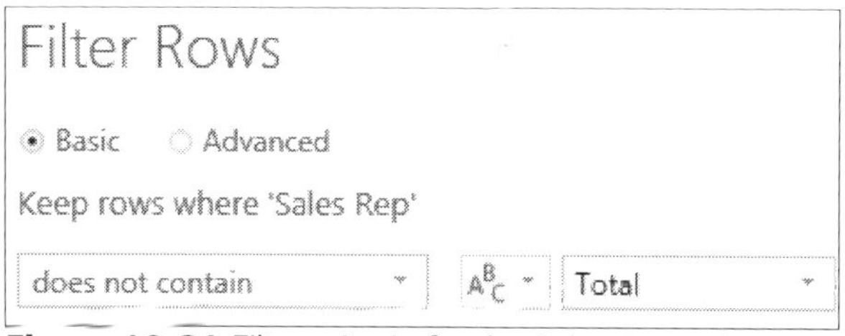

Figure 10-31 Filter criteria for the Sales Rep column

   Using "Total" will filter out all of the rows that need to be filtered out. Using "Totals", will not.

Filter The Product Column

Interestingly enough, the same criteria created for the Sales Rep column will filter out the rows that have totals for each product category, like row 5, shown earlier in Figure 10-29, that has "Bicycle Locks Total".

1. Open the Filter drop-down list for the Product column ⇒ Text Filters ⇒ Does not contain.

> In this exercise, you could use the **DOES NOT END WITH** criteria option. However, if the label gets renamed and the word "Total" is not at the end of the label, the criteria will not filter out the row. For example, if the label on row 5 was changed to "Total for Bicycle Locks", the Does not end with criteria would not work.

2. In the field across from the Does not contain option, type `Total`.

The table should now have 163 rows. On your own, you would probably rename some steps to indicate the columns that were used or filtered.

> While the steps in the exercise that you just completed work, the **ONLY** reason that they work is because each subtotal row has the word "Total". If the word "Total" is removed from any subtotal label, that row of data will not be filtered out. This would also be the case for the Grant Totals row.

Summary

This chapter covered the Pivot column and Unpivot Columns transformations and how they can be used when the data that is imported, comes from a table that was poorly designed. Like many of the topics covered in Chapter 8, the Pivot and Unpivot transformations are also ways to **MASH UP DATA**. The pivot and unpivot transformations are used to change the structure of the data. Knowing how to unpivot data is important when working with data that does not come from a database.

While initially the Pivot Column and Unpivot Columns transformations may seem overwhelming, in particular the Unpivot Columns options, my advice is to take your time and look at the data, either in the data source file or when you first import it into Power Query. Doing this will help you make a list of all of the tasks that need to be done.
The two unofficial rules that I follow for the Unpivot Columns transformations were discussed earlier, right before Exercise 10.4.

You also learned how to create filters that filter out subtotal and total rows of data. Keep in mind that while the solutions that were covered in this chapter are better then selecting the individual filter filters, as they can fail, if the labels in the data source change and no longer meet the filter criteria that was created.

Hopefully, you see how the pivot and unpivot transformations can get the data that is stored in elaborate and complex spreadsheets, that seem to have data all over the place, into rows and columns that can be used to create reports.

At the beginning of this chapter, the **TRANSPOSE TRANSFORMATION** was briefly discussed. If this transformation was applied to the table shown in Figure 10-32, it would look like the query shown in Figure 10-33.

	Column1	Column2	Column3	Column4	Column5
1	Jams, Preserves	Dried Fruit & Nuts	Condiments	Canned Fruit & Vegetables	Cereal
2	1	0	1	7	2

Figure 10-32 Data that needs to be transposed

	Column1	Column2
1	Jams, Preserves	1
2	Dried Fruit & Nuts	0
3	Condiments	1
4	Canned Fruit & Vegetables	7
5	Cereal	2

Figure 10-33 Data that has been transposed

PROBLEM SOLVING

After reading this chapter and completing the exercises, you will start to understand how to fix or avoid some of the problems that can arise when transforming data.

CHAPTER 11

Overview

This chapter covers topics that may cause you a problem at some point. You will learn how to resolve them. If you have worked through the exercises in the previous chapters, you have seen how things are "suppose" to go. For the most part, on your own, you should have the same or similar experience. However, we all know that things can and will go wrong from time to time. The goal of this chapter is to bring up problems that I have encountered and how I resolved them.

By no means do I think that I have encountered every problem that can happen in Power Query. My hope is two-fold: One, to provide a realistic view of how easy it can be to get into trouble and two, how to start thinking about how to resolve problems that come your way.

The topics and exercises covered in this chapter take concepts that were covered in the previous chapters and either show another way to use a transformation, take the concept up a notch or how to resolve a problem.

Exercise 11.1: Maintain The Excel Sheet Name When Appending Data

In the Excel append exercises that were covered up to this point, each sheet in the file had a unique name. That name was automatically included as a column in the query. So even after queries were appended, each row had the sheet name. More than likely, you will not always import Excel files, that have a descriptive sheet name.

Instead, they will have names like "Sheet 1, Sheet 2" etc. When that is the case, you may be thinking that renaming the sheet once it is imported will solve the problem.

1. In a new file, import the Sheet 1 sheet in the following workbooks: Customers USA.xlsx and Customers Canada.xlsx.

   Notice the query names, as shown in Figure 11-1. Sheet 1 is the name on the tab in both workbooks. Remember that when importing from an Excel file, that the initial query name comes from the sheet name.

   If for no other reason, then to keep your sanity, you would rename these queries. In the Query Editor, Sheet 1 should be USA Customers.

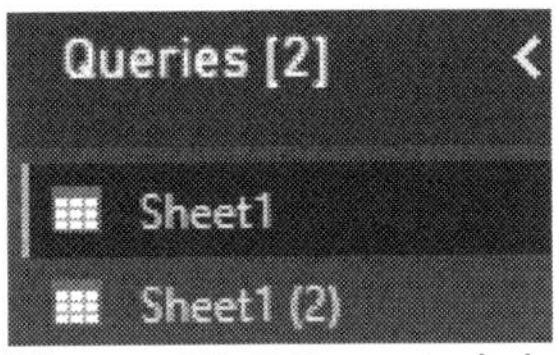

Figure 11-1 Imported sheets from two workbooks

2. Rename the first query to `USA Customers` ⇒ Rename the second query to `Canadian Customers`.

Append The Queries

1. Select the USA Customers query ⇒ Home tab ⇒ Append Queries button ⇒ Append Queries as New.

2. In the second drop-down list, select the Canadian Customers table.

The Append 1 table should have the data from both queries. Notice that there is no way to tell which query each row of data came from, even though you renamed the queries. So renaming the queries that have a generic name, is not the solution.

3. Rename the Append 1 query to `All Customers`.

4. Save the file as `E11.1 Maintain the Excel sheet name`.

Add A Column To Store The Sheet Name

The heading of this section should be a give away as to how to solve the issue of having the file name or query name listed for each row. By adding a column to both of the customer queries, means that the current rows in the query will get a table name and when the data is refreshed, any new rows that have been added to either data source file, will have the query name filled in, when the row is appended.

In this part of the exercise, you will create a formula to add the query name to the new column.

1. Select the USA Customers query ⇒ Add Column tab ⇒ Custom Column button.

2. In the New column name field, type `FromQuery`. On your own, you can name the new column anything you want.

   In the Formula field, after the equal sign, type `"USA Customers"`, as shown in Figure 11-2 ⇒ Click OK.

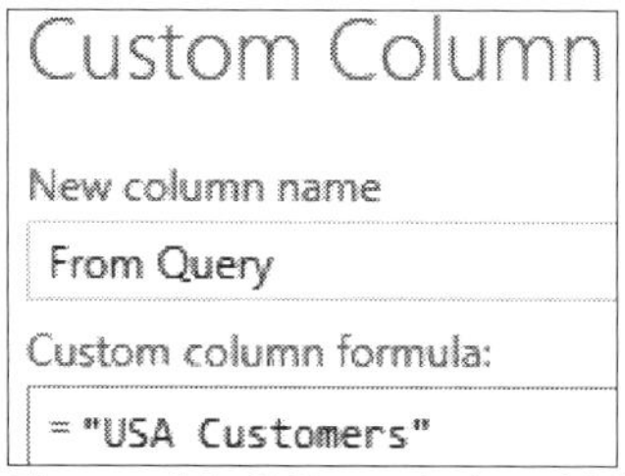

Figure 11-2 Formula to add the query name to the new column

3. Move the new column to the beginning of the query, as shown in Figure 11-3.

	From Query	CustomerID	CompanyName
1	USA Customers	1	City Cyclists
2	USA Customers	2	Pathfinders
3	USA Customers	3	Bike-A-Holics Anonymous

Figure 11-3 New column with the query name

4. Repeats steps 1 through 3 above, for the Canadian Customers query. In step 2, change "USA Customers" to `"Canadian Customers"`.

5. Display the All Customers query ⇒ Scroll down to row 43.

   You should see the query name filled in for all of the rows, as shown in Figure 11-4.

	From Query	CustomerID	CompanyName
43	USA Customers	43	Insane Cycle
44	USA Customers	44	Our Wheels Follow Us Everywhere
45	Canadian Customers	45	Cycles and Sports
46	Canadian Customers	50	Crazy Wheels

Figure 11-4 From Query column filled in with the query name

Exercise 11.2: Append Multiple Sheets In A Workbook

In the previous exercise, you imported sheets in different Excel files that did not have a descriptive name for the table (the tab). In this exercise, you will import data from all of the sheets in a workbook, similar to the workbook used in Chapter 9, Exercise 9.3. The difference is that the sheets in the workbook used in this exercise, do not have a descriptive name.

1. In a new file, import the Multiple sheets with no sheet names workbook.

2. On the Navigator dialog box, you should see three tables, as shown in Figure 11-5 ⇒ Right-click on the workbook name and select Edit.

   In the Query Editor, the values in the Name column will be added to the query. Once the tables have been expanded, you will create a conditional column to give the sheets a unique and descriptive name.

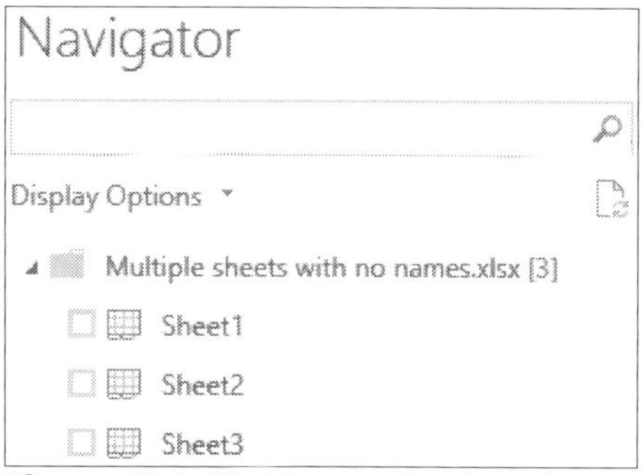

Figure 11-5 Workbook with tables that do not have descriptive names

3. Delete the Item, Kind and Hidden columns. They are not needed.

4. Click the Expand button at the end of the Data column ⇒ Clear the check mark for the Use original column name as prefix option ⇒ Click OK.

5. Promote the first row to headers.

6. Display the filter options for the Invoice Nbr column ⇒ Filters ⇒ Does not equal ⇒ In the field across from the filter criteria, type `Invoice Nbr`. This will filter out the column header rows for all tables, except the first table.

7. Save the file as `E11.2 Import multiple sheets without names.`

Create The Conditional Column

In this part of the exercise, you will create a formula that adds a different value to the new column based on the value in the Sheet 1 column.

If you look at the dates, you will see that all of the dates on each sheet, are for the same month and year, and that each month and year are unique to the sheet. Those values could be used to create the new name that will replace the sheet name.

1. Add Column tab ⇒ Conditional Column button.
2. In the New column name field, type `From Sheet` ⇒ Create the criteria shown in Figure 11-6.

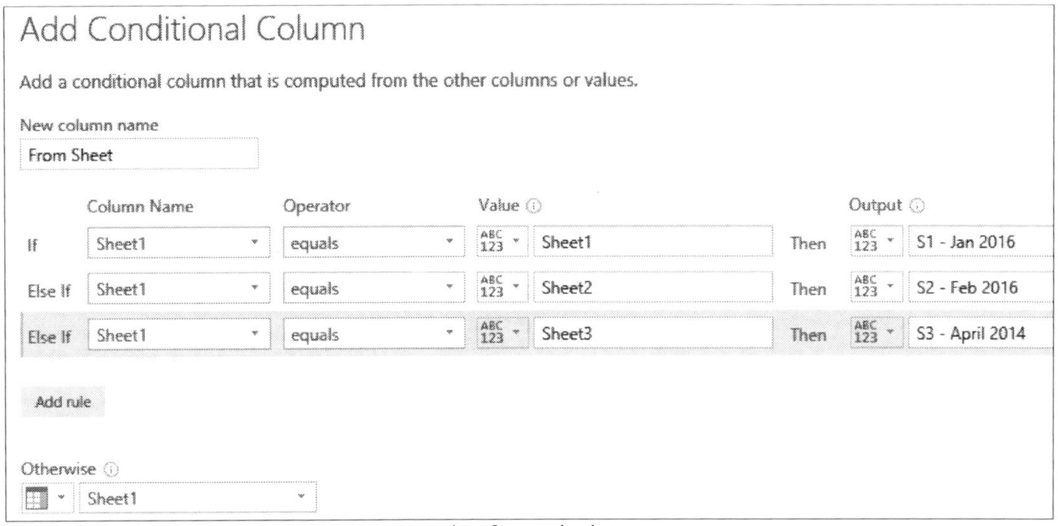

Figure 11-6 Criteria to create a custom value for each sheet

The three rows at the top of the Add Conditional Column dialog box, create the conditions, that check the value in the Sheet 1 column. Based on the value (Sheet 1, Sheet 2, or Sheet 3), a descriptive name (the value in the Output column) is added to the From Sheet column that is being created. The S number at the beginning of the field, corresponds to the sheet number in the data source.

The reason that I used the Sheet 1 value in the Otherwise field is because the contents on the sheets that were imported, indicate that more sheets will be added to the workbook. When that happens, the criteria on the first three rows will not place a value in the From Sheet column. As you may have guessed, when new sheets are added to the data source, you will need to add more criteria to this dialog box, to give the new sheet(s) a descriptive name.

In addition to that, you need to pray that no one renames the existing sheets in the data source workbook. If that happens, the criteria in Figure 11-6 will not work. While annoying, on your own, you may want to check the Excel file to ensure that the current sheets have not been renamed or deleted, before you import it.

3. Click OK ⇒ Move the From Sheet column to the beginning of the query.
4. Scroll down to row 28. You should see the data shown in Figure 11-7.

	From Sheet	Sheet1	Invoice Nbr
28	S1 - Jan 2016	Sheet1	6134
29	S1 - Jan 2016	Sheet1	6135
30	S2 - Feb 2016	Sheet2	6240
31	S2 - Feb 2016	Sheet2	6241

Figure 11-7 Column with a descriptive sheet name

While this solution is not perfect, it will work, but you will have to maintain it. In this scenario, it isn't worth it, to take the time to create an M formula, because you cannot control what the new sheets in the workbook will be named to.

Exercise 11.3: Selecting Columns vs Removing Columns Transformations

Both transformations have the functionality to let you discard columns in the query, that you do not need. Because there is no option to select the columns that you need, before the data is loaded into Power Query, you have to delete columns after the fact. We are use to deleting a lot of things on our own computer, without having to think about whether or not it will cause a problem, someplace down the road. Because data in Power Query needs to be refreshed on a regular basis, especially when the data is used for reporting purposes, you do have to take into consideration how or if the data that is deleted from the query can cause a problem.

As I said earlier, the Rename and Select Column transformations achieve the same result on the front end (the part that you can see). On the back end, these transformations work differently. The **SELECT COLUMNS TRANSFORMATION** (the Choose Columns button on the Home tab) keeps the columns that you want. The **REMOVE COLUMNS TRANSFORMATION** deletes columns that you do not want. Removing columns from the query can cause the refresh to fail, if the removed column in the query, is deleted from the data source.

During the refresh, the removed columns are marked as missing if they are not in the data source file. During a refresh, the select columns are less likely to cause the refresh to fail.

Fortunately, the functions for both of these transformations, the **TABLE.SELECTCOLUMNS** and **TABLE.REMOVECOLUMNS** functions, have arguments that can be set to ignore errors, which will keep the refresh from failing. The **MISSINGFIELD.IGNORE ARGUMENT** will ignore the missing column. The **MISSINGFIELD.USENULL ARGUMENT** adds a null value to the column when there is an error. It makes the most sense to add this argument to the formula, because the column will still be in the query, just without data. Hopefully, this would get someone's attention, when the column is viewed on a report and that they will look into why the column does not have any data. While both arguments work, the formula can still fail.

The purpose of this exercise is to demonstrate how each transformation works by viewing the formula that the transformations create.

Delete The Columns

1. Save the E2.4 file as `E11.3 Select vs Delete columns`.

2. Duplicate the Customers table ⇒ Rename it to `1 Delete columns`.

3. Select the Company and Job Title columns ⇒ Press the Delete key.

The **REMOVED COLUMNS STEP** created the formula shown in Figure 11-8. If either of the fields shown in the formula is deleted from the data source, this query would fail, when it is refreshed. A field that is renamed in the data source would be recognized as a new column in the query.

```
= Table.RemoveColumns(_Customers,{"Company", "Job Title"})
```

Figure 11-8 Formula created by deleting columns

Select Columns

After completing this part of the exercise, you will see a formula that shows which columns from the Customers table to keep in the query.

1. Duplicate the Customers table ⇒ Rename it to `2 Select columns to keep`.

2. Home tab ⇒ **CHOOSE COLUMNS BUTTON** ⇒ Choose Columns ⇒ Clear the check mark for the Company and Job Title columns, as shown in Figure 11-9 ⇒ Click OK.

Notice that the step name is **REMOVED OTHER COLUMNS**. This name indicates that columns were selected to keep, which is what the formula shown in Figure 11-10 shows. If either of the columns in Figure 11-9, that is not checked, is deleted from the data source, the formula in Figure 11-10 will not cause the refresh to fail.

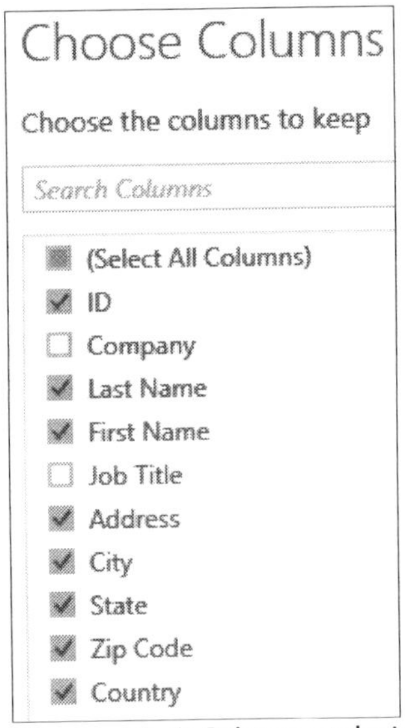

Figure 11-9 Columns selected to keep

```
= Table.SelectColumns(_Customers,{"ID", "Last Name", "First Name", "Address", "City", "State", "Zip Code", "Country"})
```

Figure 11-10 Formula created by selecting the columns to keep

Changing The Order Of Columns In A Query

On more than one occasion in this book, you have changed the order of the columns in a query. I don't know about you, but I change the order because there are some columns that I want to see by default, without having to scroll to see them. Most of the time, I had you move columns that were created, next to a particular column, either for comparison reasons or to demonstrate that the new column was working as expected.

If you move a column for either of these reasons, the recommendation is to delete the **REORDERED COLUMNS STEP**, once you have confirmed that the data in the new column is correct. Doing so, will reduce the chance of the refresh failing.

In other cases, like creating a pivot table, moving columns around is sometimes a requirement. If you have to change the order of columns in a query, do it after you have selected the columns to keep. One reason is because it is possible that once you select the columns to keep, the column(s) that you wanted to move, are now in the place that you want them in.

The logic behind the **REORDER COLUMNS TRANSFORMATION** is similar to the **SELECT COLUMNS TRANSFORMATION**, in that it is best that the formula only contains the action that you take and leave everything else out of the formula.

Exercise 11.4: Reorder Columns

Yes, I know that it is hard to believe that rearranging the order of columns can cause the data refresh to fail. Keep in mind that this, like many of the other topics covered in this chapter, pertain more to data that is not in a database. The names of columns and data types, etc, rarely, if ever change in a database. These types of changes can be and often are a frequent occurrence in text based files, including spreadsheets, because they are free form.

In this exercise, you will learn how to modify the Reorder Columns formula so that it only captures (contains) the columns that are moved. That way, if new columns are added to the query or if any of the other columns are renamed or deleted, the refresh will not fail, because columns were moved.

1. Save the E2.4 file as `E11.4 Reorder columns`.

2. Duplicate the Orders query ⇒ Rename it to `1 Reorder columns`.

3. Move the Ship Name column left, after the Employee column ⇒ Move the Shipped Date column after the Ship Name column.

Figure 11-11 shows the formula, that was created, for the Reordered Columns transformation. As shown on the first row of the formula, the Ship Name and Shipped Date columns are in the third and fourth positions. If any of the other columns are moved, deleted or renamed in the data source and then this query is refreshed, the refresh will fail.

```
= Table.ReorderColumns(_Orders,{"Order ID", "Employee", "Ship Name", "Shipped Date", "Customer", "Order Date", "Ship Via", "Ship Address", "Ship City", "Ship State/Province", "Ship ZIP/Postal Code", "Ship Country/Region", "Shipping Fee", "Taxes", "Payment Type", "Paid Date", "Notes", "Tax Rate", "Tax Status", "Status ID"})
```

Figure 11-11 Reordered Columns transformation formula

The goal is to modify this formula, so that the only columns that are referenced in the formula are the two that were moved. Yes, if any column that is reordered, is deleted or renamed, in the data source, the refresh will fail. To accomplish this, the following functions are needed.

The **LIST.INSERTRANGE FUNCTION** takes the values from the list and inserts them into another list, at the location that is specified in the formula.

The **LIST.DIFFERENCE FUNCTION** returns the items from the offset argument of the function, from the first list, that are not in the second list.

The **TABLE.COLUMNNAMES FUNCTION** requires a table as input. It returns the names of columns from a table.

4. Change the formula shown above in Figure 11-11, to the one shown below. You can type it all on one line. I used multiple lines to make the formula easier to read.

```
= Table.ReorderColumns(_Orders, List.InsertRange (List.Difference
(Table.ColumnNames (_Orders),{"Ship Name", "Shipped Date"}), 2,
{"Ship Name", "Shipped Date"}))
```

Translated, the formula above moves the Ship Name and Shipped Date columns and inserts them starting in the third position. Remember that the offset in the M language, starts at zero, so the third position (column) has an offset value of 2.

Splitting Columns

This transformation is most often used to split one column into two or more columns. This transformation can also be used to split a column into two or more rows. What may not be obvious is that when a column is split into rows, a new table can be created.

Sometimes the new table is needed to create a report that needs to display a sum or count for each entity.

For example, a count of products by size, can't be accomplished when one column has two or more values, like column C, in the table shown in Figure 11-12.

	A	B	C
1	ProductID	ProductName	Size
2	1101	Active Outdoors Crochet Glove	x-small
3	1102	Active Outdoors Crochet Glove	small, medium, large
4	1103	Active Outdoors Crochet Glove	medium
5	1104	Active Outdoors Crochet Glove	large
6	1105	Active Outdoors Crochet Glove	x-large
7	1106	Active Outdoors Lycra Glove	small, medium

Figure 11-12 Table with two or more values in one column

Exercise 11.5: Split A Column Into Rows

As shown above in Figure 11-12, the Size column has multiple values. In that layout, there isn't much that can be done with the data in the Size column, the way that it is currently. Each entry in the Size column needs to have its own row, in order to be useful, to create reports.

1. In a new file, import the 10 Products table in the More Data Files workbook.

2. Save the file as `E11.5 Split column into rows`.

3. Select the Size column ⇒ Transform tab ⇒ Split Column button ⇒ By Delimiter.

4. Select Comma, as the delimiter ⇒
   In the Advanced options section, select **ROWS**, as shown in Figure 11-13.

   The table will now have a row for each size option. For example, Product ID 1102, shown in Figure 11-12, will have three rows in the table. One for each value listed in the Size column.

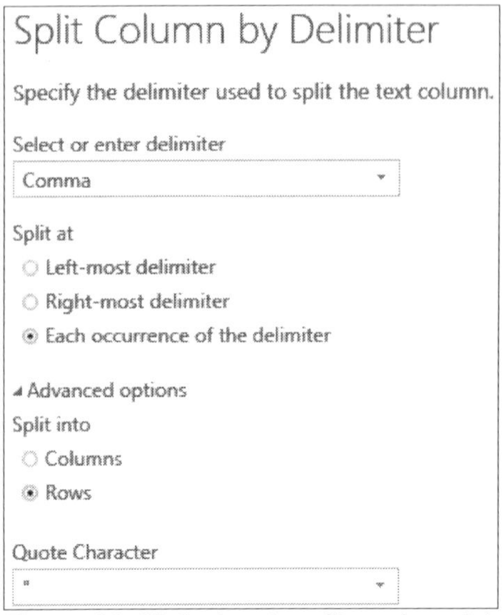

Figure 11-13 Options to split a column into rows

Using Report Titles To Identify The Table

In Exercise 11.1, you learned how to append the data on sheets in Excel files, that did not have a descriptive name. In that exercise, the sheets did not have a descriptive name, so you learned how to create a column that would add a descriptive name, by hard coding the names.

Usually, it is best not to hard code. Using a generic way to get information is better, when it is available. That is because if the value changes, the hard coded value in the formula will have to be changed. Using something like a report title, will be dynamic and will work because each sheet will have a different title, hopefully. <smile> And if the title is changed on a sheet after you create the formula to capture it, you will not have to modify the formula, unless the title is moved to a different cell.

Figure 11-14 shows the top of a sheet in Excel. More than likely, you have come across sheets like this, that have something like a report title above the data.

If the sheet has a default name like Sheet 1 or Sheet 2, you can use the report title as a way to identify which file or sheet within a file that the rows of data are from.

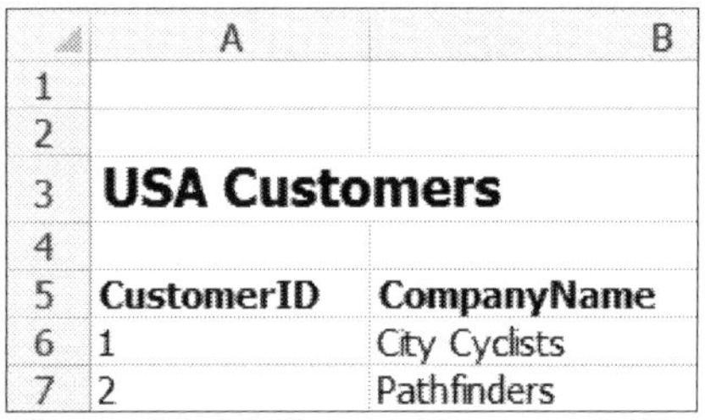

Figure 11-14 Sheet with a report title

> **Using Report Titles**
> This technique is not limited to Excel files. Report titles are often used in .txt and .csv files. They can be used, as long as the title is above the data, as shown above in Figure 11-14.

Drill Down On A Cell

In this scenario, the Drill Down option will be used to capture the report title shown above in Figure 11-14. The formula shown in Figure 11-15 is the result of right-clicking in a cell and selecting Drill Down. This formula extracts the value from the cell (in the table), that was right-clicked on. This step is done before the data in different tables are appended.

Source {0}, returns the first row in the table. "Source" refers to the name of the table.

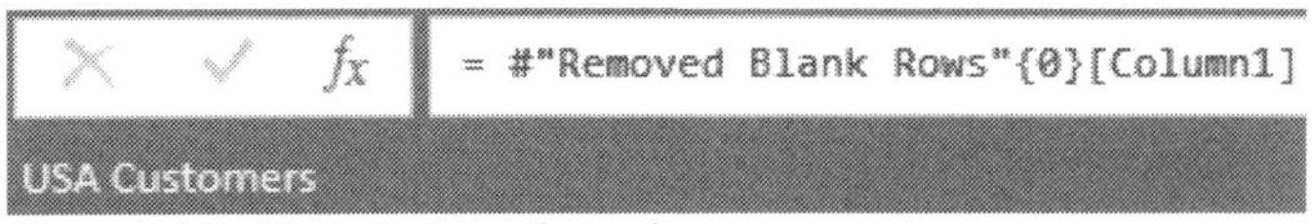

Figure 11-15 Drill down formula

Exercise 11.6: Use The Drill Down Option To Capture The Report Title

As you may have guessed by now, capturing the report title and using it as the value to denote what data source, the rows in the query are from, is a little on the advanced side of Power Query. That is true, but once you complete this exercise, you will have the blueprint to be able to do this on your own, even if you do not fully understand what each step does.

This exercise will show you how to create a process that will extract the report title dynamically from a cell that was used as the report title on the Excel worksheet and add it to each row in the query, as the way to indicate the file that the row comes from. You complete this process for each table that you import, including .csv and .txt files, before you append the queries together. In Exercise 11.7, you will learn how to apply this technique to all of the files in a folder. The good thing is that the cell with what I call the "report title" does not have to be in a specific cell on the worksheet.

1. In a new file, import Sheet 2 from the Customers USA workbook.

2. Rename the query to `Customers`.

3. Delete the Promoted Headers and Change Type steps. With your own data, you may only have one of these steps.

It is not a requirement to delete the Change Type step, but keeping it does not provide any value, because the column data types cannot be recognized at this point in the process. The reason that the data type is not recognized is because the first few rows contain the report title and blank rows.

4. You should see the report title, USA Customers, on the first row. Home tab ⇒ Remove Rows ⇒ **REMOVE BLANK ROWS**. This will remove all of the blank rows in the query. The column headings should be Column 1, Column 2, etc.

5. Save the file as `E11.6 Use the drill down option`.

Drill Down To Get The Report Title

The main reason to drill down to get the report title value is so that you do not have to hard code the words on the spreadsheet. If it isn't hard coded and the person that maintains the sheet, changes the report title in the cell, when the query is refreshed, it will not fail because the title was changed. The new title will overwrite the existing title.

1. Right-click in the cell that has the report title (USA Customers) ⇒ Drill Down.

On your own, the report title may not be in the first column. That's ok, just right-click on it, regardless of the column and cell that it is in.

You should see the formula and report title, shown earlier in Figure 11-15. The #"Removed Blank Rows" portion of the formula comes from the previous step.

2. Rename the Column 1 step to `GetReportTitle`, all one word.

3. With the Get Report Title step still selected, click the fx button. It is to the left of the formula bar. You should see = GetReportTitle ⇒ Replace it with = `#"Removed Blank Rows"`.

   Doing this lets you bypass the report title step and go back a step. When you press Enter, you will see the table again.

Create The Custom Column

In this part of the exercise, you will create a column that adds the report title to each row in the query. This is the equivalent of creating a custom column, like you created in Exercise 11.1.

1. Home tab ⇒ Remove Rows button ⇒ **REMOVE TOP ROWS** ⇒ On the Remove Top Rows dialog box, in the Number of rows field, type `1` ⇒ Click OK. On your own, you may have to remove more than one row.

2. Transform tab ⇒ Click on the top half of the Use First Row as Headers button.

3. Add Column tab ⇒ Custom Column button.

4. On the Custom Column dialog box, type `FromFile` ⇒

   In the formula box, after the equal sign, type `GetReportTitle`, as shown in Figure 11-16.

   This is the step that has the report title value.

   I used "From File" as the column heading to indicate which file the row of data came from. On your own, you can use any name that you want.

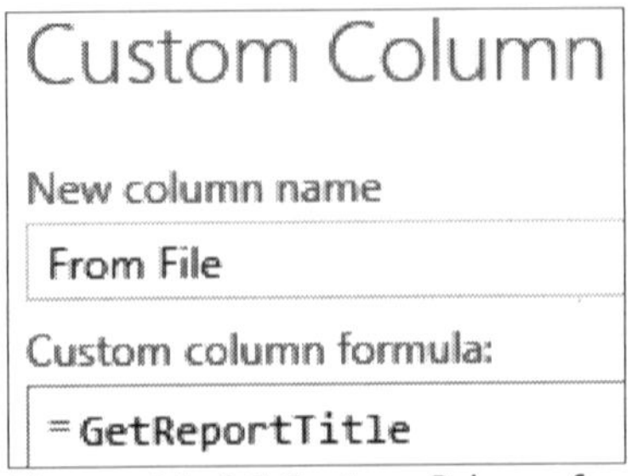

Figure 11-16 Custom Column formula

5. Click OK. You should see the report title (USA Customers) in the From File column.

You would repeat the steps in this exercise for every sheet of data that is imported into the query, then append the queries into a new query.

Exercise 11.7: Use The Report Title As The Table Name

In Chapter 9, Exercise 9.1, you learned how to append the data in all of the files in a folder. In Exercise 11.6, you learned how to use the report title on an Excel sheet as the value to indicate which file the data on each row came from. In this exercise, you will combine the functionality of both of those exercises.

Combine The Files In A Folder

1. In a new file, open the Get Data dialog box and select the **FOLDER** option.
2. On the Folder dialog box, select the Import files with report titles folder. This folder is in the folder for this book.
3. On the next dialog box, you should see three Excel files ⇒ Combine button ⇒ Combine & Edit.
4. On the Combine Files dialog box, open the **EXAMPLE FILE** drop-down list and select any one of the three Excel files ⇒

   Click on the Sheet 1 table, shown in Figure 11-17 ⇒ Click OK.

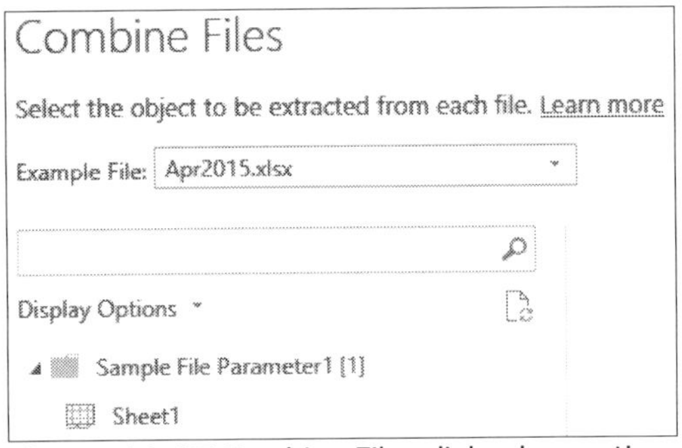

Figure 11-17 Combine Files dialog box options

5. Save the file as `E11.7 Add a report title to multiple files.`

Drill Down To Get The Report Title

Even though each table has its own report title, the process to capture all of them is the same as if you were doing it for one file.

1. In the Query Editor, click on the query, **TRANSFORM SAMPLE FILE FROM IMPORT FILES WITH REPORT TITLES** ⇒ Rename the query `Invoice sample file.`
2. With the Invoice sample file still selected, if you have a Promoted Headers step, delete it.
3. Home tab ⇒ Remove Rows button ⇒ Remove Blank Rows.
4. Right-click in the cell that has the report title. Depending on the file that you selected in the Example File drop-down list, on the Combine Files dialog box, determines the report title that you will see in the query ⇒ Select Drill Down ⇒ In the formula bar, you should see the formula shown earlier in Figure 11-15.
5. Rename the Column 1 step to `GetReportTitle` (all one word).

6. Click the fx button, next to the formula bar ⇒ Change the formula to `=#"Removed Blank Rows"` ⇒ Press Enter.

7. Home tab ⇒ Remove Rows button ⇒ Remove Top Rows ⇒ In the Number of rows field, type `1` ⇒ Click OK.

8. Transform tab ⇒ Click the top of the Use First Rows As Headers button.

Create The Column To Store The Report Title In

1. Add Column tab ⇒ Custom Column button.

2. On the Custom Column dialog box, type `FromFile` ⇒ In the formula box, after the equal sign, type `GetReportTitle`, as shown earlier in Figure 11-16. This is the step that has the report title value.

3. Delete the Changed Type step.

4. In the Queries panel, click on the Import files with report titles query ⇒ Delete the Changed Type step.

If you display the filter drop-down list for the From File column, you should see a title for each table that was imported and appended, as shown in Figure 11-18.

Having an entry in this list for each file, lets you know that the import, append and drill down worked correctly.

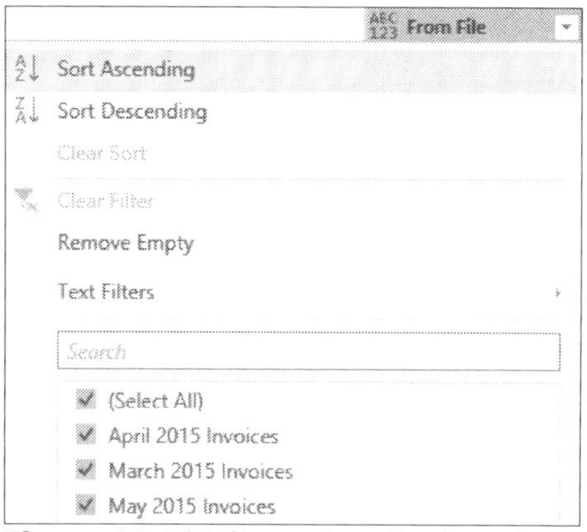

Figure 11-18 Filter options for the column that stores the report title

Summary

This chapter covered a variety of topics. Hopefully, they will be the answer to some of the "How Do I" questions that you may have. There should be no question that data comes in a variety of layouts and unique situations. I suspect that when you first read about the Drill Down option in Chapter 4, you had no idea that this option could be used to navigate to a report title in a text file, to use to indicate the table that the data came from.

This chapter also covered some solutions to prevent refreshing data from failing. I suspect that there are other ways that a refresh can fail, but so far, the ones that I covered, are the only ones that I have encountered.

Other Things To Look Out For

In addition to the Changed Type step and renaming a column issues that were covered in Chapter 9, below are some other things to look out for. They may or may not cause an error in every file, but are important, just the same.

☑ **DELETING AND SELECTING COLUMNS** Sadly, the import process does not have functionality that allows you to select the columns (in each table) that you want to import. Often, you will have to delete columns that you do not need. On the surface, it seems harmless to delete ("Remove" in Power Query terminology) columns in the query.

When creating the data files for this book, I needed to delete columns from one of the data files. I thought "no harm, no foul" . . . right up to the point, where I refreshed the data in a query that used the data source table that I deleted columns from. When I got the error, shown in Figure 11-19, I was stumped for a few seconds because it was a few days between the time that I deleted the fields in the data source file and refreshed the data in the query. That is what prompted this chapter. A solution for deleting and selecting columns was covered in Exercise 11.3.

- ☑ **CHANGING THE ORDER OF COLUMNS** As you have seen, in many exercises you moved columns. That was done for illustration purposes only. On your own, you probably will not have a need to change the order of columns on a regular basis. The exception may be to pivot or unpivot the data, which was covered in Chapter 10.

  The Reorder transformation uses the **TABLE.REORDERCOLUMNS FUNCTION**, which creates a list of all of the column names in the query. This increases the chance of the refresh failing. If you change the column order for the same reason that I did in this book, when you have finished confirming the data, delete the **REORDER STEP**, to remove this from being a cause of the data refresh from failing. A solution for changing the column order was covered in Exercise 11.4.
- ☑ **SPLITTING COLUMNS** Using the **SPLIT COLUMN BY DELIMITER** transformation was covered in Chapter 4. I suspect that most of the time, splitting a column into two or more columns is a good option. Depending on the report that you need to create, the split data may need to be in rows instead of columns. A solution for splitting columns was covered in Exercise 11.5.
- ☑ **CREATING FILTERS** This topic was discussed in Chapter 5, but it bears repeating here. While it is easy and tempting to check or uncheck values, at the bottom of the Filter panel, it is better to create filter criteria by using the **FILTER ROWS DIALOG BOX**.

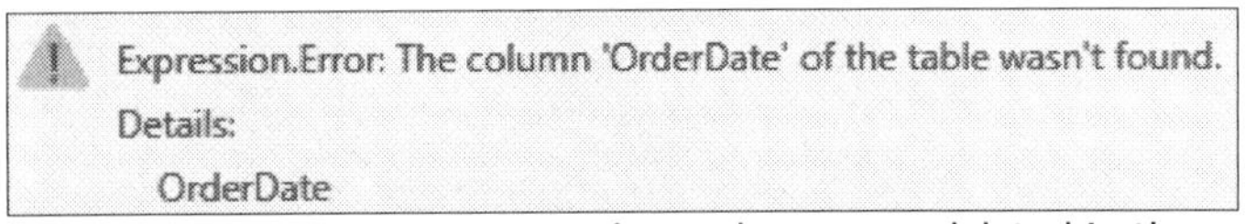

Figure 11-19 Error message when columns are deleted in the source file

> I just do not understand why there is no option to select columns during the import process. Microsoft already has this functionality built into SQL Server Management Studio (SSMS). This software has an import and export wizard, that in addition to being able to connect to a variety of data sources, allows you to select the columns that you want to import, instead of having all of the columns imported, whether they are needed or not. I don't know about you, but I would prefer not to import columns that I don't need, during the import, instead of after. My hope is that they add this functionality to Power BI Desktop, sooner rather then later.

While the focus of this book is not learning the M language, I hope that the times that I have mentioned it or displayed a line of code, that you looked at it. The reason that I am saying this is because even if you do not know how to create a formula from scratch on your own, that looking at the formulas that the transformations create, you will understand more than you realize. This may sound strange, but looking at the formulas in the formula bar can be your best friend because it displays the logic used to create the transformation.

For example, in the filter options shown in Figure 11-20, if you cleared the check mark for the Online option, you are thinking that all other Customer Types will be displayed, even new customer types that are added in the future.

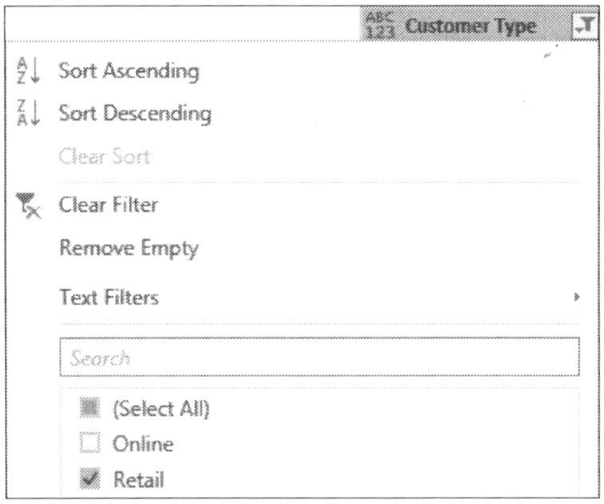

Figure 11-20 Customer Type filter options

Figure 11-21 shows the formulas for the Filtered Rows transformation that was created. As you can see, the only rows that will be displayed in the query will be the records that have a customer type equal to Retail. This means that if next month a new customer say, named Phone for example, was added to this column, non of the records with that customer type would be displayed in the query. Not quite what you were expecting. More than likely, you were expecting to see the formula shown in Figure 11-22.

If you created a report based on the rows retrieved by the formula shown in Figure 11-20, the report would not include all of the rows that it should. The formula in Figure 11-22 would return all of the rows that do not have the Online customer type. Not to scare you, but are you starting to see why I say that you need to start looking at the formulas that are created? It is things like this why many IT people (like yours truly) cringe when we hear that users (people that do not have a technical background) are creating reports.

```
= Table.SelectRows(#"Promoted Headers", each ([Customer Type] = "Retail"))
```

Figure 11-21 Formula created by the options selected in Figure 11-20

```
= Table.SelectRows(#"Promoted Headers", each ([Customer Type] <> "Online"))
```

Figure 11-22 Formula that selects all records that do not have the Online Customer type

As we have come to the end of this book, hopefully, you have a good understanding of the Query Editor and how it can be used to import, transform and combine data, to get the data ready for the analysis step of the report process. I hope that you have enjoyed learning about the Query Editor.

INDEX

T

U

V

W

X

Y